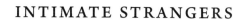
INTIMATE STRANGERS

University of Nebraska Press

LINCOLN

Intimate
Strangers

A HISTORY OF JEWS

AND CATHOLICS IN

THE CITY OF ROME

FREDRIC BRANDFON

The Jewish Publication Society
PHILADELPHIA

Franz Wasner's translation of the poem by Cardinal
Gaetano Stefaneschi in chapter 3 is from "The Popes'
Veneration of the Torah," *The Bridge* 4 (1962): 281. The
poem by Petrus Mallius in chapter 4 was translated
by Ra'anan Boustan and Marie Thêrése Champagne,
published in "Walking in the Shadows of the Past: The
Jewish Experience in Rome in the Twelfth Century,"
Medieval Encounters 17 (2011): 464–94; and by Ann
Vasaly, published in *The Lateran in 1600: Christian
Concord in Counter-Reformation Rome*, by Jack Freiberg
(Cambridge: Cambridge University Press, 1995), 205n1.
The sonnets by G. G. Belli in chapter 8 were translated
by Lynn Gunzburg and previously published in
Strangers at Home: Jews in the Italian Literary Imagination
(Berkeley: University of California Press, 1991).

Library of Congress Cataloging-in-Publication Data
Names: Brandfon, Fredric R. (Fredric Richard), author.
Title: Intimate strangers: a history of Jews and
Catholics in the city of Rome / Fredric Brandfon.
Description: Philadelphia: Jewish Publication Society;
Lincoln: University of Nebraska Press, [2023] |
Includes bibliographical references and index.
Identifiers: LCCN 2022031519
ISBN 9780827615571 (hardback)
ISBN 9780827619029 (epub)
ISBN 9780827619036 (pdf)
Subjects: LCSH: Judaism—Relations—Catholic
Church—History. | Catholic Church—Relations—
Judaism—History. | Antisemitism—Rome—History. |
Christianity and antisemitism—History. |
Rome—Ethnic relations—History.
Classification: LCC BM535 .B66 2023 | DDC
261.2/609—dc23/eng/20220709
LC record available at https://lccn.loc.gov/2022031519

Set and designed in Arno by N. Putens.

For Shirley and Ben

CONTENTS

ILLUSTRATIONS

ACKNOWLEDGMENTS

This book is about family, and without the help of my special extended family, it would not have been written. I wish to thank them all.

My editors at The Jewish Publication Society, Rabbi Barry Schwartz (director) and Joy Weinberg (managing editor), who took the utmost care in making sure I produced my best work and whose advice was indispensable, deserve praise as well as thanks. I was also guided by the numerous and valuable suggestions of the anonymous peer reviewers who took care with every word in the manuscript they were given. At the time, I mistakenly believed that I had written a close to finalized text. Their notes as well as Barry and Joy's generous editorial comments were my most valuable teachers for this project. I must also thank the University of Nebraska Press and its staff, Haley Mendlik, and Amy Pattullo. Amy Pattullo was another diligent reader that this project needed.

Other teachers must be acknowledged as well. Claudio Procaccia and Gabriele Franzone at the Archivio Storico "Giancarlo Spizzichino" della Comunità Ebraica di Roma had no reason to believe, when I first met them, that a complete stranger coming to their offices would ever actually make good on his promise to write a book about the Roman Jewish community. They nevertheless gave me books to read, helped me track down references, and of course welcomed me to the archive and showed me the work they were doing. Jane Gerber was also generous with her time and her assistance in reading an earlier version of the book.

My dear friend Ze'ev Herzog, who taught me to think like an archaeologist, has influenced this book more than he might imagine. He and Hannah Herzog always enriched my heart and mind during the hours of conversation we have shared. Other Israeli colleagues, now deceased, were often in my mind while I wrote. Anson Rainey was deeply concerned with the discipline of history and encouraged me to critically assess everything I read. Yohanan Aharoni, for too brief a time, was a mentor in field archaeology. Shmuel Moskowitz made me laugh when I was just beginning to pursue a scholarly profession. I miss them all.

Others helped me in part because they were with me in times of shared grief. David Bonanno, who published some of my earlier work in the *American Poetry Review*—works of history, not poetry—was with me at almost every moment of heartbreak and joy throughout my life. And at similar times for him, I gave what humor and solace I could. His wife, Kathy Sheeder, was the best storyteller I ever met—and many of the hilarious stories she told were about Dave and me. Just before they died, I visited them in Philadelphia on my way to and from Rome to begin the research for this book. I also shared the good and the terrible times with David Bonanno's family, Suzanne Alex Sheeder and Joe Borelli and Richard and Norine Bonanno. My continuing friendship with them has been a treasure. Similarly, Deborah Wiley has always had my back, especially during those difficult times.

Recently I have been lucky to have the help of Josh Loeb and his family. Josh's grace and interest in my work has been nurturing and unflagging. Gabriel Loeb, too, has offered a sense of humor and humanity to put this work in perspective.

Three people have been instrumental in bringing me to write this story. Rosa Lowinger informed me ten years ago that Rome was a city I would fall in love with. She got that right. Mark Smith repeatedly encouraged me to write a book, just not this one—but I cannot forget his support. Andy Ross, an expert on writing book proposals, gave generously of his time.

I would have achieved nothing without my family. My parents, Aaron and Lillian (Babe and Lily), are constantly with me even though they died when I was a teenager. My aunt and uncle, Beatie and Paul Schwartz, helped me immeasurably after my parents died. I doubt I would have had a graduate education without them. Their beloved daughter Sylvia was more a sister than a cousin, and I wrote this book constantly wishing she could read it. I so deeply regret that none of them will read even one word.

Finally, there is the laughter and joy brought to me every day by Shirley Loeb and Ben Brandfon. I thank them and dedicate this book to them. Their gifts to me far exceed whatever I have achieved here.

INTIMATE STRANGERS

Introduction

Giannina's Glance

On October 18, 1960, a United Jewish Appeal Study mission met Pope
John XXIII in the Vatican Throne Room. After some formalities were
exchanged, the Pope stood up, stepped down from his throne, and
addressed his Jewish visitors, "I am Joseph, your brother."

—*L'osservatore Romano*, October 19, 1960

Before I began writing this book, I took a tour of the Vatican Museum,
guided by an art historian who, it turned out, was also a member of the
Jewish community in Rome. Early in our tour, we headed down a gallery
leading to the Sistine Chapel. Behind us was an equally long corridor lined
with scores of marble busts, but sealed off from visitors by a purple velvet
rope. At regular intervals along the length of the closed gallery there stood
fireplaces, once necessary to keep the drafty corridor that connects the
Pio Clementino Museum with the Sistine Chapel less chilly. Our guide
stopped and pointed to the second fireplace on the right: "That is where my
grandparents slept during World War II. They were hiding from the Nazis."
At that moment, I realized the Jews of Rome had a story to tell. And their
story was inextricably bound to the history of their Catholic neighbors.

This book, then, begins with a question: How do you describe two ven-
erable peoples, Jews and Catholics, who have lived side by side as Romans
since the first century, in anger, adversity, and intermittent admiration?

I call them "intimate strangers." The oxymoron that is the title of this book encapsulates a contradictory relationship through which, despite real difficulties, two very different communities have managed to live together, uninterrupted, for almost two thousand years.

In this book I identify this relationship as familial. So did Pope John XXIII in 1960, when he welcomed his Jewish visitors by reenacting the biblical story of Joseph and his brothers. When Joseph, recently elevated to power in Egypt, greets his brothers, who had sold him into slavery some years back, as if they were strangers, they fail to recognize him. Only when the time is right does Joseph address them as family: "I am your brother Joseph" (Gen. 45:4). With that revelation, the brothers' long estrangement begins to heal.

While the circumstances in the biblical tale and the Jewish-Catholic meeting in the papal palace were different, Pope John (Angelo Roncalli) wanted to evoke intense emotion and the hope for healing expressed in the story they all knew and shared. After the horrors of the Holocaust—during which Roncalli himself, then an apostolic delegate to Turkey and Greece, provided Jews with false identity documents to pass as Catholics and avoid deportation and death (see chapter 11)—John XXIII emphasized the language of family. I might add that before my guide's grandmother found refuge in the Vatican, she sought protectors for her daughters (including the guide's mother) in a convent. Before leaving her children, the grandmother told her daughters, "This is the Mother Superior. Until I return, she will be your mother." The guide's grandmother, like the pope, used words of family to intensify and make sense of a Jewish-Catholic encounter.

Of course, Jews and Catholics were never an actual family. In fact, once Rome became a Catholic city, intermarriage between Jews and Christians was forbidden. However, they often used the language of family to create a feeling of extended kinship. Large families are not always comfortable associations. In extended families, some people are so distantly related, they do not even think of themselves as family. Often enough there may be no love lost between relatives, but the people in such families still have to learn to live together, and even depend on each other. Indeed, when push comes to shove, in a time of crisis, a family can expect to see the best come out in people, and the worst as well.

At no time was that more evident in the metaphorical Jewish-Catholic family than during the years of Fascism in Italy and the Nazi occupation of Rome (1922–44). Many Roman Jews felt that despite the genocide unfolding elsewhere in Europe, Rome would be safe. They had faith that Pope Pius XII would not let similar outrages happen in his Eternal City. They were wrong. In the midst of that pope's inaction, over a thousand Roman Jews were deported to Auschwitz on October 16, 1943; only fifteen would return. Another thousand Jews were deported in the subsequent months, in large part because individual Catholics throughout the city turned hidden Jews over to the Fascist and Nazi authorities to gain monetary rewards.[1] At the same time, Jews were fiercely protected from the Nazis in monasteries, convents, churches, individual Roman households, and even the Vatican itself. Catholic betrayal and protection of Jews occurred in Rome simultaneously.

This book is the story of how seemingly contradictory circumstances existed side by side—and not only during Nazi-occupied Rome, but throughout two thousand years of Jewish-Catholic history in the city.

GIANNINA'S GLANCE

In the opening pages of *The Garden of the Finzi-Continis*, Giorgio Bassani's novel about the fate of Italian Jewry under Fascism, the time is post–World War II, 1957, fourteen years after the Nazis' brutal 1943 roundup of Jews in Rome. The wounds of that atrocity have not fully healed, but it is a happier time, and Bassani's Jewish narrator sits in the back seat of a friend's car on a Sunday drive from Rome to the Etruscan tombs. In the front seat are his hosts, a non-Jewish couple, and sitting between them is their young daughter, Giannina. The father, one hand on the wheel and the other stroking his daughter's curls, asks the girl what she learned about the Etruscans in school, to which she replies: "In our history book the Etruscans are at the beginning, next to the Egyptians and the Jews. Tell me Papa, who do you think were more ancient, the Etruscans or the Jews?"[2] Amused, her father motions toward the back seat: "Ask the gentleman back there."

Giannina, who we imagine as a charming, even precocious child, turns and glances at the narrator, her look "severe and filled with mistrust." Then, quickly, she turns back to silently stare out the front window.

So it is that Bassani introduces us to a Roman family (father, mother, and child) on an idyllic outing with a guest who has a special identity—Jewish—and sits alone in the back seat. Is the guest a close friend, much like family, or is he not? Giannina wishes the guest were not there. Her one-second hostile glance in the context of a seemingly welcoming situation epitomizes much of the Jewish-Roman experience of two thousand years.

Giannina's fictional hostility was presaged by actual events four hundred years earlier. In the mid-sixteenth century three young girls of about Giannina's age living in the heart of Rome had a similar response to a Jewish guest. Their father, a lute maker, ran a shop beneath his residence on the Via dei Leutari (lute-makers' street). Whenever Bonaiuto, an elderly Jewish customer from the Ghetto, entered the shop, the girls, watching from the upstairs apartment, would shout down the slur: "*Cagnaccio sciattato*" (Judaeo-Roman street slang for "kosher slaughtered ugly dog," which three preadolescent Catholic girls had somehow absorbed). Bonaiuto was the father's friend, but his daughters, like Giannina, treated him as an interloper. (Nevertheless, cursing someone in his own peculiar dialect demonstrates both intimacy and disgust simultaneously.)[3]

Indeed, if the lute maker's daughters managed to curse Bonaiuto in his own language, Jews were often happy to return the favor, and in equally unusual ways, as the following story attests.

KADDISH FOR MUSSOLINI

The Hebrew words *Yitgadal veyitkaddash sheme raba* (magnified and sanctified be God's great name) begin the Jewish prayer for the dead known as the *Kaddish*, which is most often recited in the synagogue, the home, or at the graveside.

In 1939, the Jewish janitor Romeo Bondi recited *Kaddish* each morning at the Villa Celimontana, a Jewish high school hastily organized by Rome's Jewish community a year after the Fascists had enacted a series of so-called Racial Laws prohibiting government-supported education of Jews (see chapter 9).[4] Donning his black skullcap and in the presence of students hurrying to class, Bondi chanted *Kaddish* in remembrance of the Fascist dictator Benito Mussolini.[5] Of course, in the fall of 1939 Mussolini was very much alive; but, as Romeo probably mused, one could always hope.

For Romeo, the *Kaddish* was a chance to spit in the dictator's eye, even if he was in the basement of a school opposite the Colosseum while Mussolini was several miles away at the Villa Torlonia, a nineteenth-century estate perched atop an ancient Jewish catacomb dating from the third century CE. In his novel, Giorgio Bassani used the villa grounds as a model for the gardens of the wealthy Jewish Finzi-Continis; in real life, Mussolini utilized the Jewish tombs as a bomb shelter. In fiction and reality, and in death and life, Jews and Catholics in Rome were never far apart from one another. Thus the Italian government's aim to segregate Jews from the rest of Italian society could not readily be accomplished. Jews had lived in Rome too long—since 139 BCE, over two thousand years. In fact, the janitor's family may have existed in Rome since 1538, when persons named Bondi—Moise and Menachem—are mentioned in the Jewish notarial records.[6]

As such, Bondi's *Kaddish* for Mussolini was a small personal reversal of the Racial Laws. Bondi dragged Mussolini away from his grand palace and into the Jewish community in the only way he could, with tongue in cheek. The Jewish prayer for the dead is a quintessential family ceremony, establishing connections between generations and among parents, children, brothers, and sisters. In effect, Romeo Bondi was saying, "If you, Mussolini, do not want us in your family, we, nevertheless, will include you in ours. We are still Romans."

THE TWO TRIBES OF ROME

The stories of Giannina, Bonaiuto, and Romeo Bondi exemplify, in brief, Jews and Catholics who are not quite family, but who speak to each other, or act with each other, as if they were family. Whether they share a dialect or a holiday, whether they curse or bless one another, they are pushing up against the boundaries of family. Full entry is always barred, and is usually not the goal to begin with. Instead, this liminal circumstance, living at the boundary line of family, characterizes their existence.

The approach and avoidance strategies practiced by Catholics and Jews in Rome were not specific to them. In most societies there are strangers among the locals. From an anthropological or sociological point of view, such strangers are a necessity, bringing newness in the form of ideas, commercial contacts, even genetic material, all vital to a community's growth. However, strangers are simultaneously a source of anxiety, first, due to differences with their hosts and, second, due to the real possibility that they may appropriate for themselves, through intermarriage if nothing else, accumulated family and communal wealth.[7] Further, sexual or even close relations between stranger and host invite a fear that through contact, the stranger's worst traits may become contagious—that is, once infected by the stranger, the host will slowly but invariably become more and more like the stranger.[8] Whether this fear was stated or unstated in the case of Jews and Catholics—and during two thousand years in Rome it was both—it meant limiting, or even prohibiting, by law, custom, and edict, social and sexual contact between them.[9]

Still, as we will see in the pages to follow, there existed a codependence between Jews and Catholics which, while often the basis of hostility, also fostered cooperation. As the historian David Nirenberg has reported about Jews and Catholics in thirteenth-century Spain, the impulse to "divide the world into opposing categories of tolerance and intolerance, mutual interest versus mutual hostility, open society or closed" is not altogether apt. Jews and Catholics in Spain often "depended one upon the other" and often "produced and co-produced themselves through a process of simultaneous identification and dis-identification with their rival 'siblings' and neighbors."[10] The same happened in Rome. The line separating Roman Jews and Catholics was always shifting. Jews created their own story when that was possible, and Catholic Romans kept redrawing the line between themselves and Jews, as much to compose their own identity as to marginalize or persecute the other.

Our story, then, proceeds like a historical dance, Jews and Catholics approaching and avoiding each other across the millennia. If Roman Jews and Catholics are like a very extended family, then that dance involving many people across the generations is like the traditional Jewish hora, in which people link arms, change partners, go in different directions, sometimes crash into each other or at least step on each other's feet. In Rome the dancers could be poets and prelates, notaries and swindlers, legislators and mystics, rabbis and popes. In Rome the dance could be uncomfortable, or joyous, or even a matter of life and death.

We begin the story of that dance with a couple—a Jewish queen and a Roman emperor—in a marriage that was not meant to be.

ROME

Villa Borghese

20

F

17

VATICAN CITY
14

3

D

E

B

10
C/11

8

Tiber River

13

7

15

A 12
16 6

1

5

G

Isola Tiburina

TRASTEVERE

4

9

Aventine Hill

19

Places of Historic Interest

1 Arch of Titus
2 Ardeatine Caves/Fosse Ardeatine
3 Castel Sant'Angelo
4 Circus Maximus
5 Colosseum
6 Ghettarello
7 House of the Catecumeni
8 Italian Military College
9 Lateran Church
10 Piazza Navona
11 Piazza Pasquino
12 Porticus D'Ottavia
13 Regina Coeli Prison
14 St. Peter's Basilica
15 St. Pietro in Vincoli
16 Tempio Maggiore (Great Synagogue)
17 Tiburtina Railroad Station
18 Vigna Randanini (Jewish Catacomb)
19 Villa Celimontana
20 Villa Torlonia

A Largo Stefano Gaj Tachè
B Ponte Sant'Angelo
C Via dei Leutari (Street of the Lute Makers)
D Via del Corso
E Via Rasella
F Via Sicilia
G Via Tasso

JEWISH GHETTO

Via della Reginella

Piazza Giudea

Cinque Scole

Via del Portico

Piazza Pescaria

d'Ottavia

12

Tiber River

Parco della Caffarella

0   1 km

18

2

MAP 1. Map of Rome and the Ghetto. Erin Greb Cartography.

1

An Inconvenient Liaison

The Triumph of Titus and His Affair with Berenice

Today, there is still a neighborhood in Rome known as "the Ghetto." Any guidebook to Rome has a section with recommendations for visiting the Ghetto and any Roman taxi driver knows exactly where to take you if you utter the words *il ghetto* when you get in the cab. You are headed to the Jewish neighborhood that was enclosed by walls upon order of Pope Paul IV in 1555. The walls are gone, but it remains the heart of Jewish Rome.

Fronting the main street that runs through the Ghetto's center is a large restaurant, Da Gigetto. It is almost one hundred years old. You can grab one of the many tables near the curb and watch visitors strolling past nearby kosher milk bars while munching on traditional crusty fruit cakes from the nearby iconic bakery, Boccione. Don't make that mistake.

Instead, ask for a table in the rear, in the small garden behind the large dining rooms. If you are lucky, you will be escorted to an outdoor patio. After you take a seat, inhale the aroma of the embowering flowers, and glance at the menu, look up. You will be in the shadow of a monumental gateway: the Portico of Octavia. Towering over you is the twenty-meter-high entrance to the portico, originally built as a gateway to the temples of Juno and Jupiter in 146 BCE. (Destroyed in late antiquity, it was rebuilt and renamed after Augustus's sister Octavia in roughly 27–25 BCE.)

Unfortunately, the sacred area with its temples has been obliterated. We know of its existence from Suetonius's *Lives of the Caesars* and the *Forma Urbis*, an ancient map of Rome.[1] A fire in the late second or early third century CE destroyed the area, but the Emperor Septimius Severus and his son Caracalla restored the gateway in 203 CE. In the eighth century the remains of the entrance were adapted as part of the atrium of the Church of St. Paul in the circus,[2] now known as St. Angelo in Pescheria (the fish market). Consequently, you are now looking at a monumental gate, which these days leads only to the garden you are sitting in and the adjacent street.

After your meal, take the time to walk through the modern restoration of the portico. When you emerge, you will be near the spot where a temporary platform was erected in 71 CE. From that platform, the Emperor Vespasian and his son Titus announced the victory of Rome over Judaean rebels and the destruction of Jerusalem and the Jewish Temple. And from that platform, after prayers and sacrifices had been offered, Titus began his triumphal march through the streets of Rome.

In 1885, Lawrence Tadema painted what he imagined that scene looked like. His painting *The Triumph of Titus*, now in the Walters Art Museum in Baltimore, is, no doubt, based upon the ruined gateway in Rome, along with historian Josephus's eyewitness description of the event in *The Jewish War*:

> At break of day Vespasian and Titus emerged garlanded with laurel and dressed in the traditional purple costume, went over to the Porticus of Octavia. . . . A platform had been erected in front of the colonnade with thrones of ivory set on it. . . . Vespasian gave the signal for silence. When it was completely quiet everywhere, he rose, covered most of his head with his robe, and uttered the customary prayers. Titus prayed likewise. After the prayers Vespasian briefly addressed the assembled company all together. . . . He and Titus first had a bite to eat and then, putting on their triumphal dress and sacrificing to the gods whose statues are set up by the gate, they sent off the triumphal procession, riding through the theatres.[3]

It had become a custom to award Roman generals for their victories a "triumph," a procession through the city to the acclamation of all Rome.[4] Titus, having captured Jerusalem and having destroyed the Jewish Temple, was about to enjoy this honor.

But before we follow Titus on his day of glory, a little background is necessary.

It is said that King Solomon built the Temple in Jerusalem in the mid-tenth century BCE (1 Kings 6–8). The biblical description of the glories of that Temple is surely an exaggeration, and the exact date of its building is fiercely debated. However, there is no doubt that by the seventh century BCE there was a Temple in Jerusalem, and that the Babylonian empire utterly destroyed it in 587 BCE.

The later biblical books of Ezra and Nehemiah then describe the building of the Second Temple. By that time, in the sixth century BCE, it was understood that animal sacrifices could only be carried out in the Jerusalem Temple, and not anywhere else in the world, as commanded in the Torah. Specifically, the order of sacrifice had been set forth in the biblical books of Leviticus, Numbers, and Deuteronomy, which, according to Jewish belief, God had delivered (along with Genesis and Exodus) to Moses on Mount Sinai.

That is not to say that Jews did not transgress this Law and offer sacrifices elsewhere. At the banks of the Nile in Egypt on the island of Elephantine, Jews had their own understanding of the Law that did not prevent them from building their own sacrificial temple during the sixth and fifth centuries BCE.[5] Nonetheless, notwithstanding some variation in practice, the Jerusalem Temple was undoubtedly central to Jewish worship in the several centuries before the Common Era. This did not prevent the Seleucid Syrian ruler Antiochus Epiphanes from profaning the Temple in 168–167 BCE—and the Maccabees from restoring it just a few years later (1 and 2 Maccabees). Then, during the reign of Herod the Great in Judaea (37 BCE–4 CE), the Temple was considerably elaborated, making it an alleged wonder of the ancient world. Even so, Judaea was a province of the Roman Empire, and Herod accommodated himself to Roman rule.

The Jewish Revolt against Rome (66–70 CE) unfolded against this backdrop. While hard fought, given Roman imperial might the defeat of

Judaea was a foregone conclusion. What was uncertain was the fate of the Temple.

Josephus depicts the siege and destruction of the city of Jerusalem in book 6 of *The Jewish War*. When it came time to decide whether to spare or destroy the Temple, Josephus pointedly lets Titus off the hook. He describes a council of war where Titus demands that his subordinates advise him on what should be done about the "holy house." Some counsel burning it according to the rules of war, so that it could never again become a focal point of a new uprising. Others recommend sparing it, unless the Jews used it as a citadel from which they made a last stand—at which point it should be burned, and the blame put on the Jews who had used their own Temple as a battlefield. Not surprisingly, since Josephus wrote his history while living in Rome in the good graces of Titus's family, Josephus gives Titus the last word: "'Although the Jews should get upon that holy house, and fight us from there, yet ought we not to avenge ourselves on things that are inanimate, instead of the men themselves?' And that he was not in any case for burning down so vast a work as that was, because this would be mischief to the Romans themselves, as it would be an ornament to their government while it continued."[6]

However, in the fourth century CE, the Christian historian Sulpicius Severus—apparently relying on a lost passage from Tacitus's *Histories*—left us an entirely different story: "Titus summoned his council, and before taking action consulted it [as to] whether he should overthrow a sanctuary of such workmanship.... For if preserved it would testify to the moderation of the Romans, while if demolished it would be a perpetual sign of cruelty. On the other hand, others, and Titus himself, expressed their opinion that the Temple should be destroyed without delay, in order that the religion of the Jews and Christians should be more completely exterminated."[7]

These two contradictory witnesses serve as a reminder of the fragility of our historical understanding. It is almost certain that we will never know what Titus actually said, or even if there ever was such a council of war. Neither Josephus nor Sulpicius Severus pretend to be eyewitnesses to that meeting. Nevertheless, when it comes to Titus's triumphal procession through Rome, Josephus was an eyewitness—albeit one who must always be viewed critically because of his unusual status as both a Jew and a privileged Roman citizen.

Josephus was born in Jerusalem in 37 CE into an elite priestly family that also claimed royal Hasmonaean ancestry (the Hasmonaeans took credit for having established, through force of arms, an independent Jewish kingdom in Judaea in the second century BCE).[8] In approximately 61 CE, Josephus traveled to Rome to petition Emperor Nero on behalf of certain Jews whom the governor of Judaea had sent to Rome for imprisonment. His mission failed, and upon his return to Jerusalem, he joined the Jewish revolt against Rome, at which point he was ordered to defend the Galilee. He notably failed in his new task as well: the Romans captured him in 67 CE. Josephus later admitted that, defeated, he had considered suicide, but he also claimed he was privy to divine guidance in his dreams. Those dreams, he said, required him to become an emissary to the Romans (and thereby conveniently exculpated him from being a traitor). He used those dreams to present himself as a prophet to his Roman captors. Rome, he predicted, would be victorious in Judaea, and Vespasian, commander of the Roman forces, would ultimately be elevated to emperor.

To Josephus's good fortune, Vespasian shortly became emperor, defeating several rivals. He left his son, Titus, behind in Judaea to complete the conquest, and when, sometime later, Titus, upon his father's death, acceded to the imperial palace, he gave Josephus his Roman residence on the Quirinal Hill. Josephus, in turn, took the name of his benefactor, Vespasian, whose family name was Flavius. In so doing he changed his name from Yosef ben Matityahu to Flavius Josephus, the name by which he has since been known.

Then he embarked on a project that would consume the rest of his life: that is, the justification of Judaism and the explanation of Jewish history to the Roman elite. He chronicled that history in four books: *Jewish Antiquities*, *The Jewish War*, *Against Apion*, and his autobiography, the *Life of Flavius Josephus.* Among the innumerable episodes he recorded is Titus's triumphal parade through Jerusalem. Titus had completed the conquest of Judaea and the destruction of the Temple—though this, according to Josephus, was more accidental than intentional. He blames a simple soldier for setting the Temple aflame through unbridled zeal.[9]

TITUS'S TRIUMPH

Nevertheless, Titus did not balk at returning to Rome with the spoils of war, including the Temple treasures. Josephus describes Titus's triumph as consisting, in part, of parading through Rome with those treasures on full display. In addition to the soldiers, captive Jews, and heaps of gold, ivory, and gems, the parade was a marching depiction of the war itself. Titus and Vespasian had ordered the construction of "pageants," or what in today's parades would be called floats—three-dimensional representations of the conflict, its horrors and its glory:

> But what afforded the greatest surprise of all was the structure of the pageants that were borne along; . . . for many of them were so made that they were on three or even four stories one above another. . . . There was also wrought gold and ivory fastened about them all; and many resemblances of the war. . . . For there was to be seen a happy country laid waste, and entire squadrons of enemies killed; . . . with the strongest fortifications taken, and the walls of most populous cities upon the tops of hills seized on. . . . Fire also sent upon temples was here represented . . . and the art and magnificent workmanship of these structures now portrayed the incidents to those who had not witnessed them, as though they were happening before their eyes.[10]

Finally,

> The spoils in general were borne in promiscuous heaps; but conspicuous above all stood out those captured in the Temple at Jerusalem. These consisted of a golden table, many talents in weight, and a lamp stand,

FIG. 1. Arch of Titus. The interior frieze shows spoils taken from the Jerusalem Temple in the first century CE. Zev Radovan / BibleLandPictures / Alamy.

likewise made of gold, but constructed on a different pattern from those which we use in ordinary life. Affixed to a pedestal was a central shaft, from which there extended slender branches, arranged trident fashion, a wrought lamp being attached to the extremity of each branch; of these there were seven. . . . After these and last of all the spoils was carried a copy of the Jewish Law.[11]

Josephus's description could serve as an extended caption to the Arch of Titus erected by his successor Domitian to honor the short-lived emperor. The arch, which has survived in restored form as an attraction near the Roman Forum, displays two original reliefs in its interior.[12] The English poet Shelley described them: "On the inner compartment of the arch of Titus is sculptured in deep relief, the desolation of a city. . . . The foreground is occupied by a procession of the victors bearing in their profane hands the holy candlesticks and the tables of shewbread, and the sacred instruments of the eternal worship of the Jews. On the opposite side, the reverse of this sad picture, Titus is represented standing in a chariot drawn by four horses, crowned with laurel."[13]

The ceiling of the arch is dedicated to Titus's apotheosis. He is riding the wings of an eagle, being transported to the heavens, where it is said he had taken his place among the gods, or at least among the former emperors who had been deified. Atop the arch, and now entirely lost, stood a bronze four-horse chariot driven by Vespasian and Titus.

Titus was so glorified for the conquest of Jerusalem that coins bearing the inscription "Judaea Capta" (conquered Judaea) and images of a victorious Titus along with a dejected female Judaean were minted in his honor. A second arch extolling Titus was erected about a mile away at the southeast end of the Circus Maximus. That monument is long gone, but a preserved stone includes the inscription: "With the instruction and advice of his father, he subdued the race of the Jews and destroyed the city of Jerusalem which had either been attacked in vain by all leaders, kings and people before him or had not been attempted at all."[14]

Whoever wrote that inscription was willfully ignorant of the prior desecrations of Jerusalem and the Temple or was willing to forget inconvenient facts in order to favor the deified emperor. In either case, Titus's victory over Judaea was the keystone of his imperial career.

Finally, upon the destruction of the Jerusalem Temple, Vespasian took onerous steps to drive home the point that the Temple was no more. Prior to the demolition, Jews throughout the empire were allowed to pay annual monies to Jerusalem for the Temple's maintenance. Afterward, Vespasian redirected those monies to the city of Rome by creating a tax in the same amount, specifically for Jews, to finance the rebuilding of the Temple of Jupiter on Capitoline Hill. If Jews were not fully aware that Titus had demolished their Temple, the tax was intended to make the disaster perfectly clear.[15]

A BRIEF BIOGRAPHY OF BERENICE

There is more to Titus's story than the glorious triumph and ultimate deification depicted in his arch. There is a second track to his career as general and emperor, one which also concerns Judaea and the Jews. It is the story of Berenice, a Jewish woman who was both sister of King Agrippa II of Judaea and consort to Titus, the despoiler of Jerusalem.

Berenice has a minor role in the New Testament presiding, along with her brother Agrippa, at a trial where the apostle Paul tries to convert them to his belief in the resurrection of Jesus. Berenice and Agrippa demur.[16] Only after this cameo, in sources other than the New Testament, does Berenice gain her notoriety. In 64 CE Nero appointed a new procurator of Judaea, Gessius Florus, who persecuted the Jews and, according to Josephus, acted with both barbarity and depravity, including executing Jews by crucifixion.[17] In response, Berenice sent delegations of her guards to Florus to beg for an end to the killings. Florus refused, and his soldiers appear to have threatened Berenice herself to the extent that she fled to the palace of her brother the king of Judaea. There she performed a vow whereby she shaved her head and abstained from wine for thirty days, after which she walked barefoot through Jerusalem to Florus to personally deliver the same plea. Vows were common Jewish undertakings, to the extent that an entire tractate of the Jewish oral Law, the Mishnah, *Nedarim* (Vows), was devoted to them. They were made to avoid a catastrophe, but in this case Berenice's vow did not achieve the desired result. She failed to stop the inevitability of the coming rebellion.[18] A further request to Cestius Gallus, the legate of Syria, also received a disappointing response. Gallus sent a fact-finding tribune to Judaea with no authority to alleviate the suffering. Again the tempest was not stilled.[19]

Florus's violence had incited the Jews to the point of revolt, forcing Berenice's brother, Agrippa II, to implore the people of Jerusalem to relinquish the fantasy of a successful war against Rome. Just as Berenice was unsuccessful with her entreaties to the Romans, Agrippa II failed to dissuade the Jews from revolting.[20] At the end of Agrippa's speech, Berenice is said to have wept along with the king. The war followed.

It began in Jerusalem, where, among other assaults, the revolutionaries attacked and burned the palaces of Agrippa and Berenice.[21] Apparently, brother and sister fled to the Galilee and surrendered to the Romans while awaiting the outcome of the war. Nero sent Vespasian to quell the rebellion, and subsequently Vespasian's son Titus joined him. Together, commanding sixty thousand Roman soldiers, they subdued the Galilee, where Berenice, obviously no shrinking violet, met Titus.

In her youth she had married three times. Her first two husbands, Marcus Julius Alexander and Herod of Chalcis, had died young, and she deserted the third one, Polemon II of Pontus.[22] The marriage to Polemon was considered a necessity, to dispel rumors of an incestuous liaison with her brother the king. Polemon, who was not Jewish, had to be circumcised and take up the Jewish religion as conditions of their marriage.[23] Once Berenice forsook the marriage, Polemon forsook Judaism.

Undaunted by her own checkered career, Berenice entered into an affair with Titus and simultaneously supported Vespasian's candidacy for emperor.[24] After Nero's suicide in 68 CE, several notables vied for the office of emperor, and Vespasian was ultimately successful.[25] Having several victories behind him, but with the war not yet won, his army acclaimed him emperor and, armed with, among other things, Josephus's prophesy, he returned to Rome, leaving Titus behind to complete the conquest of Jerusalem. Once that was accomplished, Titus returned to Rome to aid his father, and Berenice remained in Judaea.

There may have been some resistance among Romans to Titus's affair with Berenice, but in 75 CE she came to Rome, lived with him as his wife, and exercised considerable power.[26] Quintilian, a Roman rhetorician from Hispania (ca. 35–ca. 100 CE), reports that upon pleading a case on her behalf, he discovered that she was also the judge.[27] Such abuses, or purported abuses, must have caused certain Romans to oppose her. Moreover, her foreign origins and her Jewish identity probably irked many more. It is not reported, but the stipulations prior to her marriage to Polemon that he convert to Judaism and be circumcised might have raised concerns that Titus would do the same. The specter of a Jewish emperor, and Jewish heirs, could not have been ignored, and possibly became too much for Rome or Titus to bear. Even if Titus did not become Jewish, his children by Berenice, if any, could very well be Jewish according to both Jewish and Roman law.[28]

In the first century CE, the Roman world may not have been fully conversant with the notion of conversion from pagan to Jew.[29] However, one hundred years prior, the poet Horace (65–8 BCE) jokes that poets are like Jews, they will compel you to join them.[30] Similarly, the Stoic philosopher Seneca (ca. 4 BCE–65 CE) complains that Jewish customs, if not Jews, are prevalent everywhere.[31] It is therefore unlikely that the implications of the imperial heir-apparent consorting with a Jew went unnoticed.

Senator and historian Cassius Dio (ca. 155–235 CE) reports that two Cynics—philosophers and their adherents who disdained convention and material possessions—namely Diogenes and Heras, spoke against Berenice in the theater.[32] While the content of those tirades is not preserved, they were apparently virulent enough to issue in the flogging of Diogenes and beheading of Heras.

When in 79 CE, upon his father's death, Titus became emperor, he sent Berenice away, exiled from Rome.[33] This should have put to rest the fear that Titus would have Jewish heirs, although the Talmud claims that Titus's nephew Kolonymos (or Kolonikos) converted to Judaism sometime later. (Supposedly he was arrested for that misstep but avoided execution; however, there is no independent corroboration outside the Talmud for this incident.)[34]

Aside from its prurient fascination, what are we to make of this story? Undoubtedly, various political factions in Rome would have attempted to use her liaison with Titus to discredit him and nip the new Flavian dynasty in the bud.[35] But her role in Jewish history is less mundane. The queen of Judaea, aggressive both sexually and politically, carried on a thoroughly public affair with the man who had defiled and demolished the Temple in Jerusalem. No doubt she is remembered for the glamor with which she carried off that betrayal of her people. As a lover, her story has been retold over the years in romantic plays, operas, and novels.[36] As a Jew, she may be a traitor, but is she any more of a traitor than Josephus or, for that matter, the revered Rabbi Yohanan ben Zakkai? The Talmud relates that during the siege of Jerusalem, the rabbi had himself spirited out of the city disguised as a corpse, only to revive in the presence of Vespasian and declare, "Long live the Emperor," thus being the second Jew to prophesy Vespasian's imperial destiny.[37]

And surely even Berenice's treason was outdone by her first husband's brother, Tiberius Iulius Alexander, a Jew who actively effectuated the Temple's destruction by serving as Titus's second in command during the siege of Jerusalem.[38] The satirist Juvenal, in an aside, expresses what Jews worldwide no doubt also believed: that it was permissible to urinate on Tiberius's triumphal statue.[39]

Regardless, for us her significance lies in the fact that, as a Jew, Berenice is the first, and the prototypical, "intimate stranger" in Rome. She was both an intimate with the prospective emperor and a despised foreigner in the eyes of many Romans. As such, she foreshadows the role that the Jewish community itself would come to play in Rome's future. Her narrative can thus be read as symbolic as well as factual. As a figure in the popular imagination of the ancient world, she operated as a mediating figure between the cities of Rome and Jerusalem.

ROME AND JERUSALEM

That Rome and Jerusalem, separated by considerable geography, were nevertheless fatally connected became a mainstay of both Jewish and non-Jewish thought. Berenice became one early link in the chain that bound the two cities.

In order to discover other such links and put Berenice in context, we enter the realm of popular lore and legend. Jewish tales and traditions in the Talmud and other rabbinic literature of the second and third centuries CE constitute a narrative about Jerusalem and Rome. When they are read alongside the story of Berenice, a mosaic image develops from which it is possible to reach an understanding of how Romans and Jews perceived their relationship. The depiction of Roman-Jewish ties that follows is complicated, mythological, symbolic, and perhaps overstated—but it may also be instructive. The mosaic ultimately provides a glimpse of feelings more than facts, which nonetheless may help in understanding how, from the beginning, Jews and non-Jews in Rome concocted a portrait of their mutual identities.

The first piece in the mosaic is a Jewish legend concerning the origins of Rome. It is said that the foundation of Rome came to pass in the tenth century BCE, when in ancient Jerusalem King Solomon chose opportunism (and maybe lust) over obedience to God's Law. *Canticles Rabbah,* a book that contains Jewish traditions from the second and third centuries CE, states that the city of Rome was founded on the very same day King Solomon took the Pharaoh of Egypt's daughter as one of his brides.[40] That marriage, but not the founding of Rome, is recorded in the Bible: 1 Kings 3:1 says that it took place in Jerusalem, before Solomon had started building the Temple. Whether the nuptials actually occurred is doubtful,[41] but the biblical author, in attempting to glorify Solomon, depicts him as marrying into one of the world's most illustrious families: the Pharaoh's.

Indeed, for the Rabbis of the second and third centuries CE, the biblical story could have been nothing but true, and they take Solomon to task for a match that never should have been made. Consequently, hundreds of years after the biblical story was written, the Rabbis comment that Solomon's taking a foreign bride from Israel's former slave masters was sufficient apostasy to have planted the seeds that would grow into the Roman Empire, a nation that would eventually devastate Solomon's own yet-to-be-built Temple. The rabbinic story states that on the day of Solomon's wedding to the Pharaoh's daughter, the angel Michael (or Gabriel) plunged a reed into the sea that eventually became the city of Rome.[42] And, of course, from the historical account we know that some thousand years later, Rome made its way to Jerusalem and destroyed the Temple.

If that tradition isn't ironic enough, there is another piece of the mosaic: a talmudic tradition that admonishes, "If a man asks you 'Where is your God?' the answer is: 'In the great city of Rome.'"[43] This tradition is ascribed to Rabbi Joshua ben Levi of Lod (third century CE), who claimed to have met Elijah, and was told that the Messiah had already come and was sitting among the lepers at the entrance to the city of Rome.[44] The implication of these bitter words is that God, who had previously dwelled in the Temple, also known as the House of the Lord (1 Kings 6:1), allowed that House to be destroyed because Solomon married a foreigner. God was now living in Rome, the city responsible for that destruction, and Jewish taxes now had to fund the building of a different Temple, to a different God.

The Solomonic tale reverses the story of Berenice. Here the king, Solomon, a Jew, takes as his bride an outsider from Egypt, the very nation that God and the Hebrew people had humiliated and demolished. With Solomon married to an Egyptian, an unstated fear lurks in the background. What if Solomon has a son with his Egyptian queen and that Egyptian prince, the Pharaoh's hypothetical grandson, ultimately becomes king of Judaea? For Jews, the disaster is incomprehensible.

In the story of Berenice, instead of a Jewish king we have the non-Jewish Roman emperor, Titus. He takes as a presumptive bride a Jew and an outsider, the queen of a nation he has recently humiliated and demolished. Again, the fear that their Jewish progeny could become emperors is not unfounded, though in this narrative, the Romans are the ones who would have been appalled. The Berenice story is a variation of the Solomonic tale, with a Jew switching roles from male to female and from insider to outsider.

In the Jewish legend, Solomon's extreme exogamy (in anthropological terms) or apostasy (in religious terms) had dire consequences for the nation of ancient Israel. On the other hand, in 79 CE Rome, once Titus exiled Berenice instead of marrying her, his extreme exogamy was aborted, and any consequences that might have ensued—a Jewish, or more than one Jewish, emperor—were averted as well; Rome was saved once more. Titus would go on to become a beloved emperor who was deified upon his death. The self-deprecating story of Solomon is preserved in Jewish tradition, and the self-aggrandizing story of Titus is memorialized in stone and still visible in the Arch of Titus.[45]

However, the Jewish narrative continues and does not let Titus off the hook so easily. There is yet another piece of the mosaic. The story of the heroic Emperor Titus that comes to us from Josephus and Suetonius is contradicted by the rabbinic legend that unsurprisingly gives us a villainous Titus, subject to the wrath of God. According to Jewish tradition, during the destruction of Jerusalem, Titus entered the Temple and defiled the Holy of Holies, the room reserved only for the High Priest. In total desecration of God's House, Titus brought with him two Jewish whores, whom he raped upon an open Torah scroll, after which he gathered the Temple treasures and conveyed them by sea to Rome, mocking God along the way. Nevertheless, after his triumphal parade through Rome, while he was bathing, God caused the tiniest of creatures, a mosquito, to fly up his nose and lodge in his brain. Eventually, in agony, he called for doctors, who split open his skull to find there a dove. The dove, having grown from a mosquito, caused Titus's death, and then flew away.[46]

This rabbinic tale may be interpreted, among other things, as a commentary on the story of Berenice and Titus.[47] Instead of Titus marrying a Jewish queen, he rapes two Jewish prostitutes. Moreover, he defiles the Temple. This act is mirrored by the Roman fear that their emperor and his lineage will be defiled by a foreigner if Berenice is allowed to become empress.

The second part of the story is even more interesting. It starts with Titus being penetrated by a mosquito. In Hebrew, a mosquito is a *yitush*, which sounds like, and is a play on, the name "Titus." The story ends with a dove lodged in Titus's brain. The dove often appears in rabbinic literature as a symbol of the people of Israel;[48] thus Israel has nested inside Titus himself. In the end, contrary to the story told in the Arch, Titus does not ascend to heaven on an eagle's wings. Rather, he is killed by the wings of a dove that represents Israel.

And with that, the story of Solomon has come full circle. Solomon's extreme exogamy with the Egyptian queen has resulted in the establishment of Rome, and ultimately in Titus's destruction of the Jerusalem Temple: an act of desecration that involves the rape of Jewish prostitutes—and, implicitly, cohabitation with a Jewish queen—that fittingly leads to Titus's own downfall.

Further, beyond orchestrating this tragedy, God finally takes up residence in Rome. What Berenice aspired to do—that is, to move from Jerusalem to live in Rome—God now accomplishes. At the same time, Rome's emperor, Titus, may have banished a single Jew, Berenice, but once a dove lodges in his brain, he finds himself literally inhabited by all of Israel. Thus it is that the heroic story of Titus's triumph, his love affair with Judaea's queen, and his ultimate divinity is countered by Jewish tradition.[49]

Taken together, the Roman story of Titus's triumph and apotheosis and the Jewish tale of Titus's desecration of the Temple and his ultimate demise concretize the idea that Jews and Romans were intimate strangers. Not only is Berenice an intimate stranger—Titus's lover and foreign queen—but the people of Israel, symbolized by a dove, come to live intimately inside Titus's very body and brain. In a sense, the thought that Titus might have to convert to Judaism or that his heirs by Berenice would be Jewish and, thereby, Rome might become Jewish is substantiated by the talmudic tale. Israel inhabits the emperor of Rome. In symbolic terms, if the *yitush*, mosquito, has been transformed into a dove, then the near-homonym of *yitush*, Titus, has similarly been transformed into Israel. As a result of his crimes against the Temple and by his liaison with Rome's first Jewish intimate stranger, he has become a Jew.

However fragmentary and speculative, the picture we now have of the early relationship between Rome and Jerusalem depicts the Jewish presence in Rome in terms of courtship, sexual intimacy, transformation of insider into outsider, and banishment. The story of Titus and Berenice encapsulates that experience with the expulsion of Berenice the stranger.

Nevertheless, it is here that the symbolic stories, legends, and traditions diverge from historical events. As much as some Romans wanted the Jews expelled from Rome, and as much as the Jews felt exiled even while in Rome, they were there to stay.

2

"Who Is a Jew?"

Jews, Pagans, Proselytes, and God-Fearers in the Roman Catacombs

At the height of World War II, during 1943 and 1944, the United States and Britain conducted bombing raids on Rome and its environs, forcing Italian families to shelter underground. Several families found safety thirty feet beneath a hilltop, close to the Via Appia (Appian Way) south of Rome, in two rock-cut cubicles, each between seven and eight feet from floor to ceiling. To arrive at either cubicle, they had to walk about a mile underground through a narrow, lightless passage illuminated solely by flashlight, candle, or torch. Upon arrival, the space was cramped. Neither cubicle had been constructed as an air raid shelter.

Painted on the ceiling of the first cubicle is a winged victory placing a garland on the head of a nude youth. The goddess holds a palm branch in her left hand; the boy holds a leafy bough and possibly a quiver. Surrounding the pair are figures of peacocks, birds, and flowers. Painted images of pegasi (winged horses), again peacocks and birds, a sheep, and a caduceus (staff with two entwined snakes and two wings at the top) appear on the walls.

The second room, too, has an elaborately painted ceiling. Its central figure, the goddess Fortuna, carries a cornucopia in her left hand and a libation dish in her right. Arrayed around her are paintings of fish, ducks, cupids, two dolphins, and a hippocampus (a creature with the body of a horse and the tail of a fish). On the walls are paintings of flowers and a badly damaged image of a man standing between two horses.[1] The families who huddled in those rooms in fear of the bombing added their own drawings and scrawls to the chamber walls almost two thousand years after they had been cut from the rock.

Today, the cubicles lie beneath a vegetable farm, but in antiquity they were part of an extensive underground cemetery: a catacomb. The particular catacomb where the two painted rooms were found has been identified as a Jewish burial ground, given that Jewish symbols such as the *menorah* and, very occasionally, a Hebrew inscription, were found marking the less prepossessing burial niches nearby. The catacomb in question, known as Vigna Randanini (because it was discovered in 1859 beneath a vineyard owned by Giuseppe Randanini), consists of a series of haphazard branching tunnels cut into the rock underground. Further dug into the tunnel walls are burial niches of varying sizes, each intended to hold a single corpse. In some places, a side passage leads to individual cubicles also cut into the rock. One such side passage, near the western end of the catacomb, leads to the two painted rooms described above.

Since its discovery in the nineteenth century, the "cubicle of the pegasi," as it has come to be called, has been the subject of some controversy. Could it possibly be a Jewish sepulcher, given the extensive mythological decoration on every surface? Jews are commanded to refrain from making "graven images" (Exod. 20:4–5). While apparently this commandment was often breached in antiquity—for instance, among other images, the painting of David as Orpheus in the third-century CE Dura Europos synagogue found in Syria—each discovery of such a breach always seems to provoke debate.[2] Given the ambiguity of the evidence, the debate about the cubicle of the pegasi encompasses a wide range of interpretations.

One theory holds that the "cubicle of the pegasi" and the nearby "cubicle of the palms" could not have been Jewish and were pagan tombs pure and simple.[3] Or maybe they were originally pagan, but reused by Jews who, in cutting through the rock underground, happened upon an earlier pagan tomb.[4] On the other hand, they could have been originally Jewish with no pagan use whatsoever.[5] It is even possible that the nearby burials that used Jewish symbols were not Jewish but evidence of pagans borrowing Jewish symbols. If that were the case, the catacomb at Vigna Randanini would not be particularly Jewish at all.[6] This last suggestion appears the least likely, but it cannot be ruled out.

It is not my purpose to judge which of these theories is correct. It is sufficient to note that the state of the evidence supports this general conclusion: in second-, third-, and fourth-century Rome, in death as in life, it was not always self-evident who was a Jew and who was not.

JEWISH BURIAL IN ROME

In ancient Rome, there were five Jewish catacombs, although all five might not have been in use simultaneously. All were outside the city walls. That there were separate locations for specifically Jewish burials, where Jews would be buried next to Jews, appears to have been established by the talmudic tradition that it is most desirable for the Jewish righteous to be buried together.[7]

Much is to be discerned from the catacombs—for starters, the Jewish presence in Rome in late antiquity. While precise population numbers are unknown, the community was sufficiently large to support several cemeteries.[8] Possibly, multitudes of Jewish slaves were brought to Rome after the 135 CE Bar Kokhba revolt failed in Judaea, to add to those taken after the destruction of Jerusalem in 70 CE—but that is only speculation.[9] Nonetheless, while Jews were a minority in Rome, they were not negligible.

Second, we learn not only from Cicero, Suetonius, and other ancient authors, but also from the catacombs, that this considerable community had a public presence. Short inscriptions on the walls in the catacombs identify the person interred and, sometimes, that person's synagogue. Thus we learn that Rome in the second through fourth centuries CE was home to eleven synagogues (the Agrippesians, Augustesians, Calcaresians, Campesians, Elaea, Hebrews, Secenians, Siburesians, Tripolitans, Vernaclesians, and Volumnesians), although, again, not all eleven were likely operating at one time.[10] The word "synagogue" probably referred to congregations composed of persons. Another word, *proseucha*, which has not been found in any of the catacombs but appears in Jewish inscriptions elsewhere, likely referred to Jews' physical place of worship.[11]

Notably, archaeologists have not found even one of the eleven Roman synagogues or any partial remains. We only know of their existence from the funerary inscriptions in the catacombs.[12]

In all likelihood, these synagogues organized the funerals, maintained the cemeteries, and, along with the families of the deceased, arranged the funeral processions that carried the dead through the streets of Rome and outside the city walls to the catacombs.[13] Jewish law mandated that Jews of the priestly class (*Kohanim*) not touch the dead (Num. 19:11) or approach a cemetery except to bury their own dead. More generally, contact with the dead made all Jews unclean.[14] Consequently, while we cannot track any specific route for a Jewish funeral procession in the second through fourth centuries CE, we can say that the route would have passed through Rome, where the Jews lived, to burial grounds outside the city, and that as a matter of Jewish belief, the route carried the mourners from pure to impure space. We can also say that the city of Rome that had to be traversed at least in part to get to the catacombs had an overwhelming street life full of festivals, oratory, theatrical performances, and public feasts, not to mention other processions. Likely traffic did not stop for a Jewish funeral. But just as surely, the dead were carried through the crowded streets and past pagan temples to the Jews' final resting place.

We have no description of an ancient Jewish burial procession, but once it reached the catacombs we are on a slightly firmer footing. Undoubtedly, prayers were said for the deceased prior to interment, and although we have no record of what was said, we may know where the prayers were said, or, at least, one place where funeral prayers and orations could have taken place. At the entrance to the Vigna Randanini catacomb there was a vestibule paved with mosaic and divided by a central wall. Similar vestibules have been found at the Monteverde catacombs and at Villa Torlonia. These vestibules appear to have been meeting places, although late in the period of the catacombs' use, the Vigna Randinini vestibule included burials, possibly for the priestly families. At Vigna Randanini, a room off the entrance hall surrounded by benches and marked by a well in its center prompted the suggestion that the vestibule had been used for a funeral service and the side room for a funeral banquet, with the well providing water for purification.[15] That said, the idea of a funeral banquet does not comport with any known rabbinic custom of the time.

Once one entered the catacombs, the underground pathways were narrow and the ceiling low. The graves were niches in the wall or floors, sealed and usually marked with painted or engraved memorial inscriptions. Some—very few—burials were in coffins or sarcophagi.

The inscriptions were mostly in Greek, with some in Latin, and a very few in Hebrew or Aramaic.[16] Almost exclusively, the inscriptions named the deceased with an accompanying blessing and a few words concerning his or her accomplishments in life. Occasionally, an inscription was adorned with a carving or painting of a group of symbols, including menorahs, amphorae, palm branches, *lulavs, etrogim,* incense shovels, baskets of loaves or fruit, lamps, Torah scrolls, and circumcision knives.[17] Rarer were depictions of living things such as doves, grapes, trees, and even a bull and a dolphin.[18] Several inscriptions mentioned the deceased's occupation. One person, Eudoxius, was described as a painter of living things; another, Alexander, was said to have been a butcher.[19]

Prominent Jews were buried in the stone coffins called sarcophagi. These, too, were decorated and inscribed, often in elaborate ways common to pagan sarcophagi as well: strigilated (carved with a wavy pattern) and adorned with figures of griffins, masks, small children representing the four seasons, lions, and dolphins.[20] Apparently, generic sarcophagi were carved for Jews, pagans, and Christians. When a Jew purchased such a sarcophagus, certain areas were left blank so that particularly Jewish symbols could then be added along with an inscription.

In one instance, for example, as shown in figure 2, a Jewish owner had purchased a sarcophagus with symbols of the four seasons and a specific space initially left unadorned. Similar Christian sarcophagi would have had a cross—and pagans, perhaps a head of Medusa—carved into that space, but on this sarcophagus the owner arranged for the carving of a menorah.[21] From this example we get a picture of the coffin maker's trade. The craftsman, maybe not Jewish, sold a standard-issue blank sarcophagus, useful for

FIG. 2. *Season Sarcophagus,* contemporary with Jewish catacombs, provenance unknown, now in the Museo Nazionale Romano, Rome. Dmitriy Moroz / Alamy.

Jews, Christians, and pagans, to his Jewish customer. At this point either the original seller or another craftsperson decorated the sarcophagus in an appropriately Jewish manner.

Further evidence of Jewish accommodation with non-Jewish practices comes from small, round glass objects with gold inlay found in the catacombs. The inlaid decoration had a Jewish theme, mainly the menorah, but the technique of combining gold and glass was a local Roman fashion.[22]

From the catacombs, then, we may conclude that Jews in Rome had achieved a certain comfort with their neighbors.[23] On the one hand, they were allowed to remain a separate community that was recognized and respected at least enough to allow for their separate burial sites in Jewish community tombs. In Rome, from the beginning, these catacombs were the property of the Jewish community. By contrast, in Palestine, where most of the Roman Jews originated, burials were in private family sepulchers.[24] Similarly, the Jewish community worshiped in its own synagogues, and to a certain extent retained the Hebrew language. That said, only three inscriptions from the catacombs, all from Monteverde, are in Hebrew, and these only say *shalom* or *shalom al Yisra'el* (peace, or peace on Israel).

Another five or six tack the word *shalom* onto the end of a Greek inscription.[25] Most of the inscriptions in the Jewish community's catacombs are in Greek or Latin. Moreover, Roman Jews' familiarity with the winged victory, the dolphin, the bull, the griffin, and the ram—all, in a funerary context, possibly representing a pagan vision of heaven—is particularly striking because these emblems appear side by side and intertwined with menorahs, *lulavs*, Torah scrolls, and other Jewish symbols. The catacombs provide such overwhelming evidence of Jewish familiarity with pagan iconography that one scholar characterized the Jewish and pagan symbols as having a remarkable "intimacy": "Jews used pagan motifs, indeed, in such intimacy with Jewish symbols, that one must come to the obvious conclusion that the pagan motifs were as important symbolically for the Jews as were the menorahs, ethrogs, and Torah shrines beside which they stand."[26]

And if the symbols crossed over from one community to another, undoubtedly so did the people for whom the symbols held meaning. The catacombs are testimony to both Jewish separateness from and integration into the wider Roman community. That ambiguous status would set in motion Roman Jewish history through the next two thousand years.

JEWS DURING THE EARLY EMPIRE

In first century CE Rome, Jews were outsiders. They had come to Rome as slaves and maybe merchants. In today's terms, they were immigrants. Two or three centuries passed, and they were still Jews. In the streets, in the courts, in the catacombs, Jews were known as a distinct people. But what made them Romans as well?

We begin that story with events 210 years prior to Titus.

Ironically, the earliest—and, apparently, much exaggerated—story we have about Jews in Rome tells of their expulsion. Valerius Maximus, a first century CE collector of historical anecdotes, wrote *Factorum et Dictorun Memorabilium* (Memorable deeds and sayings) in approximately 131 CE describing what he claims happened back in 139 BCE. At that time, before Titus, before Augustus, and before Julius Caesar, he says, a praetor (magistrate of the Roman Republic) expelled astrologers and also the Jews:

"Gnaeus Cornelius Hispalus, praetor peregrinus . . . ordered the astrologers by an edict to leave Rome. . . . The same praetor compelled the Jews, who attempted to infect the Roman customs with the cult of Jupiter Sabazius."[27]

Yet the Jews never worshiped any iteration of Jupiter.[28] Perhaps the author mistook a Jewish name of God, YHVH Sabaoth (Lord of Hosts), for the Phrygian Jupiter Sabazius. Or perhaps Valerius somehow mistook Judaism for the mystery cult of Sabazius that existed in Rome and other places in the empire.[29]

More important than such a mistake is the fact that, according to Valerius, the administrator who issued the expulsion was a *praetor peregrinus*—that is, an administrator charged with cases involving citizens against non-citizens. In effect, Valerius is asserting that the Jews subject to Hispalus's order were persons traveling through Rome and not residents.[30] While it is possible that these were the same Jews who reportedly came to Rome as part of a Hasmonean delegation from Judaea in 140 BCE to renew a treaty negotiated twenty years earlier, that remains speculative.[31] Even if the Jews subject to the decree were more settled than travelers, the decrees of a *praetor peregrinus* were valid only during the single year of his appointment, in this case 139 BCE. After that, any Jews who had left Rome could return. In other words, the supposed first-century expulsion noted by a popularizer of history, who relied on more proficient historians for his information, was a one-year expulsion at most and probably no expulsion at all. It would have been ironic if the two-thousand-year continuous residency of Jews in Rome began with an expulsion—but the evidence does not support such an irony.[32]

Of more import, this earliest reference to Jews described them as "infectious," a danger to Roman customs. As such, from their earliest identification, Jews are described as a contagion that must be contained. If not, Rome may become, in some measure, "Jewish."

The first indication of a Jewish community living permanently in Rome comes from the orator Cicero (106–43 BCE), who does not hide his contempt for Jews. In 59 BCE, Cicero became defense counsel for Lucius Valerius Flaccus, the Roman governor of Asia Minor, who had been criminally charged with having confiscated gold that Jews in Asia had sent legally to Jerusalem to support the Temple. The outflow of gold to Judaea was a vexing issue at the time, because it could be seen as enriching a colony conquered by General Pompey just four years earlier. Flaccus, defending himself as a patriot, claimed that he was seizing funds legitimately en route to Judaea in order to prevent the support of barbarous rites practiced in Jerusalem. He was nonetheless brought to trial for withholding lawful payments by Jews to their Temple.[33]

As defense counsel, Cicero was not above playing on popular prejudices when it came to foreigners. An audience of Jews attended the public trial, and Cicero described this audience as a politically influential group that "unanimously . . . stick[s] together." To top it off, Cicero accused the prosecutor, Decimus Laelius, of purposely packing the audience with enough of a Jewish "mob" to pose a threat to justice: "We come now to the libel involving the gold, the Jewish gold. This is obviously the reason why the present case is being tried close to the Aurelian Steps. It is because of this particular charge that you have sought out this location, Laelius, and that mob. You know what a large group they are, how unanimously they stick together, how influential they are in politics."[34]

Undoubtedly the Jews in attendance were concerned should their annual contributions to the Temple be misappropriated. Fortunately, those fears would prove unfounded, despite the fact that Flaccus was eventually acquitted.[35] For our purposes, we may conclude from Cicero's invective that Jews were a well-known, substantial community residing in Rome by 59 BCE.

The Hellenistic Jewish philosopher Philo of Alexandria (also known as Philo Judaeus) observes that the Roman Jewish community may have originally consisted of Jewish prisoners of war whom Pompey took from Jerusalem to Rome in 61 BCE and then forced to march in his triumphal parade.[36] The apocryphal *Psalms of Solomon* may preserve a memory of that parade of captives:

The beauty of his glory was despised before God;
It was completely disgraced.

The sons and daughters were in harsh captivity,
Their neck in a seal, a spectacle among the gentiles.[37]

Nonetheless, just two years later, in 59 BCE, the community of Roman Jews seems to have consisted of freedmen comfortably attending Flaccus's public trial.

Jewish antipathy toward Pompey may also account, in part, for Roman Jews' support of Julius Caesar in his civil war against Pompey in 49 BCE, during which the Egyptian king Ptolemy III killed Pompey and then besieged Caesar in Alexandria. The siege was lifted in 47 BCE when Jewish forces led by Herod the Great's father, Antipater (113–43 BCE), came to Caesar's rescue.[38] The victorious Caesar responded by granting the Jews of the Roman Empire unusual freedoms. Despite Roman law strictly governing assemblies, Jews were allowed to meet and celebrate as their traditions required; thus they were free to worship as Jews.[39] The Temple tax paid to Jerusalem was also permitted, and Jews were exempted from military service, given that they could not march on the Sabbath nor partake of unkosher military rations. Furthermore, Caesar sanctioned the operation of separate Jewish courts where disputes between Jews could be adjudicated.[40]

In Rome, Jews lived on the west bank of the Tiber in an area known as *Transtiburinum* (across the Tiber) separate from the center of the city. They did so without recorded incident not only during the reign of Caesar (49–44 BCE) but also during the reign of his adopted son Augustus (27 BCE–14 CE), who reaffirmed their freedoms.[41]

At about this time (35 BCE), the poet Horace (65–8 BCE) describes an incident so universal and so comic that the characters would be at home in a novel by Balzac or an episode of *Seinfeld*. The incident only obliquely concerns Rome's Jews, but they are used as an excuse for a failure of camaraderie. In one of his comments on Roman society and its devotees of money and fame, Horace reports being accosted by a boor who will not take no for an answer (*Satire* 1.9.67–72). He wants Horace to introduce him to Horace's wealthy patron, which Horace is loath to do. While still trapped by his interlocutor, Horace spies a welcome passerby: his friend

Aristius Fuscus. Dragging Fuscus into the conversation, Horace pointedly asks him, "Wasn't there something you wanted to talk to me about, *in private*." Horace clearly hopes that Fuscus will take the hint and extricate him from the boor's incessant requests, but Fuscus is either oblivious to Horace's not-so-subtle entreaties or he is enjoying seeing his friend squirm. He replies that the conversation Horace suggested is not suitable for the moment because it is the "thirtieth Sabbath" (whatever that means), and surely Horace does not want to insult the "circumcised Jews." Horace, showing his desperation, answers with some irritation that he has no "religious scruples" and again offers a silent plea for Fuscus to get him off the hook. But Fuscus is adamant. *He* indeed has religious scruples, he says, thereby one-upping Horace. He leaves to let Horace fend for himself.

There may be more amusement than historical value in this story, but it does indicate that some (even if inaccurate) knowledge of Jews and their customs was sufficiently prevalent in first-century BCE Rome that they could be a source of humor.

Other documents indicate that Judaism was imperfectly understood. Augustus, who, as noted, acted favorably toward the Jewish community, and whose wife, Livia, had a Jewish handmaid named Acme, nevertheless believed the Sabbath was a weekly fast day.[42] Among some Romans, including the satirist Persius (34–62 CE), the Sabbath was known as the "Day of Herod," named after the most prominent Jew in the empire.[43] On the other hand, the poet Ovid (43 BCE–18 CE) may have had a better understanding of Jewish customs. He understood the Sabbath to be a day unsuitable for business as well as an inauspicious day for a trip.[44]

Upon Augustus's death and the accession of the Emperor Tiberius (14–37 CE), unforeseen hardship befell the Jews of Rome. Four separate historical sources attest to an expulsion of Jews from the city. The best witness to this troubling event is the first-century historian Tacitus (56–120 CE), despite the fact that he virulently despised Jews and their customs:

Once during a plague in Egypt, which caused bodily disfigurement, King Bocchoris approached the oracle of Ammon and asked for a remedy whereupon he was told to purge his kingdom and to transport this race [the Jews] into other lands, since it was hateful to the gods.

They [the Jews] dedicated, in a shrine, of that creature [the ass] whose guidance enabled them to put an end to their wandering and thirst.

The Jews are extremely loyal toward one another, and always ready to show compassion, but towards every other people they feel only hate and enmity. . . . Though a most lascivious people, the Jews avoid sexual intercourse with women of alien race.[45]

Tacitus explains that under Tiberius, a senatorial edict forbade Jewish ritual and expelled four thousand Jewish descendants of slaves to Sardinia in the hopes that they would die from the "pestilential climate" there. The remaining Jews would have to leave Italy unless they renounced their religion.[46]

The historian Suetonius (69–ca.122 CE) corroborated Tacitus's account: "He suppressed foreign cults and the religions of the Egyptians and the Jews, obliging those who practiced such rituals to burn their religious garments and all their paraphernalia. The young men of the Jewish people he sent to regions where the climate was severe, ostensibly on military service. The rest of that people, and others of similar beliefs, he banished from the city, with the penalty of slavery for life if they did not obey."[47] A later historian, Dio Cassius (155–235 CE), wrote of an expulsion of the Jews to Sardinia in 19 CE, attributing the Jews' banishment to their "converting many of the natives to their ways."[48]

Finally, Josephus, too, informs us of the banishment under Emperor Tiberius and links it to Jewish proselytism. He tells the story of an unscrupulous Jew who had been banished from Judaea. Upon arriving in Rome, he enlisted the help of three other Jews in bilking a noblewoman out of her money. The four scoundrels persuaded Fulvia, a woman of "great dignity" who had converted to Judaism, to remit gold to the Jerusalem Temple by first giving them the money; they, of course, absconded with the gold. Josephus goes on to explain that when Tiberius heard of this crime, he carried out the expulsion.[49]

Josephus's explanation is too similar to the story of Flaccus, and too much in the style of a folktale, to be credited as a correct understanding of Tiberius's actions. However, taken together, the four narratives indicate that Tiberius had concerns about foreign influences in Rome that could undermine or even replace longstanding Roman traditions. As we shall see, emperors, who sought the honor of deification, were displeased by a people in their midst whose beliefs could not countenance such imperial aspirations. One can understand the expulsion under Tiberius as grounded in these reasons. Further it is also not clear that, at the time, Roman historians or other Latin authors, such as poets, fully comprehended the concept of a conversion from Roman religion to Judaism. The idea that an individual decision concerning cultic matters could result in membership in what they considered an ethnic group like the Jews does not seem to have been fully grasped. While Jews accepted proselytes in the first century CE, there is no mention of converts as an identifiable group in the concurrent Roman literature. That said, it appears that by 19 CE, some Romans did believe that Jews posed a threat to Roman mores.[50]

As a result, if one was not Jewish, being mistaken for a Jew was best avoided. The Roman philosopher Seneca the Younger (4 BCE–65 CE) wrote that during the time of Tiberius, in order to achieve tranquility of mind, he had adopted an Epicurean diet, one based on moderation that required he abstain from meat. After extolling the excellent results of such a diet, in particular the clarity of mind it afforded, he nonetheless took his father's advice to return to dining "more comfortably." Seneca notes that "some foreign rites were, at that time, being inaugurated, and abstinence from certain kinds of animal food was set down as a proof of interest in the strange cult."[51] Yet, at the same time, Seneca is at pains to tell us that his father did not fear he would be "prosecuted" for adhering to the prohibition against "certain foods." Only his father's hatred of philosophy, including Epicureanism, had made him advise his son to resume eating meat.

It is not stated in the text, but we may surmise that during the reign of Tiberius, appearing to follow some Jewish customs—refraining from pork in particular—might have resulted in one's prosecution—that is, an order of exile. If we take Seneca's word as true, his father harbored no such fears. Nevertheless, the text attests that such fears existed.

During the following reigns of Caligula (37–41 CE) and Claudius (41–54 CE), there was a considerable Jewish presence in Rome, despite the probable expulsion of some Jews under Tiberius. Both emperors affirmed the rights of the Jewish community throughout the empire with the exception, according to Suetonius, of "the Jews he [Claudius] expelled from Rome since they were constantly in rebellion at the instigation of Chrestus."[52] In apparent corroboration of this account, Acts 18:2 tells of Paul arriving in Corinth and there meeting the Jews Aquila and Priscilla, because, Aquila says, "Claudius had commanded all the Jews to leave Rome." However, Cassius Dio plainly states that Claudius did not expel the Jews from Rome because their number had become too large.[53] What are we to make of this contradictory evidence?

The Suetonius passage has been heavily interpreted due to the possibility that "Chrestus" may be a reference to Christ. That may not be the case, but if it is, "the Jews . . . constantly in rebellion at the instigation of Chrestus" would refer to the earliest Christian community in Rome, which indeed could have been instigating conflict within the wider Jewish community. In that instance, Claudius might have exiled only those followers of "Chrestus" and no other Jews. If so, then the statement attributed to Aquila in Acts that all Jews had been expelled would be exaggerated and wrong.[54] Because many Jews actually stayed in Rome during and after the reign of Claudius, the suggestion that the expulsion was only partial is convincing. Even if Suetonius was referring to a Roman Jew named Chrestus who had nothing to do with Jesus Christ, it is likeliest that the expulsion under Claudius was only partial.

Nonetheless, prior to Claudius's reign, Emperor Caligula's well-known erratic behavior extended even to Jews. When in 38 CE the governor of Alexandria required Jews to display images of the emperor in their synagogues, Alexandrian Jews sent a mission, headed by the philosopher Philo, to Caligula entreating intervention on their behalf—but Caligula upped the ante: Instead of placing his image in Alexandrian synagogues, Jews had to put it in the Jerusalem Temple itself. That disaster was averted when Caligula was assassinated in 41 CE.[55]

Jews were in the emperor's good graces during the reign of Nero (54–68 CE), given that his wife, Poppaea, was an admirer of the Jewish religion, indeed a Judaizer, if not a convert.[56] The Jewish quarter was also far away from the fire that destroyed much of Rome in 64 CE.

The condition of Rome's Jews changed dramatically in 70 CE with the destruction of the Jerusalem Temple and the defeat of the Judaean revolt. After suppressing the revolt, Emperor Vespasian took two further steps. First, he financed building the Colosseum, the legendary site of circuses and gladiatorial contests, from the spoils of war taken from Judaea. The remains of a fragmentary inscription found in the Colosseum states, "The Emperor Vespasian ordered this new amphitheater to be constructed from the booty . . ."[57] While the rest of the inscription is lost, it most likely refers to the treasures captured from Judaea and Jerusalem, given that those treasures were the most conspicuous spoils acquired by Vespasian. Accordingly, Jews involuntarily financed the symbol of the Eternal City found today on T-shirts, kitchen magnets, napkins, and salt and pepper shakers in a thousand Roman souvenir shops.

Second, Vespasian redirected the monies previously collected by Jews for the upkeep of their Temple to renovate the Temple of Jupiter on Capitoline Hill (portions of which can still be seen inside Rome's Capitoline Museum).[58] He collected the tax commonly called the *fiscus judaicus*— two denarii annually—from all Jews throughout the empire.[59] Effectively, Vespasian weaponized the longtime grant to the Jews allowing them to practice Judaism. They could still do so, but now they had to pay for the privilege.

Nonetheless, such a tax was not exclusive to Jews. Vespasian imposed a similar tax on Alexandrians (*fiscus Alexandrinus*) and on Asiatics (*fiscus asiaticus*).[60] The *fiscus judaicus* would be abolished in 361 CE when Emperor Julian (361–63 CE) had the tax rolls burned. In the interim, and certainly well before 361, the *fiscus judaicus* also served to focus attention on the question of who in fact was a Jew.

During the reign of Domitian (81–96 CE), Suetonius records that some Jews tried to hide their Jewish identity in order to avoid the tax: "Those who lived as Jews without being registered as such were indicted, as were those who concealed their origins and did not pay the tax imposed on their race. I remember when I was a youth being present when an old man of ninety was inspected by a procurator and a very crowded court, to see whether he was circumcised."[61]

Here we learn that Domitian's procurators did not hesitate to humiliate and persecute even aged Jews in order to collect the tax. That said, Domitian did not single out Jews for abuse. He tried to wring every penny from all Romans due to an economic crisis partly of his own making: he had overspent on public buildings and gladiatorial games.[62]

More importantly, from this passage we also learn that in Rome, Jews were considered an *ethnos*, a race, persons of Jewish "origins." In addition, others "lived as Jews," but had not been born Jews. Therein we see a distinction that persists to this day in Rome and elsewhere. For some, Judaism was a race, a birthright. The epitaphs in the catacombs indicate that the vast majority of Roman Jews were born of Jewish parents who passed some form of Jewish tradition onto their children. For others, however, Judaism was a religion, a collection of beliefs and traditions that could be freely adopted or rejected.

Both definitions of what it meant to be a Jew were made explicit as early as Domitian's Rome, when being a Jew was a financial liability. Some would try to avoid the tax by saying "Don't tax me, because although I was born Jewish, I have given up my religion." At the same time, certain Romans were converting to Judaism or taking the easier path of sympathizing with Judaism, adhering to some of the practices such as Sabbath observance and abstention from pork, while failing to convert to the extent of circumcision or attending synagogue. These latter Romans who "lived as Jews" were called "God-Fearers."[63] It was thus relatively easy to enter the Jewish world, given a variety of forms of partial membership. Moreover, at the time there was no specific Jewish ceremony akin to baptism in the

Christian community to confirm a conversion to Judaism.[64] And decisions were constantly being made concerning which of these groups would bear the financial burden by being officially deemed Jewish.

Cassius Dio writes that at its inception, Vespasian only imposed the *fiscus judaicus* upon practicing Jews—although Cassius Dio may have been simply describing the circumstances of his own time (second and third centuries CE) as if they obtained in the first century.[65] But it appears that under Domitian things took a turn for the worse for the Jews. He imposed the *fiscus judaicus* not only on persons born Jewish (of Jewish "origin") who practiced their religion, but also on apostates and possibly on God-Fearers.[66] Moreover, in some cases "living a Jewish life" could result in dire consequences. Cassius Dio tells the story of Domitian executing his cousin, the consul Flavius Clemens, and Flavius's wife Flavia Domitilla: "The charge brought against them both was that of atheism, a charge on which many others who drifted into Jewish ways were condemned."[67]

By atheism, Domitian did not mean a failure to believe in God or the gods of Rome. He meant a failure to believe that *he* was a god. For a Roman, to reject the gods of Rome meant an explicit rejection of Julius Caesar, Augustus, Claudius, Vespasian, and Titus as deities. Domitian took that rejection personally—as an implicit rejection of his claim that like his father (Vespasian) and his brother (Titus), he, too, deserved deification. In short, the import of atheism in Domitian's Rome was treason.[68]

Persons born Jewish were in a class by themselves. They had been given a dispensation to practice their religion; gentile Romans had no such grant. If Flavius and Flavia drifted away from Roman beliefs and into "Jewish ways," they did so at their peril.

Whether Flavius and Flavia were converts to Judaism or only God-Fearers is not certain. There is, however, a parallel if not corroborating tradition in rabbinic texts. The Babylonian Talmud mentions a nephew of Titus, Kalonikos, who converted to Judaism, as well as a senator, Keti'ah bar Shalom, who, with his wife, were God-Fearers and who died either by execution or by suicide.[69] Although the names in the Talmud are different, the rabbinic stories might refer to the same events. These events signal

Domitian's increasing hostility toward Jews at the end of the first century. It is even said that the second-century Jewish sages Gamaliel II, Joshua ben Hananiah, Eleazar ben Azariah, and Akiva traveled from Palestine to Rome on a mission in response to this crisis, though the story of the Rabbis' visit is uncorroborated historically.[70]

In any event, Domitian's execution and exile of his cousins points to a possible inconsistency in his policies. On the one hand, Domitian was casting a wide net by including in his definition of Jewry persons who, while not born Jewish, chose Judaism and its lifestyle. Ultimately, his decision regarding who qualified as Jewish was pragmatic: Domitian needed the *fiscus judaicus* income from as many people as possible, since the Flavian building projects, including the Colosseum and the Arch of Titus, were accruing expenses he could not easily pay for. On the other hand, Domitian's need to be treated as a deity led him to execute and exile at least some of those very same converts and God-Fearers. Taken to its logical conclusion, Domitian appears to have exiled or killed off some of the persons constituting the tax base he desperately needed.

And the dilemma he created was not his alone. It was a dilemma for Roman gentiles attracted to Judaism as well. If they had already converted, they could hide their Judaism to avoid persecution—but that was also tax evasion, which had its own penalties. If they paid the tax, they were admitting not only to Judaizing but to "atheism," which was even more dangerous. The dilemma appears to have been so acute that some have said it never happened: that Domitian was not taxing the God-Fearers, but only those Jews, born Jewish, who claimed to have abandoned their Jewish practice.[71]

For reasons having nothing to do with Jews or the *fiscus judaicus*, Domitian was murdered in the fifteenth year of his reign. A senator, Cocceius Nerva, succeeded him as emperor (96–98 CE). Nerva issued a coin bearing the words "Fisci Iudaici Calumnia Sublata," a slogan compressed to a point of being obscure to modern scholars. It may have meant "abolition of the unjust enforcement of the Jewish tax" or "The malicious accusation [brought by] the treasury for Jewish affairs has been removed."[72] Practically, it may have signified that under Nerva, the tax on the Jews initiated in 70 CE was abolished, or it could have had a more limited meaning of abolishing the tax unjustly imposed upon Jews who no longer practiced Judaism.[73] In any event, the commemorative coin, which circulated solely in Rome, was a happy one for Jews.

Nerva was considered an enlightened ruler. The fifth book of the Sibylline Oracle (a collection of Greek prophecies ascribed to the sybils but actually composed by Jews) describes Nerva as a "mortal of reverend bearing."[74] However, his reign was short, just two years, and after his death, if not before, the Jewish tax continued to be collected.

His successors, Trajan (98–117 CE) and then Hadrian (117–38 CE), took a dimmer view of Judaism. Both had to deal with Jewish uprisings, some outside Rome in North Africa and Cyprus, and finally one in Judaea. To the extent that Nerva had abolished or moderated the *fiscus judaicus*, Trajan reinstated it. That was enough to incite a Jewish revolt (115–16 CE) of considerable violence in Cyrenaica (modern Libya) and Egypt. Trajan's reaction was equally brutal, but it does not appear to have affected the Jews of Rome.[75]

The Hadrianic persecution of Judaea's Jews and the brutal suppression of the Bar Kokhba revolt in 135 CE also had few repercussions in Rome. One exception was Hadrian's prohibition of circumcision throughout the empire, including Rome. However, upon his death in 138 CE, his successor Antoninus eased the order, allowing Jews to circumcise their own children but no one else. This relaxation of a rule that struck at the heart of Jewish practice may have been accomplished by a visit to Rome from Rabbis Simeon ben Yohai and Eliezer ben Jose.[76]

At the beginning of the third century CE, Jews and Judaism enjoyed a time of some favor. The Severans were in power. Septimius Severus (145–211 CE) allowed Jews to hold public office (although he also prohibited conversions to either Judaism or Christianity). Alexander Severus (208–35 CE), the last of the Severan dynasty, was sufficiently favorable to Judaism that his enemies nicknamed him "archisynagogus." Some believe this meant that he founded one of Rome's synagogues, but this is unlikely.[77]

It is more reliably reported that he included an image of Abraham among his Lares (household gods).[78]

Thus the history of the Jews of ancient Rome (139 BCE to the third century CE) begins with an expulsion and ends with a synagogue founded by an emperor—both events that probably did not happen. These two bookends display the fragility of our knowledge of Rome's Jews in antiquity. They also point out the vicissitudes and the fragility of the Jewish community. "Fragile" is one way of saying that the boundaries of the Jewish community were fuzzy. Who, in fact, was a Jew?

THE JEWISHNESS OF THE CATACOMBS

If the question "Who is a Jew?" crops up in the works of Seneca, Suetonius, and others, it can also be found underground. Proselytes, whose status was much the subject of debate and even litigation during Domitian's time, also appear in catacomb inscriptions.[79] But if the individual proselytes found in the catacombs possibly caused controversy during their lifetimes, in death they had a secure place in the community.

The graves of proselytes are known because the inscriptions that bear their names identify them as such. One notable inscription (number 523 in Leon's catalogue) reads: "Veturia Paulla F consigned to her eternal home who lived 86 years, 6 months, a proselyte of 16 years, named Sara, mother of the synagogues of Campus and Volumnius. In peace her sleep."[80] From these brief lines on a sarcophagus we learn that as a proselyte Veturia Paulla took the name of "Sara" and converted to Judaism when she was seventy years old. We do not know anything about the duties, if any, of a "mother of synagogue" (*mater synagogue*) beyond the fact that the title is an honorific. We can surmise that this woman was remarkable for having been so honored by two synagogues.

A similar inscription (number 462) identifies a woman named Felicitas who took the Jewish name of Peregrina, which translates the Hebrew word for convert, *ger* (literally "stranger"), into Latin. Peregrina died at age forty-seven, having been a proselyte for six years.[81]

A rather mysterious inscription from the Torlonia catacomb states: "Irene, foster child, proselyte, her father and mother Jewish, an Israelite, lived three years, seven months, one day."[82] It is hard to imagine a three-year-old proselyte both of whose parents were Jewish. It is equally hard to imagine the pain of her foster parents who ordered this inscription.

Another inscription (Leon's Document 72), on a sarcophagus found near the Torlonia catacomb, may identify not a Jew but a God-Fearer. It reads: "To Julia Irene Arista, his mother, preserved through the power of God and the devotion of her family, a pious observer of the Law, Atronius, Tullianus, Eusebius, vir optimus, her son in due tribute, aged 41."[83]

That Julia Irene Arista was buried in a sarcophagus and not a simple burial niche indicates the family's wealth, status, or both. Like most funereal inscriptions, hers is condensed enough to be cryptic. Julia could very well have been Jewish, but because the label "pious observer of the Law" is unique in the catacombs, she might instead have been an admirer of Judaism who observed the Law but never converted—in other words, a God-Fearer. It is also not clear whether her son, Atronius, was Jewish, a God-Fearer, or even a gentile who nevertheless sought to honor his mother and her wishes to be buried in a Jewish cemetery. (In another circumstance recorded in a non-Jewish source, the father was a God-Fearer and the son a convert.)[84]

Regardless of whether a person was a Jew by birth, a proselyte, or a God-Fearer, the Jews of Rome made another distinction within the community. At least three inscriptions indicate that the deceased being honored was a member of the synagogue of the Vernaclians. It appears, therefore, that one of the eleven synagogues in Rome was reserved for the *Vernacli*, or native-born Roman Jews. In like vein, Rome's synagogue of the Tripolitans appears to have been founded by Jewish immigrants from the city of Tripolis, either in Phoenicia (now Lebanon) or North Africa. Other Roman synagogues seem to have been named after the area in Rome where the building stood, or the hometowns or occupations of the members.[85] However, with the Vernacli there appears to have been a desire to assert the pedigree of the congregation: to identify its members as longstanding locals as opposed to interlopers and immigrants.

If Jews were already intimate strangers in Rome, it seems the Vernacli wanted to be more intimate than strangers. However, that was probably wishful thinking. Even when Jews were accepted, including as citizens, in ancient Rome, they still were strangers. Their most prominent customs—circumcision, Sabbath observance, and the prohibition against eating pork—were not considered quaint or exotically mysterious; more often these were cause for jokes. Petronius, believing circumcision was a self-imposed deformity, said of a slave: "He has only two faults and if he were rid of them he would be simply perfect. He is circumcised and he snores."[86]

The Talmud, on the other hand, records the following story, which more accurately reflects the ambiguous circumstances of Jews in Rome: "Rabbi Abba bar Zemina [fourth century CE] used to work as a tailor for a Gentile in Rome. The latter wished to compel him to eat meat not slaughtered according to Kashrut, and threatened to kill him if he did not do so. R. Abba said to him, 'If you wish to kill, kill, for I shall not eat unkosher meat.' The Gentile said to him, 'Now I can tell you that if you had eaten, I should have killed you. If one is a Jew let one be a Jew.'"[87]

This possibly apocryphal story nonetheless illustrates the dilemma of being Jewish in Rome. You could be despised for your traditional customs, but you could also be despised if you tried to disown those customs and assimilate. Do not be a stranger, but do not try to be too intimate either.

PORK AND CIRCUMCISION

The anonymous gentile who supposedly threatened R. Abba was not the only Roman who struggled to understand Jewish customs. Many non-Jews viewed the Sabbath as a fast day and a sign of laziness. Ovid warned that the Sabbath was no excuse for avoiding a spurned lover. If one had to leave the country to get away from her, "Hope not for rain nor let foreign Sabbath stay you."[88] The kashrut laws concerning pork also occasioned humor. Macrobius reports, with tongue in cheek, that when Augustus learned King Herod had ordered his own son put to death, the Emperor joked, "I'd rather be Herod's pig than Herod's son."[89]

Beyond jokes, Jewish customs were sometimes considered an impurity or a potential infection of the body politic. When describing the expulsion of Jews under Tiberius, Tacitus stated that those expelled were "four thousand descendants of enfranchised slaves, tainted with that superstition [Judaism]."[90] He also reported that the Jews had left Egypt because during a plague, the god Ammon advised the king to purge his land of a people hateful to the gods.[91]

Saint Augustine later stated that according to Seneca, the Jewish people had turned the world upside down: "When speaking of the Jews he [Seneca] says: 'Meanwhile the customs of this accursed race have gained such influence that they are now received throughout all the world. The vanquished have given laws to their victors.'"[92]

Juvenal went so far as to describe the process of how this reversal occurred:

> Some who have had a father who reveres the Sabbath worship . . . and see no difference between eating swine's flesh, from which their father abstained and that of man; and in time they take to circumcision. Having been wont to flout the laws of Rome, they learn and practice the Jewish law, and all that Moses handed down in his secret tome, forbidding to point out the way to any not worshipping the same rites and conducting none but the circumcised to the desired fountain. For all which the father was to blame, who gave up every seventh day to idleness, keeping it apart from all the concerns of life.[93]

Juvenal depicted a generational slippery slope whereby a father "worshiping" the Sabbath eventually led to the son avoiding pork and ultimately falling all the way into circumcision—that is, full-on Judaism. At that point, the newly converted Jew could be counted on to favor only his fellow Jews and not even to help anyone else to a drink of water.

Elsewhere Juvenal spoke of Jews living as beggars at the Porta Capena, a gateway to Rome and a spot traditionally said to have been visited by Rome's legendary second king, Numa, in order to commune with a goddess. The historian Livy described it as a grove watered by a perennial spring.[94] However, Juvenal writes that in his time, it had become the haunt of poverty-stricken Jews whose women, "palsied fortune tellers . . . will tell you dreams of any kind you please for the minutest of coins."[95]

Juvenal's images of Jews are both vicious and symbolic. Jews live on the periphery of the city, the borderline between inside and outside, at the gateway. But even as they are liminal, they are said to have appropriated Numa's sacred grove for their begging, thus implicitly befouling Rome at its origins. They are both palsied and possessed of Romans' most intimate knowledge: their dreams.

They are also insidious, sick, and knocking at the door. They are strangers whose seemingly harmless customs could eventually take over a family and lead to the abandonment of Roman law and fellowship. They are intimate strangers whose intimacy is dangerous.

That said, not all Romans shared Juvenal's animosity. Nor did his ideas gain favor over time. He wrote in approximately 100 CE. About a century later, between 222 and 235 CE, Emperor Alexander Severus, known for his appreciation of Judaism, is said to have exclaimed about the Jewish religious tradition: "what he had heard from someone, either a Jew or a Christian, and always remembered, and he also had it announced by a herald whenever he was disciplining anyone, 'What you do not wish that a man should do to you, do not do to him.' And so highly did he value this sentiment that he had it written up in the palace and in public buildings."[96]

The emperor's favorite "sentiment" was the so-called Golden Rule, attributed in the Talmud to Hillel (at Babylonian Talmud, *Shabbath* 31a) and to Akiva (in *Avoth de-Rabbi Nahan* B-26). At the same time, it is also attributed to Jesus in Matthew 7:12 and Luke 6:31, but there it appears in positive form, "As you wish that men would do to you, do so to them." The negative formulation quoted by Alexander Severus is particular to the rabbinic tradition, which is the source from which he apparently "heard" it.

Although it is claimed that Severus had that sentiment written on public buildings, no such inscription appears in the archaeological record. However, two inscriptions from the Jewish catacombs bear Severus's name. One mentions a woman, Alexandria Severa, named after him; another refers to a mother and son named Severa and Severus.[97] It seems Alexander Severus's affection for Jewish wisdom did not go unrequited. The parents of these long dead Jews gave the emperor the honor they wished he and his descendants would give them and theirs.

FIG. 3. *The Ephemeral Display for the Façade of the Cinque Scole,* a pencil and water-color painting by Leopoldo Buzi, circa 1814. Photo by Araldo De Luca. Copyright Historical Archives of the Jewish Community of Rome, Giancarlo Spizzichino.

3

A Torah for the Pope

Jewish Participation in Papal Processions

To better understand the Jewish community's social position in Catholic Rome during the Middle Ages, let's jump ahead in time to confront a remarkable postmedieval image (fig. 3). It's a shocking image, if you know what you're looking at. This 37 x 57 centimeter pencil-and-watercolor architectural drawing, executed around 1814, depicts a scene from the Ghetto in Rome, specifically the façade of the Cinque Scole (the five schools or five synagogues), a well-known building in the heart of the Ghetto.

After Pope Paul IV established the Ghetto in 1555, it was ordered, and then reordered in 1566 and 1581, that there be only one synagogue for the entire Jewish community. In antiquity, there had been eleven synagogues in Rome, and at the beginning of the sixteenth century there were at least nine scole—many of them housed in the same building since 1549. Yet once the Ghetto was established, in technical compliance with the papal decree, five scole—the Scole Castigliana, Catalana, Siciliana, Tempio, and Nova—were crammed together in one three-story building, where they existed literally one on top of the other. To all outward appearances, there was only one synagogue—what was known as the Cinque Scole—in the Piazza Mercatello, but inside the building, five communities were bumping elbows.[1]

The building is no more. About thirty years after the Ghetto's final dissolution in 1870, the Cinque Scole was torn down, and plans were made for a new synagogue to be built nearby. Eventually completed in 1904, the Great Synagogue (Tempio Maggiore) of Rome still stands towering over the banks of the Tiber and across from the Isola Tiberina in the middle of the river.

But in 1814, the year of our drawing, the Cinque Scole was still standing. The drawing shows the front entrance to the synagogue with four columns on a raised platform. The doors are open, and inside, a perfect seven-branched golden menorah, luminous as it is solitary, occupies the very center of the frame. The four columns hold up an architrave and tympanum, above which are garlands, and crowning the Cinque Scole, triumphantly perched on the roof, is a concrete rendition of a huge papal seal—that of Pius VII. The crossed keys of Saint Peter and the miter, the ceremonial papal hat, dominate the synagogue. Across the architrave is a Latin inscription celebrating the pope's felicitous liberation and restoration.

With that inscription, we understand what we are seeing. The drawing does not depict either a reality or some chilling alternate history where the only synagogue in Rome has become a basilica. Rather, it shows a drapery covering the actual front of the Cinque Scole in the manner of the modern artist Christo, who used cloth to wrap the Reichstag in Berlin and the Pont-Neuf in Paris. What covered the front of the Cinque Scole in 1814 was also a work of art: a painting on cloth, an ephemeral embellishment presented in commemoration of the liberation of Pope Pius VII from imprisonment at the hands of the French army.

Napoleon had conquered Rome first in 1798 and again in 1809. Both times Jews were freed from the Ghetto and given equal rights as subjects of the French Republic. And, both times, a pope was taken captive by the French. In 1809 it was Pius VII. With the collapse of Napoleon's power, Pius VII returned to Rome in 1814. There was to be a citywide celebration, and even the Jews who, no fools, realized that their own liberation was to be short-lived, had to participate and hail the returning pope. Leopoldo Buzi, an artist and architect, painted the false façade, the platform and the pillars, the architrave and the papal seal, on a cloth that was then hung in front of the Cinque Scole, hiding the real façade. It was, in effect, a Potemkin village made of boards, painted cloth, and papier-maché that probably stood in front of the synagogue building for no more than a week.[2]

We have no idea what ultimately happened to that set dressing. This drawing, also by Buzi, is all we have of the enforced gaiety wrung out of the Jewish community. Once back in the Vatican, the liberated pope reinstated the Ghetto.

RITUAL PRESENTATION OF THE TORAH

If you think it unusual for the Jewish community to come out publicly to celebrate a pope, that's because you are not living in the twelfth century. Back then, more than four hundred years before the creation of the Ghetto, and six hundred years prior to Buzi's drawing, a series of events led to the first-known acclamation of a pope by the Jews.

In 1130, the Catholic Church, acting through a small group of six cardinals, elected Pope Innocent II to the papacy in the Lateran Church in Rome. However, within two hours, the remaining cardinals elected another pope, Anacletus II, who was of Jewish descent some generations back, to oppose Innocent.

Anacletus had the backing of a powerful Roman family, the Frangipani, and so Innocent fled north to Paris, where his supporters included the influential abbot and soon-to-be-canonized St. Bernard of Clairvaux. During Easter week, Parisian Jews marched with Innocent II through the streets toward the Abbey of St. Denis, the influential church named after the first bishop of Paris, where Innocent II had chosen to celebrate Easter. As part of the celebration, and in the French tradition of giving gifts at the coronation of a king, Parisian Jews offered Innocent II a "veiled" or covered scroll of the Law. Paris's Jewish leaders might have so introduced themselves to Innocent hoping that he would remember them and favor them with gifts in the future, but instead Innocent caustically replied by quoting 2 Corinthians: "Would God the Omnipotent, tear the veil away from your hearts" (3:15–16). This brief exchange in which Innocent II chastised the Jews for being "blind of heart" is the earliest-known instance of Jewish participation in a procession glorifying the pope, and of Jews presenting a Torah scroll to a pope.[3] As for Anacletus and Innocent II, their dispute lasted until Anacletus's death in 1138.

When the coronation ritual was taken up in Rome starting in 1145, the procession wound its way from the Vatican on the west bank of the Tiber across the river to the Lateran Church at the southern edge of Rome. It was called the *possesso* because it marked the pope's possession of Rome as its bishop. The pope was (and is) simultaneously the leader of the worldwide Catholic Church and the local bishop of Rome; and the *possesso*, a ritual statement of that dual circumstance, took place after the pope's coronation as the supreme leader of the church at the portico of Saint Peter's Basilica, when he would proceed crosstown to the Lateran Church to officiate as the bishop of Rome.

The year 1145 was, significantly, also the first year in which the Jewish community in Rome presented a Torah to the newly elected pope: during the coronation of Pope Eugenius III (1145–53). Rome's Jewish leaders repeated the ritual for Pope Alexander III (1159–81), for Clement III (1187–91), for Boniface VIII (1294–1303), and so on, for many papal coronations until 1513.[4]

For hundreds of years, inaugural papal processions were elaborate theatrical events, with multiple smaller performances, and the Jewish community's presentation of a Torah was one of them. This performance had three parts. First, the Jews encountered the pope on his parade route. Often this happened just after the pope crossed the Tiber River on the Ponte Sant'Angelo, a bridge linking Rome's historical center with the Castel Sant'Angelo (an imposing fortress built on top of the mausoleum of the Roman Emperor Hadrian, who had quelled the Bar Kokhba revolt, leveled Jerusalem, banned all Jews from living in the city, and prohibited Jews from visiting Jerusalem except for one day a year—the ninth of the Jewish month of Av, Tisha b'Av—to mourn the Temple's destruction). As the pope and his procession crossed the bridge leaving the Castel behind, representatives of the Jewish community came to meet him. With Hadrian's tomb as a backdrop, the memory of Jewish subjugation was surely evident.

At this point the second element of the ritual occurred: the Jewish delegation presented a Torah to the pope. What was said upon the presentation of the Torah is not known, but one papal attendant at the side of Innocent VIII (1484–92) captured the spirit of what he heard: "Holy Father, in the name of our synagogue, we Hebrew men implore that your Holiness deign to confirm and approve the Mosaic Law, which almighty God gave to Moses, our shepherd on Mount Sinai, as the other supreme pontiffs, Your Holiness's predecessors, have confirmed and approved it."[5]

This may sound like a rote recitation, but it was not. The Law God gave Moses at Sinai was in the Hebrew language, whereas the Catholic Bible was a Latin translation. St. Jerome's translation of the Hebrew Bible for Catholics was venerated, but also acknowledged as a translation. As the French exegete and philosopher Joseph Ibn Caspi (b. 1280) noted in his *Shulhan Kesef*, the popes were aware that when they read their Old Testament, they were operating at a linguistic remove from God's actual words. Consequently, with their gift, the Jews were presenting the pope with the Holy Scriptures in the language and words spoken by God.[6] In addition, the copying of the biblical text in its original language was considered a sacred act.[7] As gifts go, the Torah was not to be taken lightly.

At roughly the same time, in 1488, by order of Innocent VIII, a church official, Agostini Patrizi, revised the ceremony. Thereafter, the Jewish delegations would request that the pope not only "confirm and approve" the law but also "venerate" it. According to Patrizi, they made this new entreaty in Hebrew, and it is not clear that anyone other than themselves understood the request.[8]

As for the third element of the ritual, during Boniface VIII's Easter procession, Cardinal Gaetano Stefaneschi wrote a poem about it:

See the Pope, mounted on a horse,
Crossing the Tiber on the Marble Bridge.
Leaving behind the Tower of the Field [Castel Sant'Angelo],
He is met by the Jews, singing, but blind of heart.
To him, the Prince, right here in Parione[9]
Moses' Law is shown, pregnant with Christ.
Him he adored, in this Law prefigured, over the shoulder
He then returned the scroll with measured words.[10]

In other words, after the Jews applauded the pope's accession during a personal encounter (part one) and then presented the pope with a Torah (part two), the pope rejected the Torah with "measured words" (part three).

This rejection occurred in 1295, in 1316 by John XXII (1316–34), in 1405 by Gregory XII (1405–15), in 1417 by Martin V (1417–31), and in 1447 by Nicholas V (1447–55).[11] In fact, Stefaneschi reports, Pope Boniface VIII's "measured words" were a denunciation of the Jews:

> God who you once knew, today you ignore. You are his people and you have become his enemy. When he is revealed you block him from view. Although you know how to recognize him. Now when he is present you disdain him. The nations have recognized his coming; you avoid him. You have rejected He who came among his people and put to death He who shed his blood for you. This ignorance of the meaning of the Scripture will lead you to perdition. Repent if you wish on the day of judgment to share the fate of the just who the Lord welcomes in glory because of their merits.[12]

Innocent II (1130–43) likely uttered this more prosaic statement when he accepted the Torah in Paris some hundred years earlier: "We praise and revere the holy Law, for that it was given to your fathers by almighty God through Moses. Your religious practices, however, and your worthless explanations of the Law we condemn. For the redeemer for whom you wait in vain has long since come."[13]

That a succession of popes voiced these or similar "measured words" to the Jews as this ritual encounter was reenacted for hundreds of years serves itself as a window into the theological relationship between Jews and Christians in the Middle Ages. In some instances, though probably very few, the pope may have punctuated his rejection by physically throwing the Torah over his shoulder, as Stefaneschi's poem suggests ("Over the shoulder he then returned the scroll").[14]

Probably the last time a pope tossed aside the Torah was in 1513, during the coronation of Pope Leo X (1513–21). While Leo, known as a humanist, showed considerable interest in Judaism,[15] the papal-Jewish encounter was nonetheless altered during his time and that of his predecessor Julius III (1503–13) to highlight both the acceptance and exclusion of the Jewish community. For Julius's *possesso* in 1503, the Jews met the pope before he crossed the Ponte Sant'Angleo, and Rabbi Samuel Tsarfati, the pope's physician, delivered a sermon to the pope (his words have not been preserved). Ten years later, upon Leo X's inauguration in 1513, a decorated scaffolding was in place for the encounter, and the Jews accompanied the bringing of the Torah with eight lit white-wax torches.[16] Still, again, Leo was reported to have accepted the Torah only to then throw it to the ground.[17]

But after 1513, even this ritual was no more. Henceforth, Jews in Rome would laud the pope's accession to power either in person or with banners quoting appropriate biblical verses, but without the ceremonial gift of a Torah.[18] This significant shift was probably due to the church's increasing reluctance to have even a semiequal exchange with the Jews. Under pressure from the Protestant Reformation, the church, which was heading toward ghettoization of the Jews, did not want to appear to legitimize any deviation from dogma.

There exist two portraits of Roman Jews giving a Torah as a gift, but each has its own problems. A 1725 Bernard Picart engraving entitled "The Jews Presenting the Pentateuch to the Pope near the Colosseum" appears to be an eyewitness rendition of a rabbi reaching toward the pope with a Torah in his hands, but by the 1700s, the Jews were no longer presenting the pope with a Torah, so Picart was rendering a historical rather than contemporaneous ceremony (fig. 4). In fashioning his image, he might have drawn upon somewhat similar engravings such as Hélisenne de Crenne presenting François I of France her translation of Virgil (ca. 1542), or Jacques du Fouilloux presenting his book on hunting to the king (ca. 1562).[19]

In a second illustration, the Jews appear to be presenting the Holy Roman Emperor Henry VII with a Torah as part of the commemoration festivities surrounding his 1312 coronation as emperor in Rome. The Jews are approaching the emperor, who is on horseback,[20] and the Torah appears unfurled and bearing nonsensical scribbles (the artist's ignorant depiction of Hebrew letters). The caption to the drawing mistakenly says

FIG. 4. A rabbi offers a Torah as a gift to a pope in this 1725 engraving by Bernard Picart. Archivo Storico della Comunità Ebraica di Roma, Archivio fotografico, Fondo Fornari, vol. 4, no. 248.

that the emperor is presenting the Jews with the Torah, not vice versa. Yet it was the pope, and rarely an emperor, who garnered accolades from the Jewish community in Rome.

The practice of Jews applauding the pope is mentioned as early as 1111, during the papacy of Pope Paschal II (1099–1118), who, during a controversy with the Holy Roman Empire, staged an entry into Rome replete with reminders of Jesus's entry into Jerusalem on Palm Sunday. When the Jewish community came to greet the pope, the representatives were ordered to stand outside the city gates to emphasize their social position outside the Christian community.[21] By contrast, the Catholic clergy greeted the pope from inside the city, and the Greek clergy, Christian, but not Catholic, met the pope at the city walls. The symbolism was unavoidable: the further away from Catholicism your beliefs, the further away from the city center you stood.

Accordingly, the status of the Jews was intentionally ambiguous. They were outsiders, stationed beyond the city walls, who were, nevertheless, included in the ceremony. An official reporter for Paschal II's successor, Gelasius II (1118–19), explained the Jewish presence theologically: they were confessing the truth of Christianity, although blindly and unwillingly.[22]

Less theological is the explanation given by Cencius Camerarius, later Pope Honorius III (1216–27). In his *Ordus Romanus XII* (ca. 1192), he writes that each of the *scholae* of Rome, seventeen foreign clerical and lay associations, were obliged, by their presence, to pay the pope homage while he entered Rome. The Jews, listed last among the *scholae*, were required to include a further gift of three-and-a-half pounds of pepper and two-and-a-half pounds of cinnamon. But then, Cencius says, the pope renumerated all the *scholae*, and although the Jews were listed last, they received the largest *presbyterium* (payment) of any of the *scholae*: twenty solidi.[23]

What are we to make of this scripted ritual that included the pope, the Torah, payment in silver, and even some cinnamon—a rite both honorific and degrading, inclusive and exclusive? How does this one ritual reenact the overall meeting between the Jewish world and Catholic world in Rome in the later Middle Ages? To answer these questions, let us begin with an unadorned fact: the Jews are giving the pope a gift.

A similar coronation parade including gift giving took place in England in 1559. Historical comparisons can be clumsy, but, in this case, after Queen Elizabeth was crowned, she paraded through London streets festooned with celebratory banners in a manner similar to that of the papal parade in Rome. While there were no Jews in London in 1559, the Jewish community having been expelled in 1290, a young girl identified as Truth approached the queen along the parade route and gave her an English Bible. The queen accepted the Bible, raised it above her head for all to see, and then pressed it to her breast. A later commentator gushed "how striking and meaningful it must have been to the spectators to see Truth in visible union with their new sovereign."[24]

The similarity with the papal parade and the presentation of the Torah is striking, as is Elizabeth's response. She accepts the Bible—containing the New Testament—and embraces God's Truth. The popes could never do the same with the Torah, which they also understood as God's word. Their rejection of the gift certainly had to do with the Jewish gift givers, but what exactly did that mean?

It is a commonplace in modern anthropology, and a commonplace recognizable to any of us who have accepted a gift, that a gift, more often than not, incurs an obligation. "The miser always fears presents," wrote Marcel Mauss in his famous 1925 essay, "The Gift."[25] Mauss understood that gift giving is almost always reciprocal. To give a gift is to expect one in return. This expectation and understanding, Mauss discovered, is widespread among diverse cultures, from Polynesia to Iceland to the Pacific Northwest. Yet even as early as the twelfth century, the English theologian Thomas of Chobham had stated the rule quite well: "Just as when I have given you something, I can expect a counter gift, that is to say a reply to the gift; and I can hope to receive since I gave to you first."[26]

How does this apply to the Jews' gift of a Torah to the pope?

When the Jews approached the papal procession with a Torah in hand, they were offering the pope a valuable gift. They were giving the pope God's Law, and the pope knew it. Further, as the pope no doubt also understood, should he accept that gift, he would be voluntarily and publicly incurring an obligation to the Jews of Rome. Given that this gift was God's word—its value incommensurable—the gift could not possibly be accepted. At the very beginning of his papacy, a pope could not become incalculably indebted to the Jews.

Yet everyone watching understood that, on some level, this was what was taking place. For years, every churchman in the papal procession had been giving gifts to the cardinal or noble who had now become pope, in the hopes that their gifts would incur an obligation upon the recipient. Other European monarchs, too, were given gifts on their coronation, and those kings too would often play down or deflect attention from that fact, especially if the gift came from a Jew.[27]

And so, when presented with the gift of a Torah, the pope had to reject the gift. As Stefaneschi said of Boniface VIII, "Over the shoulder, He then returned the scroll with measured words."

Still, the popes had some hesitation. As Stefaneschi also said, "To him, the Prince, right here in Parione [a Roman neighborhood where the Jewish encounter with the popes usually happened], Moses' Law is shown, pregnant with Christ." The gift every pope had to reject was nonetheless "pregnant with Christ," meaning that the Torah was infinitely valuable as God's word foretelling the life, death, and resurrection of Jesus. That is how Catholics saw, and still see, the Old Testament. How could a pope reject the word of God?

And so, in a bit of sophistry, Catholic tradition devised a clever response to the Jews' gift: the pope revered the Torah as the Law of Moses, but rejected the Jews' understanding of it.

By both accepting and rejecting the gift, a pope might think he had solved his problem. However, as anyone who has ever turned down a gift knows, a residual obligation remains. The popes were in a similar position. They could not accept the gift with no reciprocation—but even if they rejected it, they still owed the Jewish community something.

Consequently, they reciprocated in two ways: offering the Jewish community protection and paying the Jewish community for participating in the procession. Protection came in the form of the papal bull *Sicut judaeis* (As the Jews), an order allowing Jews to practice their religion. Successive popes reaffirmed that bull just as successive popes accepted and rejected the gift of the Torah. In addition, the Jewish community was paid for its participation in the papal procession. Together, the protection and the payment constituted the consideration the popes gave the Jews in return for the Torah that they had to both accept and reject. The Jews then further reciprocated by giving the popes gifts of pepper and cinnamon.

In theory, this process of giving gifts, incurring obligations, and reciprocating could go on forever, and in a sense it did, in that it was repeated at papal inaugurations for generations.[28] Indeed, the giving and receiving between the popes and the Jews existed beyond the narrow scope of a scripted ritual. As Mauss well knew, the ritual giving of gifts is part of a larger contractual relationship.[29]

SICUT JUDAEIS

While the ritual encounter between the popes and the Jews was surely theater, it was theater based on an agreement understood by both parties. The notion of a written contract between a Jewish community and its Christian hosts was commonplace in medieval Italy. As Jewish entrepreneurs left Rome in the second half of the thirteenth century, they entered into written contracts, *condotte*, with smaller communities in the north of the peninsula whereby they could settle in that community, lend money at interest when given security, engage in other types of business, and freely practice their religion. A *condotta* was a de facto grant for a synagogue to be built in the contracting community. In return, Jews had to invest capital in something like a local bank, pay an annual fee proportional to the money invested, and advance monies to the community if needed at a reduced rate of interest.[30]

The Jews who entered into these *condotte* were, in a sense, pioneers, leaving Rome for the hinterlands and settling where they were allowed (as many Italian towns refused to accept them). The *condotte* were also of short duration, often three to five years, although extensions were usually negotiated. Or Jews could remain as residents, but without a *condotta*, though this meant they were subject to common law, without the security of an agreement.[31] Essentially, the contract was a business opportunity for a Jewish entrepreneur, in some ways akin to a franchise. By way of example, in the fifteenth century a Roman Jew named Mordecai ran pawnbroker businesses in at least twelve different locales in Tuscany and central Italy.[32]

In Rome, no *condotte* were necessary between the Jewish community and the popes, because the Jews had been in Rome for centuries before the popes. Roman Jews did not need a contract to live there; they were never governed by a *condotta* and never agreed to loan money to the city. Instead, they were taxed at a higher rate.[33] (In 1524, Daniel ben Isaac da Pisa did draw up a constitution for the Roman Jewish community that Pope Clement VII affirmed, but this was not a *condotta*.)[34]

Still, if there was no *condotta*, there was a written Vatican document setting forth Jewish rights and obligations. As early as 1120, by order of Calixtus II's papal bull *Sicut judaeis*, Jews in Catholic Europe were accorded certain rights in return for their acceptance of the Christian social order and canon law.[35] A generation prior, in 1096, the People's Crusade, a popular movement in concert with the First Crusade, had brutally and indiscriminately murdered Jews in the Rhineland, north of Italy. Rome's Jews were spared that violence, but in reaction to the massacres, and perhaps under pressure from the erstwhile Roman Jewish family the Pierleonis, who after conversion to Catholicism exerted considerable influence, the church under Calixtus II issued *Sicut judaeis*, which read in part:

> Gregory, bishop, servant of the servants of God, extends greetings and the apostolic benediction to the beloved sons in Christ. . . . Even as it is not allowed to the Jews in their assemblies presumptuously to undertake for themselves that which is permitted them by law, even so they ought not to suffer any disadvantage in those [privileges] which have been granted to them. Although they prefer to persist in their stubbornness, . . . nevertheless, inasmuch as they have made an appeal for our protection and help, we therefore admit their petition and offer them the shield of our protection through the clemency of Christian piety. . . .

We decree moreover that no Christian shall compel them or any one of their group to come to baptism unwillingly. . . .

Moreover no Christian shall presume to seize, imprison, wound, torture, mutilate, kill or inflict violence on them; furthermore no one shall presume, except by judicial action of the authorities of the country, to change the good customs in the land where they live for the purpose of taking their money or goods from them or from others.

In addition no one shall disturb them in any way during the celebration of their festivals, whether by day or night, with clubs or stones or anything else.

We decree in order to stop the wickedness and avarice of bad men, that no one shall dare to devastate or to destroy a cemetery of the Jews or to dig up human bodies for the sake of getting money.[36]

A slim majority of the popes from Eugenius III (1145–53) to Nicholas V (1447–55) would reaffirm versions of this bull.[37]

The Jews relied upon *Sicut*—a contract—to keep them safe, both generally and at specific times, such as when they celebrated the Jewish holidays and buried their dead. The Jews also asked that *Sicut* be reissued, usually upon the call for a crusade. While Pope Urban II did not issue *Sicut* when he preached the First Crusade in 1095, violence toward Jews undertaken by those first crusaders may have led Calixtus II to issue *Sicut* sometime between 1119 and 1124; similarly, Pope Eugenius III may have anticipated his own call for a second crusade by reissuing *Sicut* around 1145 at the beginning of his pontificate.[38]

Yet the periodic reaffirmations of *Sicut* were not problem-free or automatic. Early versions of *Sicut* appeared to be unconditional promises to the Jewish community, but Pope Innocent III's 1199 version added a final paragraph conditioning papal protection on Jewish agreement not to plot against Christianity: "We wish, however, to place under the protection of this decree, only those [Jews] who have not presumed to plot against the Christian Faith."[39] This short paragraph evidencing Innocent III's suspicions that Jews might seek to harm Christian society was repeated thereafter in all further reaffirmations of *Sicut*.[40]

In another regressive step, in 1413 Pope Benedict XIII (1394–1417) issued a separate bull, *Etsi doctoris gentium*, that undercut *Sicut* and severely restricted Jewish life. Among other things, Jews could no longer hear, read, or preach the Talmud or act as judges—though as long as they submitted to the harsher provisions in the bull, they would not be molested or offended. Yet *Etsi doctoris* was of short duration. Benedict XIII was excommunicated in 1417, and in 1418, his successor Martin V repealed Benedict's bull.[41]

Through all this, *Sicut* remained the contractual underpinning for the Jewish papal encounters at the popes' coronations. With Innocent's addition, the papal promises became conditional and *Sicut* looked less like a set of guarantees and more like a contract between the church and the Jews. Moreover, if the popes reaffirmed *Sicut* periodically, so did the Jews by playing their role in the papal processions. The Jews took their place in the city of Rome in a recognized relationship with pope and church. A contract had been struck, and it was ceremonially reaffirmed every time the Jews, bearing the Torah, encountered the pope.

Indeed, the consecutive reaffirmations of *Sicut* appear to have been a conceptual part of the pontiffs' meetings with the Jewish delegation.[42] Pope Eugenius III, for one, presented the Jewish community with a copy of *Sicut* at his coronation in 1145. Alexander III also saw *Sicut* as an integral part of his coronation.[43] The contract was, of course, not bargained for, and the Jews could hardly refuse the offer.

Then, in 1267, upon hearing of Christians who had converted to Judaism, Pope Clement IV (1265–68) issued a papal letter or encyclical, *Turbato corde* (With a troubled heart), ordering inquisitorial action:

> With a troubled heart we relate what we have heard: A number of bad Christians have abandoned the true Christian faith and wickedly transferred themselves to the rites of the Jews. . . . We order . . . [a] diligent and thorough inquiry into the above, through Christians as well as through

Jews. Against Christians whom you find guilty of the above you shall proceed as against heretics. Upon Jews who you may find guilty of having induced Christians of either sex to join their execrable rites, or whom you may find doing so in the future, you shall impose fitting punishment.[44]

"Fitting punishment" was not defined in the letter. However, by the end of the thirteenth century, Elias de Pomis of Rome would be burned at the stake for allegedly inducing Christians to convert to Judaism.

Increasingly concerned about converts' fidelity to Christianity, in 1274 Pope Gregory X reissued an emended version of *Turbato corde*, adding words that spoke to the "blindness" of converts to Christianity returning to Judaism. "With a troubled heart we relate what we have heard: Not only are certain converts from the error of Jewish blindness to the light of Christian faith known to have reverted to their former false belief, but even [born] Christians, denying the true Catholic faith have wickedly transferred themselves to the rites of Judaism."[45]

It appears, however, that the number of actual converts to Judaism among Christians was tiny. As such, in addition to undercutting *Sicut, Turbato corde*—which, after Gregory X, would not be reissued as regularly as *Sicut*—may have been addressing another issue—curtailing social, commercial, and sexual contact between Jews and Catholics. Jews could practice their religion, but to the extent that this tolerance might encourage interaction among Jews and Christians, such connections were to be avoided.

Corroborating this idea, a further papal letter by Pope Honorius IV (1285–87), addressed to the prelates of England in 1286, enumerated Jewish misdeeds that included Jews and Christians eating together, Christians visiting Jewish homes, and Jews employing Christian domestics.[46] To the extent that Jews and Catholics were acting in a manner similar to family members, such circumstances were to be the subject of an inquisition. *Sicut* was believed to have created an intimacy—to use the terms of this book—between Jews and Christians. *Turbato corde* and subsequent papal letters put Jews in their place as strangers.

However, if *Turbato corde* was perceived as a correction to *Sicut,* a few years later the pendulum swung the other way and *Sicut* was reissued with pro-Jewish attachments. In 1272, when Gregory X reaffirmed *Sicut,* even as he added a paragraph conditioning tolerance of Jews on their refraining from attacking the church, he simultaneously appended a paragraph stating that enemies of the Jews were concocting charges against them in order to extort money. In 1281, Pope Martin IV reissued *Sicut* with an addition designed to limit inquisitorial activity against Jews. Witnesses against them had to take a solemn oath and understand that false accusations could lead to their own punishment similar to the punishment they sought against the accused Jews.[47]

Despite the popes trying to thread the needle of tolerance, in 1298 tragedy struck in Rome. Anonymous accusations arose that Jews were actively trying to win Jewish converts to Christianity back to Judaism. In order to spare the Jewish community from general reprisals, Elias de Pomis, a respected Jewish leader, took the blame upon himself alone and was burned at the stake. The next year saw a seeming concession from Pope Boniface VIII: the bull *Exhibita nobis* (It has come to our attention) that granted Roman Jews the right to obtain from inquisitors the names of their accusers and the witnesses against them.[48] In theory, innuendo and unverifiable claims could no longer hide behind a curtain of anonymity.

Finally, in 1290 Pope Nicholas IV, who had already reissued *Turbato corde* twice, urged his vicar (who carried out the pope's intentions concerning the city of Rome) to prevent churchmen from preaching "in an incendiary manner" against Jews. Nicholas went on to accuse Catholic clergy of acting toward Jews in ways that made the church odious to Roman Jewry. Jews, according to Nicholas, had to be treated moderately and justly.[49]

MONEY LENDING

In the thirteenth century, as papal and church attitudes toward Jews ping-ponged back and forth between acceptance ("Jews are to be treated fairly") and rejection ("beware of Jews taking advantage and trying to convert

Christians"), papal ambivalence toward Jews played out in another arena where Jews and Christians met: lending and borrowing money.

Lending money at interest benefits the borrower, who gains cash in the short term. The lender charges for the service of providing the cash by taking interest on the loan. In the thirteenth century, when issues of usury and lending at interest became concerns for both Christians and Jews, Dominican and Franciscan friars were preaching poverty to the very people who needed to borrow money to survive. Moreover, both Judaism and Christianity were doctrinally ambivalent about lending money at interest.

Deuteronomy 23:20 allows Jews to lend money at interest, but only to foreigners and not to their "countrymen": "You shall not deduct interest from loans to your countrymen whether in money or food or anything else that can be deducted as interest; but you may deduct interest from loans to foreigners." Exodus 22:24 states, "If you lend money to My people, to the poor among you, do not act toward them as a creditor; exact no interest from them." The talmudic sage Rav Huna (third-century Babylon) declared that no usury at all is allowable,[50] but there were exceptions. Scholars were permitted to lend at interest without restrictions—a ruling that led Rabbi Solomon ibn Adret (thirteenth-century Barcelona) to note that in his generation, every Jew considered himself a scholar.[51] A more practical approach was taken in the eleventh and twelfth centuries by the rabbinic authority Rashi (France, 1040–1105) and his grandson Rabbenu Tam (France, 1100–1171), who allowed Jews to lend at interest, ostensibly because, as a minority living among Christians, they had no other economic opportunities.[52]

For their part, Jews interpreted the biblical law that allowed Jewish money lending to strangers to mean that they could lend at interest to Catholics. But Christian scholars found lending at interest abhorrent and would have prohibited it outright.[53] To Catholics, at least in this instance, Jews and Catholics were not strangers but *proximi*—"neighbors" of a theological and legal sort—because they worshiped the same God, and thus all moneylending between them was prohibited.[54] When it suited the church legists, the line between Jews and Catholics became blurred. Jews were defined as, if not quite family or intimates, then neighbors for the purpose of outlawing usury.

While some allowed that Jews were *proximi*, other Catholic scholars portrayed Jewish moneylenders as vampires sucking blood from Christian communities or even as predatory "circumcisers" who cut and removed the savings of Christians.[55] Nonetheless, practicalities bred exceptions to even such virulent objections to moneylending, and despite their reputation as leeches, Jews were granted a major exception.

St. Thomas Aquinas opined that Jews were allowed to lend at interest in the Bible, just as they were allowed to divorce. With not-so-veiled hostility, Aquinas wrote in the thirteenth century that God took into account Jewish frailties, and in order to mitigate spousal killing and Judaic greed, He chose leniency over the stricter rules that eventually applied to Christians.[56]

To the Bolognese philosopher Alessandro da Imola (1424–77), known as Tartagni, Jewish usury was comparable to prostitution: the church had to tolerate it as a lesser and sometimes necessary evil.[57] The identification of usury with prostitution would become a leitmotif in ecclesiastical thought, as exemplified by a 1566 letter sent by an unknown writer to Pope Pius V entitled "In Which His Holiness Is Exhorted to Tolerate in Rome Jews and Courtesans."[58]

Scholarly opinions of moneylending were of theological interest. However, the persons in power, the popes, lived in a practical world where Catholic farmers, merchants, and incipient entrepreneurs needed ready cash. In short, the popes hated usury, but they loved liquidity. What were they to do?

The issue first arose during the Crusades. Papal policy needed to address the practicality that the Crusades had to be financed. Expeditions to the Middle East required small-scale loans to Crusaders that would allow them to leave their homes and workplaces for an indefinite period of time. In 1198, Innocent III declared that Crusaders did not have to pay interest on their loans, and had they already paid interest, Jewish and Christian lenders would have to pay the Crusaders back. Seventeen years later, at the Fourth Lateran Council, Innocent III wrote a letter, *Ad liberandum* (To free [the

Holy Land]), which made things a bit clearer. Jews had to reimburse any interest paid on existing loans to active Crusaders, but the actual debts and the accompanying interest were not in themselves canceled. Once the Crusader returned home, the postponed payment with interest would become due.[59] Further legislation at the Fourth Lateran Council of 1215, *Quanto Amplius* (Much more), ordered Jews to pay back only "immoderate" interest charged to non-Crusaders, and in general prohibited only "burdensome and immoderate usury."[60] Pragmatism vanquished purity in this particular doctrinal debate. Jews in particular could lend at interest so long as that interest was "moderate." The usual and allowable interest rate varied between 15 and 25 percent per year—moderate indeed, when according to the patriarch of Aquilea, some Christian lenders were charging 65 percent per year.[61] It was understood that the pope would permit usury, in the sense of taking a passive stance and not punishing usurious lenders.[62] As for the Jews, while small Jewish lenders did not make the Crusades possible, they did play a recognizable role.[63]

There was also the issue of tithes, the tax the church collected on property and profits. If a Christian's property was transferred to a Jew because it had been collateral on an unpaid loan, the church asserted the right to collect a tithe from the Jewish owner of the heretofore Christian property. Ordinarily, a tithe was an obligation to be paid by Catholics, not Jews. However, in this case, Constitution 67 of the Fourth Lateran Council (1215) ordered Jews to pay the tax obligation, which followed the property and not the property owner: "We decree, under the same penalty, that Jews shall be compelled to make satisfaction to churches for tithes and offerings due to the churches, which the churches were accustomed to receive from Christians for houses and other possessions, before they passed by whatever title to the Jews, so that the churches may thus be preserved from loss."[64]

Accordingly, the church had to implicitly recognize the legitimacy of the lender-creditor relationship between Jew and Christian, and recognize the legitimate Jewish ownership interest in the property resulting from a default on a secured loan. Only if the church made such tacit admissions could it then legitimately tax the Jewish owner.

Eventually, in the fifteenth century, the church began founding Monti di Pietà, charitable and lending institutions, which would serve the same needs among the poor as Jewish short-term lenders. Local municipalities with lay participation administered individual Monti, which the church hierarchy supervised. Each Monte required papal approval.[65]

Originally the Monti di Pietà looked like banks, although created for a charitable purpose. Deposits into the banks would not generate interest, and loans made from the Monti were interest free. The sole incentive to deposit monies into a Monte was the promise of heavenly, not earthly, rewards—a disastrous business model, exacerbated on occasion by requiring borrowers to swear that they were not borrowing monies for commercial purposes.

If the Monti were founded to wean people off Jewish lending, they did not succeed.[66] However, Jewish bankers were probably influenced by the Monti. In a nod to the Monti's lending practices, in 1540 the Jewish lenders of Rome pledged to lend two hundred scudi to the Jewish poor interest free.[67]

Ironically, too, early Monti—including the first Monte di Pietà, founded in Perugia in 1462—relied on Jewish seed money. Funding for the Monti came from church collections, religious processions, indulgences, and legacies—and also from forced, interest-free loans from local Jews.[68] This was the meaning of the *condotte* that required Jews to lend money to a local bank. Accordingly, Jewish investments in Monti were not uncommon.

In other words, in towns across Italy and in Rome, Jews had to finance their competition. Yet, because the competition was so ill conceived, few if any Monti put Jewish lenders out of business. Eventually, however, in 1542, the Council of Trent approved Monti interest payments to depositors, and the Monti, of necessity, had to invest their money to generate interest as well.[69] Still, Jewish money lending was not affected, at least in the short term.[70] In Rome, the first Monte opened in 1539, yet in the sixteenth century the number of Jewish bankers there grew from twenty to seventy.[71]

In Rome and in the medieval world, Jews were indispensable to an economy that was becoming dependent on available capital and lending at interest. The church, ambivalent about capitalism, reluctantly accepted the uses of capital. If, as the French historian Jacques Le Goff says, the controversy surrounding usury was the "labor pains of capitalism,"[72] the Jews were the midwives of that birth.

Yet another ambiguity underlay the Jews' relationship to the church. All popes had two different roles. In his spiritual role the pope was the leader of the universal Catholic Church. But he was also the ruler of Rome and the Papal States. This division allowed Romans to excoriate a pope for his civic failures, such as high taxes, while venerating the same pope as the soul of the church.[73]

Even during the encounter with the Jewish delegation during the papal processions, the pope's dual nature was on display. As the spiritual head of the Catholic Church, the pope could not possibly incur a debt to the Jews. He had to reject and return the Torah. However, as the civic leader of Rome, he required Jewish engagement in the processions, paid the Jewish community for their participation, and accepted their gifts of pepper and cinnamon. Consequently, in fourteenth-, fifteenth-, and early sixteenth-century Rome, the Jews' position was triply ambiguous. They lived on the edge of three knives.

Jews had a contractual relationship with the church through *Sicut judaeis*. But in *Turbato corde* they were also accused of breaching that contract and getting too intimate with Christians. That forced them to walk a fine line—the first knife.

Their contractual relationship allowed them to lend money at interest. But taking that opportunity left them open to accusations of prostitution and blood-sucking. They could not push their lending beyond what the church considered moderate or reasonable bounds for Jews—the second knife.

Additionally, the pope himself had to maintain a balance in his double role as spiritual and civil leader. Meanwhile, Jews had to know which pope, spiritual or civil, they were dealing with at any particular time. In a bit of sophistry, Jews were considered religious enemies of the church, while simultaneously not qualifying as civil enemies; that is, they were not considered guilty of civil or criminal infractions merely by virtue of being Jews.[74] As religious enemies, their gift of the Torah had to be rejected. However, because they were not civil enemies, they had to take part in the processions and offer the Torah in the first place. Their ambiguous position was always being negotiated—the third knife.

Despite these three challenges, both parties managed to maintain an equilibrium that allowed Jews to live in Rome relatively peaceably and find a niche in Roman society. Jews navigated this sharp-edged maze and were given a place at the Roman civic table.

Their place was at the far end of the table, but at the time, in the thirteenth through sixteenth centuries, Jews were recognized as part of Rome's civic community. When a new pope was inaugurated, all Romans, including Jews, had to participate. No one group could withhold its praises of the new pontiff. And once they were invited and were paid for the participation, Jews were accepted as Romans.

That said, the Jewish place at the table was far from privileged. Jews were living de facto under the *ius commune* (Roman common law), a status that would be made explicit in 1621 when the Roman Rota (the church's highest appellate court) affirmed it.[75] Their early de facto status integrated them, along with other Romans, into the legal system—albeit not fully. Jews held an ambiguous position at the very bottom of the hierarchy.

Still, mere inclusion in a hierarchy, even at the lowest level, creates a relationship between the least within the hierarchy and those ranked higher up. All the ranks above have to follow certain rules to make certain that those below remain in the lowest rank. Thus the Jews' lowly place in the Roman hierarchy affected the behavior of everyone else. Catholics needed to know that they could not marry a Jew or eat with a Jew, but could borrow money from a Jew. Individual Catholics could then act within the rules, or even bend them a bit for their own benefit, and maybe for the benefit of their Jewish counterparts. Here, then, is the Jew as paradoxical intimate stranger.

4

Houseguests and Humanists

Philosophers, Poets, Prostitutes, and Pilgrims
in Late Medieval and Renaissance Rome

For Jews in medieval Rome, living as long-term strangers in the heart of Christendom was daunting. One Jew, Joseph ben Gorion, imaginatively navigated the fraught hierarchical terrain by turning the hierarchy inside out—placing the Jews at the top of the social order by claiming that the Jews had originally founded Rome.

Ben Gorion was the purported translator behind the *Book of Yosippon*, a book of Jewish history written in approximately 953 CE.[1] Ostensibly, as medieval Jewish readers saw it, the *Yosippon* was his translation into Hebrew of Josephus's Greek text *The Jewish War*, as well as portions of Josephus's *Antiquities of the Jews*, but in fact, ben Gorion had added considerably to the history received from Josephus.[2] Furthermore, because the Jews of Europe believed they were reading a translation and nothing more, they viewed the *Yosippon* as authoritative.[3] And for Roman Jews, it had added significance.

According to a long fictitious story in the *Yosippon*, descendants of Esau, son of the biblical patriarch Isaac, founded Rome. After God destroyed the Tower of Babel (Gen. 11:1–9) and humanity dispersed around the world, one tribe, the Kittim, settled on the banks of the Tiber River—but these were not Rome's founders.[4]

The *Yosippon* then switches gears to relate a talmudic story (Babylonian Talmud, *Sotah* 13a). As Joseph and his brothers were bringing the remains of their father Jacob out of Egypt, intending to bury him in Canaan, the descendants of Esau—in particular, Zepho, Esau's grandson—stopped them in Edom (Gen. 36:11). The *Yosippon* elevates the obscure Zepho to epic status by describing a skirmish between him and Jacob's sons, which he lost. Zepho was imprisoned, but escaped and fled to Carthage (the North African city ruled by Aeneas, originally of Troy). Here the *Yosippon* makes use of material in Virgil's *Aeneid*. According to Virgil, Aeneas, a member of the Trojan royal family, founded Rome. The *Yosippon* gives that honor to Zepho's family.

Zepho joined Aeneas in his expeditions to Italy. Eventually, Zepho defected to live among the Kittim, who asked that he kill a beast called Janus. Zepho succeeded and became king of the Kittim. Several generations later, one of Zepho's descendants, Romulus, founded the city of Rome.

The point of this tale was to demonstrate that Romulus descended from Esau, thereby making both Romans and Jews descendants of Isaac. Jacob and Esau were Isaac's sons, with Jews being the family of Jacob (Israel), and Romans being the family of Esau. As a result, Jews and Romans were cousins of a sort.[5] Thus the *Yosippon* transformed the biblical story of Jacob and Esau's rivalry into a story of Jews and Romans.[6] The Jews' status as intimate strangers, apparent outsiders who were actually family, was expressed in the *Yosippon*'s unique history.[7]

BOCCACCIO, ABULAFIA, AND LEGENDS OF JEWISH POPES

In or about 1350, the Italian writer and poet Giovanni Boccaccio (1313–75) described Rome through the eyes of a fictional Jewish visitor. In his *Decameron*, Abraham, a Parisian Jew, travels to Rome in order to decide whether to convert to Catholicism. Upon arrival, he quickly sees, within the church, lechery, gluttony, greed, and every other vice imaginable. He rushes home to Paris and requests to be baptized immediately, for the satiric reason that if Christianity can flourish where there is sin of such magnitude, it must be God's chosen religion.[8]

A true account of a Jew visiting Rome in 1280 takes up a similar, but opposite, theme. The noted Jewish mystic Abraham Abulafia (1240–ca. 1291) came to Rome to try nothing short of converting the pope to Judaism. After traveling to the Levant in search of the Ten Lost Tribes of Israel,

Abulafia returned to Europe, spent years in study, arrived in Rome in 1280, and on the eve of the Jewish New Year presented himself to the papal palace with the stated intent of making the pope a Jew. Unbeknownst to Abulafia, Pope Nicholas III (1277–80) had preemptively ordered him burned at the stake. Equally unknown to Abulafia, Pope Nicholas then, abruptly, died. When Abulafia turned up at the Vatican, there was no one on the papal throne to convert.[9] And because the papal see was vacant, while the killing ground was ready, the execution could not be ordered. Abulafia was imprisoned for twenty-eight days, but without a pope, there was no authority for keeping him longer. He escaped to write of his adventures in *The Book of Testimony*.[10]

Several legends about Jewish popes succeed where Abulafia failed. In medieval Europe there existed a persistent tradition concerning a Jewish pope, born Elhanan, in Mainz, Germany, who, after being kidnapped by a Christian servant, was brought up in the Vatican and ultimately elected Pope Andreas. Aware of his Jewish background, Andreas decided upon a ruse to locate his illustrious father, Rabbi Shim'on ben Yishaq. He ordered the Jews of Mainz persecuted, causing his father to travel to Rome to plead for mercy. When Rabbi Shim'on ben Yishaq arrived at the Vatican, Andreas/Elhanan recognized him but at first maintained the charade, only finally revealing his true identity during a chess match with his father. In the end, Pope Andreas (who never existed) renounced Christianity to return to Judaism and to Mainz.[11]

The tale assumes that a Jew is so physically indistinguishable from a Catholic that he can pass as a pope and even fool his father. At a deeper level, the story flirts with the notion that Jews and Catholic are secretly a single family that could conceivably include a pope. That notion was ultimately insupportable, even in a legend. The story resolves with the pope reverting to Judaism, or, in another variant, committing suicide.

A similar Jewish legend, from the eleventh century, concerns the first pope, St. Peter, who supposedly remained secretly Jewish, even when leading the Christian community. To better the lives of his Jewish brethren, he infiltrated the earliest Christian community, becoming the "rock" upon which Jesus built his church (Matt. 16:13–20). He then created a religion—without kosher laws and without a Sabbath—that Jews would reject, thereby preserving Judaism from the challenge of Christianity. In the legend, the Jewish pope secretly authored the *Nishmat Kol Chai*, a common Jewish prayer.[12]

The further significance of these fictitious stories about Jewish popes is in their evidencing a belief, fantasy, or aspiration that Jews could be completely assimilated into the Catholic world where they lived as second-class citizens—and then even secretly rule that world.

BENJAMIN OF TUDELA

Another account of Jewish aspirations to power comes to us from an actual Jewish traveler in Rome. Traveling from Spain to Rome in or about 1166, Benjamin of Tudela (1130–73) was welcomed by a Jewish community of approximately two hundred families. There he met Yehiel, grandson of Rabbi Nathan ben Yehiel (1035–1106), the author of an enduring encyclopedia of the Talmud called *'Aruch*. A distinguished scholar, Rabbi Nathan was also a member of the Anav family, who claimed to be one of the four families Titus had brought to Rome from Jerusalem in 70 CE.[13] A fragment of a pillar incised with the name "Natan" may be seen today in Trastevere, a Roman neighborhood on the western bank of the Tiber, near a *mikveh* (Jewish ritual bath) that purportedly dates to the Middle Ages. The association of the *mikveh* and the pillar lends some credence to the supposition that the inscription refers to Nathan ben Yehiel.

While the earlier inscriptions in the Jewish catacombs were mostly Latin and Greek, the pillar is inscribed in Hebrew, which revived as a language in southern Italy in the early Middle Ages.[14] In another example of Hebrew writing, an amulet from Rome quoting the Priestly Blessing (Num. 6:24–26) and dated to the fifth century CE was also in Hebrew.[15]

At any rate, Benjamin of Tudela reported that Yehiel, Nathan's grandson, had "free access to the Papal court" by virtue of his being the administrator of the pope's household—a self-aggrandizing and presumably exaggerated depiction.[16] Accordingly, Benjamin's description of Rome appears to be a mixture of fact and legend that informs us, mostly, of how the city's Jewish inhabitants—like Yehiel, who claimed to be an intimate of the pontiff—viewed their place in Rome and how they wanted to present the city, and themselves, to visitors.[17]

THE JEW-BADGE

In the eleventh century, a Jewish banker converted to Christianity and married into Roman nobility. For one hundred years, during power struggles between nobles and popes, the newly Christian Pierleoni family chose sides shrewdly. Then, in 1130, Peter Pierleoni, a cardinal whose great grandfather was undeniably Jewish, became Pope Anacletus II. Most of Christendom opposed his papacy, but Italy supported it. Despite vicious antisemitic attacks, Pope Anacletus II remained the pontiff until 1138, when he died of natural causes.[18]

Many other Italian Jews would have longed to similarly assimilate, not to the point of becoming the pope, but at least to the point of being treated more or less like their neighbors. But for the most part, the Vatican required Jews to be identifiable as Jews. In 1215, the Fourth Ecumenical Lateran Council ordered Jews to wear distinguishing clothing of some sort: a badge, a hat, even a complete garment. In Rome Jews were identified by a red coat.[19] Pope Innocent III (1198–1216) explained the purpose of the *sciamanno* or Jew-Badge: "It sometimes happens by mistake Christians have intercourse with Jewish or Saracen women ... [which is] a grave sin."[20] The Jew-Badge would keep Jewish men from "wicked mingling" with Christian women.[21] Such a prohibition, it was believed, prevented contamination: otherwise, physical contact with Jews could infect all Catholics, who together were conceived of as a body, the body of Christ.[22]

In theory, the body of Christ took three forms. First was the physical, human form (*Corpus Christi*) of Jesus who lived and died in Judaea. However, after his resurrection, all those who believed in him became the church (*Corpus Mysticum*), the second body of Christ (1 Cor. 12:12–27). The third was the Eucharist, the sacramental wafer or Host that miraculously transformed into the body of Christ (*Corpus Verum*) during the communion ritual (1 Cor. 11:24). Just as it was believed that Jews caused the death of the physical body of Christ (*Corpus Christi*), so Jews were thought to threaten the *Corpus Mysticum* and the *Corpus Verum*. Carnality between a Jew, who was impure by definition, and a Catholic, a living part of the *Corpus Mysticum*, defiled and infected the entire church (1 Cor. 12:14–27). Therein lay the gravity of "wicked mingling."[23]

Thus the reality that Jews and Catholics were often physically indistinguishable and sometimes had the same names presented problems for the church. Most often, Jews looked like any other Roman, and furthermore, Jews with biblical or Rabbinic names often took Italian names to be less conspicuous. For example, Jews named "Gershom"—a popular Jewish name referring to Moses's son Gershom and meaning "I have been a stranger in a foreign land" (Exod. 2:21)—also used the name "Pellegrino," Italian for "pilgrim."[24] Consequently, church leaders viewed the Jew-Badge as a necessary defense in the battle to maintain church purity. At least theoretically it could prevent the intimacy of strangers.

Thus the Jew-Badge was not allowed to lapse. In 1257 Pope Alexander IV reordered it (at which time the liturgical poet Benjamin Anau wrote a stinging poem expressing his humiliation at the demand), and in 1311 the Council of Ravenna repeated the requirement.[25] In 1360 Roman municipal statutes ordered male Jews (except doctors) to wear a red tabard (men's short coat) and female Jews a red petticoat and other identifying trappings, perhaps a yellow scarf.[26] Inevitably, Jewish women wearing required clothing became compared to prostitutes (although in Rome, unlike other Italian cities, prostitute attire was not consistently regulated).[27] In all, the church intended that the world of appearances—where Jews and Catholics were indistinguishable—correspond to what the church thought was reality: Jews being impure and different from Christians. The Jew-Badge was also a palpable reminder that the church could enforce that reality.

Jews were identified by dress for other reasons as well. Some church leaders feared their church was being Judaized, a fear that manifested itself in intrachurch rivalries. In the Middle Ages, two churches dominated Rome: St. Peter's in the Vatican and the Lateran Church. St. Peter's Basilica was supposedly built where the Apostle Peter was crucified (ca. 64 CE), and the church was founded during Pope Anacletus's reign (ca. 90 CE). The Lateran Church was built later, ca. 314 CE, at Emperor Constantine's direction, and probably sited on the land owned by Titus Sextus Lateranus. As an unknown canon of St. Peter's wrote in his guidebook, *Mirabilia Urbis Romae* (The marvels of Rome, ca. 1143):

> During the days of Pope Sylvester, Constantine Augustus built the Lateran Basilica. . . . He put there the Ark of the Covenant, which Titus had carried from Jerusalem with many thousand Jews, and the Golden Candlestick of Seven Lamps [the Temple Menorah] with vessels for oil. In the ark are these things: the golden emeralds, the mice of gold, the Tablets of the Covenant, the Rod of Aaron, manna, the barley loaves, the golden urn, the coat without seam, the reed and garment of Saint John the Baptist, and the tongs that Saint John the Evangelist was shorn with.[28]

The Lateran and St. Peter's competed over which church had the most prestigious relics. St. Peter's took glory in housing the bones of the saint, and when the Lateran claimed the tablets of the Law, St. Peter's retorted that most of the relics found in the Lateran were Jewish, and hence the Lateran was more of a synagogue than a church. Bolstering St. Peter's claim, Roman Jews would flock to the Lateran on Tisha b'Av to mourn the destruction of both the Solomonic and the Second Temple. Jews believed that the Lateran possessed two pillars named Jachin and Boaz mentioned in 1 Kings 7:21 that featured the inscription, "Solomon son of David." Titus had supposedly taken the pillars as loot from the Jerusalem Temple. On Tisha b'Av, it was said, water flowed down the columns like tears—a demonstration of grief by mere stone.[29]

Around 1175, the Lateran controversy inspired Petrus Mallius, a canon at St. Peter's, to pen a chauvinistic poem:

> Here let the people venerate the throne of Peter,
> Let them honor the church of the Prince [Christ]

Let them revere the head of the world and of the city.
I was established as the first parent, the mother, the head of churches, . . .
I glory in Peter and Paul but you [Lateran Church], Synagogue
Rejoice only in signs and ancient anointings.
I consider those men at the same time Jews and followers of Moses
Who believe the old Synagogue to be the head of the Church
For that old figure says nothing about the Prince without equal.[30]

The poet's rhetoric, accusing a Catholic of being a Jew (whether a former, hidden, or actual Jew), was not uncommon. In such a hostile environment the Jew-Badge might, paradoxically, have lowered anxieties. Theoretically, everyone would know who was the "other" and who was not, and fears arising from uncertainty could be blunted by such knowledge.[31]

Jews were also a threat to the *Corpus Verum* (the Eucharist, the third Body of Christ)—allegedly by their very proximity to the Host, the wafer used during the communion ritual. During Holy Week, Roman Jews were forbidden to leave their homes to preclude the supposed contagion that could corrupt and infect the wafers used that week. A corrupted, infected Host was worthless, and consequently Jews, by their impurity, could deprive Catholics of a means of salvation.[32]

Catholics were likewise anxious about consuming anything else purportedly contaminated by Jews. Was it permissible for them to eat meat slaughtered by Jewish butchers? For Jews, the laws of kashrut stipulated that only certain parts of a slaughtered animal were fit for consumption. Consequently, they were constrained to sell—or even give—the unkosher cuts to non-Jews,[33] even as Catholics were sometimes prohibited from accepting that gift, because it was considered an infectious carrier of Judaism. In fourteenth-century Avignon, when the popes resided there, Jews could not butcher meat on Good Friday for fear it would contaminate the sacrifice of Jesus.[34] A Catholic legist from Padua, Angelo di Castro (ca. 1404–ca. 1485), asserted that such a restriction was nonsense, and a form of Judaizing itself: if Catholics could not eat the unkosher cuts, they might as well be keeping kosher along with the Jews.[35] Catholics were on the horns of a dilemma. If they ate meat from a kosher butcher, they were in danger of contamination. If they did not eat that unkosher meat, they were no better than a Jew. The fear of Jewish contamination was logically reduced to absurdity.

STOLEN JEWISH HONOR

Some sociologists and anthropologists speak of the Mediterranean world as having a culture of honor as defined by wealth, status, and virility.[36] Or, it has been said, there are two types of honor: honor of social position based on possessions, and moral honor based upon reputation among peers.[37] For our purposes, it is enough that honor was considered an asset, even a scarce one, and that as an asset, it could be stolen.[38] A man could never be secure in his honor because conflicts or other circumstances could deprive him of it. Honor stolen resulted in shame, the opposite of honor.[39] Both honor and shame were externally—not internally—assigned.[40]

Within the Jewish community, fellow Jews might confer honor on a Jew, but in the broader medieval Roman world, honor for a Jew was a rare commodity. In Catholic legal tradition, Jews were ineligible for honor, and overall, a Jew's honor was little more than a prostitute's.[41] As the jurist Alessandro da Imola (1424–77) said, both Jewish usury and the practice of prostitution were occupations without honor—lesser evils, tolerated by the church, necessary in a fallen world for the greater good of Roman society. In Rome, there was always a limited amount of cash, a limited number of sexually available women, and a limited amount of honor. It was, therefore, socially valuable to have persons in your midst without honor who were able fill the needs for cash and sex. Jews and prostitutes supposedly had no shame about how they made a living.[42] Therefore, like Jews, the prostitutes could be set apart by wearing identifying clothing, in their case a scarf known as the *spurniglia*. And like Jews, they were compelled to attend sermons aimed at their betterment (see chapter 7).

In the sixteenth century, Jews and prostitutes were again ignominiously linked by the church's creation of a second ghetto for prostitutes modeled after the first one for Jews. A decade or so after the Jewish Ghetto's establishment in 1555, Pope Pius V created what became known colloquially as the *ortaccio* or "ugly garden" (just as the Jewish cemetery in Trastevere was known as the *Ortaccio degli ebrei*, the "ugly garden of the Jews") in the Campus Martius, in the center of Rome. Apparently, the walls were built hastily, probably of wood and plaster, with a single gate allowing entrance to a few enclosed streets. Women were locked in during Lent, forcing the pope to feed them, given that they were deprived of their livelihood for weeks. If the *ortaccio* was meant to discourage prostitution, it was undoubtedly a failure. For one, Rome had too many prostitutes to be kept in one small area. Eventually, the prostitutes outgrew their ghetto's flimsy walls, and were allowed to live in several separate areas throughout Rome.[43]

Because Jews, like prostitutes, lacked the currency of honor, they could be exploited for their purported lack of honor. One such incident concerned Cola di Rienzo, also known as Nicola Gabrini, a non-Jewish political reformer who seized power in Rome in 1347, ruled for less than a year, fled, and was assassinated upon his return. On October 8, 1354, his headless corpse was dragged from the Capitol to the home of his rivals, the Colonnas, who ordered the Jews of Rome to burn his corpse in the Mausoleum of Augustus and scatter his ashes in the Tiber.[44] The Jews, considered both impure and without honor, had to obey, despite their own beliefs concerning impurity and dead bodies.

A second instance took place yearly from 1466 to 1668. Previously, Jews had to serve as horses—human mounts—for mock tournaments in the Circo Agonale. This was so degrading that in 1312 the Jewish community agreed to pay ten gold florins annually to the Capitoline Chamber to cease the practice.[45] Certainly, Jews gained no honor by bribing their way out of their humiliation. A Roman senator noted that the ten florins reminded him of the thirty gold pieces paid to Judas for his betrayal of Jesus.[46]

Then, in 1466 Pope Paul II instituted Carnival footraces running from the Piazza San Pietro to the Castle of S. Angelo (traversing what is today the Via Della Conciliazione in Vatican City). Boys, old men, buffalos, asses, and also Jews ran the races.[47] Early on, the race of the Jews took place with some fanfare. A 1512 letter described "the Festival of the Jews" wherein a company of one hundred Jews marched immediately behind Rome's governor and police chief, followed by an additional fifty Jews, two *fattori* (Jewish community officials) on horseback, and twelve Jewish runners trained by the pope's Jewish physician. The winner, along with others, was fêted at the pope's residence.[48] In succeeding years, however, the race turned ugly. Jews were made to run naked, except for a loin cloth, with mounted men wielding goads to spur the runners on. In 1581, French Renaissance philosopher Michel de Montaigne, found the race puzzling, but explained it as traditional.[49] Anthony Munday, a British visitor to Rome in 1581, described it:

> The first day of their Carne-vale, the Jews in Rome cause an ensign to be placed at the Capitol where likewise they appoint wagers at their own costs; and then they run stark naked from the Porto Populo unto the Capitol for them, the which I judge above a mile in length. And all the way they gallop their great horses after them, and carry goads with sharp points of steel in them, wherewith they will prick the Jews on the naked skin, if so be they do not run faster than their horses gallop, so that you shall see some of their backs all on gore blood.[50]

In later years, the Jewish racers were fattened so that they became torpid. Nevertheless, they still had to run naked, making the race a comic festivity for unfeeling spectators.[51] They ran in the rain, mud, and even snow, with difficult conditions adding to the Carnival comedy, and the nudity of the Jews in sharp contrast to the exquisitely costumed audience.[52] In 1547, one of the Jewish racers collapsed and died.[53]

Munday also noted that the following day, "certain Christians run naked likewise." But these ran unmolested and their winnings were supplied by a tax of eleven hundred florins paid by Jews—except the pope's physicians—throughout the Papal State.[54] Finally, in 1668, Pope Clement IX (1667–69) ended the race of the Jews, but the tax continued in a new form that financially supported the Carnival.[55]

Anti-Jewish street theatre, *giudate*, took place during the Roman Carnival as well. Catholic actors posing as Jews performed farces mocking Jews, the players traveling the city on carts, stopping, performing in a piazza, and then moving on to another. Often during Holy Week, leading up to Easter, Jews were banned from being outdoors, but "virtual Jews," Catholics performing street theatre as Jews, were welcome everywhere.[56] Popes Leo X and Clement VII would ban *giudate*, but in the latter half of the sixteenth century, with the establishment of the Ghetto, the *giudate* were revived.

One widely reported humiliation of Jews during Holy Week appears to be legend. That each year a Jew would be crammed into a barrel on Rome's Testaccio Hill and rolled downhill is unlikely to have happened, there being no contemporaneous descriptions of such an outrage. The humiliation Jews did face at this time of year held other meanings. The Roman Carnival was a period of orchestrated anarchy during the weeks before Lent in the Christian calendar.[57] It was a limited opportunity for the poor to mock the rich, for the disenfranchised to grab some moments of esteem and power. During Carnival, the social world was turned upside down. Participants got a glimpse of what a revolution might look like. Nonetheless, despite its topsy-turvy appearance, Carnival was actually a mechanism for maintaining the social hierarchy. Soon it was over, and order restored in time for a season of repentance before Easter.[58]

Not so for Jews. They were restricted from participating in Carnival, save for the enforced races, and if they ventured out to celebrate like everyone else, they risked a public flogging. While Catholic shopkeepers and merchants might have dressed like their betters and enjoyed acting like aristocracy for a day, the message for Jews was simple: at Carnival, Jews remained Jews. If the average Carnival participant hoped to momentarily ascend the social ladder, Jews were forced in the opposite direction: classified and treated like beasts running their races along with buffalo and asses. Although originally Catholics also raced, at least until 1581, Jews would be the only "bipeds" in the contests from 1581 through 1668.[59]

Ultimately the Carnival message to Jews was that they had a place in Rome, but it was a station without honor. Everyone knew that the gentile baker, no matter his Carnival costume, was not a king; likewise, everyone knew that the Jew, no matter how naked and running with donkeys, was not an animal. However, during Carnival, social distances were shortened. The gap between a baker and a king became a bit less, and the gap between a donkey and a Jew was also diminished.

CATHOLIC RESPECT FOR JEWS

And yet, all the while Jews were being shown their place through the Carnival races, there were simultaneous indicators of a surprising respect for Jews and Judaism. In these instances, Jews were even granted a portion of honor.

In 1238, the Church of Santa Maria brought a case before the Masters of the Buildings of the City against a Jewish dyeing business whose dyed runoff water was flowing downhill to the church. Agreeing with the church, the Masters prohibited that practice, and ordered the Jews to build a conduit directing the runoff to Rome's main sewer. However, neither the Jews nor their business were impugned in the process. The Jewish dyers surely realized that their chances of prevailing against a church were slim. Nonetheless, they had a right to work in the neighborhood, and the church had to deal with them.[60]

Less mundane was a dispute some fifty years later. In 1289, the Papal Curia (a group of various bureaucratic organizations aiding the pope in the administration of the church) heard a complaint by two Roman Jews. A Frenchman, Solomon Petit, arrived in Italy inveighing against the works of the Jewish philosopher Maimonides in hopes of persuading both Jews and Catholics to burn all of Maimonides' writings because of their anti-mystical bent. The Jewish petitioners sought papal support of Maimonides against Petit. In response, the Vatican issued a proclamation that was read in Roman synagogues: there was nothing prejudicial to faith in Maimonides and persons burning his writings risked a fine.[61] Surprisingly, the church took sides in a Jewish dispute, and rather than disparaging the Jews, it decided to preserve Jewish learning.

Two hundred years later, in 1492, a great many Jews expelled from Spain arrived at the gates of Rome, eager for admittance, and Pope Alexander VI

(Borgia), who was rumored to have Jewish ancestors, opened the gates. Furthermore, according to two accounts that may be more legend than fact, Roman Jews inside the walls had appealed to Pope Alexander VI to send their brethren away—the new arrivals might try to reconvert Jews previously converted to Catholicism back to Judaism, thereby endangering the entire Jewish community. According to these suspect accounts, the pope not only opened the gates, but fined the Roman Jews for failing to come to the aid of their fellows.[62] In fact, Jewish notarial records from Rome indicate that the Roman and Spanish Jews intermarried almost from the start—an indication of little hostility between the two groups. By 1524, the Jewish community was sufficiently united that it accepted a charter and bylaws, composed by Daniel da Pisa, a Tuscan Jewish banker with ties to Rome, that treated all Jews in Rome as a single community.[63]

At roughly the same time the pope was opening Rome to Jewish exiles, a churchman opened the doors of his Roman home to a single Jewish family. In 1514, Cardinal Giles Antonini, commonly known as Giles of Viterbo, took in a Jewish scholar, Elijah Levita, and his family for almost thirteen years.

Giles was a student of Hebrew who was interested in Jewish mysticism. In 1530 he wrote *Scechina*, a Latin treatise commissioned by Pope Clement VII and addressed to Holy Roman Emperor Charles V (1500–1558).[64] The title refers to the Jewish mystical belief that God's presence on earth is a female principle called *Shekhina*, which Giles identified with the Holy Spirit. More broadly, Giles held that Jewish mystical traditions, Kabbalah, were divine revelations to Adam, then to Moses, then passed from one Jewish sage to another, including Jesus, for centuries. Armed with a kabbalistic understanding of the Hebrew language and alphabet, Giles saw each Hebrew letter as laden with meaning, and each word freighted with spiritual significance. Accordingly, he created a Christian Kabbalah.

Giles wanted to understand the *Zohar*, the classic thirteenth-century Jewish mystical work, but to make headway through its obscure text, he needed a teacher. Enter Elijah Levita, a grammarian and poet newly arrived in Rome from Venice.[65] Giles proposed himself as a pupil to Elijah, resulting in Giles, Elijah, and Elijah's family living under Giles' roof for some thirteen years, until the 1527 sack of Rome (discussed later in this chapter) brought their relationship to an end.

Another Jew visiting Rome was also welcomed by the Catholic Church, with sizable fanfare. In 1524, David Reuveni (1490–1541?), describing himself as David the son of Solomon, of the tribe of Reuben, brother of Joseph the Jewish king of Tabor, an Arabian kingdom situated in the Islamic heartland, made his entrance to seek papal support for his brother back in Arabia. His brother's kingdom, nonexistent in actuality, but described by Reuveni in glowing terms, was poised to fight the Turks and harry them from the rear as they prepared to attack Vienna. All they needed was Christendom's military support.

Reuveni was a con artist who, upon his arrival, stopped at Giles' house, where Elijah had long been residing. Reuveni reported yet another Jewish scholar, Rabbi Joseph Ashkenazi, living with Giles. Giles arranged an audience for Reuveni with Pope Clement VII. When Reuveni asked that the pope broker peace between the king of France and the Habsburg Empire to better fight the Turks, Clement demurred. However, the pope did offer him safe passage to Portugal, where he might convince the king to use his navy for Reuveni's advantage. That was never going to happen either. However, Reuveni managed to stay in Rome for exactly one year, lodging in the homes of several generous, and credulous, Jews. Eventually, he convinced the Vatican to house him in a spacious apartment outfitted, in part, as his personal synagogue. Eventually Reuveni went to Portugal but his time there ended disastrously. Accused of reconverting new Christians back to Judaism—there were rumors of a clandestine circumcision—Reuveni fled to France, and while his story did not end there, it has no more to do with the Jews of Rome.[66]

RENAISSANCE JEWS

Reuveni was a scoundrel; not so Judah Romano (ca. 1293–ca. 1330), who produced commentaries on Maimonides fifty years after the church gave its approval to the philosopher. Yet Judah Romano's most inadvertent contribution to Western culture is found in a short reference to a type of Jewish bread. In his *Glossario giudeo-italiano dei termini difficili che si trovano ne Mishna Tora* (Glossary of Jewish-Italian difficult terms found in the *Mishneh Torah* [by Maimonides]), Romano defines the Hebrew word *harara* (in the *Mishneh Torah* at *Mishnah Shabbat* I.10) as *focaccia* (flat bread) cooked on coals, or *pizza*. Romano's manuscript identifying pizza (Hebrew letters: *p-y-tz-h*) is the first written record of that now ubiquitous dish.[67]

Pizza aside, Judah Romano was a humanist and a rationalist. Absorbing Maimonides' love of Aristotelian philosophy, he believed that if both the Jewish and Catholic traditions were approached rationally, they could lead to the same universal conclusions. Consequently, he immersed himself in Christian Scholasticism and translated the work of Thomas Aquinas into Hebrew. In turn, the Italian humanist Pico della Mirandola (1463–94) translated Judah Romano's works into Italian.[68]

Judah Romano's ultimate life's work was a Bible commentary, though at first he was stymied by his rationalism. His *Commentary on Kaddish and Kadisha* discusses his inability to say *Kaddish* (the Jewish prayer for the dead), or pray at all. He found prayer revolting, given its lack of rational philosophical content. Consequently, he resolved to study Jewish prayers, even with the help of the works of Catholic Scholastics, hoping to discover their philosophical basis. Ultimately, he had something like a prophetic vision allowing him not only to pray but to comment on the Bible.[69] For Romano, the Bible was God's word, and it had an infinite number of interpretations. He would generate numerous interpretations of various biblical verses, all recorded in no particular order.

Romano also loved poetry, which he believed was derived from the same impulses as biblical interpretation. Especially fond of the poetry of his contemporary Dante, he translated portions of the *Divine Comedy* into Hebrew to be read publicly to Jews in Rome.

Romano had a cousin, also a poet, known as Immanuel of Rome (1261–1328), who composed *Tophet and Eden*, a Jewish version of the *Divine Comedy*.[70] Beginning in hell or Tophet, Immanuel travels through his version of the *Inferno*, which is populated by biblical figures, including the Kings Ahab and Uzziah, and David's son Absalom. Eventually, Immanuel reaches heaven, where numerous Jewish heroes such as Jonah, Deborah, and Rabbi Judah the Prince (compiler of the Mishnah) reside. Non-Jews also live in Immanuel's heaven. Nonetheless, Immanuel reveres them, not for any Christian virtues, but for their rational rejection of Christianity and their acceptance of universal values.

Less well known than *Tophet and Eden* are the *Mahbarot Immanuel*, notebooks in which Immanuel of Rome borrowed the sonnet form from Italian literature and wrote erotic Hebrew poems. In one long poetic story, *Megillat Hahesheq* (The scroll of love), Immanuel claims that at his friend and patron's request, he courts a beautiful Catholic nun, the friend wanting to prove Immanuel's foolishness and her virtuousness. However, Immanuel uses words of seduction to win her love where all others have failed:

> Wherefore the honeycomb upon thy lip,
> if no lover's there to sip?
> What's the point of your two breasts
> if there between them no lover rests?
> Wherefore the delights of thy jewel-like curves
> if there, no grazing buck may swerve?
> Wherefore they belly like a heap of wheat
> if Gilgal and Shittin never meet?[71]

He succeeds; the young nun decides to leave her vocation for him. However, like all Jewish-Catholic liaisons at the time, this one is doomed. Immanuel's beloved turns out to be the half-sister of his patron, who is horrified by the turn of events. Immanuel then berates his beloved for succumbing to his poetry, and she, in despair, kills herself. The poem reveals the sexual attraction of Catholic and Jew, the drive to create a mixed family, and the impossibility of those aspirations, even in the relatively open Renaissance society.

Just as the cousins Judah and Immanuel made use of Scholastic philosophy, the sonnet form, and Dante's poetry, and were comfortable in an intellectual universe that included Catholic as well as Jewish art and philosophy, some Catholic artists practiced within a universe populated by Jews. Silver work owned by the Roman Jewish community is ascribed to the craftsmanship of the Florentine goldsmith and sculptor Benvenuto Cellini (1500–1571), and Cellini was probably not alone as a gentile producing work for Jews. Given that the craftsmen who made such objects had to apprentice with guilds that were closed to Jews, and that after 1555 the only sanctioned Jewish trade was the selling of used cloth, most likely Christians crafted the Italian synagogue ornaments now in museums worldwide. Pope Pius VI's 1775 edict prohibiting Catholic silversmiths from making amulets for Jewish children is evidence that, prior to the edict, such work was common practice.[72]

The artist best known for a work revered by Jews was Michelangelo (1475–1564). His statue of Moses, the centerpiece of an unfinished funeral monument commissioned by Pope Julius II (1503–13), was eventually housed in the Church of San Pietro in Vincoli (St. Peter in Chains). A massive, muscular Moses sits with the tablets of the Law in his right hand, while stroking his long beard with the left. Two projections from his head, construed as horns, bear witness to St. Jerome's mistranslation of Exodus 34:29, 30, and 35. The Hebrew refers to *qaran*—radiance streaming from Moses' visage—but instead Jerome read the word *qeren*, horn, and Michelangelo, working from Jerome's translation, created a horned Moses.

That Moses was horned meant little to Roman Jews. They were fascinated by Michelangelo's statue of Moses, created for a pope and housed in a church. According to Giorgio Vasari's roughly contemporary work, *Le vite de' più ecccelenti pittori, scultori, e architettori* (Lives of the most excellent painters, sculptors, and architects), published in two editions, 1550 and 1568: "Moses may now be called the friend of God more than ever, since God has permitted his body to be prepared for the resurrection before the others by the hand of Michelangelo. The Jews still go every Saturday in troops to visit and adore it as a divine, not a human being."[73]

Jews probably did not view Moses as "divine." However, numerous Jews were intrigued by the statue and visited it regularly, leaving us with an indelible image: Jews flocking to a Catholic church, dedicated to St. Peter, to stand before a memorial for a pope, created by a devout Christian, in order to gaze upon the face and form of their lawgiver and the greatest of the Hebrew prophets.

That scene provides a veritable definition of cognitive dissonance. Not only are Michelangelo and his Jewish admirers strangers to one another; Moses himself has been brought to Rome out of the pages of a text shared and argued over vociferously by Catholics and Jews. Moreover, Moses was revered as the most favored teacher of a long-lived traditional Jewish community residing just blocks from the Church of St. Peter in Vincoli. Thus the monumentally Catholic and (in some ways) intensely Jewish sculpture became a fulcrum around which both Jews and Catholics could publicly play out their respective and disputed beliefs.

THE SACK OF ROME

Whatever Jewish-Catholic cordiality there was ended in 1527, when Rome was sacked by a combined army of German Lutherans and Spanish soldiers.

Armies of the Holy Roman Emperor Charles V and Francis (1494–1547), king of France, had battled at Pavia, in northern Italy. Charles, the victor, set his sights on Rome, hoping to replace Pope Clement VII, who he believed was not a legitimate pontiff. Charles' army consisted of two factions: the Landsknechte (German mercenaries sympathetic to Martin Luther) and Spanish soldiers sent to Italy to support the emperor. Together they marched toward Rome, united in a bitter cause: neither had been paid. They sought loot to compensate them for their military service. Rome seemed a wealthy target.

Duped by false promises of peace, Pope Clement VII failed to prepare the city for invasion. The result was a savage attack on Rome by soldiers literally seeking payback. The Landsknechte took special satisfaction in

FIG. 5. Michelangelo's marble statue of Moses in the Church of San Pietro in Vincoli. Manor Photography / Alamy Stock Photo.

looting the Vatican and the churches whose very riches were evidence of the corruption they had been taught to abhor. Catholic churchmen were killed, kidnapped, and paraded through the streets. Nuns and noblewomen were raped, and Catholic relics such as the heads of St. Peter, St. Paul, and St. Andrew were kicked and trampled along with supposed fragments of wood from the Cross and the Crown of Thorns. St. Peter's Basilica became a stable, and the pope and his allies fled to Castel Sant'Angelo. Eventually a peace was negotiated, and Clement was spirited out of the city. Within months, the imperial troops left as well. When Clement returned, he found a city without windows, roofs, attics, or even doors.[74]

The most disturbing events are described in *The Sack of Rome* by Luigi Guicciardini (1478–1551), who was not an eyewitness but a politician and critic of Rome, which undercuts some of his more vivid descriptions. Nevertheless, Rome was pitilessly sacked and Jews were not spared. Although some were given refuge in the palace of Cardinal della Valle, many were killed despite a bribe to Charles V's army.

As for Elijah Levita, who had been living peacefully with Giles of Viterbo for thirteen years, he and his family fled the city, never to return. That exit marked the end of an era. In the ensuing years, the Jews who survived and remained in Rome would be exiled internally. The papacy that had in some measure protected them would eventually enclose the Jewish community in a squalid part of Rome and shut the gates—a humiliation that was to last three hundred years.

5

Divorce, Roman Style

The Ghetto

On August 19, 1559, a months-old statue of Pope Paul IV (Carafa) stood in the Campidoglio piazza adjacent to Rome's city hall. Paul IV had been elected pontiff on May 23, 1555. By August 1559 he was near death, and crowds of Romans, along with others throughout the Papal States, anticipated his death with celebrations.

Upon his death (or near enough to satisfy the mobs), his statue, made of stone, was capped with a yellow hat. In 1555, Paul IV had established the Jewish Ghetto and ordered all Jewish men to wear an identifying yellow hat. Affixing the so-called Jew Hat on his statue was "in memory of having placed this yellow hat on the Jews."[1]

A mock trial and execution of the deceased pope followed. The statue was decapitated and the nose cut off. The head bearing the yellow hat was reportedly dragged through the streets of Rome, or rolled down the Campidoglio hill. A satirical poem posted in the Piazza Pasquino shortly thereafter tells the story:

O blissful and dear man,
That in the Campidoglio had his head cut off,
With that nose already full of snot,
And a face like Priapus,
His triumph celebrated by kicking his head with the yellow hat
Like a ball, all over Rome.[2]

In other versions of the story, the headless trunk of the statue was also dragged to the Campo de' Fiori, "subjected to indignities," and, in the manner of many judgments against Roman criminals and dignitaries, thrown into the Tiber River.[3] (The 1562 bull *Dudum a felicis* [Happiness for a long time] enacted by Paul IV's successor Pius IV would establish a statute of limitations for any crimes committed during the desecration and trial of Paul IV's statue, along with any crimes committed by Jews during Paul IV's papacy.[4] Thus the dramatic occurrences of the summer of 1559 would be put to rest.)

If Paul IV was judged publicly and harshly only after his death—and, therefore, solely symbolically—actual trials among the living took place all the time in fifteenth- and sixteenth-century Rome.[5] One such trial, in 1621, concerned an attack on a Christian miller, who, along with five horses loaded with flour, had passed through the Ghetto from the Piazza Pescaria to the Piazza Giudea.[6] The unbridled horses were running ahead of the miller, and the streets were crowded. At the Vicolo de' Macelli, one horse barreled into a Jew, and a brawl ensued. The miller, badly beaten, died soon thereafter.

During the inquiry, the governor and Capitoline police questioned twenty-nine Jews and five Christians. Ultimately, a vagrant Jewish ruffian named Angelo di Jacob Levi was accused of the murder. As would be expected, Jews feared that the entire community would be punished, formally or informally. Whenever Jews were charged with ritually murdering children, the result was often vicarious punishment of an entire community. While no such accusations had ever been made in Rome, in the case of the miller a Catholic had been killed at the hands of a Jew.[7]

There was one mitigating circumstance. Earlier that year, the governor had banned tradesmen, specifically including millers, from allowing their horses to run free in Rome. Would the new ordinance be enforced in favor of a young Jewish tough? On November 25, 1621, Angelo Levi was condemned to five years in prison—a surprisingly light sentence given the capital crime.

If Levi served his sentence (subsequent details are unknown), he served it in a separate cell for Jews. After 1585, by order of Pope Sixtus V, Jews and Christians were separated even in Roman jails, on the theory that incarceration should rehabilitate prisoners. How could criminals improve themselves if they were in contact with impure Jews?[8]

Looking together at these two trials—Pope Paul IV's mock trial and Angelo Levi's actual one—the question arises: why was the pope judged so severely and the Jew so leniently? Of course, the trials, separated by sixty-two years, were significantly different. For one, the dead pope suffered nothing; only his statue was punished. Nonetheless, the people of Rome, whether through their representatives or en masse, treated the Jew with far more care than they did the pontiff. Why?

OTHER POSTHUMOUS PAPAL TRIALS

That Paul IV's memory was mocked and degraded in strikingly concrete terms was not without precedent:

In approximately 897, Pope Stephen VI ordered the corpse of his predecessor, Pope Formosus (891–96), exhumed and put on trial for perjury and impersonating a bishop. Unsurprisingly, the cadaver was convicted. He was reinterred, but then exhumed once again, and what was left of him cast into the Tiber.[9]

In 985, the body of the newly deceased Pope Boniface VII was dragged through Rome's streets and deposited under the statue of Marcus Aurelius in the Campus Lateranensis.[10]

In about 1100, Pope Paschal II had the bones of his predecessor, (Anti) Pope Clement III (1080–1100), exhumed and tossed into the Tiber.[11] The Church also issued an official *deletio* and *damnatio memoriae*, wiping out any record of Clement III's existence as a Pope.

In 1527, just thirty-two years prior to the indignities suffered by Paul IV's statue, the German conquerors of Rome forced the cardinal of Aracoeli, still alive, into a coffin and, after parading him through the city, gave him a mock funeral describing his life as a history of monstrous sins.[12] The same Protestant victors dressed a cardinal in the uniform of one of their soldiers, placed their distinctive cap upon his head, and carried him around the city along with an impersonator of the still living pope, Clement VII.[13]

At least some of the 1559 rioters may have witnessed the 1527 riots and modeled those events for their own acts, including satirically placing a Jew Hat on Paul IV, the object of their scorn.[14] So "crowning" Paul IV and dragging his statue through the city was, in effect, an anticoronation: Paul's coronation procession was reversed and the Jews' presentation of the Torah (discussed in chapter 3) replaced by the humiliating hat. At roughly the same time as the anticoronation, other crowds broke into the city jail and Inquisition office to free prisoners and burn legal records. By order of the mob, the pope's family coat of arms was also removed from all churches, palaces, public buildings, and gates.[15]

Contextually, when a Pope died, the time between popes, the *Sede vacante* or Vacant See, was a period of lawlessness, unrest, and inversion of social roles—somewhat similar to Carnival, although often violent, characterized more by anger than laughter.[16] At such a time, dressing the pope's image as a Jew forced the person occupying the highest rung on the social hierarchy to share an identity with those on the lowest.

What had Paul IV done to so anger Catholics (and Jews) on that August night in 1559?

ACCULTURATION IN FIFTEENTH-CENTURY ROME

Before and even after the Crusades, Jews and Catholics had achieved and maintained an intermittent equilibrium. The papacy and Jewish community existed together in a "creative dialog" or a "tense intimacy."[17] Rome's Jews were essentially "intimate outsiders."[18]

Jews, for instance, drank Christian (nonkosher) wine.[19] Each group apparently consulted the other's diviners and magicians for love potions.[20] A Roman publishing firm consisting of two Jews and one Christian printed Jewish religious texts as late as 1545, ten years before the establishment of the Ghetto.[21] In accord with historian Robert Bonfil's definition of acculturation as the continuous confrontation of cultures resulting in convergence, fusion, rejection, argument, and borrowing, Jews and Catholics swapped concrete benefits with one another.[22]

Jews were also of theological benefit to the church. St. Augustine (354–430) believed the continued existence of Jews was a theological necessity. Without Jews, God's ancient prophetic witness to the authenticity of Christ, the Old Testament, would be lost. More importantly, Jews were the prime example of the absence of faith and grace. Their existence was a perennial teaching moment for the faithful.[23] Jews were valuable economically as well. They made small, short-term loans necessitated by seasonal cycles and unpredictable emergencies.

And so Jews and Catholics managed to live together and adapt to one another throughout the fifteenth and part of the sixteenth century . . . until Gian Pietro Carafa became Pope Paul IV in 1555.

GIAN PIETRO CARAFA BEFORE HIS PAPACY

Carafa was already aged when he was elected. He'd had a career as an archconservative at a time when Protestants in northern Europe were challenging the universality of the church. Reacting to the Catholic Church's shattering, in 1542, well before he was elected pope, Carafa helped create the Inquisition in Rome, an act that no doubt contributed to his unpopularity.[24] The Inquisition was a blunt instrument aimed at suspected Christian heretics. Torture was expected if you were arrested and interrogated. The Catholic Giordano Bruno (1548–1600), for one, was burnt alive for his belief that the Earth revolved around the sun. By 1553, Carafa was the head of the Inquisition, the Chief Inquisitor. Devoted to the cause, it was said he never missed an inquisitorial session, even when ill or infirm. Romans, especially Catholics who lived in fear of the Inquisition, likely reviled him.

Jews were not the Inquisition's target. Judaism, according to St. Thomas Aquinas, was not heresy.[25] Jews couldn't be heretics because they were not Christians. Judaism was a formerly true, but now superseded, set of laws and customs that had no value, or indeed negative value, in a world redeemed by Christ.

At least that was the theory. Practically, Jews often found themselves before the Inquisition for a variety of alleged crimes including residing near a church or employing Christian domestics.[26] In 1550, two competing Venetian publishers of Maimonides' *Mishneh Torah* consulted with a different Jewish apostate to condemn the other's edition. When both of the Jewish converts to Christianity exceeded their mandate, attacking the Talmud in general on the grounds that it blasphemed against Christianity, the Inquisition intervened and ultimately ordered the Talmud's destruction.[27]

There had been earlier instances of Talmud burning in Europe. On Pope Gregory IX's order, the Talmud was burned in Paris in the 1240s, the burnt copies reportedly filling twenty cartloads.[28] Around the same time, the Talmud was burned in Rome, with the copies first being cut to pieces and trampled on.[29] And, as a result of the Inquisition's decree and Pope Julius III's bull, *Cum sicut nuper* (Since recently with sorrow), the Talmud was burned on Rosh Hashanah 1553, at Rome's Campo de'Fiore (where the aforementioned Giordano Bruno would be burned forty-seven years later).[30]

A year later, the *fattori* (Jewish community leaders) and the *qri'ah* (Jewish community council) appointed five Roman rabbis as censors of Jewish books in the hopes that self-censorship would avoid action by the Inquisition.[31] The Jewish community sought at least the right to publish Hebrew books other than the Talmud, but the Inquisition denied that request in 1557, two years after Carafa became Pope Paul IV. Another two years later, Paul IV published an *Index of Prohibited Books* that included the Talmud and all its commentaries.[32]

Surprisingly, evidence exists that in 1552 Carafa had sought a copy of kabbalistic texts, not to burn but to read. His interest was probably piqued by his millenarian beliefs that the end of time was imminent—beliefs that could possibly be corroborated in certain Jewish mystical texts.[33]

Two reasons underlay the church's order to burn the Talmud. First, the Talmud was said to contain blasphemies concerning Jesus and Mary, and therefore had to be eradicated. Second, it was hoped that depriving Jews of the books that contained their customs and beliefs would lead to mass conversions. Paradoxically, to reach both these goals, some copies of the Talmud had to remain in circulation, albeit among Catholics, not Jews. Catholics had to know what they were banning—especially since it was believed that certain talmudic passages could be used to convince recalcitrant Jews to convert. Ironically, by virtue of the church's machinations, in Rome after 1553 the Talmud was more accessible to the Catholic Church than to the Jews. (By 1564, Paul IV's successor, Pius IV, would tolerate use of a censored version of the Talmud that also deleted the name "Talmud" from the title page.)[34]

THE GHETTO

On July 12, 1555, within two months of being elected pope, Paul IV issued the bull *Cum nimis absurdum* (Since it is absurd), devoted to Jews, which began:

> Since it is absurd and improper that Jews—whose own guilt has consigned them to perpetual servitude—under the pretext that Christian piety receives them and tolerates their presence, should be ingrates to Christians, so that they attempt to exchange the servitude they owe to Christians for dominion over them: we—to whose notice it has lately come that these Jews, in our dear city and in some other cities, holdings and territories of the Holy Roman Church, have erupted into insolence: they presume not only to dwell side by side with Christians and near their churches with no distinct habit to separate them, but even to erect homes in the more noble sections, and streets of the cities holdings and territories, where they dwell and to buy and to possess fixed property and to have nurses and housemaids and other hired Christians servants, and to perpetuate many other things in ignominy and contempt of the Christian name—considering that the Roman Church tolerates the Jews in testimony of the true Christian faith and to the end that they, led by the piety and kindness of the Apostolic See, should at length recognize their errors and make all haste to arrive at the true light of the Catholic faith, and

thereby to agree that as they persist in their errors, they should recognize through experience that they have been made slaves while Christians have been made free through Jesus Christ.[35]

Paul IV took issue with Jews and Christians living as neighbors on the very same streets, "with no distinct habit to separate them." That Jews and Catholics were indistinguishable is evidenced by an incident during Purim in 1551, four years before the pontiff issued *Cum nimis*.[36] During Purim, known as the *carnevale giudeo* (the Jewish carnival), Jews donned costumes and sometimes drank heavily. In 1551, seven young Jewish men, after drinking in various Roman taverns, found themselves in the Piazza Giudea (which four years hence would be enclosed within the Ghetto walls). Around midnight they crossed paths with a Neapolitan torch maker, a Christian visiting Rome on business that he said required him to buy old ropes for the fibers to make torches. When they asked where he was going with the rope, he replied the port of Rome, but then headed in the opposite direction. To the Jews, that seemed suspicious enough behavior to grab him on the pretense of taking him to jail for rope theft. Although in plain clothes, they presented themselves to him as Roman policemen. They took him to the Corte Savelli (a court and prison under Catholic Church jurisdiction and Savelli family authority), where they pretended to call for the police captain. Of course, no captain appeared. At this point the Jewish pranksters proceeded to steer the torch maker to the Campidoglio (Rome's civic government center), but on their way they noticed a light in a baker's house, it being early morning when bread was being baked. Both the Jews and the hapless torch maker agreed that the rope would be left with the baker for safekeeping. The Jews, now deep into their roles as Roman police, knocked on the baker's door, shouting, "Open up. The police." The baker (actually three bakers) obliged, and agreed to hold the rope while the torch maker searched for the original rope seller to prove his innocence. But the rope seller, if there ever was one—maybe the torch maker did steal the rope—could not be found. Tiring of their game, the Jews let their captive go, but not before stealing his purse. Despondent, the torch maker returned to the bakers to collect his rope, only to find that they believed the Jewish scoundrels were genuine Roman policemen. They would not return his rope without authorization from the Campidoglio. At this point, the archival records cut the story off without resolution.

Pope Paul IV was probably not privy to this story. But it proves his point: Jews could masquerade as Catholics, even Catholic constables, without anyone being the wiser. That this was still the case in 1759, two centuries later, is the basis of the following humorous tale:

> A painter of some renown was commissioned to produce a portrait of a nobleman. Upon completing the portrait, the subject refused to pay for it, claiming it was not a convincing likeness. The painter in a fit of pique, altered the portrait to depict a Jew Hat on the head of the noble; the noble was powerfully annoyed. To which the painter replied, "I would never have thought that a portrait held not to resemble the original when dressed as a Christian would be recognized as a proper likeness with the device of a Jew."[37]

But in 1555, with the Catholic Church under attack, Pope Paul IV found the community of "strangers" in the midst of Rome intolerable. Having set forth the "absurdity" of Jews living freely among Catholics, his *Cum nimis* then decreed the establishment of a ghetto segregating them in Rome:[38] "All Jews should live solely in one and the same location, or if that is not possible, in two or three or as many as necessary, which are to be contiguous and separated completely from the dwellings of Christians. These places are to be designated by us in our city and by our magistrates in other cities, holdings, and territories. And they should have one entry alone, and so too one exit."[39]

Furthermore, all Jews would have to wear an identifying hat, thereby minimizing social (and sexual) contact.[40] In addition, Jews could earn money solely by dealing in secondhand clothing. Only one synagogue would be sanctioned within the area restricted for Jews. Jewish doctors could not practice medicine among Catholics. Jews could no longer hire

Catholic servants and nurses, and could not do any observable work on Sunday. Also by order of *Cum nimis*, but with some minimal exceptions requiring a permit (see chapter 8), Jews had to work inside the Ghetto.[41]

The Roman Ghetto decreed by Paul IV differed drastically from the Warsaw and other ghettos the Nazis would implement four hundred years later. While not minimizing the degradation of the Ghetto experience in Rome, the Nazi ghettos were meant to concentrate Jews in a small area in anticipation of their being killed, whereas the Roman Ghetto was engineered to forcibly convert Jews and "save" them. Paul IV expressly intended to so degrade Jewish life that Jews would convert to Christianity out of necessity. The Nazi ghettos were established under the presumption that Jews were irremediably evil and inferior—a plague for which there was no alternative but extermination. The Roman Ghetto was based upon the opposite presumption. The Jewish condition, evil though it might be, had a cure—conversion to Christianity—and the harsh Ghetto conditions aimed to produce so-called voluntary converts.

By July 23, 1555, two weeks after *Cum nimis* was issued, Jews had to begin wearing the Jew Hat; and by July 26, one day before Tisha b'Av, Jews who did not already live in the area set aside for them were forced from their homes into the restricted area near the Tiber River banks which came to be known as the Ghetto. Also on July 26, work began on the walls to enclose the Ghetto. The Jewish community paid for the approximately seven-and-a-half-acre enclosure (completed in two months), contributing approximately one hundred *scudi*.[42] (In 1824, part of the Ghetto would be extended to the north.) The Jewish population within the Ghetto at its inception is unknown, but approximately thirty years later, an estimated thirty-five hundred Jews lived within its walls.[43]

At first, Jews in Rome did not think of themselves as confined in a ghetto. Since 1516 there had been a ghetto in Venice that probably took its name from the copper slag thrown out (*gettare*) from a refinery nearby.[44] However, the Venetian senate and the Doge (duke) Leonardo Loredan—not the Catholic Church—had established the Venetian ghetto, and for economic rather than religious reasons. Venice was not under papal authority, and

Rome's Jews had no reason to use the Venetian term. Instead they referred to themselves comically as the *serraglio degli ebrei*, a *serraglio* being a sultan's harem, which for obvious reasons was kept in closed confinement. Now crowded into a closed space, Rome's Jews joked about themselves being the pope's harem.

The same term, *serraglio*, was used during the time of Popes Pius V and Sixtus V to describe a second ghetto: one devised for prostitutes that was also known as the *ortaccio* or "ugly garden."[45] The overlap in slang concerning Jews and prostitutes should not surprise. Both were intimate strangers in Rome. Prostitutes were both literally intimate with and strangers to their customers. The Jewish condition as intimate strangers was less literal, but not by much.

It wasn't until 1589 that a word playing on "ghetto" began to crop up in Jewish notarial documents. The reference was to *nostro ghet* (our *get*), meaning "our bill of divorce."[46] Jewish law stipulates that a husband who wishes to divorce his wife has to give her a *get* (bill of divorcement). By 1589 the pope's harem had become, in the Jewish imagination, the pope's divorced wife.

Of course, the term *nostro ghet* was black humor. No one, least of all Paul IV, believed that the papacy and the Jewish community had ever lived in harmonious marriage, even metaphorically. Nonetheless, conceiving of the establishment of the Ghetto as a divorce was saying, metaphorically, that Jews and Catholics in Rome were like a family—perhaps codependents, like partners in a bad marriage. And behind the metaphor was a legal reality. In 1555 Rome, self-identified Jews and Christians could not wed. Church law forbade a Christian from converting to Judaism. In short, for many Roman Jews, the sly metaphor *nostro ghet* may have perfectly expressed how they felt about their fate.

CATHOLIC HATRED OF PAUL IV

Catholics, too, had reason to detest Paul IV. Prior to his pontificate he had helped establish the Inquisition. During his four-year reign, he started a nearly disastrous war with Philip II of Spain. By 1557 the Spanish army stood

FIG. 6. Inside the Roman Ghetto area, late nineteenth century. Archivo Storico della Comunità Ebraica di Roma, Archivio fotografico, Fondo Fornari, vol. 4, no. 244.

at the gates of Rome, a sack of the city averted only when he signed a treaty of complete surrender.[47] The Roman populace resented such blundering. During the war, Rome was cut off from the surrounding hinterlands, blocking food imports. Dwindling revenue from tourists and pilgrims also necessitated emergency taxes on the populace.[48]

Paul IV was equally heavy-handed when it came to sexual mores. His General Proclamation of 1555 prohibited commerce with prostitutes in and also near churches.[49] Given the ubiquity of both prostitutes and churches throughout the city, Romans found this restriction onerous. Paul was also hated within the church. He was generally angry and tyrannical. When he called people "dreadful pigs" and "soiled and petty," he was not referring to Jews but monks and nuns respectively.[50]

With the military fiasco, his intellectual repression embodied in the *Index of Prohibited Books* (which, among other things, kept Romans from reading the Bible in Italian translation), the curtailing of prostitution, his career as inquisitor, and his confinement of Jews within what would become Italy's longest-lived ghetto, Paul IV was reviled at his death and tried, mocked, and convicted *in absentia*.

THE TRIAL OF ANGELO LEVI

By contrast, as we saw, the Jewish tough held responsible for the death of the Christian miller was sentenced only to five years in prison. That lenient judgment may be explained by the church's ambivalence toward the Jews—an ambivalence inherent even in the creation of the Ghetto.

How so, one might ask? How could walling thousands of Jews within one small area, severely restricting their mobility and choice of livelihood, and requiring them to wear identifying clothing be understood as an ambivalent act? And yet, the Roman Ghetto was by some measure ambivalent, because it was not an expulsion.

By 1555, Jews had already been expelled from England (1290), France (1394), Spain (1492), and Portugal (1496). Each of these expulsions had its own social and economic causes, but behind them all was a Pauline Christian theology of expulsion.

Although born Jewish himself, the apostle Paul had proclaimed that contact with Jews was dangerous to the budding Christian community. Such contact, he insisted, could jeopardize a Christian's salvation: "A little leaven leavens all the dough" (Gal. 5:9; 1 Cor. 5:7). To avoid even minimal contact, Paul evoked Abraham's example in Genesis 21:9–21. Egged on by his wife Sara, Abraham had expelled his concubine Hagar and their son Ishmael (Abraham's oldest son) into the desert. Abraham's younger son, Isaac, also had two sons, the older Esau, and the younger Jacob, who became known as Israel. Paul noted (Gal. 4:21–31) that Abraham expelled his older son Ishmael, and similarly noted (Rom. 9:6–13) that Isaac rejected his own older son, Esau. Paul interpreted these expulsions metaphorically. In his own day, centuries after Abraham and his sons and grandsons, God had rejected the older community, the Jews, and affirmed divine love for the new and younger community of Christians (Gal. 4:21–31). In other words, the Jews, formerly the heirs of Jacob/Israel, had been metaphorically transformed into the children of Esau, the older child. Like Esau, the Jews no longer had a claim on the birthright given by Abraham and Isaac. Christians, being the younger community, had become the new heirs of Isaac, the younger son.[51] Likewise, just as Abraham had cast Ishmael into the desert, so had the Jews suffered a similar spiritual expulsion.

While for Paul this interpretation of Genesis was a persuasive metaphor, a rhetorical device, over hundreds of years, the metaphor became reified and the Jews' position as Esau's heirs became an inescapable theological condition.[52] For Christian theologians and historians, Jews had forfeited their identity as sons of Isaac and Jacob and had become the children of Ishmael and Esau. In that light the expulsion of the Jews from Spain, England, France, and Portugal was no more than a necessary, albeit tortured, reiteration of a biblical story. Thus expulsions for socioeconomic reasons could be justified theologically as well.

However, Paul was but one of many theological founders of Christianity. Saint Augustine was another, and for Augustine, expulsion of the Jews from Christian society was inconceivable. Without Jews, he believed, God's ancient prophetic witness to the authenticity of Christ would be lost. The

Hebrew Bible, specifically the Prophets, were proof that Jesus was the Messiah. In the face of challenges to this claim—"Where did these prophetic books come from?" "Aren't they an elaborate forgery concocted by Christians to prove an obscure point about their Messiah?"—the presence of Jews was an indispensable talking point. If one needed authentication of such ancient documents, right here, living among us, are the descendants of people who wrote them.

Additionally, for Augustine and his successors, including Thomas Aquinas, Jews were the prime example of the absence of faith and grace.[53] They were a constant and necessary reminder that in our fallen world, both good (Christians) and evil (Jews) coexisted.[54] That Jews were a dispersed and despised people demonstrated that God had punished them for rejecting Jesus. In a world where God punished evil, the ultimate triumph of good was assured—but in the meantime, evil could not simply be expelled. That was a theological impossibility: evil was endemic to the world and could not be dealt with by simply forcing it to relocate.[55]

Consequently, as a matter of theology the Christian world was split when it came to the treatment of Jews. Expulsion was a less attractive option in Rome than it was in Spain, Portugal, France, and England, since the popes, who did not control those other civil societies, only those of the Papal States in central Italy, were more attuned to the theological treatises of Augustine and Aquinas than were the various kings and barons of Europe.

Nonetheless, in 1569 and 1593, Jews *were* expelled from the Papal States. In 1569, Pope Pius V exiled all Jews from the entirety of the Papal States except Rome and Ancona. In 1586, Pope Sixtus V reversed Pius V's expulsion order, but just seven years later, in 1593, the last pope of the sixteenth century, Clement VIII, again expelled the Jews from the Papal States, with the exception of Jews in Rome, Ancona, Avignon (a papal possession in southern France), and eventually Ferrara (when it became a papal possession in 1597).[56] The stated reasons for the expulsions were the alleged Jewish practices of usury, dealing in stolen goods and magical incantations, and seduction of Catholic women. Of course, those reasons do not explain why Rome, Ancona, Avignon, and Ferrara were exempted. The importance of Ancona as a trade center and the Jewish facility with trade might provide some explanation for that exception. In the exceptional case of Rome, the pontiff likely held out hope that the Jews' ghettoization there would convince them to convert, and that aim may have made ghettoization preferable to putting the Jews out of sight.[57]

As such, while almost all the Jews in the Papal States were subject to shifting policies forcing them to leave, allowing them to return, and expelling them again, Rome's Ghetto somehow protected its Jews from such edicts.

One could also view Rome's ghettoization of the Jews as a coercive expulsion *into* a limited space as opposed to an expulsion *out of* Rome. However, the very fact that the Jews were never banished from Rome gave them certain advantages. Forced residence in the Ghetto inadvertently created a kind of "homeland" where Jews sometimes felt protected.[58] (This also had historical precedent. In 1084 Bishop Rudiger had settled the Jews of Speyer, Germany, in a walled neighborhood, thereby successfully protecting them from mobs, and possible massacre, in 1096.)[59]

As Ghetto dwellers, Jews were strangely free to be Jewish as well. As we will see in the next chapter, with some—albeit severe—limitations, Jews in the Ghetto were able to live in an intensely Jewish community.[60] And the very separation from the rest of Rome forced the Jewish community to create an identity in opposition to their Catholic neighbors and self-consciously work as a community with Catholic Rome (see chapter 6).[61] Gone were the days when a Jew like Judah Romano could recite the poetry of Dante in a Roman café. Instead, Jews were forced to live separately and get by with the aid of each other. It was not easy. The large number of disputes among Jews in the Ghetto (evidenced by the detailed notarial records analyzed in the next chapter) indicate that often cooperation had to be enforced. But that too is evidence of a Jewish society thrown back on itself.

Meanwhile, Paul IV's Ghetto was disrupting the physical and social fabric of Rome. Geographically, the Ghetto lay astride a major commercial and ceremonial route. The city center's division in half by the walled Ghetto impeded municipal commerce.[62] The cheapest way for a miller to move his horses across town was to drive them through the hazardous, crowded, and tense Ghetto streets. Angelo Levi was probably not alone in feeling invaded when a Christian ran his horses with impunity through the heart of *his* Ghetto; the limited urban space had been set aside for him and other Jews. But Levi acted in the extreme, and afterward, the miller was dead.

Jews and Catholics had a common interest in his case. Jews did not want the entire Jewish community to suffer for the crime of one Jewish rogue. Roman authorities wanted to maintain order in the Ghetto, which meant not allowing violence to escalate between Catholics and Jews there. Their mutual interests were satisfied by Angelo Levi's relatively light five-year sentence, which was, on the one hand, justice, and on the other, an amelioration of a situation that could have gotten out of hand.[63] An equilibrium, even a tense equilibrium, had to be restored.

With this understanding, the stories of Paul IV and Angelo Levi bear a certain commonality. It seems that both the supreme pontiff and the Jewish vagrant had upset the social equilibrium in Rome, and that the response to each one put the balance, for a time, to rights.

However, the constant renegotiating of the contract between Catholics and Jews did not stop with either of their actions. It just took on new forms.

6

Love, Death, and Money

Daily Life in Sixteenth-Century Rome

In the first chapter of the Mishnah tractate *Bava Metzi'a*, two men hold a corner of a piece of cloth, each claiming to be its rightful owner, and neither one able to produce a witness to support his claim. The talmudic discussion goes on for pages. The obvious answer—cutting the cloth and giving each claimant half—is dismissed as patently unfair, as it would unjustly enrich the imposter and impoverish the actual owner by the same amount. Accordingly, there was no easy solution. Yet beneath the lengthy (and probably hypothetical) rabbinical debate of the second or third century CE is a subtext: an indecipherable conundrum for human beings is surely within God's ken. God certainly knows the true owner's identity, but has left the business of justice to humans—in this case, a Jewish court.

A thousand years later, in 1556, a similar, but real, case arose in Rome. A Jew, Giacobbe Abdi, claimed that he owned a coat. A "certain *goi*," unnamed, claimed the coat was his. Giacobbe testified before Roman Jewish arbiters that he had purchased the coat from Jedidiah di Fiano, but Jedidiah himself did not testify—and thus, as noted above, without a witness, the Jewish court deemed the case intractable.

In this instance, however, a higher power did intervene. The higher power was not God, but the vicar, a papal appointee with considerable authority who, on or about July 10, 1556, ordered Giacobbe to return the coat to the *goi*.

We know about this dispute because a Jewish notary recorded the resolution of the case.[1] Jewish notaries in early modern Rome not only recorded deeds, marriages, divorces, and the like; they also served as arbiters and recorders of decisions by both Jewish and Vatican tribunals when those decisions affected the Jewish community. It seems the Jewish notaries were quite busy, Jewish society in sixteenth-century Rome being one of "litigious familiarity."[2]

The Jewish notaries did not operate independently of papal authorities. As the bishop of Rome, the pope held jurisdiction over all civil matters in the city, but delegated local responsibilities to his appointed vicar. Pope Julius III's 1550 bull *Cum sicut accepimus* (As has been received) vested jurisdiction in both civil and criminal cases involving Roman Jews in the vicar,[3] and the vicar, in turn, allowed the Jewish community to arbitrate disputes involving Jews, if the Jewish parties chose that venue. Jewish tribunals could also adjudicate disputes between Jews and their Catholic neighbors, so long as the Catholic party agreed.[4] Even some disputes between synagogues went before non-Jewish tribunals.[5] The contending parties could always choose to litigate before the vicar's courts instead, because the vicar retained his original jurisdiction,[6] along with the power to enforce rulings (as when he took possession of Isaac Tedeschi's goods, in August 1542, after Isaac refused to comply with a court order.)[7] As a result, Jews sometimes swore oaths in the vicar's courts, and Catholics, on occasion, swore oaths in Jewish courts.[8]

From time to time, Jews chose to try their cases before the vicar (not necessarily literally; "the vicar" could also mean the vicar's courts). In November 1552, a certain Aron (the notarial records are incomplete) sued Elia di Joab before Juan Battista, clearly a Catholic judge, for monies Elia was holding on behalf of a *hevra* (consortium) of butchers—proceeds from a promissory note issued by a non-Jew.[9] In July 1555, an entirely Jewish matter—the Balanes family's litigation against Joshua Abbina over matchmaker's fees—went before a non-Jewish tribunal.[10]

In at least one instance we know of, a Jew had tried a case before the vicar and then proceeded to try the same case again before a Jewish court. When in this matter the vicar himself ruled in favor of Mazliah de Ceprano in a property dispute, Mazliah proceeded to press his good fortune, choosing a Jewish arbiter for a second resolution, with the explanation that he "preferred to act in the way of kosher Jews."[11] We do not know whether the gamble paid off.

Even after the Ghetto was established, Jews had the option to go before the vicar. On August 15, 1555, a Jewish litigant insisted that the contending parties turn to the Apostolic Chamber, "not to any Jew."[12] Two months later, Sabato di Joab and Aron di Meir calendared their dispute to be heard at the vicariate (the vicar's offices or courts).[13]

The Roman Jews who maintained the notarial records that enable us to know of these events were themselves thinking in Italian, even as they wrote in Hebrew. The Jewish Italian spoken in Rome then was not the Italian language we know. It was "ebraico," a Jewish version of Roman Italian. By contrast, Christians spoke their own Roman version of Italian—a dialect the Jews characterized not as "Italian" but simply as "goi."[14] Just as in English the word "Italian" can mean both a person and also a language, so goi in Rome could mean a person (such as the claimant for Giacobbe Abdi's coat) and the language that person spoke. In the Hebrew Bible, the word goi means "nation" (Gen. 10:5), and is often used to designate the Israelite nation (as in Exodus 19:6, where the Israelites are referred to as a goi kadosh or "holy nation"); but in the postbiblical world, goi (or goy) came to mean a non-Jewish nation, or "gentile" in English. Jews might use it in a derogatory manner, but not necessarily for every usage.

Meanwhile, the Jews' habit of keeping written records in Hebrew must have irritated the vicar, who was obligated to oversee the Jewish courts, but could not read Hebrew. After 1570, the Jewish notarial records were kept in Italian, probably on the vicar's order.[15] By 1640, the vicar eliminated all Jewish notaries.[16]

In sixteenth-century Rome, the power differential between the vicar and the Jewish community did not always create a strict, formal relationship between the two. On Sunday, July 14, 1563, the commander of the vicar's police, Capitano Ottavio, hosted a summer dinner at his vineyard outside the old Porta San Giovanni gate south of the city, and among the nineteen guests were five Jews: the maestro Salomone, the lutenist Abramo, and three others.[17] Strictly speaking, the guests did not dine together—the Jews sat at a separate, smaller table and ate only cucumber salad, *mozzarella di buffalo*, and bread—but that was because the meat at the Catholics' table was not kosher. Abramo entertained the entire party, and after dinner they all returned to the city on foot, crossing through the Porta San Giovanni. Abramo was serenading the Catholic judge's wife, who was singing along with him, when a scuffle ensued in the narrow confines of the gate. As a horseback rider and a muleteer transporting baskets full of wine bottles were crossing the other way, passing out of the city, they crowded the dinner guests against the gate walls. Cursing and shoving eventually led to stone throwing. While the Jews took no part in the altercation, as luck would have it the wine was a gift direct from the pope's wine cellars to Signor Colonna, the patriarch of Rome's toniest family. The scuffle became perceived as a slight against papal property and indirectly against Pope Pius IV, not to mention the Colonnas. Consequently, note had to be taken of the incident, and there was a trial.

The following Friday, before trial, Ottavio, the vicar's police chief, invited Abramo to dinner. This time, Abramo sat at the capitano's table. It being Friday, the meal, according to Catholic custom, was meatless and therefore kosher enough for the Jewish musician. He would have had to spend the night as Ottavio's guest, because the Ghetto gates were probably closed by the time the meal was over. (The Ghetto gates were locked at night, but were open during the day, allowing Jews and non-Jews to enter and leave relatively freely.)

More than likely, the Jew and the capitano were getting their stories straight before Monday's trial. This is speculation, but the circumstances of the Friday night dinner between the vicar's chief of police and a Jewish lutenist support some such calculation. Additionally, Ottavio had been warned of Abramo's impending arrest, and he probably passed that information on to Abramo during dinner, as Abramo turned himself in at the vicar's house on the Sabbath, the following day.

At the trial, the questioning commenced with what the Jews had eaten that night. Did they eat at the same table with the Catholics, and did they eat meat? The questions may have been aimed at intuiting whether the Jews could be trusted to tell the truth concerning the altercation if they were evasive about the innocent details surrounding the meal. More substantive questioning followed, but apparently Ottavio and Abramo told much the same story, and the affair was dropped.

For us there is a separate meaning to the story. From both the dinner at the vineyard and the Friday night meal at Ottavio's, we see that even in the ghetto period, Jews and Catholics—and in this case, Catholics of some power—could occasionally dine together. Meanwhile, more than conviviality was likely transpiring at these meals. The vicar would have wanted to know what was happening in the Ghetto, and the Jews could have used any tidbit of information concerning the vicar. In a nutshell, there appear to have been back-channels between the vicar and the Jewish community. How else would Rabbi Benedetto di Joab have gotten the news that informed the following case?

A housing dispute between two Jews, being tried before a Jewish court, was taking some time to resolve, from 1556 into 1557. The vicar, perhaps impatient, perhaps choosing the opportunity to exert his authority, intervened, ordering an *inhibizione* (injunction) that would prohibit the Jewish arbiter, Rabbi Benedetto di Joab, from rendering judgment. The vicar would take his jurisdiction back and render his own decision. However, Benedetto, forewarned of the *inhibizione*, hurried to publish his own decision before the vicar's order physically reached him. He obviously knew the *inhibizione* had been issued, but believed, probably on shaky grounds, that so long as it had not reached his desk, he was not bound by it.[18] We do not know the outcome of the case (including how the vicar reacted to such an act of insubordination), but clearly Rabbi Benedetto benefited from some inside information.

The church was vitally interested in retaining its power to intervene in internal Jewish matters. In 1581 Gregory XIII's bull *Antiqua iudaeorum improbitas* (Dishonesty of the ancient Jews) made that always-present church interest (evidenced in various ad hoc cases where the vicar or his offices stepped in) explicit by ordering Jews to pay fines should they be found in violation of church law.[19] With *Antiqua iudaeorum*, the Vatican did not arrogate to itself any more power than it already had; rather, it pointedly informed the Jewish community of its precarious position vis à vis the church courts.

On September 7, 1548, a lay council of Jewish officials governing the Jewish community, meeting in the Scola Nova, decided unanimously to empower the rabbis to "punish any man or woman who offended the sacred Torah." It would be up to the rabbis "to do as they desired faithfully and honestly." Yet even as this Jewish body attempted to exert its authority and delegate its authority to the rabbis, the council members knew their decision had to be couched so that "it will receive the approval of our Lord, the Vicar."[20] In other words, power was shared between the rabbis and the vicar. The vicar had the ultimate power, but Jews were not powerless.

Of course there were also Catholic notaries. Contracts between Jews and Catholics stipulating fixed quantities of goods had to involve a Catholic court and both Jewish and Catholic notaries. The Jewish notary could record the agreement terms, but the Catholic notary had to draw up the inventory. The value of the goods was a matter of public concern: these were taxable, and matters of taxation were not delegated to Jewish authorities.[21]

Living in the shadow of the vicar in sixteenth-century Rome, the Jewish community must have perceived its relationship with Catholic power as ever in flux. The Jews themselves were both the agents and the victims of those changes.

Jews in Rome did not own their homes. Almost exclusively, they rented from Catholic owners. Nevertheless, they could negotiate with their landlords a right to continued occupation of the rented premises (*hazaqah* in Hebrew, *ius cazaga* in canon law).[22] A renter paid for a *cazaga* in addition to the annual rent. Meanwhile, *cazagas* granting the right to live in the house and to sublease could be sold and inherited.[23] A Jewish holder of a *cazaga* could retain the *cazaga* but allow a third party to occupy the premises. The new occupant would pay rent to the Catholic landlord directly, but the Jewish holder of the *cazaga* could ask for the premises back, even if the occupant was current on rent.[24]

If the Catholic landlord raised the rent, the eleventh-century traditional ordinance (*taqqanah*) of Rabbi Gershom came into play: if the previous tenant was Jewish and had vacated the premises because of the rent hike, another Jew would have to wait a full year before renting that dwelling from a Christian owner.[25] Jews were often required to announce in synagogue, and record in writing, that a dwelling was off-limits to Jews for a year because of a Catholic landlord's sharp rental increase—a public declaration known as a *humrah* (ban).[26] With the *humrah*, Jews were able to assert their collective commercial power despite being unable to own property. They could hold a greedy landlord to account by simply refusing, as a group, to rent his property. That said, in December 1552, a landlord made certain that he would not be harassed by unfair enforcement of the Jewish law in his case. He recorded a document with a Jewish notary stating that his Jewish tenant was being evicted for nonpayment of rent only, and that he was "free to rent the house to anyone I want, whether Jew or *goi*."[27]

The *taqqanah* of Rabbi Gershom could also be used to the advantage of individual Jews. In 1542, a woman we know as Esther, wife of Rabbi Hadriel, purchased a *cazaga* and swiftly proceeded to rent the property to a fellow Jew.[28] (It was commonplace for Jewish women to operate their own businesses at the time.)[29] The Catholic property owner would not have been able to do what Esther did because the previous tenant and *cazaga* owner had trouble paying the increased rent. The *taqqanah* did not apply to a Jewish landlord stepping into the shoes of a Catholic owner.

The *taqqanah* applied to businesses as well as residences. In 1548, an argument between two Jewish merchants over space in a single market stall was settled in a non-Jewish court because the Catholic owner did not want to get the *cazaga* back. The Catholic owner was afraid to go to a Jewish authority because a dispute concerning his property, even if not over rental monies, could nonetheless leave him with a property that was worthless for a year.[30]

After Pope Paul IV's death in 1559, his immediate successor, Pius IV (1559–69), made changes that alleviated some Jewish hardships. Since housing within the crowded Ghetto was at a premium and all the landowners were Catholic; Pius IV's bull, *Dudum a felicis*, stabilized rents to prevent the Catholic owners from price gouging. And because Jews had experienced great losses when forced to sell their *cazagot* outside the ghetto in order to comply with *Cum nimis, Dudum* now enabled the ousted Jews to seek compensation for that circumstance from their former landlords. Further, Jews could own real property up to a value of fifteen hundred scudi in the Ghetto.[31]

The next pope, Pius V, would reverse these policies.[32]

JEWISH PROFESSIONS AND PARTNERSHIPS

Jewish businesses were simple affairs before and after the *Cum nimis* bull establishing the Ghetto in 1555. One prevalent type of business was the purchase of soiled linens (*fardelli*) from Roman hospitals to make mattresses.[33]

Catholic law, codified in 1558, allowed Catholics to contract with Jews for the purposes of legitimate business.[34] In 1641, Pope Urban VIII (1623–44) contracted with the Jewish community to provide mattresses for the papal army, which explains why the records tell us a Jew by the name of Hazzanito "went to war."[35] Surely, he was not in the papal infantry; rather, he was providing bedding to the infantry.

The pope granted Jews eleven private licenses to procure and rent the mattresses for the pontifical army. The mattress makers were ordered to prepare twenty-five hundred beds to serve the papal troops—an arrangement that appeared to benefit the Ghetto but turned out to be a bad bargain. The Jews had to rent beds to the army, but if the beds were never returned after the rental period, they had no recourse. And often enough the Vatican never paid the rent. Then in 1656, the mattress makers were offered a perpetual contract with the military if they forgave past due rents. Even that agreement was abrogated a few years later when two Catholics were given the military mattress contract.[36] A dozen years later, the church reversed course again and offered the Jews a monopoly on military bedding once more.[37]

Jews could also be kosher butchers. Jewish community inspectors would regulate the business, including fixing the price of meat, though fixed prices could be avoided if Jews and Catholics partnered so that Jews were the butchers and Catholics sold that meat wholesale out of Jewish shops.[38] Some Jews were fishermen. Fishing sites in the Tiber usually had to be leased from non-Jews, and Jews occasionally partnered with non-Jews in the enterprise.[39]

Women could partner with men in business. A September 1, 1536, partnership between two Jewish men, Joshua and Moise, and a woman, Madam Dulcia, established the men's commitment to tend to twenty-four of Dulcia's buffaloes.[40] Jewish merchants also had agreements among themselves about their Catholic customers. An apparently unofficial arrangement known as a *ma'arufia* allowed an individual Jew to claim a monopoly on business dealings with particular Catholic clients. Although informal, a *ma'arufia* was still enforceable in a Jewish court.[41]

BONDS TO FORESTALL BANKRUPTCY

The Jews of Rome not only had to meet their financial commitments to their non-Jewish neighbors and each other; they also had to make yearly payments to the Vatican. However, after a generation or so of ghettoization, that became impossible. And so, in addition to the Vatican's "subsidized" Jewish mattress business, the church issued bonds of a sort (*luoghi di monti*) to keep the Ghetto financially afloat. Jews could sell the *luoghi* and reap the income. However, the Jewish owner of the bond eventually had to repurchase the *luoghi* and pay interest on each bond owed to the church—and often that interest amount was greater than the originally owed debt. As with the mattresses, the *luoghi* did not provide the Jewish community with much relief. However, the Vatican regularly issued the bonds, and as long as the Jews sold the new bonds, they could be kept precariously above water.[42]

Moreover, popes like Sixtus V tried to manipulate the Ghetto economy so that Jews would invest in the *luoghi*. Sixtus allowed Jews to offer short-term loans to Catholic wool workers at interest rates as high as twenty-four percent so they could invest their profits in the *luoghi* and still have money left to pay the tax debt to the Vatican.[43]

In the early eighteenth century, the Vatican was once again afraid of a general Ghetto bankruptcy. A 1716 petition to Pope Clement XI had warned of an economic crisis. Consequently, in 1719, Prospero Lambertini (who was to become Pope Benedict XIV in 1740) called for reinstituting the 1689 reform that had allowed Jews to own businesses outside the Ghetto if they paid an annual tax of 12 scudi—but this reallowance appears not to have become policy until the 1730s.[44] Meanwhile, in 1731, the Jewish community suffered the closing of the *ghettarello*, a small community with its own synagogue existing just outside the Ghetto walls, which forced additional Jews into the already crowded Ghetto.[45]

BANKS

The church's ambivalence, evident in the false subsidy of the mattress makers and the false promise of selling *luoghi*, continued in its approach to Jewish banks. Jews throughout the fourteenth, fifteenth, and sixteenth centuries were allowed to lend money at interest in Rome. Even *Cum nimis* allowed Jewish lending at interest, and the number of Jewish bankers grew from twenty to seventy during the sixteenth century.[46]

Catholic lending institutions, the Monti di Pietà, did not charge interest until the seventeenth century, when interest was permitted under the theory of *lucrum cessans* (profit ceasing), which allowed a lender to charge for lost profits.[47] Once the Monti di Pietà began to succeed, a debate commenced in Rome among Catholics concerning the value of Jewish banking. Some said it was a necessary evil; some said it benefited only Jews. Others recommended prohibiting Jewish lending as a tactic to promote conversions.[48]

The debate ended in 1682, when Jewish banks in Rome were closed, ostensibly because they did not benefit the Papal State directly. They existed for the benefit of the bankers. Even though these banks were small financial institutions, with capital holdings averaging thirty-seven hundred scudi, their closing was disastrous.[49] The institutions had employed a great many Jews. Bank closures created unemployment as well as a scarcity of capital. To avoid catastrophe, to be able to work in a trade other than used cloth, and to avoid paying for the upkeep of the *Catecumeni*, Jewish families converted to Catholicism in greater numbers than at any time during the Ghetto period.[50] Rome itself did not get a modern bank until 1870.[51]

GUILDS

At least in one instance in the sixteenth century, Jews and Catholics also worked together through guilds. Roman guilds were small trade organizations (of shoemakers, violin string makers, meat vendors, etc.) that established rules for conducting their trade and labored to support their poorest members (by financing orphanages, hospitals, dowries, and the like). Since papal officials often supervised the guilds, the organizations had a religious dimension that generally forced the exclusion of Jews. And because individuals could only work in a trade if they belonged to its guild, Jews were forced to organize their own guilds.[52]

That said, in August 1541 Jewish and non-Jewish cloth artisans met in the Castilian Synagogue to discuss forming a guild of Jewish and Christian cloth dealers.[53] The joint group went on to set seven regulations for their guild, including the reasonable price of cloth, the purchase on credit from Catholic wholesalers, and the types of wholesalers who could serve as suppliers.[54] According to the notarial record of the meeting, "The goyim obligated themselves of their own free will. It was indeed they who initiated this statute."[55] Why the Catholics did so is unknown. One speculation is that these cloth dealers were former Jews who wanted to work with their friends and relatives.

The vicar, as usual, had the last word. "The cloth artisans . . . agree to the statutes as drawn pending a final decision by the court of the Vicar."[56] It is not known if the vicar ever signed off on the arrangement, but a decade later Catholic cloth workers in Rome would petition to exclude Jews from dealing in new clothes (also for unstipulated reasons).[57] This see-sawing of Catholic-Jewish relations was a harbinger of the restrictions Paul IV would soon impose in 1555, prohibiting Jews from dealing in anything other than secondhand cloth.

MONEY LENDING

The vicar had issued twenty licenses allowing Jewish money-lenders to operate without fear of a lawsuit—a protection called *inhibitio foeneris* (regulation of lending),[58] and so, up until 1540, Rome's Jewish community had twenty Jewish moneylenders. That year, however, Rabbino David di Sabato Siciliano lodged a formal complaint against the twenty lenders, saying that they "have had a monopoly in Rome long enough."[59] Apparently the twenty Jewish lenders had arrogated to themselves the privilege of money lending in the Ghetto and kept it off-limits for all but a select few.

Taking up the dispute in an October 1540 meeting in the Scola Tempio, the *kehillot* (community) of Rome agreed that "Anyone [meaning Jews] now residing in Rome who wants to lend at interest may legitimately do so. . . . However, anyone who engages in lending may not engage in any other profession, such as commerce, but in lending alone."[60]

The Vatican must have agreed to double the number of licenses, since in October 1542, twenty "new" lenders, in addition to the twenty "old lenders," met again in the Scola Tempio concerning yet another dispute about the number of authorized lenders. They were greeted with the news that Pope Paul III's chamberlain (a lay or clerical position of honor in the papal household) had recently reminded the Jewish community, through its arbiters, that all lending in Rome was governed by the pope and his administrators.

Here we see the give and take between the church and the Ghetto community. The church apparently did not have an interest in the particular number of lenders in the Ghetto. However, because the Vatican did issue the lending licenses, it could not allow unfettered Jewish control of the situation without asserting its ultimate power.

Additionally, papal ambivalence concerning lending is on full display. As discussed (in chapter 3), church scholars had concluded that the Bible forbade money lending. Consequently the pope deplored the practice and could not actively permit it, but given the necessity of such lending in Rome, he could issue orders that, in this case, exempted Jewish lenders from being sued or punished for plying their trade. The borrowers were mainly Catholics, the majority of the church flock being modest merchants and farmers in need of continued cash to stay afloat.[61] Thus the pope exercised his control over the Jewish community by allowing Jews to engage in conduct he found despicable.[62]

Meanwhile, since Jewish law forbade Jews from lending money to other Jews at interest, Jews could avoid this prohibition by lending to a non-Jew who acted as an intermediary between lender and borrower.[63] In other instances, Jews guaranteed loans to a Jew from a Christian, as in the case of Giacobbe di Piglio, who borrowed fifteen scudi from the "*goyah* Giuditta" with Eliezer di Miccinella guaranteeing that debt.[64]

MARRIAGE

Catholic tradition forbade marriages between Catholics and Jews. For a Jew to receive the sacrament of marriage with a Catholic, he or she would have to have previously received the sacrament of baptism. Therefore, for Catholics, marriage to a Jew was an impossibility. It was also punishable by death.[65] That said, Jewish betrothals and weddings in sixteenth-century Rome were probably influenced by contemporaneous Catholic practices.[66]

Jewish marriages in Rome followed a prescribed order of four stages. First, the marriage was arranged, the families of the bride and groom having reached a verbal agreement in principle. Matches could be made by a *shadchan* (matchmaker) or a rabbi.[67] Second came the *shiddukhin* (engagement) with its *shetar hittun* (prenuptial agreement) that usually included the amounts of the dowry and the *tosefet* (additional money paid by the groom), as well as the future dates of the *qiddushin* (betrothal) and the *nissu'in* (wedding). Such was one prenuptial agreement of the time: "Cibona widow of Dalamone di Balanes, and mother of the bride, Esther and the groom Angelo Raffaele de Gabriele di Tagliacozzo make a contract of engagement. Esther's dowry will be 100 sc. And the *tosefet* will be 30 sc. The wedding is to be held by Shabbat 'Nahamu.'"[68]

The third stage was the betrothal, when the groom gave a ring to the bride and made a personal recitation sanctifying his bride. The groom's recitation undoubtedly varied, because the crucial agreement was to appear in the *ketubah*. Finally, six months to a year later was the wedding, officiated by a rabbi under a *huppah* or marriage tent symbolizing the groom's house. The actual marriage contract or *ketubah* was given to the bride before the ceremony.[69]

Notably, the various nuptial stages follow the form of a Catholic Roman marriage manual by Marco Antonio Altieri (1450–1532), *Li Nuptuali*.[70] According to the manual, the first stage was an informal although written agreement to marry sealed by a kiss—*abocamento*. The second stage, corresponding to the *shiddukhin*, was the *fidanze*, a notarized agreement detailing the terms of the marriage. Catholic Ring Day, the third stage, corresponded to the Jewish betrothal: in both instances a wedding ring was gifted to the bride. Another notarized agreement (*instrumentum matrimonii*), which might be compared to the *ketubah*, was also issued. Finally, in the fourth stage several months or more later, the Catholic couple stopped at a church to receive a priest's blessing, and proceeded in public to the groom's house, where the marriage was consummated.[71]

However, even if Roman Jews and Catholics followed similar marriage customs, there were considerable differences. First, Jews had more room for choice concerning their marriage partners than their Catholic counterparts. In brief, Jewish brides and grooms were routinely able to refuse a match, a privilege rarely allowed in Catholic Rome.[72] Second, Jews' and Catholics' respective concepts of marriage strongly diverged. The Jewish marriage was contractual while the Catholic marriage was sacramental. Consequently, a Jewish marriage could be dissolved like any other contract, while a Catholic marriage took place in the presence of God, who was a third party to the marriage and whose participation precluded the marriage from ending in divorce.

DIVORCE

In keeping with traditional Jewish practice, a Jewish divorce required a husband to give his wife a bill of divorce, a get. A wife might seek a get from her husband, but she could not initiate divorce on her own. For her own protection, then—to insure, at least in principle, that she would not be trapped in marriage to an absent, sick, or chronically inconsiderate husband—her possible grounds for divorce (e.g., her future husband's gambling, habitual disappearances for lengthy times, even serious illness) could be specified in the prenuptial agreement (*shiddukhin*). One prenuptial agreement of the time stated: "If Angelo becomes seriously ill, he is to give Esther a get. If he goes to a far-off land, he is to write a *get zeman*."

In effect, the *shiddukhin* contractually bound Angelo to give his wife a get if he could not be a good husband in the stipulated ways. If he traveled, thereby incurring a risk of never returning, Esther was insured against abandonment by a *get zeman*, a preemptive divorce document that Angelo would give her before traveling and which would take effect after an unreasonable absence. The meaning of "unusual absence" could be negotiated. In Angelo's case, the *get zeman* he gave to his bride in January 1538 stated that it would be valid if he did not return from Modena by Shavuot several months hence.[73]

An unusual inversion of both Jewish and Catholic beliefs surrounded the divorce of Jews who had converted to Catholicism. Catholic law prohibited divorce, but nevertheless allowed a Jewish convert to divorce his wife who decided to remain Jewish, and encouraged second marriages. Jewish law allowed divorce only with a get, but if a husband converted, the church would not allow the giving of a get, thereby keeping the blameless convert's wife from remarrying. The Jewish community responded by drafting a streamlined get with few ritual specifications in the hope that the church would approve it, to no avail.[74]

Shiddukhin also set forth the conditions upon which the bride's father (or kin) was to give a dowry to the groom (and, possibly, to see it returned), such as:

> A certain Isach engages his daughter Laura to Menahem the son of Mazliah di Ceprano. If Laura dies during Menahem's lifetime, he will return half the dowry, unless there is a child that survives for 30 days. If there is a child, Menahem keeps all the dowry. If Mehahem dies without issue, Laura will be given back her dowry, *ketubah* and *tosefet*. If there is issue she will receive the *ketubah* but not the *tosefet*. Also if Menahem dies without issue, his brothers will accept *halizah* [an agreement by the late husband's kin that the widow could remarry someone not related to her husband] at no cost. Laura may not be divorced against her will, nor will she ever be asked to accept a second wife.[75]

Dowries were not gifts outright to the groom. They were more like loans secured by the marriage and by the resulting children.[76] If the wife died within a certain time or there were no children, the dowry or a portion of it might revert to the bride's family. Further, upon the wife's death, a portion or the complete dowry could go to her children. Meanwhile, if the marriage was not plagued by death, the dowry, held in trust by the groom, could be invested during the marriage.[77]

If, however, Menahem died without children, Jewish law required the dead husband's nearest relative to marry the widow in order to provide her and her deceased spouse with a child (Deut. 25:5–6; Ruth 4:3–6). Such a brotherly duty could be onerous, especially if the nearest kin was already married, and even if he was not. Accordingly, the late husband's kin could accept *halizah*, which would free the widow to marry who she wanted and release the next-of-kin from his obligation.

Menahem also pledged not to take a second wife while married to Laura. At the time a Jewish husband could petition the pope for a dispensation to take a second wife if after ten years the marriage did not produce children and the wife was considered sterile. Thus the Catholic Church had a direct hand in Jewish family life.

ARBITERS OF TROUBLED MARRIAGES

Beyond the premarital agreement, spouses had some recourse within the Jewish courts if husband and wife developed an antipathy for each other. The stormy story of Sabato and his wife Laura is one example.

Before the arbiters got involved, Laura had left Sabato for her father's house, taking some of their belongings with her. At arbitration, she was ordered to give her husband an inventory of the objects she had taken and Sabato was to pay her for that service. Sabato agreed not to hit her while she was staying with her father, and she was exempted from all "marital duties" while separated. She was free to return to her husband, but any reconciliation had to be mutual.

This somewhat "liberated" ruling was, however, accompanied by the stipulation: "If she does return [to Sabato], then he is freed from his guarantee and may beat her in the way women, virgins and girls are hit." Three months later, Laura agreed to go back to Sabato, and he in turn agreed not to give her cause to leave him again through "acts of cruelty or other improprieties." Nevertheless, two-and-a-half years later, a second agreement was necessary. Laura agreed to return to her husband and "Behave properly"; Sabato allowed that the one hundred scudi dowry would go to Laura upon divorce or his death, and moreover, that he would not call Laura a whore nor strike her, "except at appropriate moments, when he may strike her occasionally and punish her with a light strap."[78]

Thus was the thorough ambiguity of the woman's situation in sixteenth-century Jewish Rome. She was free to leave her husband, make demands, receive a promise of payment, and reconcile if the feeling was mutual. Yet once the marriage was reconstituted, she was in danger of being beaten. Striking one's wife was allowed.

That said, there were limits on spousal abuse, and the courts, not the husband, set those limits. In the troubled marriage of Beniamino and Marchigiana, for example, the agreement "to restore marital peace" stated: "If the two fight and Beniamino hits her, whether with a stone or his fist or whatever else, Marchigiana has the power and right to raise a hue and cry in the markets . . . and she may approach the arbiters who will see that justice is done."[79]

POSSIBLE SEXUAL ABUSE OF CHILDREN

Child sexual abuse and its cover-up may also have occurred in the Roman Jewish community of the time. Many documents published in Kenneth Stow's *The Jews in Rome* certify that certain young girls remained virgins despite their loss of the "signs of virginity" due to an accident. Dolce di Giuseppe di Tivoli fell from a ladder while gathering chestnuts from the roof. Marchigiana, the twelve-year-old daughter of Aron, was playing on a ladder when she fell. Five-year old Stella fell from a bench during a *Havdalah* service marking the end of the Sabbath. The four-year-old unnamed daughter of Moise di Menasce fell from a trunk, as did Miriam, daughter of Samuele. Ten-year-old Graziosa fell from a chair; Diana, daughter of Nissim Pinchas, fell from an attic; seven-and-a-half-year-old Malca di Elia Corcos fell out a window. These are just a sample of the girls said to have lost their signs of virginity due to accidents.[80]

This accounting, albeit only suggestive, seems revealing:

> In the house of the young man called Giuseppe di Samuele Zadich Tedeschi (Ashkenazi), a six year old girl, going on seven, named Simhah the daughter of the Illustrious Shalom di Bologna, now of Rome, was standing on a *banca* (bench) and held in her hand a pomegranate. Also present was a young man and Angelo Giuseppe di Acquapendente, a tailor by trade. This fellow wanted to play with the girl and he put out his hand and took her arm. But she did not want to play and she refused to play with him, until between one thing and another she fell from the bench on the floor and began to cry out loud and her virginity was lost.[81]

There were pragmatic motives behind these notarizations. A girl's virginity was essential to a successful marriage, and if doubt could be cast upon a bride's condition, the marriage might be annulled. Thus a notarized document going back to the girl's childhood was used to preempt any objections by the groom on or before the wedding night.

A more overt case of child sexual abuse occurred in Rome just before and after the establishment of the ghetto. The case is not found in the Jewish notarial records because Catholics were the victims and victimizers, but one Jewish woman played a crucial role. The victims were the daughters of Christoforo Gramar whom we met in the introduction, when they were shouting curses at the Jewish lutenist visiting their house. The victimizer was Alessandro Pallantieri, the chief prosecutor of the Papal States, who lived across the street.

Pallantieri used his judicial authority to threaten his way into the girls' home. He raped the oldest daughter, Lucretia, in the presence of her mother, and then continued to abuse her until she became pregnant at age fifteen. Pallantieri kept Lucretia at his house but made her return home to give birth to a boy named Orazio. Orazio was immediately taken from his mother and placed in a Catholic home, but his upbringing was supervised by a Jew, identified in the record of Pallantieri's eventual trial as Fiorina. Evidently Fiorina was Orazio's de facto guardian for several years, Pallantieri having paid her to insure Orazio had both food and a home. Pallentieri may have felt it was prudent to employ a Jew instead of a Catholic to cover up his crimes. However, Fiorina became attached to Orazio, and when Pallantieri stopped paying her in 1551, she sold her share of an inn in the Jewish quarter to feed the boy.

Pallantieri also raped the middle daughter, who eventually gave birth to a daughter. He became a shadowy part of the Gramar family and paid the dowry of the youngest daughter, Livia, who, with some effort, avoided his clutches.

From the testimony preserved of Pallantieri's trial, we see an extended and deeply dysfunctional family that, in its penumbra, included a Jew like Fiorina. According to her testimony, Fiorina knew Pallantieri quite well, and may have helped to raise other illegitimate children he fathered. The trial record does not include a sentence for Pallantieri, but we know he was officially beheaded in 1571.

In a dark way, the Pallantieri-Gramar "family" may serve as another sociological model: of a larger, deeply problematic family of Jews and Catholics in early modern Rome. If Giles of Viterbo and his tutor Elijah Levita can be seen as the model of the Jewish-Catholic "family" before the Ghetto, the Pallantieri-Gramar was more the model afterward. Jews were outsiders, and precisely as such could be employed as insiders when it was to the advantage of the powerful.

TRIAL OF AN IMPUGNED WIFE

In a somewhat related matter entirely within the Jewish community, Isach "Shem Tov" Sopporto—and his mother!—attempted to impugn the virginity of Ricca, Shem Tov's wife.[82] According to trial testimony, Shem Tov discovered on the marriage night that he had been "tied," meaning he could not function sexually, because someone had cast a spell on him, preventing him from taking his wife's virginity.[83] The cure for Shem Tov's troubles ostensibly came from a gentile versed in magic, who led him to the banks of the Tiber, where there lay a ladder made of millstones. The gentile prescribed that Shem Tov urinate upon the millstones, and having done so, he claimed to be cured and able to "do the job." Just as Pallantieri used a Jew from outside his community to help cover up his disgraceful acts, Shem Tov consulted a gentile from outside his community to help alleviate his shame at being "tied." While Shem Tov and Pallantieri were in no way equals, both saw the value in discreetly employing a stranger concerning intimate family matters.

The following Sabbath, Shem Tov's female relatives boasted to friends that the groom had "bought the honey pot"—that is, deflowered Ricca. The proud women produced a garment supposedly marked with Ricca's virginal blood. However, Shem Tov soon decided he did not want to be married to Ricca. He began spreading the rumor that she was not a virgin when she married him, and Ricca's family countered by accusing him of defaming a daughter of Israel. A trial ensued, during which the above testimony was taken, along with the expert testimony of Gemma di Bonanno, an elderly widow who had inspected Ricca prior to Shem Tov's "cure" to see if "her lid was off." Gemma testified that it was not. Gemma was also called in to see the soiled robe and a bloody sheet. The evidence of Ricca's virginity was beyond a reasonable doubt. Consequently, it was announced in the Scola Tempio, Shem Tov had to pay one hundred scudi (probably to Ricca or her family) as a *tosefet*.

GAMBLING

A number of pledges not to gamble are testimony to a gaming addiction among some Jews in sixteenth-century Rome.

One Giuseppe promised not to gamble for two years. R. Hashan pledged before his Christian landlord (who, no doubt, wanted the rent paid) that he would not gamble for three years upon penalty of one scudi per violation. Aron loaned his brothers Elai and Joab four hundred scudi to be paid back in eighteen months, during which time the brothers swore "not to gamble nor to eat in any *osteria* [a tavern serving wine and simple food] whether [the owner] is a Jew or a *goi*." Others pledged not to gamble "until Purim" or "until Passover."[84]

That the fines for violation of the promise ranged between one and four scudi may indicate that the gambling was on a small level. A gambler doing a cost-benefit analysis might have concluded he could earn more by gambling than the fine, and thus his continued gambling would pay off. Israel di Elisha's arrangement—to be able to gamble for a small measure of wine despite his overall pledge not to gamble from November 1554 through Purim of 1555—evidences the intersection of two vices: Jews in Rome were known to gamble so that they could afford a drink. Benedetto di Salomone promised not to gamble during the coming year, "except for one game called *maglio abbozzo o all'amore* (hammer for the statue or for love) so that he could drink at a pub with friends." Moreover, to add a third vice, when Benedetto or Israel drank wine with friends, it was not necessarily kosher wine.[85]

As for the nature of the gambling bets, it is well known that habitual gamblers will bet on anything from the weather to the sex of an unborn child. Gambling in sixteenth-century Rome was no different, except for the specialized nature of certain bets.[86] Starting in the late fifteenth century, upon the death of a pope there was active betting on who would become the next pope. During the papal interregnum known as the Vacant See, brokers, including Jewish pawnbrokers, set up stalls across the river from the Vatican and provided each bettor, again including Jews, with a ticket as a receipt.[87] Other times, Romans engaged in monetized speculation on which churchmen would be elevated to cardinal. In 1592, four masked men broke into the home of a Jewish astrologer and, brandishing daggers, warned him to stop predicting the papal election of Cardinal Tolomeo Gallio (who ultimately would not become pope)—possibly because if Gallio were elected, they would have to pay out on significantly more bets than if the astrologer had kept quiet.[88]

After the church's futile attempts in 1555 and 1567 to curb the betting, Pope Gregory XIV's 1591 bull *Cogit nos* (We are compelled) finally outlawed all betting on the outcome of papal elections, the duration of pontificates, and the promotion of cardinals on pain of excommunication, which would cut off the perpetrator from the Body of Christ and the comfort of the sacraments, including marriage and last rites.[89] For their part, Jewish bettors on papal matters could be sent to the galleys for life.[90]

JEWS AND JAILS

When Jews went behind bars, they shared the same jails with Catholics until 1569, when Pope Sixtus V segregated the prisons.[91]

If Benjamin Nehemiah ben Elnatan's account is accurate (he reported on his experience of being imprisoned in both the Prison of the Inquisition and Corte Savella Prison in 1555, when his town of Civitanova chose to rid itself of Jews), the Prison of the Inquisition consisted of thirty-two courtyards, each with a garden and orchards. Some of the courtyards housed prisoners, others, the prison administrators. There were also rooms in the basement, where Benjamin Nehemiah was kept. Each room held two prisoners. Each day, a guard brought food in the morning and took away the dishes in the evening. Benjamin Nehemiah was freed from prison during the riots that took place upon Pope Paul IV's death.[92]

In 1542, Abramo di Caivano was imprisoned for not delivering horses that Aron di Meir had paid for but which a gentile apparently owned. In the Jewish community, aggrieved parties customarily paid jailers to free their fellow Jews, but in this case, Aron did not do so and Abramo had to pay another person, Joab Katzav, one scudo to make the payment (or bribe).[93]

The Jewish community also tried other ways to release Jewish prisoners from jail. In 1555 a Jewish community tax on kosher meat, collected by the *fattori* (body of community officials) from the kosher butchers, was used for general charitable services, including *pidyon shevuyim*, release of prisoners.[94] Later, in December 1556, after several Jewish artisans had been imprisoned for unnamed offenses, the Jewish community met to discuss how to approach the vicar "to set the matter aright." This may have been the first step toward the community's establishment of a fraternity for *matir 'assurim*, freeing the imprisoned.[95] Instead of its somewhat ad hoc collections from the kosher butchers, the *fattori* was now trying to establish a more formalized process to fund the release of Jews from jail.

WILLS

Samuele Levi Zarfati was worried about being repaid the one hundred scudi he had loaned to Abramo di Modigliano. Having been refunded only thirty-two scudi, he anticipated not being reimbursed in full by the time he died. Consequently, his will stipulated that any payments still owed him postmortem go to his (unnamed) sons, minus ten scudi for Michele di Tagliacozzo, who had helped him record the will. Samuele also left four scudi to an orphan girl, eight scudi to keep the *ner tamid* (eternal light) lit in his synagogue, one scudo to the *gemilut hasadim* (voluntary Jewish burial society), which presumably would prepare his body, and six scudi to purchase a shroud and a coffin. Samuele left nothing to his wife, who no doubt received her dowry, which was not subject to a will.[96] Of course, in some wills the husband made sure his wife was cared for.[97]

A dispute arose over the will of David da Fondi. For reasons unknown, he had provided dowries for two girls, and his will specified that the monies were to be held in trust until they married. However, the girls' parents wanted the monies paid ahead of time. Ultimately, the *fattori* decided that the money was still to be held in trust, but the interest on it could be distributed to the girls' relatives before marriage.[98]

Both these wills were entirely Jewish affairs. However, on at least one occasion a Jewish will is notarized by a Jewish notary but witnessed by two Christians, Pietro Civili della Stamps and Paolo Isbargaimi the German, who may have been converts to Catholicism.[99]

BURIALS

From 1363 until 1645, Rome's Jews were buried in the Porta Portese cemetery, which Jews called the *kerem* (vineyard) and Catholics the *Ortaccio degli ebrei* (ugly garden of the Jews). Once Porta Portese become consistently overcrowded, the Jewish burial grounds were moved to the Aventine Hill.[100]

In 1556, there was no room for Joshua Bina because all of the burials inside the *kerem* were too fresh. The usual remedy for lack of burial space was "secondary burial": bones were removed from a grave and interred elsewhere to make room for the new burial. But at the time of Joshua's death, no remains had disintegrated to the point where a grave could be emptied. Meanwhile, Joshua's widow, Simha, would not take no for an answer. She sufficiently harassed the members of the *gemilut hasadim* that they threw aside their shovels and left. (At least three *gemilut hasadim* societies functioned in sixteenth-century Rome.[101] Each society had a governing board of ten men who paid token dues monthly to sustain the society.) Evidently Simha and those close to her then appropriated the discarded tools to bury Joshua inside the *kerem*—but probably inside someone else's grave, a somewhat grisly resolution to the dispute.[102]

A 2017 excavation in Rome's Trastevere neighborhood, conducted during the renovation of the Palazzo Leonori, uncovered thirty-eight graves from the same Jewish cemetery that had refused Joshua entrance.[103] In or around 1644, Pope Urban VIII expropriated land from that Jewish cemetery to build a new wall for the city of Rome. Technically, as we saw, *Sicut* prohibited violating Jewish graves. There could be exceptions to that rule, especially if a church was to be built on a Jewish gravesite, but Urban VIII created his own exception.[104] The wall was completed during the succeeding pontificate of Innocent X, and some graves were moved at that time, possibly to the new Jewish graveyard on the Aventine Hill.[105] The Palazzo Leonori was then built over the old Jewish graveyard. However, we now know that not all the graves were removed. The 2017 excavation uncovered evidence of graves remaining from the old Jewish cemetery.

JEWISH PARTICIPATION IN THE NON-JEWISH WORLD

One indication of Jewish participation in the non-Jewish Roman world was the Jewish community's use of the term "Christmas" or *Natale* (in Hebrew, *n-'-t-l-y*) in reference to Jesus' birth in the notarial records. A payment to a butcher for monies owed him by a *hevra* (consortium) of butchers had to be made by Christmas or Carnival (the following February) at the latest.[106] In November 1554, Moise promised that his prospective wife's dowry would be invested "with a Jewish banker by Christmas."[107]

In other words, sixteenth-century Roman Jews inhabited both Catholic and Jewish time. Notarial records were often dated so as to be understood in both worlds—for example, both the Jewish and the non-Jewish month, "26 Iyyar May 1541," might appear in a single record; or a date of Jewish significance would appear alongside the commonly used date ("44th day of the Omer, May 1541"); or, on occasion, the weekly Torah portion would be part of the date ("Parashat Matot, July 1541").[108]

And so it was that after being ghettoized in the sixteenth century, Rome's Jews continued to live as Jews despite hardship. As we will see, that adversity only increased as the church, bent on converting Jews and faced with a lackluster record of success, turned to more extreme and aggressive methods.

7

"Till the Conversion of the Jews"

Church Attempts at Forced Baptism

To the English poet Andrew Marvell (1621–78), the conversion of the Jews en masse was an event so unimaginably far in the future that in his poem "To His Coy Mistress," it served as a comic metaphor for his lover's frustrating delay in consummating their desires:

> I would
> Love you ten years before the Flood;
> And you should, if you please, refuse,
> Till the Conversion of the Jews.[1]

For centuries, papal policy concerning conversion differed little from Marvell's sly understanding of Christian expectations. As Pope Innocent III stated in the 1205 bull *Etsi non displiceat* (Even if it was not bad), Jewish conversion would occur "at length."[2]

However, the sixteenth- and seventeenth-century popes clung to the hope that Jewish capitulation would occur forthwith, and during their lifetimes. For a time after 1555, they believed that the misery being meted out to the Jewish community in the Roman Ghetto would result, sooner than later, in a change of heart. Yet by the seventeenth century, that change had not only failed to materialize, but was calling unwanted attention to the indigent but steadfast Roman Jews—drains on society and markers of resistance to Vatican policy, all in the pope's own backyard. By the eighteenth century, the popes were pondering justifications for forcibly baptizing Jews. A Jewish conversion was a sign of Vatican success, and celebrated publicly.

ANNA DEL MONTE

In at least one instance we know of, things did not go as the church had planned. In May 1749, papal authorities kidnapped Anna del Monte, eighteen, near her home in the Ghetto, in order to convert her to Catholicism.[3] Anna subsequently described the encounter in a "diary."[4] "They did not even give me the courtesy, or the time, to change my clothing, or to say a word to my mother and father, as though I were a whore, slapping everybody around and paying no attention to people's rank or even their state of health. They snapped me up like a *giutta* [buffoon, or person of no account] in such haste that I still had on my apron."[5] The kidnappers whisked Anna to the Casa dei Catecumeni (House of the Catechumens, a home for Christian converts under instruction before baptism), outside the Ghetto and about a mile-and-a-half from her house.

At the suggestion of the Spanish theologian Ignatius Loyola (1491–1556), Pope Paul III's 1543 bull *Illius qui* (That is) had called for the founding of the Catecumeni as part of a larger plan aimed at conversions, mostly the conversion of Jews.[6] By 1554 the Jewish community was required to support the Catecumeni to the tune of ten ducats per synagogue per year, according to Pope Julius III's edict, *Pastoris eternis vices* (The eternal shepherd). Between 1555 and 1778, one-third of all Jewish community payments to the Apostolic Camera (treasury) and Roman Civic Camera went to the Catecumeni and associated projects.[7]

The demand for Jewish support was not merely mean-spirited or arbitrary. The church believed that most Jewish converts to Catholicism were indigent and lived off Jewish charity, and Jews should not be allowed to palm off their expensive public charges onto the Catholic Church. In this, the church willfully ignored its own role in creating Jewish poverty through ghettoization. Its generalization about the converts was also mistaken. Many of them after 1554 were wealthy Jews who chose to convert in order to avoid paying the Catecumeni taxes—a financial burden that in some cases could seriously reduce Jewish wealth. The community's payment for the Catecumeni's upkeep became all the more difficult once more well-off Jews converted out of the faith.

And so it was that after being kidnapped, Anna was sequestered in a church institution that her family and friends had fiscally maintained for almost two hundred years. In a building next to the Church of Madonna ai Monti, the Catecumeni housed candidates for baptism who, once converted, became *neofiti*, new converts. Anna, and other involuntary candidates, were sequestered there among willing converts. The length of incarceration varied according to the circumstance.[8] An involuntary candidate like Anna could only be held between twelve and fourteen days if she did not convert within that time. A voluntary candidate was held for forty days to make certain he or she really wanted to convert. An involuntary candidate who was betrothed to a voluntary candidate was held for forty days.[9]

Anna's internment lasted thirteen days. Upon arrival, a prioress led her to a small room furnished with a bed, table, and drawer. A sequence of encounters between Anna and church functionaries followed. At first, one Cardinal de Rossi questioned her about her sexual relationships in the Ghetto. It soon emerged that Sabato Coen, a young man she knew from the Ghetto who had been born Jewish but had since converted, had falsely told the church that Anna would convert as well. (Perhaps Sabato had asked Anna to marry him, and when she refused, he schemed to wed her despite her wishes.) Once baptized, new converts could claim that people they knew had similar desires to convert. The church had little interest in verifying new converts' claims against other Jews. If the unsuspecting individuals had no interest in converting, that fact would become evident after their interrogation at the Catecumeni.

In Anna's case, Cardinal de Rossi's personal questions were intended to ascertain the nature of her relations with Sabato. If she acknowledged having had intercourse with Sabato, the church would consider them betrothed and, as noted, by its own rules could have kept her for forty days.

Anna admitted to no such thing. There followed three days of intermittent confrontations in her room with priests who tried to ply her with promises of salvation. Anna said as little as possible: "Leave me in Peace. I was born a Jew and want to die the same and I don't need your preaching so please be silent and go."[10] Anna was told that Pope Benedict XIV himself was anxious for her conversion. She was also promised a glorious baptism, complete with a procession through Rome on a bejeweled carriage.

On the fifth day, a young preacher threatened Anna with a lifetime of incarceration and declared confidently that she would convert before his eyes. He then poured a pitcher of holy water over her: "For my part I struck my face with my hands and began to shout. 'It will never happen that either my flesh or my face will accept a drop of this water as long as I am a Jew. I will have nothing to do with your water or your superstitions. For my part, a dog may just as well have pissed on me.'"[11]

Later that day, six more priests visited her, along with Sabato Coen's sister, Sarra, herself a convert. While Sarra extolled her life as a Catholic, the priests sermonized on biblical passages and supposedly misguided Jewish ritual. After thirteen days, Anna was released, still a Jew. She returned home a hero, but may well have been deeply wounded by the experience. She died shortly before 1779 at the age of forty-six.

PIOUS LASHES

Between the time of Giles of Viterbo, the Catholic cleric who had welcomed a Jewish family into his home ca. 1514, and 1749, when Catholic clerics were routinely kidnapping and incarcerating Jews, in this case Anna, there had been a revolution in the church's policy toward Jews.

One year before Giles welcomed Elijah Levita and his family, the monks Paulus Justiniani and Petrus Quirini published *Libellus ad Leonem Decem* (Petition to [Pope] Leo X), a book, directed at the pope, detailing measures the monks believed would maximize conversions to Catholicism. As they well knew, given the fairly recent discovery of the New World (1492), Pope Leo was determined to convert Jews and infidels.[12] The Americas were teeming with persons unacquainted with the Gospel—a state of affairs crying out for immediate missionary work.

The *Libellus* expressed contradictory attitudes toward conversion. Surely, according to Pope Gregory I (going back to the sixth century), no one should be forced to the faith. The thirteenth-century bishop of Ostia, Henry of Segusio (also known as Hostiensis), had agreed, writing in his *Summa aurea* (The most golden) that Jews should not be forced into baptism, "because a compelled service does not please God."[13] Yet the *Libellus* made exceptions to that rule. Monetary or material incentives were not considered coercion. Moreover, if hearing the Gospels or receiving monetary blandishments did not result in the desired conversion, sterner measures were warranted: "With a certain measure of paternal piety, those whom we were not able to soften with blandishments we can force, in a manner of speaking with threats and pious lashes to return to the heart."[14]

The *Libellus* detailed such "pious lashes" aimed at the Jewish community as prohibiting Jewish usury and commerce, limiting the number of synagogues, and preventing Jews and Catholics from social mingling, in part by requiring Jews to wear a distinguishing badge. Additionally, the *Libellus* exhorted Pope Leo to designate preachers to "incessantly" teach Jews the truth of Christianity.

Leo X did not follow the suggestions in the *Libellus*. He was certainly under no obligation to make the theories of two monks Vatican policy. However, a reading of *Cum nimis* demonstrates that Paul IV acted on almost all of the *Libellus*'s recommendations when he established the Ghetto in 1555. He limited the number of synagogues to one, although the Cinque Scole actually included five. He required the wearing of distinguishable Jewish attire like the Jew Hat and a Jew-Badge. And of course, the Ghetto in general was a radical attempt to prevent Jews from mingling socially with Catholics.

Simultaneous with the establishment of the Ghetto, Francisco de Torres, a Jesuit theologian and scholar of the church fathers, published the tract *De sola lectione* (Of reading alone), wherein he allowed that although the church had permitted the Jews to observe their own laws in accordance with *Sicut judaeis,* it is nevertheless "one thing for the Jews to profess the Law, another to corrupt the Law which they are permitted to profess. The Church permits the profession of the Law so that perhaps we may win them; the corruption of the Law it does not permit."[15] Published by the church, the *Lectione* urged the inquisitors to take such actions as deliver weekly Catholic sermons in synagogues—and, as a final measure, force Rome's Jews into poverty and hunger in order to bring them to baptism through despair.[16]

As an initiator of the Roman Inquisition, it is likely that the *Lectione* came to Paul IV's attention. His bull *Cum nimis* seems to be cognizant of all these recommendations. As with the *Libellus,* he put many of them into practice, although he did not require conversionary sermons.

In 1558, the Italian jurist Marquardus de Susannis's *De judaeis et aliis infidelibus* (*Of the Jews and Other Infidels*), a handbook for judges concerning Jewry law that also served as a summary and guide to Paul IV's policies, gave Paul IV's policy legal sanction.[17] The handbook explained that converts must be received in the church with love. If a Jew expressed a desire to convert, he was not to be baptized immediately; a forty-day waiting period was necessary to insure the convert was acting out of sincere devotion. Money could be used to bring a potential convert to the baptismal font, but baptism obtained by absolute force was forbidden. That said, "predisposing force"—force that might stimulate conversion—was allowable. If the New World natives had been subject to "predisposing force" in the service of conversion, the same rule needed to apply to Jews. "Predisposing force" was behind *Cum nimis,* which had enclosed Jews in the Ghetto. Still, if absolute force was used, and no objection raised after a long (unspecified) time, the baptism was also valid.

De Susannis's 1558 handbook, which to a great extent codified what Paul IV had already done, was available in the Vatican and perhaps other libraries, and could be referenced in individual cases. *De judaeis* thus gave Paul IV's policies concerning Rome's Jews legal authority, becoming a guide for dealing with the Jewish presence in Catholic society.

In the Papal States from 1555 to 1600, eight hundred Jews converted—a substantial number that nonetheless failed to meet Vatican expectations.[18] As a result, Pius V's successor, Gregory XIII, (1572–85) instituted organized preaching to the Jews of Rome.

The idea of conversionary sermons had been proposed as far back as the thirteenth century. Popes Nicholas III (in his 1278 bull *Vineam Sorec*) and Benedict XIII (in his 1415 bull *Etsi doctoris*) had suggested such sermons.[19] In 1434, the Council of Basle ruled that Jews were required to attend conversionary sermons, but the council did not have papal approval.[20] In 1565, Charles Borromeo, archbishop of Milan, prescribed that missionary sermons be preached to the Jews, with attendance mandatory, but his opinions had no force in Rome.[21] All this prior theorizing came to fruition in 1577, with Pope Gregory XIII's bull *Vices eius nos* (Our changes) stating: "We have ordered . . . that on each Sabbath in a specified oratory in Rome, Christ be preached and announced to the Jews."[22]

Then in 1584 Gregory XIII's bull *Sancta mater ecclesia* (Holy mother church) went into greater detail. It mandated preaching the gospels in Roman synagogues, and weekly attendance by at least one-third of the Jews above the age of twelve. Gregory XIII's successor, Pope Sixtus V (1585–90), required all Jewish men in the Papal States to attend three sermons per year.[23]

By 1581, the French philosopher Michel de Montaigne could write in his diary of his experience on a Jewish Sabbath in Rome: "Amongst other pleasures I enjoyed in Rome during Lent, mention must be made of the sermons. There were many excellent preachers, for instance the renegade Rabbi who preached to the Jews on Saturday afternoons in the church of the Trinità. Here was always a congregation of sixty Jews who were bound to be present. The preacher had been a famous doctor amongst them, and now he attacked their belief by their own argument, even out of the mouth of their rabbis and from the words of the Bible."[24]

The preacher whom Montaigne so appreciated was Andrea de'Monti, born Josef Zarfati. The church trained *neofiti* (new converts) like him to preach to Jewish audiences, believing that their knowledge of Jewish traditions would be persuasive. Although ordered to be in synagogues, generally the sermons took place at the church of Santissima Trinità dei Pellegrini, a few blocks from the Ponte Sisto (the bridge over the Tiber named after Pope Sixtus IV).[25]

However, enforcing the weekly attendance mandate was not easy. Noncomplying Jews could be cut off from their already limited contact with Catholics or, as suggested in the *Lectione*, they could be expelled from wherever they were living,[26] but the church never acted so punitively. Moreover, there was the issue of holidays. The church recognized that Jews could not be expected to attend coerced sermons during the weeklong holidays of Hanukkah and Passover and on the Sabbaths before and after Purim. Sabbaths after a fast were exempted, as were Sabbaths before Tisha b' Av and Sabbaths coinciding with Rosh Hashanah. The funeral of a rabbi took precedence over the church-ordered sermons, and Catholic holidays, such as Easter and Pentecost, also provided a respite if the latter fell on a Sabbath or the former on the Sabbath before the holiday. There were even snow days, although in Rome those days must have been few and far between.[27] As a result, roughly half the year's Sabbaths were exempted from mandatory sermons.[28]

Generally, Jews tried to avoid hearing the sermons. Upon entry into the chapel, they were searched for balls of wax, wool, or cotton that could be used as earplugs. Or in something called *cambio* or exchange, a Jew would pay another Jew to take his place at the sermon, both risking a fine of five scudi if caught.[29]

Meanwhile, Jews walking in a group, against their will, to attend church would attract unruly crowds. A placard published in June 1620 threatened a fine of five scudi, three lashes, or any other applicable punishment if anyone attacked the Jews on their way to the Oratorio of the Trinita di Ponte Sisto.[30] Notwithstanding all the difficulties of preaching to a resistant and inattentive congregation of Jews, coerced sermons persisted for almost three hundred years until 1847, when Pope Pius IX (1846–78) ended the practice.[31]

At the end of the sixteenth century, Pope Clement VIII (1592–1605) issued an *Absolutio* that gave Rome's Jews a pardon: "We, desiring of the Jewish Community of Rome that it recognize the way of truth and then observe it, therefore . . . release and pardon you and each member of the Community of whatever transgressions excesses or delicts, excepting however, homicides, counterfeiting, sacrileges, *lèse majesté* [insulting the King] and infractions against the Inquisition done or committed by you up to the present day."[32]

This particular pardon made it clear that it was based firmly upon the hope of mass Jewish conversion. Popes Paul III and Julius III had given Rome's Jewish community similar pardons, although Paul did not link the pardon to Jewish conversion.[33] Clement's pardon made the connection between the pardon and conversionary policy explicit. That said, Clement VIII did not make this pardon conditional on conversion; he merely stated that his conversionary hopes spurred him to issue it. Despite the pope's aspirations, Jewish conversions did not increase.

FORCED BAPTISM

In 1743, an edict consisting of sixteen declarations concerning Jews and *neofiti*, written by the Vice Regent Ferdinando De Rossi (Anna del Monte's interrogator in the Catecumeni), was posted on the Ghetto gates and throughout Rome. *Neofiti* could no longer contract or socialize with Jews without permission, enter the Ghetto to attend Jewish ceremonies, buy or receive kosher meat, or even leave Rome without permission. Jews, in turn, were prohibited from dissuading prospective converts or approaching the Catecumeni. Most importantly, if a converted Jew "offered" a relative or acquaintance to the Catholic faith, other Jews could not hide or aid the "offered" person.[34]

The conversion of a Catholic to Judaism was punishable by death and almost never occurred. Still the pressure continued concerning Jewish conversion to Catholicism. In 1643, Ferdinando Alvarez, a Portuguese Jew who had ostensibly converted to Christianity, was accused of "falling

[back] into Hebraism" and executed—although, in a manner of speaking, he executed himself. Since Ferdinando refused to abjure his Judaism even at the gallows, it was decided that he should not be hung but burned alive. However, since his head was already in the noose, Ferdinando kicked over the stool he was standing on and was hung "without the aid of the executioner."[35]

In 1747, Pope Benedict XIV penned his *Lettera a Monsignor Arcivescovo di Tarso Vicegerente sopra il battesimo degli ebrei o infanti o adulti* (Letter to Archbishop of Tarso, Viceregent, concerning the baptism of Jews, infants, and adults), which addressed not only the offering of a child for baptism but also the secret baptism of a child without a parent's consent. While St. Thomas Aquinas had concluded that baptism of Jewish children under the age of reason, and without parental consent, was illicit, hundreds of years later, Benedict called for exceptions to Aquinas's rule.[36] First, if a Catholic found a Jewish baby in danger of death, a baptism, clandestine or not, was meritorious. Second, if a Jewish child was abandoned outside the Ghetto, baptism was enforceable against subsequent pleas by the parents. Third, when a father converted to Catholicism, he could offer his child for baptism despite the Jewish mother's objections—in this case, the father, not the mother, had the right of *patria potestas* (ancestral power). That said, if a mother converted to Catholicism and offered her child for baptism despite the father's objections, the child could still be baptized.[37] Even as the father held ancestral power over his child, that power was negated by *il favor della Fede*, "the favor of the Faith"—a concept (actually, a catch-all excuse for baptism in questionable circumstances) used whenever the honor of the faith was threatened.[38] Finally, if both parents promised to convert and offer their children, but later reneged on their promises, the children were to be baptized despite parental objections, to protect the faith from any mockery.[39]

In 1755 a case came before the ubiquitous Monsignor De Rossi. A neophyte offered his nieces, Deborah, ten, and Ricca, six, for baptism. Their widowed mother objected. Deborah had reached the age of reason (seven) and could not be baptized without her own consent. Ricca had not reached the age of consent, but the late father's *patria potestas* had passed to the mother, who argued that when their uncle offered Ricca, he had no authority to do so. Nonetheless, the children were taken to the Catecumeni. Monsignor de Rossi recommended that Ricca remain at the Catecumeni and be fully instructed. Upon reaching the age of reason, she could be baptized consensually. Pope Benedict agreed, and so ordered. By the time of Benedict's decision, and according to the Catecumeni, the older sister Deborah had already "firmly resolved to receive Baptism."[40]

HUSBANDS, WIVES, AND FETAL BAPTISMS

The *Lettera* also considered conversion of adult Jews. If a husband converted but his wife refused to follow him, the marriage was to be dissolved, allowing the neophyte husband to marry a Catholic woman. However, since church law forbade the neophyte from giving his wife a get, the Jewish woman could not remarry. Benedict probably hoped that the harsh outcome would induce more conversions.[41]

As it turned out, the *Lettera* did not cover all possible circumstances. In 1751, Benedict wrote a second *Lettera*, *Lettera della santità di Nostro Signore Benedetto Papa XIV a Monsignor Pier Girolamo Guglielmi assessore del San'Officio* (Letter of the sanctity of Our Lord Pope Benedict XIV to Monsignor Girolamo Guglielmi, assessor of the Holy Office), to decide a controversial case in which a neophyte, a paternal grandmother named Giuliana, had offered her grandchildren. Their father Salomone, Giuliana's son, had died, but the children's mother, Perla, was living. Complicating the matter, Salomone had anticipated his mother's subsequent offering and named Perla as his children's tutor in his will. Ultimately Benedict ruled that the offering could not be enforced under *patria potestas* because the grandmother, a woman, could not have acquired *patria potestas* from her deceased son. However, *favor fidei*, the favor of the faith, trumped *patria potestas*. In such cases, a legal fiction was warranted: "For the favor of the faith, the woman can be said to become a man, and the [grand]mother to become the father."[42] As for the mother, her rights concerning her children could only be asserted if she were a Christian. A mother's natural right, under *ius della natura*, natural law, did not apply to Jews. And since the mother held no rights to assert, the grandmother's offering could be accepted in favor of the faith.[43]

In the following years, similar cases all concluded with the children being baptized, and all rulings referenced the letters of Benedict XIV and the doctrine of *favor fidei*.

In 1783, an explosive case came before Pope Pius VI. The pope's forces had entered the Ghetto and kidnapped eleven-year-old Angelo Terracina and his seven-year-old sister Sara. They were without any family, as their parents, paternal grandparents, and paternal uncles had all died. In that vulnerable state, they were offered by two *neofiti*, their father's cousin and their great aunt.

Never before had an offering been made by such distant relatives. If a great aunt and a remote cousin could successfully make such a "donation," then no Jews would be safe. The Jewish community objected on the grounds that the offering was void because Angelo and Sara had closer relatives than the *neofiti* who had offered them—there existed a living maternal grandmother and two paternal aunts. The objection also included a warning: such offerings jeopardized the peace and stability of the ghetto. "We ask these things in order to ward off such disorders as might occur and, more broadly, in the interest of the common quietude, to avoid the irreparable and palpable tumults that might arise, given what is involved is something that offends even Nature herself and heats the blood, and [also relying on] the Supreme prudence that Your Eminence has always shown in view of preventing [such tumults]."[44]

The community also requested that in the case of all further offerings, the Jewish community be consulted beforehand. The vice regent's reply, although couched in technical terms, ultimately said that both children had achieved the age of reason and were willing converts. Moreover, *favor fidei* supported the distant relatives, which gave them precedence over the closer aunts and grandmother.[45] In any event, by the time their objection reached the pope, the children had already been baptized and could never return to the Ghetto. Once baptized, their souls could not be jeopardized by living with Jews.

In 1762 another case arose concerning two sisters, Stella and Ester. Their parents, Isacco and Allegrezza, were still alive, but nevertheless, the paternal grandmother appeared at the Catecumeni to convert and offer her granddaughters. The church accepted the offering and agreed to baptize the children, grounding the decision in Benedict XIV's letters and the doctrine of *favor fidei*.[46]

However, one issue remained. At roughly the same time the grandmother offered her granddaughters, their mother was pregnant. Consequently, the grandmother also offered "the unborn fetus, currently existing in the womb of the pregnant Daughter-in-Law."[47]

The status of a fetus had previously arisen in 1712 when a Jewish woman, Chiara del Borgo, offered herself as a convert, along with the child she was bearing.[48] Chiara subsequently reneged on that offering; nevertheless, she was kidnapped and kept in the Catecumeni until the child was born. The infant girl was immediately baptized on the pretext that her life was in danger, and Chiara then converted to be with her child.[49] That ended the controversy—that is, until the issue of fetal conversions reemerged in the case of the grandmother and her pregnant daughter-in-law.[50]

Monsignor Veterani, *assessore* (secular officer) of the Holy Office (the Inquisition), made the argument against conversion. Saints Augustine and Thomas Aquinas, among others, had long held that a fetus was not a person as long as it was in the womb, for at that stage it was a part of the mother's body. Accordingly, the grandmother could not offer an unborn child to the church, because there was no person residing in the uterus to offer; that person came into existence only at birth. He further argued that if the church exercised a right to take unborn children from Jewish mothers, the birthrate in the Ghetto would plummet. Jewish families would forego having children under the limitless threat of abduction, which would discredit the church in the eyes of both Jews and Catholics. In short, the offering had to be rejected.

Opposed to that argument was an idea, new in the eighteenth century, that the fetus was a person independent of the mother. With that new understanding, an offered child could be baptized in the womb in cases where the unborn child was in danger of dying before birth. Even if that danger was not present, where a third party had offered her unborn child, the Jewish mother had to be brought to the Catacumeni to protect the offered child until it was born. Such precautions were warranted because, in the minds of the Catholic legists, the Jewish mother might abort her child or kill it at birth rather than allow it to be baptized. After the birth and baptism of the child, the mother remained Jewish, and the child was taken from her if she did not convert. The rate of maternal conversion in these cases was high. Even if not many mothers gave birth in the Catacumeni, such mothers almost always converted to stay with their children.[51]

In Allegrezza's case, she gave birth before the Vatican reached a decision, and thus the church no longer needed to decide the issue of the fetus. Eventually, the grandmother's offering was rejected for all three children. The baby was returned to its parents, but the two older children, having spent years in the Catecumeni, agreed to baptism, supposedly of their own free will.

Allegrezza's story demonstrates that today's Catholic position on abortion—the fetus is a person at conception—developed, in part, out of debates concerning the forced baptism of Jews close to three hundred years ago. Undoubtedly, other factors also contributed to the church's conclusion, but that conclusion should not be separated from its role in the debate about forced conversion. The church found it advantageous to target young women like Allegrezza and Anna de Monte because they were of childbearing age, they might be pregnant, or they might become pregnant after conversion and produce Catholic children.[52]

Another case raised the issue of whether a Catholic husband could offer his Jewish wife to the church. A recently baptized husband, Angelo, offered his wife Mazaldò (also known as Bonafortuna) despite her violent objections. Mazaldò's defense argued that a marriage did not give either party any additional rights over the other except those concerning childbearing. As to the "Soul" and "things Divine and supernatural," husbands could not dictate such matters to their wives. Nonetheless, in 1770 Pope Clement XIV decided in favor of the husband's rights. After some time in the Catecumeni, where she reportedly broke down the door of her cell, Mazaldò finally relented and converted to become "an obedient sheep in the Fold of Jesus Christ."[53]

The success of conversionary efforts aimed at Roman Jews can be measured in numbers. From 1614 through 1797, 1,197 baptismal ceremonies for Jews were conducted in Rome, some of the ceremonies including more than one baptism.[54] Given the Jewish population of the Ghetto, which grew from fewer than a thousand in 1600 to close to three thousand in 1800, the conversions did not destroy Rome's Jewish community, but a thousand conversions were not negligible either.[55]

CELEBRATORY CONVERSIONS

One reason some Jews converted was the celebrity accorded the converts and the elaborate public ceremonies accompanying the conversions.[56] Often the pope performed the baptism; pontiffs such as Gregory XV (1621–23), Innocent XII (1691–1700), Clement XII (1730–40) and Benedict the XIV (1740–58) conducted very public baptisms of Jews. And if the pope was unavailable, a cardinal performed the rite.

In most cases, the neophytes became literally "new men," taking the name of the pope or cardinal who baptized them. As a result, Jewish converts became disengaged from their families. In the case of the wealthy Corcos family, Elia was baptized by Pius V (Ghislieri) to become Michele Ghislieri. Salomone and his son Lazzaro Corcos were baptized by Gregory XIII (Boncompagni) and took the new names of Ugo and Gregorio Boncompagni.[57] Their family had been nullified.

Important baptisms—that is, for illustrious Jews, if that's not a misnomer in the Ghetto, such as Rabbi Mosé di Cave, the Corcos family, and the four minor children of Rabbi Giuseppe Ascarelli—took place at St. Peter's Basilica or the Basilica of St. John Lateran.[58] The church intentionally crafted the baptismal rites to resemble Roman and papal triumphs. The neophytes progressed through the Ghetto and across the city of Rome "with a following of many Carriages with Trumpets and Drums . . . with great rejoicing of the People and confusion of the accursed and obstinate Hebraic rabble."[59] Sometimes the neophyte's sponsor footed the steep bill for the elaborate affair; other times the Catecumeni bankrolled the event, drawing from its own taxes on the Jewish community.

One such procession took place in 1704. Angelo, a wealthy Jewish merchant from Livorno, agreed to convert and hoped to convince his wife Bianca and their fourteen-year-old daughter Anna to do the same. They agreed to follow him to Rome to attend his baptism, though then planned to return to Livorno as Jews. But on the trip, mother and daughter were plied with jewels, gifts, and an ornate wardrobe. Bianca could not hold out for the length of the journey; Anna agreed to be baptized after one day in Rome.

The baptism was scheduled at St. Peter's Basilica. The three catechumens (aspiring converts) proceeded to the church, followed by eighty prelates and one hundred carriages. The former Queen of Poland also made an appearance. Once inside St. Peter's, Pope Clement XI arrived, escorted by seventeen cardinals. Upon Bianca's baptism, she received a diamond-studded clock. Anna was gifted with a diamond ring. Last baptized was Angelo, who had a crucifix bearing seven large diamonds draped around his neck. At the dinner that followed, the pope gave the three former Jews red velvet purses containing a hundred gold scudi and three figurines in the pope's image. Finally, Bianca and Anna each received stock in the Papal States (luoghi vacabili) that accumulated 120 scudi per year, and Angelo reaped a lifetime annuity of twenty scudi per month.[60]

Such lavish gifts represented generosity on the part of the church and the individual popes. However, the gifts also redounded to a pope, who was hoping for sainthood. After his death, the conversions of important Jews under his tutelage were claimed as qualifying miracles.[61]

After conversion, even if a neophyte was not showered with gifts, life necessarily improved. According to Marquardus de Susannis, a convert was not to lose any of the property and inheritance rights he had as a Jew, and gained rights previously denied him. He or she even gained rights denied other Catholics. For instance, a former Jew, upon conversion, could collect his inheritance from his living Jewish father, a privilege that contradicted *ius commune* (Roman common law).[62] *Neofiti* lived outside of the Ghetto, and were allowed to work as tailors, mattress makers, hat makers, chicken vendors, fruit vendors, green grocers, stone sawyers, shoemakers, and wagon makers, professions that were all, except mattress maker, prohibited for Jews.[63]

That said, Jews did lose certain rights when they converted. A Jew with two wives could not remain married to both after conversion. Also, as codified in *De judaeis*, before baptism a Jew had to return all usurious gains to the so-called victims of his usury in order to take the sacrament free of sin. It is not clear under what circumstances this latter rule was enforced.[64]

In fact, the church's enthusiastic welcome masked a suspicion that *neofiti* were prone to backsliding. Both male and female neophytes had to marry persons of Catholic origin, in order to prevent two newly married converts from establishing a Jewish home. (This rule may not have been known to Sabato Coen when he offered Anna del Monte in the hopes of marrying her as a Catholic. As for the cardinal who wanted to know if Anna and Sabato had had sex, if Anna said yes, the two would have been considered betrothed, not married; and as betrothed, Anna would have been kept longer in the Catecumeni. Had Anna gone on to convert, she would have married someone else, probably a born Catholic.)

Church concerns regarding backsliding resulted in the creation of the Confraternita di San Giovanni Battista (Confraternity of John the Baptist) in the early seventeenth century. Converted Jews had to join the confraternity, which met at the oratorio on Via Baccina on Catholic holy days in order for the *neofiti* to hear special sermons: readings from a "devout book." Catholic men who had married *neofiti* were also obliged to attend, pursuant to another de Rossi edict in 1743.[65] This latter rule kept *neofiti* and their spouses from using the meeting as a gathering of Jews.

The story of forced conversion is one of the darkest chapters in the history of Jews and Catholics in Rome. The church's actions cannot be justified, but they may be understood.

To start, we may look at the gifts bestowed by the popes upon certain converts. It's worth looking at those gifts against the backdrop of Jewish gift-giving to the pope, which we discussed in chapter 3. With the pope bestowing gifts upon Jews, albeit converted Jews, the gifts now proceeded in the opposite direction. As we learned from the anthropologist Marcel Mauss, gift giving is quasi-contractual.[66] Each gift entails an implicit or explicit agreement that the gift will be paid back through a system of reciprocal gifts, which may have effects across generations.[67]

These conventions were certainly at play in early modern Rome, where husbands explicitly or implicitly offered their wives as gifts, and grandparents donated grandchildren to the church as well. When Angelo was preparing to convert, he did not explicitly offer his wife and daughter to the church, but given the ensuing events as Bianca and Anna traveled to Rome to attend his baptism, one could say that his gift was nonetheless implicit—and the whole family benefited financially.

The more obvious meaning of conspicuous gift-giving to a single Jewish family was that each diamond and sum of money given to the *neofiti* symbolized the spiritual gifts they concurrently received from the church for having accepted baptism. Just as the gift to the pope of the Torah, God's word, had been of incommensurable value, so the gift of salvation upon a Jewish family was of similar incalculable worth. Of course, the gifts were not exactly reciprocal. The Jews were giving the pope a gift; the pope was giving gifts to converted Jews and not the Jewish community. For the church, no individual Jew deserved the gifts showered upon Angelo and his family; but a converted Jew did. A Jew was deemed despicable; a convert was treasured. Therein the church demonstrated one aspect of its ambivalent feelings toward Jews.

Moreover, in Angelo's family's case, Pope Clement was conveying, to all who could see, that the church conferred incalculable spiritual wealth, not only on certain Jews who decided to convert, but on all its people. No amount of treasure could equal the gift of salvation that this family, by joining the Catholic family, came to possess.

But the material rewards were hardly beside the point. What was conferred on Angelo would recycle eventually through the Catholic ambit. Prior to his conversion, Angelo had become a wealthy merchant in the town of Livorno. Had Angelo not converted, his personal fortune would have circulated within and solely benefited the area's Jewish community. With his conversion, the Jewish community was not only deprived of his previous wealth, but the money and jewels given to his family at baptism would ultimately redound to the Catholic world through inheritances, dowries, and real estate transfers. Angelo's daughter's eventual marriage to a Catholic would enrich that family, and they would pass that wealth on, maybe even through investments in Catholic bonds and banks and charities. Thus, at least by Mauss's interpretation, the pope was not only being generous. He was confident that his exuberant giving would come around again to the ultimate enrichment of the church.

And so it was that Pope Paul IV and his immediate successors, whose policies can be seen as reactions to the Protestant Reformation, were so preoccupied with growing the church, they repeatedly justified harsh acts that disrupted Jewish families against the contrary teachings of saints like Thomas Aquinas. Even if the majority of Jewish families escaped the kidnapping of their children, the threat posed by papal orders and judicial decisions that countenanced taking children from their parents and adult spouses from their homes must have seriously destabilized life in the ghetto.

Ultimately, the church could not prevent its further isolation and loss of power, a reality that was to unfold in the following century, and which would finally liberate the Jews from their Ghetto.

8

Trading Places

Papal Exiles and Jewish Emancipations during the Nineteenth Century

In 1870, the armies of the newly constituted nation of Italy broke down the gates of Rome, entered the city, and ended the Papal State that had ruled Rome for hundreds of years. Pope Pius IX was confined to his palace and its environs, and soon considered himself a "prisoner" in the Vatican.[1] Simultaneously, the Ghetto was abolished and Rome's Jews were liberated and emancipated, meaning they were given equal rights under the law, the same rights as other Romans.

Our story of how the pope came to be "imprisoned" as Rome's Jews were simultaneously freed after 315 years in the Ghetto begins in 1621 with the legal status of Jews in Rome.

IUS COMMUNE

The law in papal Rome was not a simple matter. Canon law governed Catholic marriages and testamentary matters, as well as complaints against the clergy. Civil law, based in late classical codes such as the Code of Justinian, governed daily life.[2] Additionally, Roman common law, or *ius commune*, derived from Roman statutes, governed nonreligious matters and also applied when no specific statute covered the circumstances.[3] Finally, Roman Jews followed Torah law in their own ritual matters (e.g., marriage, divorce, burial, and kashrut).

In 1621, the Roman Rota (highest apostolic court), decided to include the Jewish community under *ius commune* jurisdiction. Jews could still use Torah law to govern themselves ritually, but otherwise *ius commune* became the binding authority—meaning the procedural aspects of Jewish life were now subsumed under the common law. By 1640, by order of the vicar, Jewish notaries could no longer operate in Rome.[4] *Ius commune* now governed business dealings and even loans between Jewish family members, as well as the number of witnesses required for a will. Thus, put differently, the rights of Roman citizens were extended to Jews.

What is more, and surprising: Jews were now considered among the faithful (*fideles*) of the church. They were not *fideles* of the Church Triumphant (consisting of those who are in Heaven), but they were protected and sustained by the church, and as such they were considered *fideles* of the Church Militant (those who struggle against sin). Given the Jews' status as religious enemies, but not civil enemies, Jews could not claim any benefits from canon law, but in civil disputes, they could use *ius commune* procedures even against Catholics. Thus it was that Jews were accorded justice under the law so long as they were not granted any privileges, such as the honor of holding offices or judgeships, otherwise denied them under local laws or canon law.[5]

If this Jewish legal status sounds unsure, that is because in Rome, the Jewish circumstance was always ambiguous. Jews were both enemies and citizens: intimate strangers.

After 1621, it could have been hoped that putting Jews under *ius commune* jurisdiction would be a first step toward emancipation—and it was, but emancipation did not follow swiftly. On the contrary, in the late 1600s and early 1700s forced baptisms increased and Jewish banks were shuttered. Much of Ghetto life was a battle with the papal authorities in order to keep Jewish heads above water.[6]

MEO PATACCA

We get another glimpse of Ghetto life from the epic poem *Il Meo Patacca ovverro Roma in feste nei trionfi di Vienna* (Meo Patacca, or Rome in jubilation because of the triumphs of Vienna). Written by the Catholic poet and playwright Giuseppe Berneri in the Romanesco dialect and published in

1695, the poem told the story of a fictitious rake, Meo Patacca, during the time the Ottoman Turks besieged Vienna (1683). Meo, short for Bartolomeo, a renowned swordsman, has every intention of defending Christendom until he discovers his help is not needed: the Austrians have already been victorious. Celebrations break out in Rome, and the festivities target the Ghetto, which the revelers perceive as a den of infidels similar to the Turks and seek to set on fire. While concocting this story out of whole cloth, the poet describes the Ghetto:

> The Ghetto is a small place next to the Tiber,
> On one side, and to the Fish-market on the other;
> It's a rather miserable enclosure of streets,
> As it is shady, and rather saddening.
> It has four huge gates, and a small one;
> During daytime it is open, to let people out,
> But from evening until break of dawn
> It is kept locked by a porter guard.[7]

Young toughs head toward the ghetto, intending to set it afire with "piggy banks" (*dindarolo*) turned Molotov cocktails. They spy a Jew and begin to beat him:

> Many people form a crowd to see who he is,
> Why he is being treated in that way
> And some serious persons who happen to be there
> Feel very sorry about the mistreatment.
> They beg the braves not to harm him any longer,
> Because such a beating is enough;
> So, they stop and, while more people join the crowd,
> The Jew stands up and runs away.[8]

Finding another Jew hiding in a barrel, the crowd rolls the barrel around the streets until several more sober Romans save the Jew inside. He stumbles toward the Ghetto but is forced to seek refuge in a tavern, where the Catholic innkeeper tries to protect him from the mob. Just then, Meo Patacca appears on the scene. He calms the crowd, rescues the Jew, and through the force of his reputation as a swordsman, peacefully saves the Ghetto from being attacked. Subsequently, the Jewish community compensates Meo with a suit of fine clothing delivered personally by a rabbi:

> He hands over the gift and Meo unveils it,
> Only looking at it, and turning towards him says:
> "I accept it, appreciate it, and give it back to you.
> Because I do favors as a gift, I don't sell them."[9]

In the same breath, however, Meo demands that the Jews join in celebrating the Christian victory, on pain of the Ghetto being burned if they refuse.

Meo's simultaneous acceptance and rejection of the gift—"I accept it, appreciate it, and give it back to you"—mirrors the manner of the medieval popes upon being gifted a Torah from the Jewish community. Even as the popes accepted the Torah as the word of God, they then "returned the scroll with measured words."[10]

As for Meo, even as he returns his gift, he instinctively knows he is owed something for his heroism. Upon the briefest of reconsiderations, he makes the brusque demand: celebrate with us, or bear the consequences. The same could be said of all prior celebrations by Jews at papal coronations. Here, the contractual nature of Catholic-Jewish relationships in the Middle Ages is reiterated as early modern noblesse oblige.

In 1793, a century after *Meo Patacca*'s publication, an actual drama similar to the one described in the poem took place at the Ghetto walls. A mob of antirevolutionaries murdered the new French Republic's representative in Rome, Hugo de Bassville, then sacked the French Academy in Rome (at the time on the Corso) and headed toward the Ghetto. It was rumored that Pellegrino Ascarelli, a Jew and hence necessarily a Ghetto resident, was storing weapons for the revolutionary French Republic; consequently, he was the mob's next target. Ascarelli escaped injury by convincing Vatican authorities the rumor was false, but the following day a crowd again headed toward the Ghetto. Two monks supposedly dissuaded them to return home—twice—but nevertheless, some persistent agitators set fire to three carts at the Ghetto gate opposite the Piazza Mattei. Finally, at about 11 p.m. a powerful lightning storm drenched the city and the mob, extinguishing the fires, and over two thousand papal militia sent to restore order dispersed the crowd.

Still, the Ghetto was locked for eight days while Pope Pius VI hedged his bets. On the one hand, he dispatched four preachers to churches in the Roman neighborhoods of Trastevere, Monti, Regola, and the Piazza del Popolo to quiet passions. On the other, he reissued the *Edict on the Jews* that required, among other things, that Jews wear the hated yellow badge, even inside the Ghetto walls.

This incident soon became known as the *Moed di Piombo*, the Festival of Lead.[11] While the event hardly foreshadowed emancipation, nonetheless, conditions in Jewish Rome would dramatically improve five years later.

NAPOLEONIC ROME

After invading northern Italy in 1796, Napoleon Bonaparte, acting for the French Directory,[12] allowed his general, Louis-Alexandre Berthier, to take Rome in February 1798 and establish the Roman Republic, a sister republic of revolutionary France. The social, legal, and religious distinctions that constituted the Ghetto were swept away. Jews tore off their yellow badges and planted a Liberty Tree (a symbol of the French Revolution borrowed from its American predecessor) in the piazza in front of the Cinque Scole. On February 18, 1798, Antonio Pacifici, a Jew, addressed a crowd of Jews and Catholics: "From here on, if you [Jews and Christians] are good citizens ... [a single] law will judge us both; in civil life all that will distinguish us one from another is virtue, and not religious belief."[13]

Within days, Pope Pius VI was taken captive to France, where he died a year later.[14] Jews carrying French flags soon assembled on the Quirinale Hill and listened to Berthier's edict granting Jews all rights as citizens of the new Republic.[15] In turn, Jews would be taxed three hundred thousand scudi and were expected to support the Republic by enlisting in the national guard and providing the guard with uniforms. A Jew, Ezechiele Morpurgo, was elected a senator of the city, serving next to a Borghese prince.[16] It seemed things would never be the same.

Nonetheless, this radical change in Jewish fortunes was short-lived. An invasion from Naples in September 1799 ended the Roman Republic and restored the papacy in the person of Pope Pius VII the following June. Jews welcomed him with gifts, and he lowered the Jewish community's taxes[17]—but they were still required to live in the Ghetto.

Jews were also viciously reminded that in welcoming Napoleon they had chosen the losing side. As a barometer of the reactionary resentment against the Jews (with unknown effects), the 1799 song "Canzonetta nuova sopra gli ebrei" (A new song about the Jews) took twenty-two verses to fully vent its (anonymous) author's wrath. It concluded:

Listen to the people scream
Vendetta against the Jews . . .
The Day of Wrath has come.
It is useless to flee
Invoking the Messiah.
Let him [rather] kill them in the street. . . .
On gibbets they repose
Either hung or impaled, [who cares]
As long as they breathe no more.[18]

Both the Jewish community and the papacy had learned something from the Roman Republic: they were at the mercy of international events happening far from their city. In particular, circumstances in France in the first decade of the nineteenth century and for a hundred years thereafter would reverberate in Rome and make a difference in the lives of both Jews and popes.

In 1804, Napoleon replaced the *ius commune* that had been the law in France with the Code Civil or Napoleonic Code, a product of the Enlightenment that codified Jewish emancipation and made all French citizens equal under the law.[19]

Two years later, Napoleon, as emperor, convened an Assembly of Jewish Notables in Paris that would turn out to be more propaganda than substance. Italian communities sent delegates, but Roman Jews, under papal rule, could not attend. Nor could they agree to, or celebrate, the assembly's declaration that in the new Napoleonic Europe, Jews would have all the rights of citizenship, so long as they assented to the laws of the state.[20] To formally ratify that agreement, in 1807 Napoleon assembled a second group of Jews, a "Sanhedrin" (a clumsy attempt to recall the Jewish assemblies of Second Temple times), which did its part by pledging Jewish obedience to the state. In return, Jews were to be given religious freedom. However, within a year, that freedom was hedged with imperial decrees limiting where, in France, Jews could live, and requiring a license for the practice of any trade or business, especially farming and artisanal crafts.[21] Roman Jews were then exempt from these strictures, because Napoleon had been ousted from Rome. In 1807 they still remained under papal rule, which was even more oppressive.

Yet French forces retook Rome in 1808, and (again) spirited the pope to France. In 1809 the French Republic declared the papacy to be a spiritual power only, without temporal clout of any sort, and forced Pope Pius VII to sign a concordat with Napoleon that stripped the papacy of its secular powers. Some Catholic Romans, despairing at the pope's surrender, were heard to exclaim, "If this is true, let us go to the ghetto and become Jews." As reported by Cardinal Paca, pro-secretary of the Papal States, this cry, satirically proclaiming the impossible—that is, the conversion of Christians into Jews—expressed a widely held anxiety that the worst could in fact happen. If the pope could surrender to Napoleon, the rest of Christian Rome might as well surrender to the Jews.[22]

Italian Jews, on the other hand, enthusiastically supported Napoleon. It was said that in 1812, Italian Jewish soldiers fighting for the emperor in Russia would sit around campfires singing Hebrew Psalms to the tune of the Marseillaise.[23]

The Ghetto was opened again in 1808, allowing Jews to open shops and businesses outside the gates and live elsewhere as well. And this time, in 1810, Rome and most of central Italy became part of the French Empire.[24] Jews in Rome gained legal equality under the Napoleonic Code, and Jewish taxes to pay for Carnival, the Catecumeni, and the Monti di Pietà were abolished. Unlike the rules Napoleon imposed on French Jews in 1808, these boons to Rome's Jewish community did not come with similar restrictions. In France Jews were prohibited from further settling in the regions of Alsace and Lorraine; Italian Jews were not subject to a similar order. French Jews could not practice many professions without a license, but in Italy exceptions were made in order to stimulate trade. The City of Livorno was exempt from any such orders, and that exemption eventually covered the entire kingdom of Italy.[25] In addition, for health reasons, Jewish burials that for centuries had taken place within Rome were moved outside the city walls to the newly designed Verano Cemetery that included both a Jewish and a Catholic burial ground.[26]

THE GHETTO ECONOMY

British forces finally defeated Napoleon at Waterloo in 1815. With his demise came the Congress of Vienna, a conference of ambassadors from the major European powers that restored Italy to a hodgepodge of small kingdoms (Piedmont-Sardinia), duchies (Tuscany and Modena), and papal holdings. In fact, the restored papacy was one of the big winners at the Congress of Vienna.[27]

Pope Pius VII made a triumphant return to Rome to be welcomed by a Jewish community who knew they would be ghettoized again. They produced the painted façade for the Cinque Scole pictured in chapter 3, and an (unknown) artisan crafted a gift to the pontiff: a commemorative ring bearing the Hebrew inscription "Emanuel"—perhaps a reference to the closing lines of the Gospel of Matthew as well as to Matthew 1:23, meaning "God is with us"—along with a cameo portrait of Pius VII.[28]

The Jewish community then asked the Supreme Council of the Papal State not to reestablish the Ghetto. The French colony of Rome had allowed the Ghetto gates to remain, in all likelihood because removing them would have been a complex and expensive proposition, as we will see later in this chapter. The Papal State refused the Jews and closed the gates again every night at sundown.[29]

Small Jewish shops had been established outside the Ghetto while the French were still in charge. After 1815, all Jews had to operate their businesses from within the Ghetto, so those shops had to be moved, and any Jewish properties outside the walls sold within five years. According to an 1816 census, a majority of Roman Jews, were engaged in commerce, which meant small shops. A fifth of the population were artisans, and a tenth were servants or public servants like porters and garbage collectors. Jews were heavily invested in the textile businesses, largely dependent on Catholics to produce the textiles while they handled the sale and marketing.[30]

More generally, Christian merchants feared competition with Jewish entrepreneurs, and some churchmen were on a mission to cease the new contacts between Catholics and Jews that were, by definition, "scandalous"; Jews, it was said, were seeking sexual connections with Catholics, and would use their freedom to convert Catholics to Judaism.[31] Hence, in 1815 Jews were ordered to vacate the businesses they had started in greater Rome—but certain exceptions were tolerated. A few Jewish shop owners were able to operate on Via Reginella, Via de' Falegnami, and Via delle Tartughe just outside the Ghetto gates, if they received one-year (probably renewable) licenses certified by Cardinal Annibale della Genga. Concurrently, the cardinal expelled Jewish students from the Sapienza (University of Rome) and reinstated conversionist sermons.[32]

The cardinal's contradictory policies continued in 1823 when he was elevated to the papacy. As the new Pope Leo XII, he began preparing for a Jubilee in 1825 by clearing the streets of any Jewish businesses, especially those streets where Jubilee processions would take place. For Leo, the Jubilee project was intended to reconsecrate Rome after the Napoleonic interlude, a celebration of the triumph of religion over revolution. Returning the Jews to the Ghetto was part of that endeavor. The renewed Catholic city would exile its Jews internally once again.[33] Plans were additionally prepared for a new ghetto in the Rione de Borgo neighborhood, cheek by jowl with the Vatican—but the logistical and financial difficulties attendant to relocating both Jews and Catholics were prohibitive and the new ghetto never materialized.[34]

Instead, the crowded and unhealthy Ghetto conditions were only exacerbated when Jewish merchants had to bring their businesses back inside the walls. Meanwhile, Catholic merchants benefited from the loss of competition, and that economic justification continued to drive the relocation of Jewish shops.[35]

Another contradiction in Pope Leo's policies is evident in his 1824 order to alleviate Jewish suffering through a small expansion of the Ghetto. Possibly as a result of pressure from the Rothschild family, two streets north of the Ghetto were added to accommodate the shopkeepers ordered to return. Yet Ghetto overcrowding was not much reduced; rather, the two-block addition became equally crowded. For his part, the pope may have been agreeable because the additional streets were not near the proposed Jubilee parade routes.[36]

A second census of 1827, after the Jubilee, reveals the return of a smattering of Jewish shops existing outside the Ghetto, and reveals, surprisingly, that Jews both inside and outside the enclosure were engaged in supposedly prohibited activities, such as carpentry and tin working. A significant number of small business owners were women (17 percent), many—but not all—widows who had inherited the businesses from their husbands. Some women operated businesses independent of their spouses.[37] In business, Jews also employed a considerable (unreported) number of Catholic staff. (In the home, Jews would not have been able to hire Catholic domestic servants.)

Eventually, the papal antirevolutionary vision had to confront events outside Italy. In 1830 Parisians revolting to establish a constitutional monarchy deposed the Bourbon king Charles X (whom the Congress of Vienna had installed on the French throne) and replaced him with the more liberal Louis-Philippe d'Orleans. Like previous French upheavals, the revolt reverberated in Rome—a brief revolt in Rome opened the Ghetto gates, and on February 10, 1831, Jews were given the rights of citizens[38]—but Austrian forces that had long opposed the tide of liberal democracy emanating from France swiftly reestablished papal rule.

A tenuous order was restored, but several foreign powers presented Pope Gregory XVI, elected in 1831 in the midst of the revolt, with a memorandum requesting such reforms as representative governance of municipalities, a partially elected board to regulate finances, and lay participation in judicial and legislative bodies. When Gregory rejected those calls to moderation, the Austrians withdrew, but returned to occupy Bologna for six years, while France followed with a similar occupation of Ancona.[39]

VERDI AND HAYEZ

Gregory was only one of several Italian rulers who, after 1815, fought a rearguard action against modernity with the help of foreign interference. Italy was a jigsaw puzzle of small principalities that resisted both unification and Italian independence from Austrian rule. However, the historical trend toward independence counterbalanced that conservatism.

During this time of revolutionary ferment termed the Risorgimento (rising again), two Italian artists identified the tribulations of the Italian people with the plight of the Jews. Giuseppe Verdi (1813–1901), born near Busseto, Italy, became the most beloved composer of Italian opera of his generation. *Nabucco*, his 1842 work that initially brought him success, was very loosely based on the Babylonian king Nebuchadnezzar's destruction of Jerusalem and the First Temple in 587 BCE.[40] Verdi and his librettist, Temistocle Solera, recreated the sad event of the Israelites being led captive into Babylon (told in 2 Kings 24 and 2 Chron. 36:5–21). "On the banks of the Euphrates. Jews in chains and at hard labor" (as the scene was set), the chorus of Hebrews—performed by Catholic Italians—sang the song known as "Va, pensiero":

Fly my thought on golden wings
Go and settle on hills and dales
Where the soft and warm airs
Of our native land smell ambrosial
Greet the banks of the Jordan
And the fallen towers of Zion
Oh my country, so adorable and lost
Oh my country so dear and full of pain.[41]

Verdi, an intense supporter of the struggle for Italian liberation, expressed the Italian longing for freedom and independence by putting "Va pensiero" into the mouths of a chorus of Jewish captives. The exiled Israelites' yearning for their homeland simultaneously gave voice to the Italians' desire for their own nation. By bringing together the Jewish and Italian struggle for freedom, Verdi articulated the historical circumstances of mid-nineteenth-century Italy—and soon "Va pensiero" became the anthem of the Risorgimento. As Italy moved toward unification, the cause of Jewish emancipation advanced simultaneously.[42]

Francesco Hayez's painting, *The Destruction of the Temple of Jerusalem*, also conflated Italian and Jewish aspirations. Primarily a commentary on the historian Josephus's depiction of the Jewish revolt in 70 CE, Hayez painted the Temple courtyard filled by a monumental altar upon which Jewish rebels fought valiantly—individual rebels dangled from the altar top—but all in vain, as Titus burned the Second Temple. Displayed in 1867, the painting was then also understood as a commentary on Verdi's understanding of the contemporary plight of the Italian and Jewish people.[43] The sympathetically portrayed first-century Jewish freedom fighters were stand-ins for the nineteenth-century Italian freedom fighters. Interestingly, those first-century Jews were fighting against Romans—a fact that lends confusion—or, better, ambivalence—to the work.

While Verdi and Hayez were deeply involved in the Risorgimento throughout the Italian Peninsula, another artist spoke particularly for the city of Rome. Giuseppe Gioachino Belli (1791–1863), a Catholic known as the people's poet of Rome, wrote 2,279 *Sonetti romaneschi* (Sonnets in Roman dialect) chronicling Roman life.

Belli's interest was less revolutionary and more sociological. He wanted to encompass, in satire, all of Roman life. A poet not so much of politics as of morals, he saw hypocrisy everywhere.

Among other things, Belli had an enduring fascination with religion, the Bible, and the Jews of Rome. Writing at a time when several virulent antisemitic pamphlets were circulating in the city, Belli searched for an understanding (albeit crude) of his Jewish neighbors.[44] As a satirist, he composed sonnets depicting Jews as sly moneylenders (Sonnet 1979, "La vennita der brevetto" ["Pension for Sale"]) and retailers of defective dry goods (Sonnet 1221, "La bbona spesa" ["The Bargain"]). Those and other sonnets reveal a coarse antisemitism that was commonplace in Rome. However, as a freethinker, Belli saved his choicest invective for the popes, whom he often described as Jews. In Sonnet 833, "E ppoi?" ("And Then?"), Belli described Pope Gregory XVI (1831–46) as a patient listener, similar to a "Jewess who cuts and sews, mending here and patching there."[45] By contrast, when derogating Pope Pius VIII (1829–30) in Sonnet 11, "Pio ottavo" ("Pius VIII"), his description was vicious:

> A boon to mommies and aunties to scare [their] children into behaving,
> He's got herpes all over, he's lost all his teeth, he's cross eyed,
> He drags his feet, he lists to one side and I'd be surprised if he could even manage to find sinecures for his relatives . . . A real mess of a Pope.
> What a beaut of a Pope they've elected! Damn! With all due respect he's the image of the rabbi.[46]

In other sonnets, Belli elucidated the lurking dangers if popes and rabbis spent time together. In the case of Rabbi Moisè Sabbato Beèr, known as "l'amico del papa" (friend of the pope), the chief rabbi of Rome tried unsuccessfully to convince his friend Pope Gregory XVI to emancipate the Jews. To that end, upon Gregory's election in 1831, Rabbi Beèr wrote a sonnet venerating the new pontiff. The rabbi prefaced his poem with an adulatory invocation:

Blessed father, adored sovereign,

Far from the tumultuous arena of the day's cares, there is in words a silent refuge, where contemplation and meditation abide, where study has eclipsed the day, the lamp has illumined midnight's work and the tranquil application and the sweet repose, invited by the brilliant labor and efforts of genius. It is then that the Temple is consecrated to the Muse. . . .

Heavy with profound veneration and at the feet of the most August Throne, I genuflect, prostrate myself, pray to Heaven a solemn prayer from my heart "God Save Gregory," Amen.

Your humble, devoted, obedient servant and faithful subject
Mosè Sabbato Beèr, Chief Rabbi, Rome on November 15, 1833.[47]

When Rabbi Beèr died on May 9, 1835, Belli wrote Sonnet 1544, "La morte der Rabbino" ("The Rabbi's Death"), which concluded:

He was the Pope's friend,
In fact the very day the Pope was elected
He took pen in hand and wrote him a sonnet,
Half in Hebrew, half in Latin.
So when he died the Pope cried huge tears
Even though he's the Pope, and felt his heart break.
I tell you, had the Rabbi lived a bit longer,
Either we would have seen him become a Christian,
Or the Pope would have ended up a Jew.[48]

Here, in explicit terms, we find the persistent belief—stated previously in the papal bull *Turbato corde*, and evident in *Cum nimis*—that propinquity between Jews and Catholics would result in some sort of unavoidable conversion. Belli was joking, but on another level, the tug of war between Catholics and Jews was perceived to be so strong that even if one party was a pope, he might still fall prey to becoming a Jew. Simultaneously, Belli's admission that the bonds of Jewish-Catholic friendship could create an involuntary family spoke to the perceived familial closeness of Jews and Catholics in Rome. Whether Gregory and Rabbi Beèr truly were close friends is not as germane as the belief that such a relationship was both possible and dangerous.

Various Belli sonnets portrayed the pope's transformation into a Jew. Two years after the 1830 revolt, the Papal State needed money—in Belli's words, the treasury was so empty, "crickets were dancing where once there had been gold"—so Gregory XVI negotiated a loan from Karl Rothschild of the Jewish banking family. In Sonnet 316, "La sala di Monziggnore Tesoriere" ("Monsignor Treasurer's Ante-chamber"), Belli excoriated both the pope and Rothschild:

> Well it's a great miracle that in order to save the Church
> God touched the heart of a Jew.
> But [to get his own back] the Pope will have the Sacrament explained
>   [to Rothschild, hoping]
> To convert to sweet Jesus the man who helped him out at 61 percent.[49]

Was Belli hoping for the prominent Jew's conversion to Catholicism? In Sonnet 622, "Er motivo de li guai" ("The Source of Our Troubles"), he voiced the opposite concern:

> You want to know why Rome is in such trouble,
> Why God is trying her so hard with such suffering? I'll tell you.
> It's because the Pope has become a Jew
> And all that's left of his Papal nature is the vestment.

This is because [since the time of] Pius VIII the Jews no longer wear
    their badge.

. . .

Too bad for us. [And nothing will be done]
Because by borrowing so much money from a stinking Jew,
Pope Gregory sold him Rome and the Papal State![50]

More often, Belli's satire focused on the transformation of Catholics
into Jews. "Er còlera mòribbus II" ("Deadly Cholera II"), a sonnet written in 1835, lamented the Jewish bailout of the Vatican, because Rome was
being turned into a ghetto. Another sonnet warned that Catholics and
Jews living together as neighbors would lead to sexual escapades with
dire consequences. In Sonnet 848, "Nono, nun disiderà la donna d'antri"
("Ninth [Commandment]: Thou Shalt Not Covet Thy Neighbor's Wife"),
Belli admonished his son for whoring in the Ghetto:

Maybe Rome doesn't have enough whores
So you have to go look for Jewish ones in the Ghetto?
You want sex? Get it on with your own Christian girls
So you don't offend God.
Here out of every dozen Roman women
Eight or ten will go to bed with you.
And, after all, what does it cost? Half a lira, a lira
And you'll still have some change left
Look you're baptized aren't you.
Don't you know that a baptized Christian
Can't touch a Jewish woman?
And once you have committed this sin,
You can wait all you want for absolution
You'll be excommunicated my son, permanently.[51]

Belli replaced a key word in the ninth commandment that was the title
of his poem. While the Hebrew word *rāecha* in Exodus 20:14 is translated

as "neighbor," and in Italian as *prossimo* or *vicino*, meaning "neighbor" as well—in other words, "Do not covet your *neighbor's* wife"—Belli translated the ninth commandment as "Do not covet *another's* wife."[52] In his poem, the "other" (*antri*) is pointedly Jewish; for Belli, intimacy with a Jew was more intimacy with a stranger than with a neighbor.[53]

Sonnet 2118, "Sesto, nun formicà" ("Sixth [Commandment]: Thou Shalt Not Commit Adultery") exposed the practical consequences of Christian men indulging in extramarital affairs with Jewish women:

> But without being married,
> If a man and a woman, do what I do
> Every night with my wife Rosa,
> Isn't that always a deadly sin?
> And the hermit replied,
> I wouldn't want to tell you that such behaviour isn't sinful,
> But the Church, our generous mother,
> Knows how to distinguish, six from half a dozen.
> For example, if a [baptized] Christian
> Is caught in the act [*in flagrante*] with a Jewish woman,
> It's automatically a sin which stays on his conscience.
> If, on the other hand, he's caught with a [Christian] woman,
> We can look the other way.
> It's all a matter of the eventual offspring: A Jew bears a Jew and a
> Christian, a Christian.[54]

In other words, the proliferation of Jewish children was a threat, whereas making Christian babies, even those out of wedlock, was a boon to the church.

Thus Belli voiced a continuing Roman fear—not only that living next door to Jews invited sexual relations, but that those sexual relations would result in a Jewish population explosion. Longstanding Vatican policy had aimed to reduce Rome's Jewish population through ghettoization and forced baptism, but now, if the Ghetto was being liberated (albeit intermittently), was it not logical to fear that the Jewish population would expand?

A LIBERAL PIUS IX

Pope Gregory XVI died in 1846. During the Vacant See, the Ghetto had to be protected from unrestrained violence, and frivolous contact between Catholics and Jews also had to be avoided. Therefore, Catholics and Jews met ad hoc to establish a schedule of opening and closing the gates.

Two weeks later, Pius IX assumed the papacy. Pius was young for a pope (fifty-four), and his youth raised hopes that he would commence an era of liberalism. The Jewish community responded to the election with lavish events, including two nights of torchlit celebrations and a cloth façade hung from the Cinque Scole extolling God's selection of Pius. Official Jewish praise for the pope did not prevent some Catholics from harassing Jews by throwing stones and punches when they could. All the while, the Jewish community also admonished Jews, in a written notice, to restrain themselves, and allow the Roman government to protect them.

Pius IX did not disappoint. Shortly after his election, he declared an amnesty for political prisoners. In November 1846 he approved construction of five local railroad lines, and in December, after an extensive flood of the Tiber, he allowed some Jews to live outside the damaged Ghetto.[55]

In February 1847, perhaps spurred by the flood and a letter from Baron Salomon Rothschild, whose family was financing the Vatican, Pius IX appointed a commission to review the Jews' condition in Rome. The pope then relieved Jews of some onerous, long-lived traditions: canceling conversionist sermons and abolishing the annual tribute that had financed Carnival for generations. Jews were now allowed to place tombstones over their graves, and Jewish appointments to the Guardia Civica (citizens guard) were considered.[56] The commission also weighed making architectural repairs to protect the Ghetto from Tiber floods, but ultimately rejected the project, given the expense and the difficulties of relocating Jews and Catholics to effect the necessary changes.[57] Still, by June 25,

1847, Pius agreed that a limited number of Jewish families could petition to live outside the Ghetto. Hoping that their final emancipation from the Ghetto was near, Jewish appreciation for these measures was considerable, and in at least one instance, outside the bounds of reason. In May 1847, Pius baptized three young Jews who believed that the pope was the long hoped-for Messiah.[58]

Catholics, too, were energized by the possibility of real liberal reforms in the Papal State. Pius had introduced gas streetlights for Rome and initiated the railways as well (the latter financed by the Rothschild family).[59] It felt like a Golden Age was about to dawn.

Perhaps the most famous Catholic activist pressuring the church to modernize was Angelo Brunetti (1800–1849), also known as Ciceruacchio, a Roman innkeeper and populist leader. A handbill circulating in Rome and Ancona described a meeting Brunetti had called with residents of Trastevere and Regola, who were then reviving anti-Jewish beliefs in response to the changes in papal Jewry policy. According to the handbill's author, a self-identified "spectator," Brunetti told the residents, "Let us see if I cannot dissuade you from this crazy hostility against men who in the end of the day are no better or worse than us."[60]

The handbill then described an encounter the next day in the Ghetto, where a group of men, apparently moved by Brunetti, invited Jews to drink with them in a local tavern outside the Ghetto. The Catholic instigator of this camaraderie, having forgotten to bring money, gave the key to his house to a Jew called Abramuccio and told him where to find the cash for the drinks. Then, the handbill related, the following day, yet another group of Catholics entered the Ghetto and invited Jews back to their neighborhood for supper. After sharing drinks, Jews and Catholics gathered on the banks of the Tiber and sang hymns of praise to Pius IX, accompanied by further torchlit festivities.[61]

It appears unlikely that the "spectator" who authored the handbill really witnessed all these events. All the same, the handbill's effusiveness speaks to the enthusiasm some Romans apparently felt for any sign of fraternity and modernity.

The high-water mark of this enthusiasm came on April 17, 1848, on Passover, when, during the seder in the Ghetto, Jews and Catholics broke through the walls and began tearing down the enclosure.[62] Pius had ordered the dismantling of the Ghetto, and according to historian Vogelstein's 1940 account, Jews joined Brunetti in destroying the three-hundred-year-old walls.[63]

Yet documents from the Jewish Archive in Rome offer a more nuanced account. The previous day, the Vatican had notified the Jewish community's secretary that the walls were to come down at the community's expense. The news was met by "tears of joy." However, two practicalities intruded upon the celebration. First, money was needed to pay for the demolition, and second, the dismantling of the gates would require planning because they abutted, and may even have been connected to, Jewish apartments and shops. Damage to those shops had to be minimized and the owners compensated. On April 19, the Jewish community leaders consulted with a friend of Brunetti on how best to accomplish the demolition. There is no doubt that the gates were removed quickly, because everyone wanted the matter expedited. But it was not done hastily.[64]

Afterward, Jews faced new threats from Catholic Romans who resented Jewish progress.[65] Papal forces were sent to quell disturbances against Jews and their property, but the troops may have joined in the looting instead.[66] For example, in response to a knife fight between a Jew, Angelo Moscati, and a Christian (unnamed) in October 1848, the Civic Guard was called to keep the peace, but Moscati proceeded to injure not only the Christian but several guardsmen as well. The Captain of the Guard then reported that he had to convince his comrades to refrain from rioting and maintain the peace. Things got worse from there, with a crowd storming the Ghetto, shouting, "Send the Jews to the flames." For several days civic guardsmen had to exercise riot control.[67]

1848 REVOLUTION

Nonetheless, the forces of liberalism would not be denied. Again, events in France echoed in Rome. In February 1848, King Louis Philippe was overthrown and replaced by a democratic republic. Already in January, the people of Palermo, Sicily, had forced the king of the Two Sicilies, Ferdinand II (1810–59), to approve a constitution, and in March, Prince Metternich (1773–1859), the Austrian statesman who had engineered the shape of post-Napoleonic Europe, was driven from Vienna. Within a span of three months, France and Austria, the foreign powers that had propped up the Papal States and Rome's nearest neighbor, Naples, had fallen to revolutionaries, leaving Rome exposed to a wave of popular uprisings sweeping the Continent.

Pius IX managed to hang on a bit longer. On February 12, 1848, he agreed to reform his government. One month later, he signed a Roman constitution. However, Pius would not be forced to join the Kingdom of Sardinia in a war against Catholic Austria—a war in which Roman Jews had volunteered to fight in the papal army—and with that refusal, Pius's relations with his new liberal government soured. Luigi Brunetti, son of Angelo, assassinated the prime minister under the new Roman constitution, Pellegrino Rossi, in November 1848. Within days, Pius IX fled Rome in the carriage of the Bavarian ambassador disguised as a simple priest.[68]

A month later, the republican and revolutionary Giuseppe Garibaldi led an army into Rome, and, after being met there by Italian statehood advocate Giuseppe Mazzini, declared a Roman Republic in February 1849.[69] For the delighted Jews, the most important parts of the new Roman Republic's constitution appeared in articles 7 and 8:

> Article 7. The exercise of civil and political rights does not depend on religious belief.
> Article 8. The Head of the Catholic Church will receive all the necessary guarantees from the Republic for the independent exercise of his spiritual power.[70]

In other words, the constitution emancipated Rome's Jews. Soon thereafter, two Jews were elected to the Constituent Assembly, and three Jews served on the city council.[71]

The constitution also stripped the papacy of its temporal powers. In response, Pius, from his exile in Gaeta in the Kingdom of Naples, also known as the Kingdom of the Two Sicilies, beseeched the Catholic European powers to restore the Papal State. Both the French and the Austrians agreed, and while the republican French were reluctant to reinstate papal rule in Rome, realpolitik forced their hand: they could not leave papal Italy to Austria.[72]

Under Louis Napoleon Bonaparte, or Napoleon III (1808–73), the French decided to restore Rome to the pope, although Napoleon was coy about stating his intentions directly. Many of his soldiers believed their mission was to protect the new Roman Republic and not destroy it. However, in May France elected a conservative government, easing the way for France's field commander Charles Oudinot to justify capturing Rome for the pope. The French expedition succeeded in occupying Rome in July 1849.[73]

Garibaldi retreated toward Venice with a few adherents, including Angelo Brunetti and his two sons, Luigi and thirteen-year-old Lorenzo. However, the Austrian army was waiting for them. Shortly after August 5, 1849, they were captured, and with the exception of Garibaldi, who escaped, all were executed.[74] The Roman Republic had existed for six months.

A REACTIONARY PIUS IX

In his 1849 New Year's address, the exiled Pius IX declared that Romans who supported the new Roman state were committing a grave sin. This sounded like a threat of excommunication, and its severity created anxiety.[75] Moreover, Pius survived the 1848 revolt a changed man. Any liberal tendencies he may have harbored before 1848 had been eradicated by the bitter experience of exile. The restored pope believed that the forces of modernity, including the Jews, had declared war on the Catholic Church, and he responded in kind. Even before returning to Rome, he reestablished the Inquisition.

Still, there was the question of money. The pope wanted to return from exile to the splendor he felt was his right, along with retaining the means to address practical problems. But to do that he needed cash. Again he approached the Rothschild family for a loan. This time they conditioned the loan on Jewish emancipation from the Ghetto. The gates had been removed, but in Pius IX's post-1848 Rome, Jews would still have to live within the impoverished Ghetto area. The Rothschilds demanded an end to the Ghetto itself, as well as papal permission for Jewish ownership of real estate and Jewish attendance at universities.

A Roman Jewish delegation met with both the Rothschilds and the pope in Naples. The pope was intransigent. Eventually, with the mediation of Louis Napoleon, he agreed to lift some restrictions on Roman Jews, but only after the transfer of the loan funds and then the passing of some (unspecified) time. The Vatican did not want it to appear that Pius had agreed to a quid pro quo. Meanwhile, James Rothschild, reluctant to jeopardize his relationship with his other clients, the heavily Catholic French and Austrian governments, relented on his demands. The Rothschilds loaned the Vatican fifty million francs, and Pius returned to Rome on April 12, 1850.

Upon his return, the pope issued an amnesty supposedly pardoning the Roman citizenry for rebelling against the papacy. However the pope's generosity was limited because the amnesty did not extend to active participants in the rebellion and the Roman Republic. Given the Rothschild loan, the pontiff also gained a measure of solvency; however, he would never live up to his end of the bargain. The Ghetto would remain a Roman fixture for twenty more years.[76]

Instead, in 1851 Pius appointed another commission concerning the Ghetto, and with that commission's recommendations, he allowed a small number of Jews to reside in restricted areas outside the Ghetto. However, the Jewish community was living with two masters, the Vatican and the French occupying army. On October 25, 1849, French soldiers ransacked the Ghetto in search of rumored stolen treasures that did not exist. (The real crime was the Jews' former support of the defeated Roman Republic.)[77] Then in 1861, the papal police entered the Ghetto, ostensibly to enforce a Vatican rule prohibiting Catholic servants from residing in Jewish homes. Nothing was accomplished by these intrusions other than intimidation.

In the decades after 1850, Ghetto life remained as unpleasant as ever. The renowned historian of Rome Ferdinand Gregorovius wrote *The Ghetto and the Jews of Rome* (1853) to describe the outrageously crowded and unhealthy conditions. His "Lament of the Children of Israel in Rome," a seventeen-verse poem written as a prayer and a dirge spoken by the Ghetto's miserable inhabitants, introduced the book:

Now, in the sweat of our faces,
Day after day we sit before
Our doorsteps; and all our toil
Lengthens with our bitter zeal—
And from every hole and corner
We hunt out our rags and patches
For with loathing hands, the world
Throws us its refuse only.[78]

In the face of this misery, events outside Rome were a storm gaining strength. Within a decade they would overwhelm the pope, the Vatican, the city of Rome, and its Ghetto. Even as the Roman Republic had been thoroughly quashed in 1849, the rest of Italy proceeded apace to unification, a constitutional monarchy, and republican government.[79]

Back in Rome, even with protection from French forces, the pope could be challenged in other ways. In 1858, a Jewish child became the focus of such a challenge.

KIDNAPPING OF EDGARDO MORTARA

Edgardo Mortara and his parents lived in Bologna and, when he was an infant, they employed a Catholic teenage servant, Anna Morisi. When Edgardo was a few years old, he had a mild illness. Anna baptized Edgardo secretly for fear that he would die without the church's comfort.[80]

In Catholic tradition, a baptism does not have to be performed by a priest. Moreover, the water used does not have to be sanctified. As long as the Catholic layperson intends to baptize the child, and as long as it is performed reasonably, the baptism is effective. The church could disapprove of "clandestine" baptisms, and the lay officiant could be punished, but the baptism itself was still recognized as a sacrament.[81]

In Edgardo's case, Anna sprinkled kitchen water over his head when his mother was not looking. Thus he was baptized. Edgardo recovered from his illness and later, Anna left the Mortaras's employ. No one but Anna was the wiser, until she told of the incident to a neighbor's house servant. Thereafter the Inquisition was tipped off concerning the baptism and Anna was summoned to testify. Within days, on a June evening in 1858, the police knocked on the Mortaras's door and, with the barest of explanations to the parents, whisked Edgardo from his home. Anguish followed, and the Mortaras made every protest they could muster, but their son was taken to the Catecumeni in Rome. When the matter came before Pius IX, he determined that Edgardo was a baptized Catholic who could not be returned to his Jewish parents, given the danger they would pose to his soul.

The pope was assailed in newspapers worldwide. The French ambassador to the Vatican intervened for Edgardo and his parents to no avail. The uproar spread to the United States, where the *New York Times* published more than twenty articles concerning Edgardo. Along with the *Baltimore American* and the *Milwaukee Sentinel*, the *Times* pressured President James Buchanan to speak out against the pope.[82] Buchanan, known for being indecisive, was loath to do so. After all, the separation of a child from his parents was a commonplace event in America's slaveholding states in 1858.[83]

The pope never budged on the issue of Edgardo, and the boy grew up to become a priest whose story brought him some notoriety. He died on March 11, 1940.[84] However, for Pius IX, the reverberations of the Mortara affair were not yet over.

A DEFEATED PIUS IX

Feeling besieged, Pius IX struck back with reactionary measures. In 1864 he issued the encyclical *Quanta cura* (How much care), and attached a "syllabus of errors" listing eighty pillars of modernity that he condemned, including, most notably, the freedoms of speech, press, and religion, separation of church and state, and the belief that the papacy was only a spiritual and not a temporal power.

The syllabus of errors was a precursor to the 1869 First Vatican Council called by Pius. After considerable debate, the council declared the pope infallible, if only on occasions when he spoke from his full apostolic power, *ex cathedra* (from the throne). Nevertheless, nine days after being declared infallible, on July 27, 1870, Pius received bad news from the French ambassador: France would be withdrawing its troops from Rome, as they were needed "elsewhere." The French garrison was all that safeguarded Rome from attack by the newly minted nation of Italy. But having lost leverage with the French due to his intransigence concerning Edgardo Mortara, Pius could only listen and shrug his shoulders.[85]

"Elsewhere" meant Paris, which had to be protected from German forces. The Roman garrison needed to come home to play its part in the Franco-Prussian War (ultimately a disaster for France).[86] After the troops' departure, negotiations ensued between the government of Italy and the Vatican for a partition of Rome that would leave the pope sovereign over the Vatican City and nothing else. But Pius IX was unyielding.

Forces of the Kingdom of Italy began to advance toward Rome. On or about September 18, 1870, Pope Pius, seventy-eight, on his knees, crawled up the *scala sancta* (holy staircase)—supposedly the same steps that had once graced Pontius Pilate's Jerusalem palace (it was said that Emperor Constantine's mother had transferred them to Rome in the fourth century). Having climbed those twenty-eight steps, Pius then offered a prayer for the safety of his city.[87]

Two days later, papal prayers notwithstanding, Italian artillery commanded by Captain Segre, an Italian Jew, punched a hole fifty feet wide through the city wall at the Porta Pia on Rome's northern edge.[88] The pope could not muster more than two hundred citizens to come to his aid.[89] On October 2, Rome became the capitol of united Italy. On October 13, the royal decree of King Victor Emmanuel II, monarch of a newly united Italy, abolished any and all religious disabilities previously prevailing in

Rome. Finally, the last existing European ghetto, the Roman Ghetto, was no more; the Jews of Rome were freed.[90]

Nevertheless, the pope, in high dudgeon, called for the full dismantling of the Italian state, an impossibility by anyone else's measure. Pius and his successors then remained confined, of their own choice, inside the Vatican for the next fifty years.[91]

9

Backyard Exiles

The Jews in Fascist Rome

"I should be grateful to Mussolini. He made me realize that I myself was a Jew."[1]

In one acerbic sentence, the Italian novelist Elsa Morante epitomized her wartime experience of surviving both Fascist Italy (1922–43) and the Nazi occupation of Rome (1943–44). Her contemporary, the writer Natalia Ginzburg, said the same: "My Jewish identity became extremely important to me from the moment the Jews began to be persecuted. At that point I became aware of myself as a Jew."[2]

A third Jewish writer, Carla Pekelis, reflected that being Jewish in Rome between 1907 and 1924 was "like nothing, nothing at all"—this despite the fact that Rome's Jewish population tripled between 1870 and the 1930s.[3] Looking back, we might say that if you have to thank Mussolini for your discovering your Judaism, there was, most likely, a problem to begin with. Or, to put it in historical terms: during the generation preceding Mussolini, many Italian Jews traded some or all of their Jewish identity for what seemed like a secure place in a modern, liberal, democratic state. That turned out to be a very bad bargain.

In the second decade of the twentieth century, Fascism, a reaction to the horrors of World War I and the Bolshevik revolution, became the totalitarian governing ideology of Italy. While initially not hostile to the tiny Italian Jewish minority, the Fascist government came to believe that antisemitism would benefit the new Italian order. From 1921 through 1943, Jewish assimilation and acculturation would be overtaken by hatred and persecution.

Even before 1870, when Italian forces took Rome, Pope Pius IX refused to recognize the legitimacy of the Italian nation—a position the Vatican would not alter for two generations. Accordingly, Jewish Romans, newly liberated from the Ghetto, now entered a severely divided polity. After 1870, Rome quickly became a secular society, and in 1871, the capitol of Italy. However, it existed in defiance of the Catholic Church, which leveled unremitting criticism at any Italian government attempts to take its place in modern Europe.[4] Meanwhile, the church considered Jews to be agents of that despised modernity, given their love for the secular world that had granted them freedom.

In short, in the conflict between the Vatican and the nation of Italy, Italy's Jews stood with the nation. Throughout Italy, Jews—who as a group were better educated than most Italians—took advantage of their country's opportunities and enthusiastically supported the new state. By 1874 there were eleven Jewish members of Parliament, and fifteen members twenty years later. The first Jewish prime minister of Italy, Luigi Luzzati (1841–1927), was elected in 1910. A minister of war, Giuseppe Ottolenghi (1838–1904), was a Jew.[5] Ernesto Nathan (1845–1921), a follower of the revolutionary thinker and activist Giuseppe Mazzini, served as mayor of Rome from 1907 to 1913, much to the Vatican's chagrin. Nathan took it upon himself to modernize Rome, with improvements in education, municipal transportation, and sanitation. A vigorous advocate for urban renewal (and fighter against corrupt real estate speculation), he once retorted to colleagues: "You talk, gentlemen, as if Rome were a corpse, and I decline to embalm her."[6] Concurrently, the Vatican criticized him in its official press for being a modernist and Freemason as well as a Jew.[7]

The Vatican's journalistic response to Nathan was part of a larger anti-Jewish campaign particularly expressed in two Catholic periodicals: *Civiltà*

FIG. 7. Italian stamp featuring Ernesto Nathan, mayor of Rome, 1907–13.

cattolica (Catholic civilization), a bimonthly Jesuit journal, and *L'osservatore Romano* (Roman observer), a daily Roman newspaper owned by the Holy See.

Father Giuseppe Oreglia di Santo Stefano, one of the journal's founders, would undertake the earliest attacks against Jews in *Civiltà cattolica* starting in 1868. For hundreds of years, Oreglia wrote, Jews had lived happily in their ghettos, protected by the church, while the Catholic community had been protected from the Jews. However, with liberation, "the Jewish race . . . immediately becomes the persecutor, oppressor, tyrant, thief and devastator of the countries where it lives."[8]

A proponent of the idea that Jews were more a race than a religion, Oreglia insisted that even if Jews rejected Judaism and converted, that change was a pretense: Jews would always remain Jews, retaining the racial proclivities they were born with. While he attempted to temper his vitriol with declarations of Christian love for Jews, these statements were themselves tempered by exhortations to, nevertheless, act against the evil Jews committed. Much of his hostility was directed at talmudic Judaism, which he slanderously maligned as requiring that Jews persecute and even exterminate non-Jews.[9]

By the 1890s, Fathers Raffaele Ballerini and Saverio Rondina, writing in *Civiltà cattolica*, were reprising many of the same canards. In 1893, Rondina promulgated this classic antisemitic trope: "It [Judaism] is the giant octopus that with its oversized tentacles envelops everything. It has its stomach in the banks . . . and its suction cups everywhere: in contracts and monopolies . . . in postal services and telegraph companies, in shipping and in the railroads, in the town treasuries and in state finance. It represents the kingdom of capital . . . , the aristocracy of gold."[10]

Many quarters of Europe were backing away from antisemitism, and so Ballerini and Rondina found it necessary to deny that they were hate mongering. They were only issuing a warning: "We do not write with any intention of sparking or fomenting any anti-Semitism in our country. Rather, we seek to sound an alarm for Italians so that they defend themselves against those who, in order to impoverish them, dominate them and make them their slaves, interfere with their faith, corrupt their morals and suck their blood."[11] Other pieces published in *Civiltà cattolica* referred to Italy as the "Kingdom of the Jews" and Rome "the capitol of Jewry."[12]

If it could be said that *Civiltà cattolica* shrank from the "antisemitism" label, the *Osservatore Romano* embraced it. In 1892, it distinguished between good and bad antisemitism. Good antisemitism was "natural, sober, thoughtful" and "Christian." Bad antisemitism resulted in the persecution of Jews; but bad antisemitism was actually a type of Judaism, since Jews provoked their own persecution in order to garner sympathy. Hence, bad antisemitism was a Jewish byproduct, and true antisemitism was simply good practice: "True antisemitism 'is and can be in substance nothing other than Christianity completed and perfected in Catholicism.'"[13]

Along with Catholic periodicals, Italian pulp fiction often used antisemitic themes. Serialized novels like Carolina Invernizio's *L'Orfana del Ghetto* (The orphan of the Ghetto), published in 1887, employed a host of antisemitic stereotypes, including Jewish avarice, filth, lust, and the blood libel, while employing such hackneyed plot devices as children switched at birth, false identities, and fraudulent marriages. Consequently, popular antisemitic literature often created a fictional single family of Catholics and Jews connected by blood, inadvertence, and mistakes, thus restating what Belli had satirically addressed half a century earlier: the dire consequences of sexual relations between Jews and Catholics. Along with the authors' moralizing was the implicit admission that Jews and Catholics often found themselves involuntarily enmeshed in familial relationships.[14]

JEWS BECOMING ITALIANS

While familial relations between Jews and Catholics were only a theoretical problem in Belli's 1830s Rome, this was not so for the aforementioned Invernizio in the 1880s. With the Ghetto's liberation in 1870, what the Catholic Church had dreaded for hundreds of years—Jewish-Catholic marriages—became reality. For its own reasons, the official Jewish community was similarly averse to the marital mixing of Jews and Catholics: Jewish newspapers featured cautionary tales of Jewish heroines falling for Catholic men, with predictably miserable results. But ultimately, free people would have their own say.[15]

Reliable numbers concerning mixed marriages in the years right after Italian unification and the liberation of the Roman Ghetto are not available, but it is clear that Jews exploded into the modern world, excelling in almost every aspect of Italian society.[16] In Rome, though, that explosion was muted by the Jewish community's abject poverty; in 1900, free matzah had to be distributed during Passover to most of the city's Jews.[17] By the 1938 census, mixed marriages accounted for 43.7 percent of all Italian Jewish marriages, but in Rome—where most of the Jews were still indigent given their long Ghetto history, and hence probably had fewer marital options—the intermarriage rate was only 8 percent.[18]

Even if most Roman Jews did not intermarry, they began to lose interest in traditional Jewish life. In 1891, the Italian Rabbinical College was moved to Rome from Padua, but it failed to attract students. The secular city, not the rabbinate, offered more opportunities to young men.[19] Roman Jewry was engaged in a confrontation with modernity. In or about 1890, in recognition of women's growing independence in Roman and Jewish society, Rome's Chief Rabbi Mosè Ehrenreich introduced the bat mitzvah ceremony to the Roman community.[20] The decision to approve a ceremony parallel to the bar mitzvah grew out of classes Rabbi Ehrenreich had inaugurated for women at the Institute for Talmud Torah. Even traditional Roman Judaism was trying to keep up with the times.

At roughly the same time, the Jewish community decided to replace the Cinque Scole, the house of worship in the Ghetto since 1555. Work started on the Great Synagogue, sited on the east bank of the Tiber, in 1901, and despite financial difficulties, the majestic building with its square cupola atop a Romanesque roof was completed in 1904. On July 2 of that year, three weeks before its inauguration, King Victor Emmanuel III of Italy visited the new temple, accompanied by all the rabbis of Rome.[21] The presence of this Great Synagogue would alter the urban plan of the surrounding neighborhood and spur urban renewal in the Ghetto area.[22]

Some Roman Jews had found ways to improve their economic circumstances.[23] Additionally, with the Ghetto's liberation, Jews across Italy arrived in Rome, bringing considerable wealth. More prosperous Jews moved away from the Ghetto area to live and do business, with the wealthier Jews going the farthest afield.[24] This population shift necessitated the establishment, in 1914, of a new synagogue: the Oratorio di Castro, just between the Esquiline and Quirinale hills.[25]

On the eve of World War I, Italian and Roman Jews were seeking to integrate themselves into the new Italian state either through assimilation (merging with the larger culture while abandoning most or all elements of Jewish life) or acculturation (adopting trappings of the Italian world while changing, but not abandoning, Jewish traditions). An example of one who straddled both worlds is Augusto Segre, a rabbi, Zionist, partisan, and author of the autobiography *Memories of Jewish Life from Italy to Jerusalem, 1918–1960*, who considered himself both a warrior against assimilation, in supporting the traditional Judaism of his father (also a rabbi), and a thoroughly modern Italian, in engaging in public life and fighting in the Italian resistance during World War II. Together, Jewish assimilation and

FIG. 8. Interior of the Oratorio di Castro synagogue. Photo by Massimo Listri. Copyright Historical Archives of the Jewish Community of Rome, Giancarlo Spizzichino.

acculturation in the early twentieth century brought Roman Jews closer to their Italian neighbors.

One measure of Jewish assimilationist success was the poet Crescenzo Del Monte's nostalgic preservation of Roman Ghetto life. His nostalgia is a recognition of what had been lost. Del Monte sought to conserve the colorful speech patterns of Ghetto residents, and composed sonnets in the Roman Jewish dialect about the poorer members of the Ghetto, sharing their imagined nineteenth-century conversations. In one sonnet, "Lo Parentato" ("The Engagement"), written in 1895 but depicting life forty years earlier, two female gossips pick apart the impending marriage of a not-very-attractive bride to an unpromising groom, and the financial arrangements underlying the match.[26]

Another measure of Roman Jewry's assimilation was the failure of modernizing Jewish movements, such as Reform Judaism. Reform was unpopular in Italy, not because Italian Jews were conservative, but because they were too busy becoming Italians. The Italian Jewish community from top to bottom saw the modern world more as an opportunity than a challenge. In the early 1900s, a survey of Italian Jews found little to no observance of kashrut laws, but considerable participation in the circumcision of infant boys. In other words, Jews were steadfast in their Jewish identity while neglecting Judaism in their everyday lives.[27] As one historian has said: "The true instrument of the transformation and modernization of the Jewish condition was Italianization."[28]

Jews who had supported Italian unification understood World War I as a defining moment for a generation. For almost the first time, Jews, along with other Italian citizens, were called to fight for their country.[29] Believing the war to be the final battle of the Risorgimento, after which Italy would take its place among the powers of Europe, Jews served with distinction throughout the Italian military.[30] Many were decorated. For that reason, and despite the church's strident antisemitism, both Jews and non-Jews commonly held that there was no antisemitism in Italy.[31] However, that was soon to be proven false.

FASCISM AND ITS JEWISH SUPPORTERS

Italianization was a prelude to the Jewish community's encounter with Fascism. Benito Mussolini (1883–1945) inaugurated his antisemitic career with writings in 1908 and 1913 that cast Jews as instrumental in the fall of the Roman Empire.[32] In 1919, Mussolini wrote about international Jewish bankers "who seek revenge against the Aryan Race."[33] Nevertheless, early on Mussolini enjoyed modest Jewish support. Some 750 Italian Jews were card-carrying Fascists, even from the days of Mussolini's 1922 March on Rome, a paramilitary demonstration wherein thousands of Fascist supporters, including 230 Jews, trekked across Italy, arriving in Rome on October 28 to seize control of the central government ministries. Dante Almansi, deputy chief of police, and Emanuele Pugliese, commander of

Rome's garrison, both Jews, awaited orders to defend Rome. Also prepared to fight the Fascists, the serving prime minister of Italy, Luigi Facta, asked King Victor Emmanuel III for his signature on an order declaring a state of emergency throughout the peninsula, but the king refused to sign. Instead, to avoid bloodshed, he capitulated and asked Mussolini to form a government.[34]

In the next few days Mussolini formed a cabinet, a coalition of Fascists and Liberals. He made sure that he occupied the twin positions of minister of internal affairs and minister of foreign affairs.[35] The Jewish community was divided on Fascism, but immediately after his takeover Mussolini made cordial gestures toward Jews, such as his letter to the Genoese rabbi, G. Sonino. The rabbi had congratulated Mussolini after the king's capitulation and Mussolini responded, "Distinguished Rabbi, I received your letter and reply to express my gratitude and positive feelings. I count upon all those who really love Italy. Consider me devoted to you."[36]

Mussolini's writings about Jews now included both philosemitic statements (delivered to Jewish audiences) and antisemitic ones (in secular papers). In 1928, Mussolini, writing in the Italian Zionist weekly *Israel*, disclaimed any antisemitism when it came to Fascism: "Fascist anti-semitism, or anti-Semitic Fascism, is an absurdity."[37] Yet that same year he wrote in the Fascist newspaper *Il popolo di Roma* (The people of Rome) that Italian Christians should be disturbed about the presence of a "guest" people in Italy who profess a different religion and who stay "among us like oil amid water."[38] His occasional philosemitic statements were apparently intended to thwart reprisals from Jewish financiers, among others. As he said in 1932, "I have no love for the Jew, but they have great influence everywhere. It is better to leave them alone."[39]

ZIONISM

Amid a headlong stampede toward Italianization and an underlying, church-endorsed antisemitism, Zionism, the belief in a Jewish homeland in Palestine, had become part of the Italian Jewish landscape. In 1904, Theodor Herzl, founder of modern political Zionism, had met with King Victor

Emmanuel III in Rome as part of his campaign for a Jewish state, and the king assured him that in Italy, no distinction was made between Jews and Christians.[40] Jews, in turn, were careful to acknowledge their good fortune in Italy, and their lack of any desire to emigrate to the Jewish homeland themselves. Early on, before the First World War, Zionism was a charitable movement in Italy—raising money for others, namely the Jews in Eastern Europe.[41] Yet during the war, when Italy was in conflict with Turkey, the notion that a Jewish presence would replace Turkish rule in Palestine gained favor with Italians in general as well as Jews. Victor Emmanuel III expressed "sympathy" for the Zionist vision, and Italy approved Britain's 1917 Balfour Declaration expressing support for a national home for the Jewish people in Palestine.[42]

As Mussolini grew to power in Italy, he changed his position regarding Zionism to the extent that it might prove useful to him as a politician. While his early publications in the paper he founded in 1914, *Il popolo d'Italia*, were pro-Zionist, once he decided, in the late 1920s, to make Catholicism the state religion of Italy, Mussolini espoused Catholicism's view that the Holy Land should be internationalized and that Catholic nations like Italy should participate, along with Great Britain, in the League of Nations Mandate in Palestine.[43] This Catholic sentiment supported Mussolini's understanding that Britain, Italy's rival for control of the Mediterranean, was using the Jewish presence in Palestine to thwart his ambitions for a new Roman Empire.[44] For Mussolini, it was more important that Italy, rather than the Jews, have a presence in Palestine.

The church's position regarding a Jewish state was summarized in *The Moncalvos*, a 1908 novel by the Jewish writer Enrico Castelnuovo about assimilated Italian Jews. The fictional Monsignor de Lucchi, a confidante of the (also fictional) Jewish banker Gabrio Moncalvo, explains to Gabrio: "The Church will not permit the rise of an Israelite Kingdom in the same place as the tomb of Christ, but it doesn't disapprove of the emigration of Hebrews toward whatever region where they can live in peace. It will be all the more probable that those who are assimilated into our civilization will embrace our faith."[45] Mussolini held the same position as the church: it was all well and good for Jews to live in the Holy Land, but they must not establish a Jewish state there. His early attitude toward Zionism reflected his desire to reach agreement with the Catholic Church as well as his global political ambitions.

Nevertheless, when it suited him, Mussolini met with the Zionist luminary Chaim Weizmann, first in 1923 and then several other times, often expressing his devotion to Zionism.[46] Weizmann, however, was not fooled. In 1923, after his first meeting with Mussolini, Weizmann warned of both antisemitism in Italy and "the tremendous political wave known as Fascism."[47]

Weizmann met with Mussolini again in 1926 when he lobbied for increased immigration to Palestine through the Italian port of Trieste. The Italian dictator expressed his support for a Jewish state in Palestine against the interests of Great Britain, but no official act was taken after the meeting.[48] Revisionist Zionists, resolutely anti-British and led by Ze'ev Jabotinsky, sent students to the Jewish section of the Maritime School at Citivecchia (a coastal town northwest of Rome) to train for an incipient Jewish navy, but after some students were caught attempting to smuggle Jews into Palestine—and their training vessel ran aground near the mouth of the Golo River on the French Island of Corsica—Italian authorities shuttered the school. Mussolini himself never met with Jabotinsky, and ultimately the Jewish leader broke off ties with him when his antisemitic policies became evident.[49]

By 1928, the Duce (literally "duke," a popular title for Mussolini) seemed to take an ominous wait-and-see attitude toward a Jewish state. Surprisingly, he felt it necessary to write an article in the Zionist newspaper, *Israel*. The article was anonymous in that it had no byline, but the author's identity was clear to most readers: "As long as Palestinian Zionism remains in what I will call its national preparation phase, we can accept in good faith that this does not disturb the relationships between the Jews and their fellow citizens in other countries; but once Zionism goes on to create a national state, such relationships will be radically reexamined by governments because you cannot belong to two homelands at the same time, or be a citizen of two states."[50]

Yet by 1934 he had switched positions again, probably in response to a public statement issued by the Rome Zionist Group. Aware that Zionism raised the specter of dual loyalties, the group had made a simple analogy. "What would I say to someone who asked me which was greater—the love and affection of a child toward his father or toward his mother? These feelings can coexist—neither one is destined to negate the other."[51] A month later, Mussolini, writing in *Il popolo d'Italia*, supported not only a Jewish home in Palestine but a "true and proper state" for Jews.[52]

However, most often Mussolini distinguished between his support for a Jewish state in Palestine, which was useful for his international aspirations, and Italian Jewish support for Zionism, which he considered a sign of disloyalty to the Italian nation and hence issued not-so-veiled threats to Jews to act only as patriotic Italians.[53] At the same time, when taking a position against Zionism, he mostly disavowed antisemitism. Many Jews agreed with Mussolini, including his foreign ministers of Jewish origin, Sidney Sonnino and Carlo Schanzer.[54]

THE LATERAN ACCORDS

The Fascist flirtation with Zionism was a sideshow compared to Mussolini's interest in the Catholic Church. Since 1860, the church had not recognized the legitimacy of Italy, and since 1870, the pope had self-sequestered in the Vatican. However, in 1926, Pope Pius XI (1922–39) seized on an opportunity. Impressed that Mussolini had jettisoned the liberal idea of the separation of church and state, and happy for Fascist Italy to be a "Catholic Nation,"[55] Pius declared in the Vatican newspaper *L'osservatore Romano* that through direct negotiations, there could be rapprochement between Italy and the church.[56]

The Lateran Accords of 1929, named after the church where they were signed, constituted a treaty between Italy and the Vatican. Italy recognized Catholicism as the state religion and Vatican City as a sovereign territory. The Vatican was also granted territorial rights to Rome's basilicas and Castel Gandolfo, the papal summer palace southeast of Rome. Catholic feast days became public holidays, and the state recognized religious marriages as valid, while Catholic religious instruction became mandatory in all elementary and secondary schools.[57] In turn, the church recognized the legitimacy of the Italian state, and Italy compensated the church for the loss of the Papal State with a payment of 750 million lire and one billion lire in bonds. Foreign governments would send separate diplomatic missions to Italy and the Vatican.[58]

The accords made Jews nervous. In New York City, it was rumored that Jews were to be banished from Italy and all Italian synagogues would be shuttered.[59] Mussolini moved to allay those fears. On May 13, 1929, the Duce addressed the Italian parliament: "It is ridiculous to think, as it has been said, that it will be necessary to close the synagogues. The Jews have been in Rome since the time of the Kings; perhaps they provided the clothes after the rape of the Sabines. They were fifty thousand at the time of Augustus and they asked to weep over the dead body of Julius Caesar. They shall not be disturbed."[60]

Then on October 17, 1929, the minister of justice and religious affairs proposed legislation to make the Jewish community part and parcel of the national Fascist administration.[61] Largely reassured that their government affirmed their community's right to exist, the Jews created a commemorative gold medal to honor the new law.[62] Still, every Jew was constrained to register with one Jewish community or another, and the age-old waffling by some Jews concerning "Who is a Jew?" became an administrative matter under a totalitarian regime.[63] Ultimately, it would become a matter of life and death.

JEWISH ANTI-FASCISTS

While the church was accommodating itself to Fascism, and while many Jews happily accepted government regimentation of the Jewish community, a significant number of other Jews were active anti-Fascists. Most notoriously, in March 1934 two Jews, Mario Levi and Sion Segre, were detained at the Italian-Swiss border for carrying illegal anti-Fascist publications. Mario escaped back into Switzerland, but Sion was captured.[64] Police headquarters in Rome then ordered the arrest of sixteen members of the non-Marxist anti-Fascist group Giustizia e Libertà (justice and liberty), eleven of whom were Jews.[65] Yet only the eleven Jewish anti-Fascists were "tried" in the press, and only two of them, Sion Segre and Leone Ginzburg, were tried in the Italian courts and given prison sentences. Thus Jewish membership in Giustizia e Libertà was heralded to the public.

A year later, the artist Carlo Levi, one of the original arrestees, was arrested again, and this time sentenced to *confino*, exile within Italy. The Fascist state used *confino* to punish political dissidents: persons considered enemies of the state were exiled to the most remote and backward Italian villages, where their confinement was enforced through daily registration at the local police station. The government would give the exiles a meager stipend, but generally they had to find a way to live in impoverished circumstances.[66] According to Levi's subsequent memoir, *Christ Stopped at Eboli*, during the two years he lived in Gagliano, 1935–36, he became the town's physician, despite never having practiced medicine (he had, however, been educated as a doctor).[67] After Italy's victory in its war with Ethiopia (1935–37), a celebratory amnesty gave Levi his release from *confino*.

In his memoir, Carlo Levi never identified himself as a Jew. Although at one point in the book he slipped into Hebrew, referring to himself as *rofe* (doctor), the villagers knew him as "Don Carlo." With his Judaism erased, *Christ Stopped at Eboli* was, among other things, a fantasy of assimilation. At a time when the Fascist regime's hostility to both Jews and liberal democrats thwarted secular Jews like Levi in their path to assimilation, Levi provided a vision of a simple, genuine Italy where he could be an Italian and nothing more.

JEWISH IMMIGRATION

After 1929, the Jews of Italy became embroiled in international politics. Of primary importance was the Nazi takeover of Germany in 1933. Jews were certainly better off in Italy than in Germany, and so immediately in 1933, immigration of German Jews to Italy began. The initially small number of refugees increased by approximately five hundred persons per year. In October 1934 German Jewish refugees to Italy totaled a thousand;

by October 1936 that number had increased to close to two thousand. Between 1931 and 1938 the number of foreign Jews in Italy grew from 12 percent to 21.5 percent of the Italian Jewish population, and roughly 50 percent of those were either Germans or Poles. While the numbers of Jews leaving Germany for other countries was much higher—annual Jewish immigration from Germany between 1931 and 1938 averaged around thirty thousand persons[68]—still, it is remarkable that at a time when Italy and Germany were becoming allies, Italy was nonetheless accepting Jews fleeing the Nazis. Until August 1939, a Jew could enter Italy from Germany on a tourist visa.[69]

Simultaneously, some Jews were leaving Italy. Among them were the Rosselli brothers, Carlo and Nello, both born in Rome. By 1924, at age 24, Nello, the younger brother, was delivering a speech at the Jewish Youth Convention in Livorno decisively rejecting Zionism, but just as passionately declaring himself a Jew:

> I am a Jew who doesn't go to the temple on the Sabbath, who doesn't speak Hebrew, who is completely unobservant. And yet I am attached to my Jewish identity. . . . I can't say that this idea of the motherland to be reconquered, of the land where the Jewish people will reunite, has moved me at all, not even once. I would add more: inside me there is the foundation of my entire being, the consciousness of a citizen who is part of his own country, who loves his homeland, criticizes it, rejects it, adores it, who really feels its presence.[70]

Nello's brother Carlo, a socialist (albeit an anti-Marxist and anti-Stalinist), was arrested in 1929 for engineering the anti-Fascist warrior Filippo Turati's escape to France and sentenced to *confino* on Lipari, an island off the northern coast of Sicily.[71] Escaping in 1929, he was able to get to Paris, where he joined his brother Nello, and the two along with others founded the anti-Fascist revolutionary movement, Giustizia e Libertà. After fighting against Mussolini's army and others in the Spanish Civil War, Carlo returned to Paris. On June 9, 1937, while visiting the resort town of

Bagnoles de L'Orne in Normandy, Carlo and Nello were assassinated by French Fascists most probably in the employ of the Italian government.[72] Jews could leave Italy during the 1930s, but if they opposed Fascism while expatriates, they were in grave danger.

Jewish life in Italy took a turn for the worse in 1935 with the Italian invasion of Ethiopia. The war in East Africa fed Mussolini's desire for a revived Roman Empire, but achieving that goal posed difficulties. Ethiopia was a member of the League of Nations established after World War I, and Mussolini's invasion, a barbarous attack on a sovereign state that would ultimately cost 250,000 Ethiopian lives, was in violation of the league's covenants.[73] In response, in 1935 the league ordered economic sanctions preventing the sale of weapons to Italy. Before quitting the league and ignoring the sanctions, the Italian government pressed Italian Jews to urge the Jewish community in Great Britain to pressure their government to loosen the sanctions—a naïve initiative evidencing Mussolini's belief in an influential and international Jewish power.[74]

Two months after the invasion began, in another effort to surmount the sanctions, the Italian government staged a *Giornata della fede* (Day of faith or Day of the wedding ring, *fede* meaning both "faith" and "wedding ring"). On December 18, 1935, Italian citizens were required to give their gold to shore up the nation's coffers. Every woman, Christian and Jewish, was to donate her wedding ring to the nation.[75] For Jews, the synagogue service on the Day of Faith featured the Royal Savoy March honoring Italy's king, the Fascist anthem "Giovanezza" (Youth), and a patriotic sermon. In Rome, Rabbi Aldo Lattes declaimed: "Falling short today in the duty we owe the Fatherland would be a betrayal not only before mankind but before the Lord! . . . Strip from your houses all foreign products, make every possible economy and give, give gold to the Fatherland."[76]

Implicit in the donation was a wedding between the Jewish community and Italy. In keeping with the concept of the gift as an exchange, many Jews likely expected that the gift of their jewelry to the state would incur an obligation on Mussolini's part to return the favor—a fateful misunderstanding of the Duce that would become evident in the years ahead.[77]

Italy's 1936 conquest of Ethiopia also changed the lives of the Beta Israel (House of Israel). These Ethiopian Jews, then commonly known as Falashas (a derogatory term meaning "landless") had never followed rabbinic tradition, but nevertheless identified themselves as Jews. When the Beta Israel became subjects of Mussolini's Italian Empire, the Italian Jewish community began a government-approved program to Italianize them.[78] Meanwhile, however, some Italian Fascists were attempting to settle Italian Jews in Ethiopia, with the African country serving as an interim Jewish homeland until Italy could create a Jewish state in Palestine.[79] Thus the Arab world would be placated, because pressure was being taken off Palestine for the moment, and Italy would resolve the ever-growing problem of Jewish refugees entering from Nazi Germany.

On February 17, 1934, Mussolini met again with Chaim Weizmann. Mussolini boasted to Weizmann: "You must create a Jewish state. I have already spoken with the Arabs. I think we can reach an agreement."[80] For his part, Weizmann pledged a "team" of Jewish chemists to create a chemical industry in Italy. Neither leader was doing more than posturing. Weizmann, massaging the dictator's ego, ended the meeting by requesting a signed copy of the Duce's photograph for his wife. Mussolini could hardly say no.[81]

Mussolini's meeting with Nahum Goldman (1895–1982), another prominent Zionist, was of real consequence. The Saar Valley, ceded to France after World War I under a League of Nations mandate, was to be returned to Germany, if ratified through a plebiscite.[82] Goldman met with Mussolini to ask that he intercede for Jews living in the Saar who wanted to leave if it became part of the Reich. They wanted to be allowed to leave with their possessions and their French currency. Mussolini agreed: "I shall force Germany to allow Saar Jews to leave with their money. That's it. Consider it done." And it was done. An agreement between France and Germany, signed in Rome on December 3, 1934, allowed Jews to leave the Saar with all their possessions within one year of the plebiscite of January 1, 1935.[83]

At the same meeting with Goldman, Mussolini spoke expansively about a Jewish state: "I am a Zionist myself. I have already told Dr. Weizmann. You must have a real state and not the ridiculous National Home the British have offered you. I will help you create a Jewish State. The most important thing is for the Jews to be confident in their future and not let themselves be scared by that idiot in Berlin."[84]

Four years later, on May 3, 1938, Mussolini hosted "that idiot in Berlin" in Rome. Adolf Hitler's ceremonial trip celebrated the Berlin-Rome Axis formed in 1936.[85] Nazi Germany's persecution of the Jews never came up, and the possibility of any civil unrest during the visit was thwarted by the preparatory arrest and imprisonment of all immigrant German Jews in Rome, Naples, and Florence. Despite his admiration for Mussolini, Hitler did not trust the Italian authorities, and so German operatives installed in Italian police offices carried out the arrests. By contrast, native Roman and Italian Jews were free to walk the streets. Some were even officers in the Italian army paraded before the Führer.[86]

THE POPE AND HITLER

The question remained: would the pope receive Hitler as a head of state? Pius XI and the Führer despised one another. Hitler referred to Pius XI as the "Chief Rabbi of the Western World."[87] The pope had made his position evident a year before this visit, when he delivered *Mit brennender Sorge* (With deep anxiety), a papal encyclical denouncing racism. It was written in German so that, after having been smuggled into Germany, it could be read from the pulpit on Palm Sunday, March 21, 1937, in German churches. It began "It is with deep anxiety and growing surprise that we have been following the painful trials of the [German] Church and the increasing vexations which afflict those who have remained loyal in heart and action. . . . None but superficial minds could stumble into concepts of a national religion; or attempt to lock within the frontiers of a single people, within the narrow limits of a single race, God, the Creator of the Universe."[88]

While the bull did not mention Nazism, antisemitism, or Jews, Hitler got the message: the Gestapo confiscated all copies of the statement it could find. Meanwhile, the 1933 concordat between the church and Hitler's Germany, an agreement similar to the Lateran Accords, was allowed to remain intact.[89]

During the Führer's visit, Pius snubbed Hitler by leaving Rome for his summer palace in Castel Gandolfo and ordering the Vatican museums closed, thus insuring that Hitler did not set foot in the Vatican. As a diplomatic civility, the church agreed to keep all foreigners with anti-Nazi sympathies residing in the Vatican under surveillance.[90]

THE RACIAL LAWS

If anyone, including the Nazis, had any doubt concerning Italian policy toward Jews, they had only to read the public announcement *Informazione diplomatica no. 14* of February 16, 1938. Written by Mussolini, it gave Italy's Jews little with one hand and took much away with the other:

> Recent journalistic disputes may have created the impression . . . that the Fascist Government is on the point of initiating an anti-Semitic policy. Responsible circles in Rome are in a position to affirm that such impressions are completely erroneous and consider that these polemics are due to the fact that the currents of international anti-Fascism are regularly directed by Jewish elements. The responsible circles in Rome are of the opinion that the universal Jewish problem will be solved in one way only: by the creation in some part of the world, not in Palestine, of a Jewish State, a State in the full sense of the word, in a position to represent and safeguard the entire Jewish masses scattered in various lands. . . . The Fascist government has never thought nor is it thinking of adopting political, economic or moral measures against the Jews as such, except, clearly in cases involving elements hostile to the regime. . . . The Fascist Government, nevertheless, reserves the right to keep a watch upon the activities of Jews recently arrived in our country and to see to it that the share of the Jews

in the national life should not be disproportionate to the intrinsic merits of the individual and the numerical importance of their community.[91]

Despite the disclaimers about Fascist antisemitism, the *Informazione* clearly stated that (1) Jewish hopes for a state in Palestine would not be supported, (2) foreign Jews were under surveillance, and (3) the Jewish role in national life was unacceptably large given the small Jewish percentage of the Italian population. Jews comprised fewer than 1 percent of the Italian people. After February 1938, if they were to appear in public life in the same proportion as their population, they could expect to play almost no role in government, the media, the military, or education.

Five months later, on July 14, 1938, Mussolini put his cards on the table with a *Manifesto of Racial Scientists*. He had tasked a previously unknown anthropologist, Guido Landra, to put forth the racial precepts that would henceforth guide the Fascist regime. Signed by Italian academics (most but not all of them obscure; Edoardo Zavattari, the prominent director of the University of Rome's Institute of Zoology was an exception), the *Manifesto* made the following points:

1. Human races exist as a scientific fact.
2. Large races and small races exist.
3. The concept of race is purely biological.
4. The population of Italy is Aryan and Italy's culture is Aryan.
5. The racial composition of Italy has not changed over one thousand years.
6. A pure Italian "race" exists in the twentieth century.
7. Italians must openly declare themselves racists.
8. Mediterraneans, like Italians, are separate from the Oriental and African races.
9. Marriage is only admissible between members of the European races.[92]

The *Manifesto* mentioned Jews in one additional paragraph: "Jews do not belong to the Italian Race. . . . The Jews represent the only population which has never assimilated in Italy because it is made up of racial elements which are not European, differing absolutely from the elements that make up the Italians."[93] With black humor, Jews nicknamed the *Manifesto* "The Decalogue," comparing its ten paragraphs to the Ten Commandments.

It is not easy to explain Mussolini's extreme turn toward antisemitism. It has been suggested that the Ethiopian war played a significant part. When Italian Jews were unable to influence their British coreligionists concerning the League of Nations sanctions, Mussolini may have felt that Jews, for all their supposed financial power, were unable or unwilling to help out Fascist Italy. At the same time, the Italian victory in Ethiopia gave rise to a virulent racism aimed at preventing "cross breeding" between Italians—the dominant race—and Ethiopians, the "negro" and "dominated" race. Once that racial view became articulated, similar attitudes toward the Jewish "race" followed. And of course, there was the issue of Nazi Germany. Italian Jews were sympathetic toward their German brethren and equally hostile to Nazism. That conflict between a portion of the Italian population and an Italian ally was intolerable.

Thus in 1938 Fascist Italy began to systematically persecute Jews.[94] On August 5, the Fascist government released *Informazione diplomatica no. 18*. A clarification of the *Informazione no. 14* of February, the new public announcement explained: "The Fascist government has no special plan to persecute the Jews. . . . There are 44,000 Jews in the metropolitan territory of Italy; the proportion would be one Jew for every thousand inhabitants. It is clear that from now on the proportion of the Jews in the total life of the state must be, and shall be, adjusted in the same proportion."[95]

Simultaneously, the Fascist government sponsored the creation of *La difesa della razza* (The defense of the race), a magazine aimed at promoting a racist consciousness in Italy. On its glossy, lavishly illustrated pages, long-standing Catholic antisemitism mixed with contemporary pseudoscientific jargon about "race" and "blood" under the guise of modern science. Like the pulp fiction of the late 1800s, *La difesa della razza* was obsessed with interracial marriages, as "The Half-Breeds of the Rhineland," "Half Breeds of the Americas," "Negro-Chinese Hybrids," and other such articles attested.[96]

Yet despite the Fascist government's claims not to have any "special plan to persecute the Jews," shortly after the first issue of *La difesa della razza* hit the newsstands, the regime began issuing decrees specifying how the persecution of Jews should be carried out. It was not sufficient to simply make pronouncements about Jews and Aryans; specific steps had to be taken. On September 5, 1938, all Jewish students (with the exception of university students) were expelled from Italian schools. All Jewish teachers and professors were suspended from teaching at every level of Italian education. Jewish university teachers were dismissed by a brief note that read in its entirety: "Your personal records show that you belong to the Jewish race. You have therefore been suspended from service beginning October 16, 1938 XVI in accordance with Royal Decree Law 5-9-1938 No. 1390."[97] On September 23, Jews were allowed to establish their own schools using the Jewish faculty fired by the previous decree.

Having put the cart before the horse, on November 17, 1938, a decree was issued defining who was a Jew. Basically, a child of Jewish parents was a Jew. If the parents' status was unclear, the definitional problem was to be pushed back a generation. However, this was rarely the case, given the government-mandated census of 1938 and the further mandated enrollment by Jews in their local congregations.

More difficult was classifying children of mixed marriages. If three-quarters of the grandparents were Jewish, the grandchildren qualified as Jewish. The date of October 1, 1938, was established as the cut-off point for Jews who had converted from Judaism to Christianity; afterward, Jews who converted would still legally be Jewish. Given the Lateran Accords, the Italian government could not prevent conversion to Catholicism—but it could devise its own legal and racial definition of a Jew that was in conflict with Catholicism's religious definition. Finally, according to the law, a person was either Jewish or not; there were no persons of mixed race. Thus children of Jewish-gentile marriages had to be determined as one or the other.[98]

The November 17 decree prohibited mixed marriages. It also expelled Jews from public offices and limited their right to own property. A decree of December 22 discharged all Jews from military service.

In February 1939, limits were set on Jewish ownership of real property and corporations. Jew were prohibited from owning commercial or industrial companies that were connected to national defense or that employed more than ninety-nine workers. A Jew could donate such a firm to an Aryan; otherwise the corporations were liquidated or sold to an Aryan with the proceeds theoretically to be paid to the former Jewish owner in registered government bonds.[99] On June 29, 1939, Jews were prohibited from being either journalists or notary publics, and Jewish doctors, pharmacists, architects, and other professionals were limited to serving other Jews.

Roman Jewish men attacked these exceptionally harsh Racial Laws by circulating a pamphlet late in 1938 that spoke of the sacrifices Jewish soldiers had made to keep the nation free.[100] To that point, there were two escape clauses in the Racial Laws. The first such clause, appearing in the November 17 law, allowed for "discrimination" of some Jews, a misleading term for a circumstance that could actually benefit Jews. Jews could be "discriminated" from among other Jews—that is, exempted from some of the Racial Laws—if their relatives had been killed serving in the Italian military, if they were Fascist Party members, or if they were of "exceptional merit." The main benefit of discrimination was the ability to retain real estate assets.[101] Discrimination was not automatic; a commission reviewed applicants. Approximately nine thousand Jewish applications were processed for discrimination, and by 1943, 2,486 applications had been granted. Because discrimination could extend to families, ancestors, and descendants, approximately sixty-five hundred persons benefited from discrimination.[102]

The second escape clause was "Aryanization," legislated on July 13, 1939. To be Aryanized a person had to prove that his or her birth certificate was false, and that one or both of the listed Jewish parents were not the applicant's actual parents. When Jews applied for Aryanization, they usually had to plead that their mother or grandmother had committed adultery with a Catholic.[103] In cases of discrimination and Aryanization, corruption, in the form of bribes, was more the rule than the exception.

With the publication of the *Manifesto* and the Racial Laws, the Risorgimento's achievements regarding Italian Jews were obliterated. For most of Italy's Jews it was a betrayal impossible to comprehend. Ettore Ovazza, for one, a prominent Jewish business man and philanthropist from Turin, could not accept what had happened. He wrote to Mussolini: "I write poorly because my hand is trembling. It is the end of a reality; that of our feeling one with the Italian people. . . . How many starting in 1919 and up until today, have followed You with love, through so many battles, wars living Your life. Is all this over? Was it all a dream we nurtured? I can't believe it."[104]

To make sense of the senseless, Ovazza wanted to believe that Mussolini had a hidden agenda that required Jewish sacrifice.[105] Fascist racism, Ovazza imagined, was really a demand that Jews sacrifice themselves for the good of Italy. He would make that sacrifice, so long as Mussolini, despite the laws, still considered him an Italian. He concluded, "If my soul is in pain—and with how many others—I give you a Roman salute and wish your High Mission a glorious triumph."[106] Of course, Mussolini did not reply to deluded souls like Ovazza.

The rest of Ovazza's life played out like a Greek tragedy. Five years later in 1943, while fleeing the Nazi occupiers of Italy, and trying to escape to Switzerland, Ovazza, his wife, and daughter were executed, the day after Yom Kippur, by the SS in the town of Intra near Lake Maggiore. Their bodies were dismembered and cremated over the course of three days in several small furnaces below the ground floor of a girl's elementary school.[107]

Another Jewish Fascist betrayed by the *Manifesto* was Margherita Sarfatti (unrelated to the historian Michele Sarfatti), Mussolini's longtime lover and confidante. Born in 1880 in Venice to a wealthy Jewish family, in 1913 she became Berenice to Mussolini's Titus. In a confirmation of just how small the Italian Jewish community was, Sarfatti was the cousin of Natalia Ginzburg, the novelist and intrepid critic of the Fascist regime.[108]

Together, Sarfatti and Mussolini edited the periodical *Gerarchia* (Hierarchy), a Fascist journal, and she eventually wrote an adulatory biography of the Duce.[109] By 1929, however, she watched as her lover sealed a deal with the Vatican making Italy a Catholic state. In response, Sarfatti converted to Catholicism and was baptized along with her children. But then came the Racial Laws. In 1938, she fled to South America and returned to Italy only after the war.[110]

Lieutenant Colonel Giorgio Morpurgo was another Jew who enthusiastically supported Mussolini until 1938. He fought with the Italian army in Spain, backing Francisco Franco. Upon the decree of December 22, 1938, discharging all Jewish soldiers from the army, he was ordered to return to Italy, but Morpurgo demanded to fight in one more battle. On December 23, as the attack began, he stepped out in front of his fellow soldiers and began walking slowly toward the enemy. Despite being wounded, he continued advancing until he was killed. To avoid scandal, he was awarded a posthumous gold medal.[111] In his final act Morpurgo was not alone. Between 1938 and 1943, more than thirty Jews committed suicide.[112]

Another account of the trauma inflicted by Mussolini's Racial Laws was penned by a child known only by the initials F. M. A daughter of a mixed marriage, F. M. wrote to Mussolini's son Romano in September 1939:

> I write to you because you are a child and I am a child too. I hope you will understand me and, if possible, help me. Lately I noticed that my mother is sad and after insisting, she told me what happened. . . . What I understood is that my father is not like us. . . . Your dad can do anything and I'm sure he will help my dad because he is a veteran Fascist and he married my mother who is Italian and Christian and because he is very good with everybody, because he loves me so much and also because he is very sick now and the doctor asked him to stay calm or he will never get better. . . . Please ask your dad to consider my dad as an Italian and a Christian and you and all your family will have the gratitude and love of a little girl.[113]

THE CHURCH AND THE FASCIST REGIME

At this time, in 1938, Pius XI met with the staff of Belgian Catholic radio and made the following statement. "It is impossible for Christians to participate in anti-Semitism. . . . Anti-Semitism is inadmissible. Spiritually, we are all Semites."[114]

By taking exception to the bifurcation of Italians into either Aryans or Semites, the pope's remarks were potentially incendiary: a rebuke of both Mussolini and Fascism. Vatican officials surrounding the pope were alarmed. Consequently, in the interests of amity between the church and the Fascist state, and apparently without the pope's knowledge, Pius XI's unambiguous denunciation of antisemitism was deleted from the summary of the meeting published in *L'osservatore Romano*, the official Vatican newspaper.[115]

The pope was even more outraged by the Racial Laws' stipulation that Jews could not change their status through conversion to Catholicism. For the church, it was an immutable position that all humans, equal before God, had the same opportunity, regardless of the circumstances of their birth, for salvation. Consequently, if a Jew converted to Catholicism, he or she ceased to be Jewish. The rub between the church and the Fascist regime was the regime's refusal to recognize marriages between Catholics and Jewish converts. The regime's November 17, 1938, decree had banned such so-called mixed-race marriages, but according to the Vatican, these were not mixed marriages at all, but marriages between two Catholics. Moreover, the pope believed, Mussolini had no business declaring valid Catholic marriages illegal, given that he was bound by the 1929 Lateran Accords. Article 34 of the accords stated that the Fascist government recognized the civil effects of religious marriages. The November 17 decree against mixed marriages abrogated that portion of the accords and consequently put the entirety of the 1929 agreement at risk.

Livid at Mussolini's flouting of the carefully negotiated accords, the pope wrote Mussolini a letter of protest focused solely on the issue of Catholics who had once been Jews. Mussolini ignored the letter even when a watered-down version was published in *L'osservatore Romano*.[116]

JEWISH LIFE UNDER THE RACIAL LAWS

The Racial Laws impoverished and degraded the Jewish community, wreaking havoc on Jewish lives.[117] When Jews were banned from all public employment, that meant they ceased being typists, tram conductors, firemen, librarians, government ministers, and military officers. In private employment, Jews could not manage apartment houses, dance schools, or typing agencies.[118] Jews were fired from positions they held in the theater, cinema, and radio. Works by Jewish writers and composers were banned from production on the stage and in opera houses. Jewish music was prohibited from being broadcast on the radio or distributed via recordings. Jewish writers could not publish their books. Jewish directors could no longer produce movies. No exhibition could contain paintings or sculptures by Jewish artists. Even dictionaries that defined "antisemitism" as deplorable were taken off the shelves. By 1942, libraries were ordered to cease loaning books by Jewish authors, and Jews could not even use a library. Every scholarly society in Italy expelled its Jewish members, and the Italian branches of the Rotary Club were dissolved because they would not discriminate against Jews.

Jews could not own banks. Jewish-owned real property exceeding the modest quota allowed for Jews was confiscated and liquidated by the government, which compensated the owners with thirty-year bonds at four percent annual interest.

After October 1938 kosher butcheries were banned in Italy, thereby depriving Jews of a traditional occupation that had persisted for two thousand years. Observant Jews had to give up eating meat—although some anti-Fascist butchers aided Jews in clandestine ritual slaughter.[119]

In 1940, the government revoked street peddling licenses for Roman Jews, creating misery for some nine hundred families.[120] Vitale A., age sixty, a World War I veteran with a measly pension of fifty-nine lire per month, continued selling souvenirs without a license, which earned him internment in the Urbisaglia concentration camp northeast of Rome until December 1942. When the Nazis occupied Rome in 1943, he was deported to Auschwitz, where he died on June 30, 1944.[121]

After the peddlers' licenses were revoked, the Jewish community sought relief from the Ministry of the Interior. The government agreed to reinstate the licenses, but in February 1941, non-Jewish haberdashers and mobile vendors sent a letter to the same ministry objecting to the reprieve.[122] The following month, the peddlers were again forbidden to sell their goods. In October 1941, fifteen peddlers in Rome petitioned the ministry once more to reinstate the licenses,[123] and by January 1942 the licenses were renewed. Many of the peddlers who resumed work were then killed by the Nazis two years later.[124]

Unsurprisingly, the Racial Laws drove Jews out of Italy. The Jewish population would shrink from forty-five thousand in 1938 to thirty-three thousand in 1943.[125]

The one Racial Law restriction from which the Jewish community regrouped quickly was the expulsion of Jewish children from Italian schools. Within weeks of the laws' institution, a Jewish elementary school and a Jewish high school on Rome's Via Celimontana 23 were in operation.[126] Additionally, in one instance Jews were allowed to study outside their own schools. The pontifical law school Pontificium Institutum Utriusque Iuris welcomed Jewish students. Sited next to the Lateran Basilica, it was not subject to the Racial Laws, given that, technically, the school was not in Italy; it was on Vatican property. All classes and exams were conducted in Latin, but for classically educated Jewish students, that could be overcome. Under the current circumstances, the students considered Latin to be a language of liberty in which they could express opinions forbidden to Italian speakers.[127]

Once Italy entered World War II on June 10, 1940, some Jews were considered enemies of the state and sent into internal exile. By 1943, more than four hundred Jews had been interned in towns or camps, including Leone Ginzburg, who was confined with his wife Natalia and their children to a town in the Abruzzi region east of Rome from 1941 through 1943. Life there was rustic and hard, but they had a small government subsidy: a biweekly payment of eight lire for Leone, four lire for Natalia, three lire for each child, and fifty lire per month for housing.[128] Natalia ended up enjoying the anonymity of *confino*, which to her meant enforced Italianization. Despite the Racial Laws and her new identification as a Fascist enemy, in *confino* she was just another Italian. She considered the Abruzzi period "the best time of my life."[129]

Others felt the same as Natalia. In exile on the island of Lipari, Marion Roselli, a courageous anti-Fascist herself, smuggled her husband Carlo's banned writings off the island beneath her dress. Still, she wrote of her early days there as "another honeymoon."[130]

For her and for many Jews, the honeymoon soon ended. On May 10, 1940, Fascists rioted in the former Roman Ghetto, beating and bloodying several Jews.[131] In 1942 Mussolini created "forced labor" programs known as *precettazione* to employ persons, Jews in particular, who were exempt from military duty. Roman Jews were forced to do manual labor, such as digging ditches along the banks of the Tiber, and they were paid at one-fourth the usual rate, because someone determined that Jews only worked one-fourth as hard as Aryans. In 1942, despite protests, Jews were forced to work during the High Holidays.[132]

THE END OF FASCISM

Fascist persecution of Italian Jews persisted until Mussolini's downfall, which began on July 24, 1943. On that date, Mussolini met with the Grand Council of Fascism, the main body of government under his rule. Orders voted by the Grand Council needed Mussolini's approval, but the council had a residual power. It could recommend to the king that the prime minister be removed from office.

Italy was now facing humiliating defeat in the war. Earlier in July, Allied troops had invaded Sicily, finding little or no resistance. The Americans and British had started bombing Italian cities on the peninsula. Knowing an invasion of the mainland was imminent, the Grand Council met on July 24. Mussolini defended himself and accused the Sicilians and his own generals of cowardice and incompetence, but Italy's former foreign minister Dino Grandi made an impassioned motion—depose Mussolini and place the country's military under royal control—and nineteen of the twenty-seven council members voted in favor.[133] Then it was up to King Victor Emmanuel III to depose Mussolini.

The following day, Mussolini traveled to the Quirinal Palace in Rome to confer with the king. Apparently, Victor Emmanuel told Mussolini that he was the most hated man in Italy and added, with some irony, "You have only one friend left . . . me." As Mussolini left the palace, the king's Carabinieri (Italian national police) surrounded and forced him into a waiting ambulance. He became a prisoner in an undisclosed location (later revealed as Campo Imperatore, a resort in the Abruzzi region east of Rome). Then Victor Emmanuel asked General Pietro Badoglio, a well-known general and strategist in the vicious and brutal Ethiopian war, to form a government.[134]

Badoglio's government continued nominally as a German ally. While clearly a separate peace with the Allies was in the near offing, Badoglio did not want to antagonize Hitler. He took almost no steps to rectify the Jews' second-class citizenship as imposed by the 1938 Racial Laws. Former administrators of those laws remained in power during his own months-long administration.[135]

On September 8, 1943, after negotiating with Badoglio, U.S. general Dwight Eisenhower announced Italy's unconditional surrender and demanded the nullification of the Racial Laws. Badoglio and King Victor Emmanuel, now officially enemies of the Germans, fled Rome for their lives the next day, intent on escaping an advancing German army ordered to take the Eternal City before the Allies had time to invade mainland Italy. Badoglio headed south to Brindisi, where he could receive Allied protection. Nominally he was still the prime minister of Italy and Victor Emmanuel III was still king, but the northern part of the peninsula was under Nazi control and the south was contested. Badoglio would not take the Racial Laws off the books until January 20, 1944, and by then it was a symbolic gesture because the majority of Italian Jews were under Nazi control.[136]

Rescuing Mussolini from imprisonment, the Nazis installed him as the leader of a puppet government in northern Italy, with its capitol in the small town of Salò between Milan and Verona. For its part, the Vatican did not recognize the Italian Social Republic, or the Salò Republic, as a legitimate state.

With the Germans advancing from the north and the Allies preparing to invade from the south, there was only one final piece to the geopolitical puzzle left outstanding. On September 11, 1943, the Vatican sought assurances that its independence would be maintained in a Nazi-occupied Rome, and Hitler agreed. The stage was set for the church to save, or abandon, Rome's Jews.

10

The Other Knock on the Door

Jews and Catholics during the Nazi Occupation of Rome

With Mussolini no longer in Italy's capitol, the Allied army approached from the south, while the Nazis flooded Italy from the north. It was a race for Rome in central Italy.

The Germans won, on September 8, 1943. The Allied invasion of the Italian Peninsula had stalled, allowing Nazi troops to ensconce themselves firmly in Rome with, among other things, the task of eliminating its Jews. Rome's Jews had lived there for approximately two thousand years. The Nazi occupiers intended to bring that story to a close, as they worked to "finally solve" the Jewish problem throughout Europe.

Some Jews tried to arm themselves by breaking into an armory on September 9, 1943, and seizing some seventy hunting rifles and shotguns. Arrests quickly followed, and like other Jewish communities throughout Europe, the Jews of Rome were left to face the Nazi terror unarmed.[1]

THE MÖLLHAUSEN TELEGRAM

The person charged with the job of liquidating Rome's Jewish community was Lieutenant Colonel Herbert Kappler (1907–78), chief of the Gestapo in Rome. An American Office of Strategic Services document would later describe him as a "cold correct and impassive Prussian militarist."[2] Between September 10 and September 24, Kappler received both a telephone call and a top secret dispatch from SS Reichsführer Heinrich Himmler (1900–1945), ordering him to round up and deport the Jewish population under his jurisdiction. Every Jew, regardless of sex, age, citizenship, or state of health, was to be sent via train to the Reich for final disposition.

Kappler was an antisemite; however, he found Himmler's orders "a new gross political stupidity." As he saw it, Himmler was utterly wrong that Rome's Jews constituted a secret spy network, and that every Jewish child and hospital patient, along with the adult men and women, had to be removed from Rome and taken to slaughter—all in order not to sabotage the Nazi war effort in southern Italy. He was of the opposite opinion. Even if Jews were working against the Nazis, they should be left in place and infiltrated as intelligence sources about Allied troops and Jewish financial connections abroad.[3]

Himmler's "top secret" orders to the Gestapo were also read by General Rainer Stahel, military commandant of Rome. Wanting no part of what was termed the *Judenaktion*, Stahel told the acting head of the German diplomatic mission in Rome, Eitel Friedrich Möllhausen (1913–88), that he would never participate in such "Schweinerei" (piggishness).[4]

Möllhausen, a civilian, had been installed one day before, due to the German ambassador's injury in a serious automobile accident. He was not a member of the Nazi Party, and his Italian girlfriend was hiding Jews in her home with his tacit approval. Therefore, he agreed with Stahel, objecting to the proposed *Judenaktion* on moral as well as political grounds. He brought his concerns to Kappler, who, in turn, agreed to take them to Field Marshall Albert Kesselring (1885–1960), Supreme Commander of the Nazi forces in Italy south of Naples, confronting the Allies.[5]

Kesselring agreed that the *Judenaktion* was not a priority, adding that he could not spare even one solider to carry it out. Rather, Jews could be used to help construct fortifications around the city of Rome.

Encouraged by the Supreme Commander's response, Möllhausen consulted with the German ambassador to the Vatican, Ernst von Weizsäcker (1882–1951), and his deputy, Albrecht von Kessel (1902–76). They both gave Möllhausen moral support, because stopping the *Judenaktion* might spare Germany embarrassment in the eyes of the pope, who could not fail to recognize what would be happening in his own city.

Möllhausen then took it upon himself, on October 6, 1943, to send a "very, very urgent" telegram to Foreign Minister Joachim von Ribbentrop in Berlin: "Obersturmbannführer Kappler has received orders from Berlin to seize the 8,000 Jews resident in Rome and transport them to northern Italy where they are to be liquidated. Commandant of Rome General Stahel informs me he will permit this action only on approval of the Herrn Reichminister for Foreign Affairs. In my personal opinion it would be better business to employ the Jews for fortification work, as was done in Tunis, and, together with Kappler, I will propose this to Field Marshall Kesselring. Please advise. Möllhausen."[6]

Upon receipt of this telegram, Ribbentrop was incensed. First, the orders to Kappler were top secret, yet here was a civilian, and an underling no less, offering his opinion on a very delicate subject. In addition, Möllhausen had used the word "liquidate" in his telegram, which, although truthful, was unacceptable even for internal Nazi communications. Moreover, the word "liquidate" was in a telegram addressed to him personally. If ever revealed, it constituted evidence of his personal knowledge of the "final solution."

Both Ribbentrop and Kesselring were thus humiliated before Himmler, and Möllhausen was recalled to Berlin. Before his recall, he was informed that, one, the *Judenaktion* would take place and, two, he was to "keep out of all questions concerning Jews."

Almost immediately, Adolf Eichmann (1906–62), charged with facilitating the mass deportation of Europe's Jews, sent his aide Theodor Dannecker (1913–45) to Rome. Dannecker had accomplished the 1940–42 roundup of the Jews of Paris, and although Kappler was not recalled to Berlin, Dannecker, in effect, replaced Kappler, on October 6, in organizing the roundup in Rome.[7]

FIFTY KILOS OF GOLD

Meanwhile, Kappler was busy with his own ideas. On September 26, he summoned Ugo Foà (1887–1953), president of the Roman Jewish Community, and Dante Almansi (1878–1949), president of the National Union of Italian Jewish Communities, for a sit-down at the German embassy. After engaging in some pleasantries designed to soften up his audience, Kappler delivered his demand: fifty kilograms of gold within thirty-six hours. If the ransom was not paid and on time, two hundred Jews would be captured for service on the Russian front or "otherwise be rendered innocuous."[8]

Foà and Almansi were privately indignant, but at the same time they considered the ransom demand a bargain. If reliable, it meant saving the lives of all Roman Jewry at a cost of approximately five dollars per Jew. Fifty kilos of gold (about fifty-six thousand dollars) was an insignificant sum for the Reich's coffers;[9] the Germans had recently emptied the Bank of Italy's gold reserves in the amount of 110 metric tons. The money could be raised.

Still, it was not easy to collect fifty kilos of gold in under two days. The ransom would burden the small Jewish community already impoverished by the Racial Laws. The available gold would be in the form of wedding rings post-dating or surviving Mussolini's Day of Faith, along with lockets, other jewelry, and gold fillings for teeth.

The next day, a collection center was established in the Great Synagogue's boardroom and Renzo Levi, president of DELASEM (Delegazione Assistenza Emigranti Ebrei, Committee for aid to Jewish emigrants), was assigned to oversee the collection. To insure success, he traveled crosstown to the Vatican to ask Pope Pius XII for a loan to cover any shortfall. Pius XI had died in 1939, and his successor, Pius XII, found himself in the middle of an unmanageable world war. His action or inaction concerning Europe's Jews is a matter of serious contention, but in this instance he offered an interest-free loan of whatever amount was needed.

No papal largesse was required. By late afternoon, more than the fifty-kilo goal had been reached. The word had spread outside the Jewish community as well, and many Catholics, including some priests, came forward and made donations.[10] Additionally, an anonymous gentile donor, a glamorous woman, drove to and from the synagogue in a long black limousine to drop off a kerchief full of gold coins. Gold came also from Rome's most impoverished, such as a street vendor of candy who provided earrings, her last bits of gold, given that her wedding ring had been donated to "the Fatherland on the Day of Faith."[11]

With the ransom in hand, there followed a bit of bargaining. Thinking to deceive Kappler into believing it was more difficult to come up with the ransom than it actually was, the Jews asked for more time and were granted more time.[12] Then, on September 28, Foà and Almansi, along with a Fascist police escort, took the gold to Kappler at the embassy. Refusing to accept it there, Kappler directed them to a building nearby. They spent hours haggling over the exact amount of the gold, which had to be weighed and reweighed several times until the gold was accepted.

In the end, the entire exercise was meaningless. After the war, the golden box of Jewish valuables and memories, along with many ounces of Catholic goodwill, was found in Berlin near the desk of chief of the Reich's main security officer, Ernst Kaltenbrunner (1903–46), unopened.[13] Why the gold was extorted and then never touched remains a mystery. Most historians do not consider it necessary to explain the actions of antisemitic administrators bent on deceiving the Jews about their ultimate fate.[14]

THE GREAT SYNAGOGUE LIBRARIES

On October 11, SS officers accompanied a pair of German scholars to the Great Synagogue to inspect the Jewish community's two libraries housed there. The Biblioteca della Comunità Ebraica and the Biblioteca del Collegio Rabbinico collections of books and documents concerning Judaism and early Christianity were priceless. One of the SS officers paged through several ancient manuscripts:

> With hands as cautious and sensitive as those of the finest needlewoman, [he] skins, touches, caresses, papyri and incunabula, [he] leafs through manuscripts and rare editions, peruses parchments and palimpsests. The varying degree of caution in his touch, the heedfulness of his gestures, are quickly adapted to the importance of each work. Those texts were, for the most part written in exotic alphabets. But when the officer opens to a page, as happens to certain particular readers, who can instantly find desired and meaningful passages, his gaze is riveted, his eyes become bright. In those aristocratic hands, the books, as though subjected to the

cruel and bloodless torture of an exquisite sadism, revealed everything. Later, it became known that the SS officer was a distinguished scholar of paleography and Semitic philology.[15]

Satisfied with his discoveries, the officer warned the Jews in attendance that he was taking possession of the libraries, and any attempt to remove even a single book would be punished by execution. No one dared save the books, and a few days later the entire collection of the Biblioteca della Comunità and a portion of the Biblioteca del Collegio Rabbinico were loaded onto three freight cars and shipped north to the Reich.[16] Other books were removed on December 21–23, 1943. That was the end of the libraries. After the war, part of the Collegio Rabbinico's holdings would be recovered, but all efforts to locate the Jewish community's complete collection would prove fruitless—an immeasurable cultural loss.[17]

The synagogue furnishings had been removed to safety before the SS arrived. They were hidden beneath Roman Jewry's *mikveh* (ritual bath).

ISRAEL ZOLLI'S WARNING

In September 1943, according to his own account, Rabbi Israel Zolli (1881–1956), then the chief rabbi of Rome, issued a blunt warning to Rome's Jewish community: cease all public Jewish functions, shutter all administrative offices, destroy all lists of Jews kept in the synagogue, disperse and hide as best you can.

A self-important man, Zolli was little loved by his congregation. Born in Austria, he had previously served as chief rabbi of Trieste as well as professor of Semitic studies at the University of Padua. His 1938 book, *The Nazarene: Studies in New Testament Exegesis in the Light of Aramaic and Rabbinical Thought*, was a work of scholarship, not piety, but it did foreshadow his future actions (see chapter 11).[18] Nevertheless, he was offered the chief rabbinate of Rome, and had stepped into that post in December 1939.

Four years later, as the Nazis were arriving in Rome, Foà and Almansi, Rome's other Jewish leaders, rejected Zolli's dire proposals.[19] Most of

Roman Jewry would not heed his warnings either—perhaps in part because of Zolli's personality. In early October 1943, according to Zolli, the Nazis ransacked his apartment and impounded the family belongings, but by then he and his family were in hiding, first with a Jewish family and then with the Catholic family of Amadeo Pierantoni, an anti-Nazi subversive who hid a cache of explosives and weapons as well. Given those perilous circumstances, he later explained, he had to be incommunicado from the Jewish community until Rome's liberation in the spring of 1944.

Yet Ugo Foà, who also survived, would vigorously dispute Zolli's account, accusing him of having deserted his post as the community's spiritual leader when the Nazis entered Rome, thereby causing confusion and dismay among the people who needed him most.[20] On the other hand, Foà was not without his own detractors, who said that had Rome's Jews dispersed as Zolli had recommended, Foà would have lost his base of power. In short, Foà was accused of ignoring the danger to the Jewish community in order to maintain his own position.

It is not worthwhile to judge between Zolli and Foà. However, their differences aside, it is worth contemplating what would have happened had Zolli's warning been heeded. Some Jews did escape to the countryside, being warned not only by Zolli, but by Italian soldiers returning from the Russian front, and even the Soviet ambassador.[21] Nevertheless, the poorest of Rome's Jews, the four thousand or so who lived in the Ghetto neighborhood, stayed at home, where they thought, disastrously, that they would be safe.

OCTOBER 16 ROUNDUP

At four o'clock in the morning of October 16, 1943, the shooting stopped. For about three hours, gunfire and explosions had kept the Ghetto residents awake and, more importantly, in their homes. Besides, with the cold autumn rain outside, who would venture into what sounded like a war zone?

Then at five o'clock, residents heard the "heavy cadenced steps" of German soldiers.[22] Dannecker had massed his troops at the Portico of Octavia, the exact spot where, almost two thousand years earlier, Emperor Vespasian and his son Titus had set forth on their triumphal march through Rome celebrating the destruction of Jerusalem and its Temple. An archaeological excavation had created a sizable pit at the foot of the portico.[23] Dannecker's men emerged from that pit at dawn and, on a Sabbath morning, began to barricade the streets of the former Ghetto.

A hundred German soldiers marched through the street near the portico, leaving guards at each intersection. Carrying lists of names and addresses, they entered apartment buildings to knock on the doors, rouse the Jewish inhabitants, and take them away. The soldiers carried cards with instructions in Italian and German giving the Jews notice that they were being forcibly moved, and they had to take with them their ration cards, identification, drinking glasses, and food for eight days. Each card allowed the deportees to take a single suitcase for blankets, linens, clothing, money, and jewelry. Finally, they were admonished to lock their homes and take the key. Most importantly, every living soul had to leave with the soldiers. The sick, even those gravely ill, had no choice but to submit to deportation. At the very bottom of the card, the Jews were told they had twenty minutes to comply after reading the last sentence.[24]

As the roundup proceeded, some Jews were able to escape. Most of these were men who, upon hearing the knock on the door, fled out a window and across the rooftops. It was still believed then that the Nazis only wanted to take the men for forced labor.[25] By the time it became clear that every Jew was subject to deportation, it was too late for the women and children. Of those arrested, almost three out of four were women and children.

In those moments, the difference between capture and escape was often a matter of luck. A mother who thought to escape but wanted to first dress her infant waited seconds too long. Another mother was clutching her eighteen-month-old baby while teetering on the back of a German transport. The child's aunt began to scream, and a Catholic bystander, without a moment to think, cried out that the child was hers and had been baptized. The Nazis believed her and gave the boy to a complete stranger who saved his life.

A Jewish woman hid in a café with her daughter, a small child. She might have been safe, but she looked out the window and saw her pregnant sister being forced onto a truck. The look of sorrow and horror on her face alerted a German soldier to her identity and both mother and daughter were taken.

In one case, a Jewish woman noticed that her name was not on the list brandished by the soldiers in her apartment house. She brazenly told them she was Catholic and that the two children from the neighboring apartment were hers. All three escaped.

Claudio Fano reports that when the Germans came to his apartment house: "They had our names on the list. . . . And this [neighbor] lady was coming down the stairs who was the wife of a colonel who had joined the Black Brigades [Fascist antipartisan units]; her son had also joined the Black Brigades, and all. And this lady spoke German. She found the Germans on the landing and asked them 'Who are you looking for? Look, they've all left.' And the Germans did not go up[stairs]. So the wife of the colonel of the Black brigades [saved a family of Jews]."[26]

In the Testaccio neighborhood, a mother and her three children had been warned the night before. They had fled their apartment late in the evening and found a taxi, but had nowhere to go. When the driver inquired of their destination, the mother said, "I don't know. I'm Jewish and the Germans are coming to get us." After a moment's hesitation, the driver took them all to his home where he, his wife, and his own children kept the family safe for eight months until the Allies entered Rome.

In the San Lorenzo district, a priest, Father Libero Raganella, took a Jewish family to a cloister where he believed they would be safe. However, the Mother Superior refused to accept the family, which included men and boys and therefore violated the vows of her convent. Father Raganella prevailed upon her by asking that she leave the gate unlocked; he could then technically "break in" to the cloister without her permission. She agreed and the Jews were given temporary refuge.[27]

Among those who did not escape were Admiral Augusto Capon, the physicist Enrico Fermi's seventy-one-year-old father-in-law (paralyzed, and therefore carried from his apartment), and a nurse, Alina Cavalieri, sixty-one, who had won a silver medal for service in World War I.[28]

Nazi soldiers led the captured Jews through the streets to waiting trans-ports, then drove them to the Portico of Octavia, where they waited in the rain to be shuttled to the Italian Military College, their prison over the weekend, just six hundred feet from the Vatican.[29] The roundup, which ended at around 1 p.m. on Saturday, October 16, had concentrated on the former Ghetto area, but Jews living in other areas of Rome were arrested as well. They all spent the night on straw mattresses provided by their jailers. At least one woman gave birth that night.[30]

That Monday morning the prisoners were put into vans and taken to the Tiburtina railroad station, where they were loaded onto cattle cars. For the entire morning, the locked and guarded train stood, unmoving, in the sweltering heat. The novelist Elsa Morante, who had escaped with her husband before the roundup, recreated the scene from eyewitnesses' testimony in her novel, *History: A Novel*:

> There were perhaps twenty cattle cars, some wide open and empty, others closed with long iron bars over the outside doors. Following the standard design of such rolling stock, the cars had no windows, except a tiny grilled opening up high. At each of those grilles, two hands could be seen clinging or a pair of staring eyes. . . .
>
> The interior of the cars, scorched by the lingering summer sun, con-tinued to reecho with that incessant sound. In its disorder, babies' cries overlapped with quarrels, ritual chanting, meaningless mumbles, senile voices calling for mother; others that conversed, aside, almost ceremoni-ous and others that were almost giggling. And at times over all this, sterile bloodcurdling screams rose; or others of a bestial physicality, exclaiming elementary words like "water!" "air!" From one of the last cars, dominating all the other voices, a young woman would burst out, at intervals, with convulsive piercing shrieks typical of labor pains.[31]

At 2 p.m. on October 18, the train with its human cargo of 1,022 Jews left Rome.[32] It arrived at Auschwitz-Birkenau the night of October 22.

The following day, 149 men and 47 women passed the selection and were admitted to the work camp. The rest were killed.[33]

The Auschwitz log for October 23, 1943, reads: "Transport, Jews from Rome. After the selection 149 men registered with numbers 158451–158639 and 47 women registered with numbers 66172–66218 have been admitted to the detention camp. The rest have been gassed."[34]

Only one Roman newspaper—the resistance paper, *L'Italia libera* (Free Italy), edited by Leone Ginzburg—reported the story:[35]

> The Germans during the night and all day long went around Rome seizing Italians for their furnaces. The Germans would like us to believe that these people are in some way alien to us, that they are of another race. But we feel them as part of our flesh and blood. They have always lived, fought and suffered with us. Not only able-bodied men, but old people, children, women and babies were crowded into covered trucks and taken away to meet their fate. There is not a single heart that does not shudder at the thought of what that fate might be.[36]

Nevertheless, the Roman public was aware of the round-up.

On October 16, Kappler, still chief of the Gestapo in Rome, despite Dannecker's appointment by Eichmann to oversee the roundup, telegrammed General Karl Wolff (1900–1984), SS commander in Italy: "Comportment of the Italian [gentile] population: evidencing passive resistance, in many cases even intervening and aiding. In particular, for example, the police found at the door of one apartment a fascist, a woman, dressed in a black blouse with documents in order that demonstrated she had recently come into possession of a Jewish dwelling at the last minute. Presumably similar episodes were repeated. During the operation there were no manifestations of antisemitism in the population, while the major part of them attempted to keep the police far from the Jews."[37]

On the day following the roundup, Jews who had escaped capture wrote urgent letters to Pius XII asking him to intervene and save the Jewish prisoners. The Vatican took affirmative steps to save Jewish converts to

Catholicism and some Jews married to Catholics. The rest remained in German hands and were sent to Auschwitz. Of the 1,020 Jews who arrived at Auschwitz on October 28, only sixteen would survive the war.[38]

CATHOLIC SHELTERS FOR JEWS

Outside the Vatican, however, Catholic churchmen, nuns, and laypersons were seizing the opportunity to save thousands of Jews.[39] Monasteries, convents, and Catholic schools usually had rooms for boarders or pilgrims. Accordingly, in the weeks both before and after the roundup, an exodus of sorts took place in Rome, as Jewish families knocked on the doors of Catholic institutions looking for safety. Not all the doors opened for them, but many did.

On or about September 29, Lea Di Nola, a young woman working for Jewish refugees in Italy, was welcomed, along with her mother, to the convent of Santa Maria Ausiliatrice. As in many cases, the Mother Superior knew they were Jews. The other sisters in the convent probably knew them only as visitors.[40]

Silvana Ascarelli Castelnuovo knocked on several convent doors before she found one that opened for her on September 8. The Convento del Sacro Cuore del Bambino Gesù accepted Silvana, her four children, and her mother.[41] The Mother Superior knew they were Jews, but the rest of the convent was told they were Sicilian refugees. Undoubtedly, many of the nuns were not fooled; however, the fewer people who knew the facts, the safer it was for all concerned.

Both Lea and Silvana, like many other Jewish refugees, paid rent to the institutions that gave them sanctuary. The Jews were extra mouths to feed. Nonetheless, there was no requirement that a Jew convert in order to gain sanctuary.

Not all the doors knocked upon by fleeing Jews opened into a convent. On October 15, a day before the roundup, a street singer warned Mirella Calò's family of the impending SS operation. Mirella, age four, had three older sisters. Her parents hurriedly dressed all four girls with two pairs of underpants, several sweaters, and coats, and left their home in Testaccio to live in a whorehouse a few blocks from the father's place of business, the madam there having told him she would hide his family. He himself escaped to the country, while his wife and daughters stayed safe in the whorehouse basement for eight months. A whorehouse was not as safe as a convent; German soldiers were often customers upstairs, and the family had to be silent most of the time. Either the madam or her husband brought them food and even played cards with the children.[42]

At the same time, the Capuchin monk Father Maria Benedetto, also known as Father Marie Benoît (1895–1990), was working with the aid agency DELASEM,[43] which the Italian Jewish community had founded in December 1938 to help foreign Jews leave Italy for elsewhere.[44] Initially the Italian minister of the interior had approved DELASEM, possibly because foreign contributions to the organization would bring international currency into the Italian economy. However, after the Racial Laws and the Nazi occupation of Italy, DELASEM transformed into a clandestine organization operating with considerable help from local Catholic churches. By 1943 it was smuggling funds across the Swiss border into Italy to provide food, medicine, false documents, and warm clothing to foreign Jews in hiding. With the monies smuggled from abroad, food and other assistance had to be purchased and distributed. DELASEM would turn over funds and lists of persons in need to churchmen and women who would carry out the charitable work.

Of these, the most active priest in Rome was Father Benedetto. In addition to providing basic sustenance for hidden Jews, he forged identity cards for refugees—usually choosing addresses in southern Italy outside of Nazi control so their authenticity could not be checked.[45] When the Nazis occupied Rome, DELASEM's leaders went underground and entrusted Rome's DELASEM branch to him. He operated the organization from the Capuchin monastery in the Via Sicilia, without financial support from the nearby Vatican. Apparently the American organization, United Jewish Appeal, had given the Vatican $125,000 to support refugees fleeing religious persecution. These funds never reached DELASEM but were used to help Jewish converts to Catholicism.[46]

How DELASEM managed to keep the necessary funds flowing to save Jews despite the oppressive surveillance of the German occupiers is a story of bravery and ingenuity. Given the SS's fierce focus on Jews, the supply line of funds from Switzerland was no longer feasible, and Mussolini's northern Italian Republic of Salo was an obstacle to travel along the length of the peninsula; so Father Benedetto and his Jewish counterpart in DELASEM, Settimio Sorani (1899–1982), devised an alternate scheme. In the spring of 1944, with the Allies slowly approaching Nazi-occupied Rome from the south, Sorani and Father Benedetto negotiated loans from non-Jewish Italians to pay DELASEM's expenses. Once the war ended, the Jewish relief organization American Jewish Joint Distribution Committee would repay in dollars the loans originally made in lire (the greater value of the dollar compared to the lira provided something like interest on the loan). Meanwhile, the loans, $120,000 in Italian currency, were secured by simultaneous deposits in a London bank in American dollars and verified by the American and British diplomatic representatives to the Vatican, Harold Tittmann and Sir D'Arcy Osbourne. After the war, the loans would indeed be paid back from that bank. However, the money crucial to DELASEM, the loaned Italian lire, was not paid directly to DELASEM. That was too dangerous. Instead, the funds were collected by a French priest, Monsignor Hérissé, who had an apartment in Vatican City. He was also trustee on the notes, promising the eventual repayment in dollars. To carry out the perilous transaction, Sorani would enter the Vatican, meet with the monsignor, and leave with thousands of lire wrapped in newspaper, under the noses of the Germans guarding the boundary between Vatican City and Rome. These escapades were repeated throughout the spring of 1944, and thus the lire spirited out of the Vatican fed and clothed Jews living desperately in hiding, as well as paying for their medicine and forged documents.[47]

Father Pietro Palazzini, assistant rector of the Seminario Romano, also helped imperiled Jews. The pipeline to his seminary began with a Catholic teacher, Maria Amendola, who directed Jews to Father Vincenzo Fagiola, a young parish priest, and from there to Father Palazzini. Ultimately more than 200 people, 55 Jews and 145 non-Jews in danger from the Nazis, found sanctuary at the seminary. After the war, Amendola, Fagiola, and Palazzini, along with Father Benedetto, received the Righteous among the Nations award from Yad Vashem, Israel's Holocaust museum.[48]

Jews were also hidden at the Seminario Lombardo, the pontifical institution where priests were trained and housed, and a few even in the Vatican itself. On June 2, 1944, just before the Allies' liberation of Rome, some forty persons—Jews, converts to Catholicism, and draft dodgers—were living in Vatican City as fugitives.[49] A few Vatican officials became skittish about continuing to provide them refuge and recommended expulsion from the Vatican. Others prevailed upon the Vatican Secretary of State Cardinal Maglione to convince Pius XII that expulsion would be an error. Ultimately, the pope agreed to keep the refugees in the Vatican.[50]

Some Roman hospitals sheltered Jews as well. At the University of Rome, Doctor Brenno Barbudieri hid Bruno Maestro in a refrigerated room holding typhoid cultures. The sign on the door, "Entrance prohibited: serious danger of mortal infection," succeeded in keeping the Nazis out.[51]

All of these efforts and many others were heroic. The rescuers faced the real danger of being captured and killed themselves.

CATHOLIC INFORMERS

Not all Jews who hid before or after the October 16 roundup remained safe. Between eight hundred and one thousand Roman Jews were deported to Auschwitz from October 17, 1943, until June 5, 1944, when the Allies liberated the city. Various informers, policemen, gang members, and ordinary Romans and Catholics turned Jews over to the authorities.[52]

After October 16, there was a months-long lull in deportations. Rome's chief of police, Ermindo Roselli, was reluctant to order the arrests of any Jews, despite a November 30, 1943, order issued from Mussolini's Salo Republic to capture Jews and send them to special concentration camps.[53] Also, the German occupiers were less interested in Jews and more concerned with the Allied landing at Anzio, the real threat to the Nazis. Moreover, after October 16, the remaining Jews were in hiding. Finding and arresting them was not an easy matter.

But in December 1943 the Nazis began to pay monetary rewards for information revealing the whereabouts of hidden Jews—five thousand lire for each Jewish man, three thousand lire for each Jewish woman, and fifteen hundred lire for each Jewish child denounced to the Gestapo in Rome.[54] The reward was a considerable temptation, given that the average Roman family made less than a thousand lire per month at the time. Some women found denouncing Jews to be as profitable as prostitution, if not more so, and credited the bounties for keeping them off the streets.[55]

The rewards also enticed Fascist criminal gangs, like the Koch gang, the Cialli Mezzaroma, and the Pantera Nera, to capture more than one hundred Jews. Pantera Nera was named after the notorious Jewish informer Celeste Di Porto, also known as la Pantera Nera, the black panther. Eighteen-year-old Celeste would walk the Ghetto streets with her non-Jewish fellow gang members, and upon seeing someone she knew, jauntily call out their name. If the person turned toward her, their Jewish identity was revealed. Other times, she simply told the gang who to capture. Eyewitness accounts from persons only identified as A. A. and V. V. report the capture of the Jewish prizefighter Lazzaro Anticoli: "While we walked the Via Arenula together with Lazzaro Anticoli on the morning of 24 March, we saw Celeste Di Porto, the so called Pantera Nera, drawing the attention of a group of Republican Fascists to us. The Fascists moved towards us to arrest us. While we managed to flee, Lazzaro Anticoli was captured and we have not heard anything from him since."[56]

Motivated by money, gang members would extort payment from Jews who thought (or hoped) they were buying their freedom; then turn the Jews in to the Gestapo, doubling their profit; then plunder the apartment where the Jews had lived. Jews were also tortured to provide addresses of other Jews.

By early 1944, with money scarce, food at a premium, and black-market prices skyrocketing due to the Allied landing at Anzio, the Gestapo's high reward made turning in a Jewish neighbor even harder to resist. After February 1944, hundred of letters denouncing Jews flooded the Gestapo offices on Via Tasso. Landlords turned in their Jewish tenants in hopes of getting both the reward and the Jews' possessions from their apartments. Catholics denounced their Jewish partners to gain full control of a business. Porters, who knew a great deal about the tenants in their buildings, turned in Jews, or blackmailed them, or both. In all these instances, the assurance that a denounced Jew would be marked for death—and thus could not return to claim compensation or seek revenge—made denunciation easier.[57]

Besides the aforementioned Celeste Di Porto, other Jews even turned in each other. One Giulio L. was denounced by his brother, allegedly in order to win Giulio's girlfriend. A tour guide for German troops who drove around the Jewish area identifying Jews to SS officers was revealed, after the war, to be himself a Jew.[58]

SECOND ROUNDUP

The second roundup of Rome's Jews took place over several months. On February 2, 1944, Rome's new police chief, Pietro Caruso, who had replaced Roselli at the end of January 1944 and was considerably more zealous in hunting Jews, ordered the arrest of all Jews in Rome.[59] At roughly the same time, Caruso transferred policemen off their usual beats and split up police teams, thereby severing personal ties between individual policemen and the people they served, as well as placing policemen with unknown partners. Some policemen, he found, were willing to protect Jews—reporting, for example, that they could not find the Jews they had been ordered to arrest. Aimed at impeding such behavior, Caruso's new policies effectively increased anxiety among the police. Before, policemen had known who they worked with, especially whether their partner was a Fascist or not. When ordered to arrest Jews, many police later claimed they were looking over their shoulders at their fellows, making sure they would not be denounced themselves for not obeying orders.

In one instance, on March 15, officer Fabrizio Contini arrested five-year-old Emma, three of her four siblings, her parents, and a nephew hiding on the ground floor of an apartment building. After deportation, they all died at Auschwitz, Ravensbruck, Buchenwald, and Mauthausen. At his postwar trial, Contini claimed he had no choice but to follow Caruso's orders—otherwise, he might have compromised his secret membership in the Italian resistance—and he was acquitted.[60] The apartment's concierge, Eufemia Agosti, was the hero. Realizing she could save a life, she told Contini that the youngest, Rina, was hers and thereby saved at least one child.[61]

Other police gratuitously beat their prisoners before handing them over to the Gestapo or, in order to augment their income, worked after hours to entrap Jews. The Germans converted a former apartment building on Via Tasso into a prison and torture chamber.[62] On the other hand, at the Regina Coeli prison, where Leone Ginzburg was tortured and killed, some doctors acted secretly to protect Jews, injecting them with a solution that led to a fever, which qualified the prisoners for transfer to a hospital where they could be sheltered.[63]

It has been claimed that the Roman police were more sympathetic to the Jews than the Gestapo, which may or may not be true. More likely, such a conclusion was reached because the postwar investigation of the 1944 arrests concentrated less on the police than on the organized gangs. However, in a few documented instances the Pubblica Sicurezza, the public security police, actively saved Jews or looked the other way. As one historian has noted, "It is then quite evident that without the aid, or instead the inertia, of various officials and functionaries of the Pubblica Sicurezza, the salvation of thousands of Jews hidden in Rome would not have been possible."[64]

Churches sheltering Jews relied on the forbearance of the Nazis in steering clear of church properties in Rome. The Vatican was its own sovereign nation, and religious institutions throughout Rome were protected by the Lateran Accords of 1929—an arrangement Hitler recognized, though local gangs did not.

On the night of February 3, Pietro Koch and his band of mercenaries, along with fifteen Germans, surrounded the Basilica di San Paolo Fuori le Mura, a major Roman institution and, according to the Lateran Accords, protected Vatican territory. Inside were dozens of persons sought by the Nazis as enemies of the Reich, including several Jews. The Koch band blocked exits, cut telephone lines, looted the premises, and enabled the roundup of sixty-four prisoners by the next morning. At least five Roman Jews were dispatched to and killed at Auschwitz.[65] Thirty people escaped, including one Jew posing as a priest.

ROMAN RESISTANCE AND NAZI RETRIBUTION

If the Nazis aroused the basest treachery among some of the Roman population, they also inspired a heroic resistance movement that included approximately fifty to sixty Jews.[66] The Roman resistance attacked Fascists during the fall of 1943 and through the spring of 1944. They also set off bombs in railway stations and movie theaters, and on bridges over the Tiber.[67] However, their most startling achievement was the March 23, 1944, ambush of a column of ss soldiers.[68]

The opportunity for the March 23 ambush arose out of the severe discipline imposed on the Third Battalion of the ss Polizeiregiment stationed in Rome. Answering to General Karl Wolff, the Third Battalion was attached to Kappler and Commandant Kurt Mälzer as ss police. The battalion's Eleventh Company, Lieutenant Wolgast's responsibility, was billeted on the Via delle Quattro Fontane. Every morning, the 160 men in the Eleventh Company crossed the city to the north, arriving at a firing range on the far side of the Milvian Bridge, and every early afternoon, they marched back to their barracks, singing all the while.

The return route from the firing range crossed the Piazza del Popolo to the Via del Babuino, past the Spanish Steps, and then past the Column of the Immaculate Conception in the Piazza Mignanelli. Like clockwork, every day at 2 p.m. the ss parade made a left turn onto the Via Rasella, a narrow, unprepossessing corridor leading to the Via delle Quattro Fontane, where the ss ranks turned right toward their barracks. A well-placed bomb detonated midway toward the Via delle Quattro Fontane would be expected to rip through the ss formation and kill tens of ss.

The bomb was created in the basement of a young physicist, Giulio Cortini, and his wife Laura Garroni. Twelve kilograms of TNT were stuffed into something like a cast-iron pail. In a separate canvas sack they poured another six kilograms, along with several six-inch lengths of iron pipe also stuffed with TNT. The pail of TNT was lowered into the sack of TNT and topped off with a detonator and a fifty-second fuse.

To get the bomb safely to its destination, the partisans decided to put it in a garbage can. Rubbish in Rome was collected from a cart with two garbage cans in front of each house. The bomb could be put into one can, and garbage in another. Both cans could be placed aboard a standard garbage cart. Thus the entire contraption could be rolled innocently through Rome to its destination on Via Rasella in front of the Palazzo Tittoni.

That task fell to an idealistic young couple, a Jew and a Catholic in their early twenties who were part of the Gruppi di Azione Patriottica (GAP), an arm of the Communist Party and the resistance. Carla Capponi, part Jewish, enough so that she was affected by the Racial Laws,[69] was romantically involved with Rosario Bentivegna, a Catholic medical student. By spring 1944, they were experienced guerillas. Rosario, dressed as a street cleaner, would place the bomb. Then, upon a sign from Carla, the lookout stationed at the top of Via Rasella, he would light the fuse and walk calmly in her direction. She would give him a coat to cover his street-cleaning outfit and both would escape. Meanwhile, other partisans would lob several shells into the SS mob and make their own escape.

The operation succeeded. Although the Germans' routine was altered that day, the bomb blast killed thirty-two Germans and wounded many others. All the partisans, including Carla and Rosario, survived.

Kappler, Mälzer, and others in the Nazi command rushed to the scene, recognizing the impending damage to their careers if serious reprisals did not ensue. An overwrought and tearful Mälzer wanted the entire street razed. When Hitler learned of the bombing, he outbid Mälzer, demanding that a full quarter of Rome be demolished and all the inhabitants slaughtered. He also ordered thirty to fifty Romans killed for every SS man killed.

However, Kappler and others in the German command in Rome soon reduced the number of Italians to be murdered in reprisal to ten for every German. Kappler and colleagues had to find approximately 320 Roman citizens to kill to appease the Führer and perhaps discourage further partisan activity in Rome. Several persons already in SS custody were to be executed anyway, and others who were accused or had been found guilty of crimes against the Fascist regime or the Nazi occupiers could be put on Kappler's execution list. Then, too, there were Jews. Sixty-five Jews, some scheduled for deportation to Auschwitz and some Jewish partisans, were added to the list of *Todeskandidaten* (candidates for death). In addition, Jews were being arrested every day through the web of Roman informers.

On March 23, the day of the bombing, the SS arrested the brother of la Pantera Nera. Not wanting to anger Celeste Di Porto, a key informer, they quickly freed him—but then the list of *Todeskandidaten* was one short. On March 24, Celeste had the Roman Jewish prizefighter Lazzaro Anticoli arrested in the manner we've already detailed. The boxer was substituted for her brother in a deadly and cold-blooded transaction.

One Catholic priest was also on Kappler's list. Don Pietro Pappagallo, age fifty-five, had been accused of "Communist activities" while serving as chaplain to the Suore del Santo Bambino Gesú convent.

Ultimately, the number of persons slated for execution exceeded the required 320 and had to be reduced. At his trial after the war, Raffaele Alianello, commissioner for public security, gave self-serving testimony that he ordered ten names, eight Jewish names and two others, removed from Kappler's list.[70] Other reports indicate that it was nine Jews.[71]

The list was finalized on March 24, one day after the bombing. The customary Nazi killing ground was the prison yard at Fort Bravetta on the southwest side of the Janiculum Hill; however, the number of bodies that would have to be disposed of required an alternate location. Kappler chose a series of tunnels and caves near the Appian Way, not far from Vigna Randanini, the Roman Jewish catacombs. On Kaplan's execution list were Aldo Finzi, Mussolini's first underminister of the interior, whose father happened to be Jewish, and Colonel Giovanni Prignani and Captain Raffaele Aversa, who had arrested Mussolini at the Quirinal shortly after he met with the king. Others were brickmakers, shopkeepers, and men from neighborhoods throughout Rome.[72]

On that day, March 24, 1944, at 2 p.m., the 335 civilians and political prisoners were driven in meat wagons from the Via Tasso in Rome to the Ardeatine Caves south of Rome known then as a group of mines for extraction of volcanic dust, useful in making cement, since the beginning of the twentieth century. Prisoners were taken inside the cave in groups of five. Each prisoner was escorted by an executioner. The victim was forced to kneel, and his killer placed a pistol behind his neck and fired through the brain. Death was intended to be instantaneous, but as the corpses piled higher, the killers fortified themselves with cognac' and their shots went awry. Some of the condemned were shot four or five times, effectively decapitating them. Unbelievably, others did not die at the hands of the increasingly inebriated executioners. They were just tossed among the dead and suffocated as further corpses were piled upon them. A nearby farm worker heard the shots from about 3:30 p.m. to 8:00 p.m. By that time, there were two five-foot mounds of bodies in the cave. The bodies had been slowly stacked up so that the remaining prisoners had to climb up a heap of dead relatives or comrades and wait for their executioner to join them at the top before they were shot and added to the pile.

When the killing ended, German engineers detonated the caves, collapsing the tunnels and entrances. It was hoped that the crime would be hidden for the duration of the Thousand-Year Reich, but the Allies captured the city of Rome on June 5, 1944, just two months later.

ALLIED LIBERATION OF ROME

While the Allied capture of Rome was inevitable, it was slow in coming. Umberto Turco, a gentile, a teenager at the time, would later recount: "[There was a] grayness and sadness that you could see in the very air, you could breathe it. . . . It was this suffering starving Rome. It was a Rome where you saw people on the run, gaunt, sad, understand? . . . That is, you might see a body on the pavement, killed but it didn't strike you that much. . . . It was someone the Germans killed. He was there on the ground, understand? And you dodged, you tried not to be involved."[73]

Finally, on June 5, 1944, Allied armies entered the city. Jews celebrated by rushing to the synagogue. In the words of Mino Moscati: "Oh, we opened the Temple. The first thing my father did was to rekindle the candle in front of the Sacred Ark, because that's a very important thing, and then hugs and kisses among the survivors. We gave it a big cleaning, straightened things up, and then in the evening, obviously we held a ceremony once again."[74]

The Nazi occupation was over.

FOSSE ARDEATINE

Within days, the pilgrimages to the Ardeatine Caves began, long lines of families carrying flowers to the now putrid caves. The site took on a new name: "Fosse Ardeatine," meaning the Ardeatine "ditches" or "graves."[75]

In response, the Allied regional commissioner for Rome ordered a commission comprising gentiles and Jews to investigate the killings. He appointed Attilio Ascarelli, professor of legal medicine at the University of Rome and director of the Superior School of Police, to exhume and identify the bodies. A Jew who had hidden during the Nazi occupation, Ascarelli was also the uncle of two victims murdered at the Fosse Ardeatine.

Working from a pile of decomposed flesh and shattered bones ridden with vermin, it took Ascarelli and his team six months to account for all the dead. The cave contained the bodies of 330 individuals, 322 of whom could be positively identified. Seventy-seven or seventy-eight were Jews. In one Jewish family, the Di Consiglios, a grandfather, his three sons and a son-in-law, and three of his grandchildren all died in the cave. All were men; the Di Consiglio women who had been hiding with their husbands in an apartment on Via Madonna dei Monti were taken to be killed at Auschwitz.[76]

Over the following months, Giacomo Debenedetti, a literary critic, wrote a postscript to the events of March 24, 1944. He took moral exception to statements claiming that when Kappler was compiling his list of *Todeskandidaten*, Raffaele Alianello, the public security official noted above, had deleted eight Jewish names from the list, thereby saving eight Jews. One might expect Debenedetti, a Jew who had survived in hiding during

1943 and 1944, to be grateful that there existed a single person in the vast murderous apparatus who took pity on a few Jews. However, Debenedetti was not grateful; he was furious. As a Jew, he did not want anyone's pity, and surely not a Fascist's. Instead, he wanted Jewish Romans to be treated like every other Roman or Italian resistance fighter. No exceptions should be made for Jews. Of course, exceptions had already been made for Jews, by adding as many Jews as possible to the list of *Todeskandidaten*.[77] Still, Debenedetti demanded that his fellow Jews be given a human face before being counted merely as Jews. He wrote: "If there is a right that Jews claim, it is only this: that those of their dead who died of violence and hunger, their infants, who after months of starvation in their places of hiding didn't survive the first sip of milk finally offered to them, their women kicked and machine-gunned to death, their newborns tossed in the air and gunned down as though they were birds, should be ranked with all the other dead—all the other victims of this war. They too were soldiers, alongside every other soldier."[78]

Debenedetti wanted Jewish fighters to be placed in the ranks of every other soldier who fought for freedom, even though he counted among the Jewish "soldiers" women and children, infants and newborns. Although the Jews' suffering had been inordinate, the recognition of that suffering, while deserved, should not be extraordinary.

Debenedetti's statements may be surprising and unconventional, but it is perhaps best to hear his words as a plea that Jews be allotted only a common humanity. Jews in every period in Rome over the last two thousand years could have uttered that same cry. If Jews and Catholics in Rome often felt that they were connected by family ties, Debenedetti voiced something slightly different: a yearning and a demand for entry into such a family.

PIUS XII

Pope Pius XII has been a controversial figure in the nightmare that played out over the nine months of German tyranny, and indeed throughout the war. Rolf Hochuth's play *The Deputy*, which reached Broadway in 1964, but was banned in Italy, was a thorough indictment of Pius's alleged inaction in the face of the Shoah.[79] Robert Katz's history *Death in Rome* (1967) alleged Pius knew in advance of the Nazi reprisals at the Fosse Ardeatine and did nothing. The pope's family sued Katz for defamation of the pope's memory and the lawsuit played out over ten years before it was eventually dismissed.[80] On the other side of the argument, *The Pope's Jews*, by Gordon Thomas, and José M. Sanchez's careful work *Pius XII and the Holocaust: Understanding the Controversy* vigorously defended the pope.

These references are mere examples of a vast literature about Pius XII and the Holocaust that is not possible to review at length here. Most important for this study is the state of the evidence. New facts have recently come to light as a result of Pope Francis's decision, effective March 2020, to make the full documentation of Pius's papacy (sealed since the latter's death in 1958) available for scholars. David Kertzer's 2022 book, *The Pope at War: The Secret History of Pius XII, Mussolini, and Hitler*, draws from a thorough investigation of the Pius XII papers, and the following discussion makes use of the new material Kertzer discovered.

Initially, the questions that need to be asked and answered concerning Pius XII are: What did the pope know about the Holocaust in general, what did he know about the October 16 roundup, what did he know about the Ardeatine massacre, and, in each instance, what did the pope do with that information?

Based upon published Vatican correspondence, it is undeniable that Pius knew, at least by mid-1943, that Hitler intended to kill as many Jews as he could and was carrying out those intentions against the Jews under his control.[81] For example, in May 1942, Abbot Pirro Scavizzi, while traveling with a hospital train through Poland, wrote directly to Pius XII, saying:

> The struggle against the Jews is implacable and constantly intensifying with deportations and mass executions.
> The massacre of the Jews in Ukraine is by now nearly complete. In Poland and Germany they want to complete it also, with a system of mass murders.[82]

Kertzer reveals several other instances, going back to 1941, when Abbot Scavizzi informed Pius, both in writing and in person, of the systematic murder of Jews in Ukraine. As we have seen, the pope did not speak out publicly in response. However, Angelo Roncalli, the future Pope John XXIII, reports that the pope questioned his own silence and Scavizzi reported the pope crying "like a child" during their meeting. In 1942, both Andrea Szeptzycky, archbishop of the Ukrainian Greek Catholic Church, by letter and Giovanni Malvezzi, a prominent Catholic, through a meeting with Monsignor Giovanni Montini, deputy to the Vatican Secretariat of State, painted a horrifying picture of the fate of Eastern European Jews to the pope. In September of that year the American special envoy to the Vatican, Myron Taylor, reported the liquidation of the Warsaw Ghetto and the "butchering of the Jews of Germany, Belgium and Holland." Nevertheless, there were those in the Vatican who were skeptical of the reports and Pius responded to Harold Tittmann, Taylor's assistant, that it was not yet possible to verify them. Consequently, the pope remained silent.[83]

In the weeks prior to October 16, it is highly likely that Pius XII knew of an impending roundup. An Italian intelligence agent informed the Vatican secretariat of state as early as October 11 that the Nazis planned a roundup in Rome on October 18. That date was wrong, and the intelligence agent did not mention Jews, but there were probably similar reports coming to the Vatican that would have put the pope on notice that an atrocity was being planned.[84]

It is certainly undeniable that the pope knew of the October 16 roundup in Rome while it was taking place. On that day, Princess Enza Pignatelli Aragona Cortes, who did charitable work in Rome, informed the pontiff in person, rushing to the Vatican and meeting with Pius XII after a friend had telephoned her to report in horror what she was seeing from her home near the Ghetto. The pope immediately called the Vatican secretary of state, Cardinal Luigi Maglione, who then summoned German ambassador Ernst von Weizsäcker to the Vatican that same day for this discussion:

I [Maglione] asked him [von Weizsäcker] to intervene in favor of those poor people. . . . I told him simply. . . . It is painful for the Holy Father, painful beyond words, that here in Rome, under the eyes of the Common Father, so many people are made to suffer because of their particular descent.

The ambassador, after some moments of reflection, asked me: "What would the Holy See do if these things continued?"

I answered: The Holy See would not want to be obliged to express its disapproval.[85]

Austrian bishop Alois Hudal, rector of the German Catholic Church in Rome, delivered a similarly passive response by letter later in the day to General Stahel of the German high command:

A High Vatican dignitary in the immediate circle of the Holy Father has just informed me that this morning a series of arrests of Jews of Italian nationality has been initiated. In the interests of the good relations which have existed until now between the Vatican and the German High Command . . . I earnestly request that you order the immediate suspension of these arrests both in Rome and its vicinity. Otherwise I fear that the Pope will take a public stand against this action which would undoubtedly be used by the anti-German propagandists as a weapon against us.[86]

Later, Ambassador von Weizsäcker did telegram the German foreign ministry asking that the Jews be consigned to a labor detail within Italy, to no response.

It is likewise undeniable that the pope was aware of the reprisals for the ss killings in Via Rasella. On the day after the resistance action, the Vatican received a report of the imminent murder of ten Romans for every ss operative killed. In a Vatican memo dated March 24, 1944, 10:15 a.m., the Vatican secretariat of state noted: "The Governatorato of Rome reports the following details about yesterday's incident: the German victims numbered 26 soldiers [an undercount], among the Italian civilians there were, unfortunately, three or four deaths; . . . the countermeasures are not yet known: it is however foreseen that for every German killed, ten Italians will be executed."[87]

The pope's public responses were tepid. Not once did he object to the wholesale slaughter of Jews. Rather, the October 25–26, 1943, edition of the official Vatican newspaper *L'osservatore Romano* reported Pius's dismay at the suffering of "so many unfortunate people":[88]

> As is well known, the August Pontiff, after having tried in vain to prevent the outbreak of the war . . . has not for one moment ceased employing all the means in His power to alleviate the sufferings that are, in whatever form, the consequences of this cruel conflagration.
>
> With the growth of so much evil, the universally paternal charity of the Supreme Pontiff has become, one could say, even more active; it does not pause before the boundaries of nationality, religion, or descent.
>
> This manifold and incessant activity of Pius XII has been greatly intensified recently by the increased sufferings of so many unfortunate people.[89]

The article did not cite any evidence of the pope's "using all the means in His power to alleviate the sufferings." A companion front-page article entitled "The Slaughter of the Innocents"—a biblical reference to Herod's massacre of Jewish children two years old and younger in the vicinity of Bethlehem (Matt. 2:16–18)[90]—spoke only generally of the sufferings of all innocents in the war, making no mention of Jews or the roundup.[91]

But did the pope act differently when not speaking publicly? Several reports by papal supporters such as attorney Ronald Rychlak and journalist William Doino have stated that both Popes John XXIII and Paul VI, and Father Pancrazio Pfeiffer, Pius's personal liaison to the German military command in Rome, attested to orders from Pius XII to save Jewish lives. According to another papal supporter, Rabbi David Dalin, when Cardinal Palazzini accepted his designation as Righteous among the Gentiles at Yad Vashem, the cardinal claimed that all credit had to go to Pius XII, who had ordered him to save Jews.

This testimony to a more active, albeit private, pope who quietly issued directives to Catholic clergy to save Jews offers a different picture than what is found in the pope's public statements. Any explicit written order, even if cautious, would cast Pius's role in the Holocaust in a more favorable light. However, historians familiar with Vatican documents have never seen such a writing. The priests and nuns who risked their lives to save Jews in Rome, and elsewhere in Italy, believed they were acting in accordance with the pope's wishes, but as Holocaust historian Susan Zucotti has stated, "Moral support is not the same as a papal directive."[92]

Numerous explanations have been offered for the pope's relative silence. Pius XII remained neutral between the Axis and the Allies in order to create a space for a negotiated settlement of the war. Even though a negotiated settlement was never a possibility, Pius was reluctant to relinquish that hope. Alternatively: inasmuch as Pius feared German Nazism, he was even more concerned about Soviet Communism. He needed a strong Germany to oppose Communism, so he was unwilling to weaken papal ties to Germany. Another, perhaps more likely, explanation: the Vatican's own political and military weakness translated into a fear for the welfare of Catholic clergy and laypeople living under the Reich. The pope did not want to jeopardize the lives of innocent Catholics by antagonizing the Nazis, especially when in 1939, 1940, and 1941 it appeared that Hitler would win the war and most of Western Europe, even Great Britain, would be under Nazi control.[93] Further, on that issue, the pope has been roundly criticized for his reticence concerning Catholic suffering in Poland under Nazi occupation, where numerous atrocities transpired separately from the persecution of Jews.[94] During October and November 1939, 214 Polish priests were executed, and by the end of that year approximately one thousand members of the Polish clergy were imprisoned in concentration camps, all without papal condemnation. In Germany the Catholic Church supported the Nazi war effort in Poland, and likewise the pontiff remained silent on the matter.[95] Thus Pius XII has been accused of being just as timid about Catholic Poles as he was about the Jews.[96]

That said, on select occasions Pius XII abandoned his studied neutrality. Although the Vatican has generally not been perceived as of great help to the Allied war effort, at the beginning of the war, Pius XII warned the Allies of German invasion plans and served as a conduit for messages—albeit no messages concerning Jews—between anti-Nazi agents in Germany and the British.[97] Toward the end of the war, Pius privately urged the Germans, through his nuncio in Berlin, to provide him with the approximate numbers of Jews awaiting deportation, to stop all deportation of Jews from northern Italy, and to allow those Jews to reach a place of refuge. The pope's urgings were ignored.[98]

In at least one case, as long as he was not voicing concerns to German authorities, the pope acted to save Jews. In April 1943 when the Germans asked the Italian army to hand over the Jews under its control in France and on the Dalmatian coast, Pius asked his envoy to protest to the Italian undersecretary of foreign affairs. The Jews remained in Italian hands, which protected them from execution at least until September 8, 1943, and the Nazi takeover of Italy.[99] On the other hand, when Angelo Roncalli, later Pope John XXIII, pleaded with the pope to intervene with the head of the Slovakian government, a Roman Catholic priest, to allow one thousand Jewish children in Slovakia to emigrate to Palestine (with British authorization) to avoid their impending deportation to Polish death camps, the Vatican's longstanding opposition to a Jewish state in Palestine overrode the call to save Jewish lives. The pope informed Roncalli that he favored a position where the "non-Aryan youths" remain in Slovakia, but not be deported to Poland.[100]

Finally, it has been argued Pope Pius may have been afraid to jeopardize church institutions across Rome, Italy, and Europe that were clandestinely sheltering Jews. Had the pope given Hitler any excuse to move against the church, even invade the Vatican, the lives of thousands of Jews in safe hiding would be risked and might well have been lost. While such an explanation is plausible, there exists no evidence that the pope had such concerns. Any apprehension Pius XII might have had regarding his own possible kidnapping would not have been irrational. Rumors circulated throughout the war that the Nazis had plans to remove the pope from Rome or even do away with the Vatican altogether. Most likely the rumors were Allied propaganda and nothing more.[101] Nevertheless, they were probably unnerving. Pius XII would have known that the French under Napoleon took the early nineteenth-century popes to France, and if it came to that, the protection Pius was giving to Jews in the Vatican and ostensibly elsewhere in Rome would have evaporated.[102]

And yet critics like Katz believe that any such concerns were merely a cover for the pope's timidity, and that bold actions would have saved lives. The pope could have publicly condemned Hitler once his antisemitic intentions had become clear. A thorough and explicit condemnation of Nazi antisemitism could have rallied the German churches against Hitler, causing Catholic Nazis to question or even abandon the Nazi Party and refuse to carry out his genocidal policies. In Rome, Pius XII probably had enough advance information about the danger to Roman Jews to issue a clear warning about the impending roundup and thereby save hundreds of lives. Historian Susan Zuccotti has also speculated that had Pius spoken out forcefully, some in the Italian resistance, armed with papal indignation, might have found a way to stop the train to Auschwitz and free the Jewish prisoners. Speculation aside, the British minister to the Vatican, Sir D'Arcy Osborne, reportedly was upset enough to ask the pope after the roundup, on October 18, how vile would the Nazis have to be—what conditions would have to prevail for him to no longer remain quiet, and would he ever leave Rome. The pope replied that he would never leave the Vatican unless forcibly removed. Osbourne then urged him to understand his considerable moral authority and its potential usefulness in the future.[103]

There is no simple answer to the question of Pius's conduct during the war. Given his background as Vatican secretary of state to Pope Pius XI, he appears to have been a pope enamored of diplomacy at a time when all diplomatic overtures to Hitler's Germany were doomed to failure. Even the language he used in his public statements about the Nazis' "Final Solution" was burdened by diplomatic jargon and evasive turns of phrase.

His decision not to use the words "Jew" or "Jewish" when referring to Nazi crimes made his statements more obscure and less powerful. And finally his fear of a Communist takeover of Europe drove him to believe in a negotiated settlement with Hitler and Mussolini that would leave the institution of the Catholic Church unscathed in a postwar world. Taken together, Pope Pius's predilections and aspirations led him to remain silent while the numbers of the dead produced by Nazi war crimes multiplied into the millions. His hopes for a viable postwar church were achieved at the expense of a deep moral deficit.

Whether an unequivocal condemnation of the Nazi policy toward Jews would have made a significant difference to the victims of Auschwitz, Treblinka, and the other Eastern European camps is a matter of speculation. That said, it appears likely that in his own city of Rome, such a statement abhorring the October 16 roundup would have been effective in saving Jewish lives. A strong, specific denunciation against the Nazis' treatment of Jews and a poignant recognition of his neighbors as innocent victims might well have prevented much Italian cooperation in the roundup and subsequent transport of the Jews by train to Auschwitz. That was a pointed opportunity for moral leadership that Pius failed to grasp.

Even his critics have described the pope as a profoundly spiritual man, a man uncommonly devoted to God and to humanity. Yet according to the available evidence, during the war years of 1939 through 1945 and specifically from September 8, 1943, through June 5, 1944—the time of crisis when the Nazis occupied Rome—Pius XII failed to live up to that image.

PROTECTORS AND INFORMERS

Contradictions in the relationship between Catholics and Jews during the Nazi occupation abound. As Liliana Picciotto, a chronicler of the Shoah in Italy, has said of the Jews there, "An estimated 23,778 were saved because of the good relationships they had with their non-Jewish neighbors and to the generosity of people who sheltered and fed them, many of them belonging to the clergy."[104] The matter in Rome has been stated more starkly: if individuals had not harbored Jews, and if the church institutions had not taken in many Jews, the two-thousand-year-old Jewish community in Rome would not exist today.[105]

The precise number of Jews rescued by the church cannot be known. De Felice calculates that over the course of the Nazi occupation, Catholics and Catholic institutions sheltered 4,447 Jews.[106] Yet, as in the case of the shelter at Basilica di San Paolo Fuori le Mura, some of the protected Jews were eventually captured and killed. Of the known informers, none were clerics, and none worked on the church's behalf. On balance, it has been said, "Every [Roman] Jew who survived owed his own life to a non-Jewish Italian, and it is also probably true that almost every Jew who died in an extermination camp owed his fate to a non-Jewish Italian."[107]

That inspiring and simultaneously sobering assessment was offered as a corrective to a narrative that developed after World War II making more of the Italians' assistance to Jews than Italian informers' betrayal of them. On December 14, 1956, Sergio Piperno, president of the national Union of the Italian Jewish Communities, spoke the following words at a public ceremony in Rome, where Jews thanked their Catholic neighbors for their assistance during the Nazi occupation: "Everyone helped; all those who in some way could follow the moves of the occupying power and its collaborators were quick to warn their innocent and marked victims; all the friends, the acquaintances, the neighbors were quick to take them in, hide them and help then; everyone labored at procuring false documents for the Jews and derailed the searches."[108]

The above is quoted in *The Jews in Fascist Italy*, a classic work by historian of Fascism Renzo De Felice, which has been seriously criticized for creating a storyline of Italian aid to Jews while ignoring some of the worst offences by Fascist collaborators.[109] Another historian of Fascist culture, Ruth Ben-Ghiat, more recently explained that after the war, Jews like Piperno contributed to a glorification of Italian bravery and generosity belied not only by the informers but also by the postwar Italian regime, which refused to identify Jews as a politically persecuted people. Jews returning to Italy from the concentration camps and death camps were not considered war heroes like the Italian partisans. Forty-six streets in

FIG. 9. Trilingual dedicatory inscription (Latin, Italian, Hebrew) to the martyrs at the Fosse Ardeatine (Ardeatine caves). The Hebrew is Psalms 130:1. Elio Villa / Alamy.

Rome were named after non-Jewish victims of the Fosse Ardeatine massacre; none were named after Jews. Italian universities were reluctant to reinstate Jews into the positions they had held prior to the Racial Laws, and the courts were reluctant to convict Italians of persecuting Jews; by the end of the 1950s, no Italian was serving time for such a crime.[110] With the active help of the Italian Jewish community the Italian participation in antisemitism was severely downplayed and the blame put almost exclusively on the Nazis. Examples for this attitude comes from such diverse quarters as the Jewish philosopher Hannah Arendt—"the great majority of Italian Jews were exempted from the Racial laws"—and the filmmaker Roberto Benigni's *Life is Beautiful*.[111]

A DISTORTED JEWISH-CATHOLIC FAMILY

The outpouring of Catholic charity toward Jews during the Nazi occupation confirms the understanding that Jews and Catholics in Rome often perceived themselves in familial terms. They both used terms of kinship to express those feelings. While the evidence presented here is anecdotal, there is a mass of it, and it cumulatively indicates that the coexistence of Jews and Catholics in the city approached the feeling of a family relationship. Over two thousand years, there were times when Jews were made to feel part of a larger Roman family and times that they were not, producing the paradox, the cognitive dissonance, of living as intimate strangers.

A person can be accorded a place in a large family and still be given less respect than others in the family. As Debenedetti, chronicler of the October 16 roundup knew well, that had been the Jewish position for millennia. After World War II, he demanded a change in the respect accorded to Jews. He believed they had earned it. After the war several popes would visit the Fosse Ardeatine. In 1949, the victims would be memorialized in Hebrew, Italian, and Latin at the entrance to the cave where they were killed. Nevertheless, as the next chapter will demonstrate, the city of Rome would only partially and ambiguously fulfill Debenedetti's hope.

11

The Arch of Titus Redux

Israel and Vatican II in Postwar Rome

Despite Germany's total capitulation in 1945, some members of the church hierarchy retained sympathies for individual Nazis, if not for the Reich. Nazi sympathizers in the church proceeded to run what would later be called the Ratline: a sub-rosa operation out of a Vatican office that forged false identities and then smuggled tens of thousands of Nazi war criminals and their supporters out of Europe to South America.[1] In Rome the operation was initiated by Austrian bishop Alois Hudal and administered by Father Joseph Gallov, whose Vatican-sponsored charity aided Hungarian refugees along with Nazi sympathizers. Gallov asked no questions, and helped provide passports for escapees. Later, Father Krunoslav Draganović led a group of Croatian priests in Rome's San Girolamo degli Illirici Seminary who were helping Croatian Nazi fellow travelers and criminals escape Italy through Genoa on their way to South America. Pius XII himself likely knew of these and other operations to foster escape through Italy and Spain, though there is little indication that he gave them active support. Monsignor Karl Bayer later recounted that Pius XII provided "driblets" of money to obtain a false passport for Franz Strangl, commandant of the Treblinka death camp.[2] It is clear that American counterintelligence in Rome was aware of the Ratline as it was operating.[3]

After the war, some of the same church institutions in Rome that had given refuge to Jews and other anti-Fascists now sheltered Nazi and Fascist fugitives. Vigilantes had been quick to seek revenge against their former

Fascist oppressors—for example, partisans in Milan summarily executed Mussolini as the Germans retreated from Italy in April 1945. As a result, some churchmen, like Father Piero Palazzini, interpreted Pope Pius XII's (alleged) desire to "save human lives on whatever side they may be" as an order to protect "the persecutors of yesterday, now being prosecuted by the purge tribunals."[4]

The Jewish trauma was different. Despite the American Joint Distribution Committee's substantial efforts to distribute food, clothing, candy, linens, and cash to the Jewish families of Rome, the community was still in severe straits. Field workers from what came to be known as "the Joint" arrived in Italy in late 1944. As documented by one worker, Reuben Resnik, in letters to his mother in 1945, Jewish orphans in Rome had frostbite, arthritis, and scabies. He arranged for an army doctor to examine them and was also able to get the children new clothes, milk, and clean linens. In addition, the international Jewish occupational training organization ORT, operating with the help of the Joint, taught tailoring to Jewish girls in 1947. A year later, trainees were mending used clothes sent to Rome from overseas.[5]

CONVERSION OF THE CHIEF RABBI

Among the travails of Roman Jewry, their chief rabbi of Rome chose to convert to Catholicism. Toward the end of the war, on February 13, 1945, Israel Zolli and his wife Emma Maionica Zolli were baptized in the basilica Santa Maria degli Angeli.[6]

Zolli would later admit that he was "a convert out of spite."[7] His earlier warnings to Rome's Jews to destroy the community's records and leave or hide had been generally ignored, as we saw in the last chapter, and after Rome's liberation, when he reemerged expecting that he would resume his duties as chief rabbi, his extreme unpopularity made that impossible. Because he had abruptly gone into hiding, Jews perceived him as having abandoned the flock during their time of need. As a compromise, the community offered him the directorship of Rome's Rabbinical College with a sinecure greater than his rabbinic salary. The Rabbinical College was barely an operating institution at that time, and Zolli, with some indignation, refused, and converted shortly thereafter.

Upon his conversion Zolli took the name Eugenio, the name of Pope Pius XII, and eventually taught seminarians at the Pontifical Biblical Institute. He justified his conversion in a memoir tracing his interest in Catholicism back to his childhood. He tried to collect the pension typically afforded a former chief rabbi, but that request was swiftly denied. As a convert, he founded a center in Rome to assist converted Jews in their transition into Catholic life.[8] The irony of establishing his own personal Catecumeni long after the church had abandoned that institution may, or may not, have been lost on him.

WAR CRIMES TRIALS

Of greater concern for Rome's Jews was bringing the Nazi perpetrators of the Shoah in Rome to justice. The Nuremberg trials of Nazi war criminals conducted by the victorious Allies after the war did not treat the roundup of Jews in Rome or the massacre at the Fosse Ardeatine. Instead, Italian collaborators who had sent hundreds of Jews to their death were tried before the Roman courts, and German officers arrested at the end of the war in Italy were tried in Italian military tribunals.

The trials of the collaborators were concerned almost exclusively with economic transgressions. Individuals were charged with collaboration and additional aggravating acts, such as theft, plunder, or extortion. The fact that most of the victims were Jewish, and being identified was often a death sentence, was not a consideration in the Roman courts. Consequently, the defendants were given light sentences, and by the end of the 1950s, not one Italian was serving time for the persecution of Jews. It would take almost fifty years for the Jewish victims of the Nazi occupation in Rome to obtain a measure of justice.[9]

Such antisemitic avoidance of the facts was clear in the most visible case to come before a military tribunal: the 1948 prosecution of Herbert Kappler, head of the Gestapo in Rome. While Kappler was sentenced to life imprisonment, the tribunal had to engage in extreme legal gymnastics to reach that result. At issue was whether Kappler's reprisal order after the Via Rasella bombing of ten dead Romans for every dead SS member was a war crime worthy of punishment, or a matter of "just following orders," or even an act justified by the partisan attack on the SS soldiers. In the end, all those issues were avoided and Kappler's fate was decided on a separate issue. He had ordered the death of ten extra men when one of the SS victims died belatedly of his wounds. That order was judged to be Kappler's alone—he was not following orders—and their deaths were deemed arbitrary and illegal. Without that additional order, the tribunal might have found him innocent. Regarding his extorting fifty kilograms of gold from the Jewish community, he was convicted of "arbitrary requisition" and sentenced to fifteen years' imprisonment in addition to his life sentence.[10] Kappler served much of that time, but escaped from prison in 1977. He died a free man in West Germany the following year.

Twenty years later, in 1998, Kappler's subordinate, SS Captain Erich Priebke, was also convicted of the murders at the Fosse Ardeatine. Initially, Priebke was to be tried with Kappler, but with the help of Bishop Alois Hudal, and possibly with support from Italian and American intelligence, he was spirited out of Genoa to Argentina, where he would live free for decades until being discovered by ABC news correspondent Sam Donaldson.[11] Then he was extradited to Italy to stand trial.

Priebke was put on trial before a military court in Rome in 1996. He was tried not only for his participation in the Ardeatine massacre, but also for the torture he had administered in the Via Tasso prison. At age eighty-four he was found guilty of murder, but in the first of three proceedings it was determined that he could not be punished given his advanced age, his good behavior in the intervening fifty-four years, and his claim that he was just following orders. The outrage from the Jewish community and the Associazione nazionale famiglie Italiani martiri (National association of families of Italian martyrs) was instantaneous. Demonstrations followed in front of the courthouse, prompting Rome's Mayor Francesco Rutelli to address the crowd:

Until yesterday I thought that . . . if I had met Mengele here, I could call the Carabinieri and have him arrested, then tried and be sure he would be punished. Now I can't believe that anymore. After this sentence, if I meet Mengele, it would be useless to call the Carabinieri because it seems it is possible to commit massacres, be found guilty and nonetheless escape justice and be free. It is a very sad day for the city of Rome. I will instruct that all the illumination of Rome's monuments be shut off.[12]

The lights went off thereafter at the Colosseum, the Roman Forum, the Quirinale Palace (residence of the Italian president) and the Montecitorio (which housed the Chamber of Deputies [lower house of the Italian parliament]). On the same night, Italy's Prime Minister Romano Prodi traveled to the Fosse Ardeatine and asked forgiveness from the martyrs buried there. Later, Deputy Prime Minister Walter Veltroni visited the Great Synagogue and declared that contrary to the decision, "Italy . . . does not forget the lessons of memory."[13] The following day, Tullia Zevi, president of the Union of Italian Jewish Communities, visited the Fosse Ardeatine to lay a wreath of red and white flowers.

The outpouring of frustration and anger marked a change in the official memory of Rome's Nazi occupation, which for the first time took careful notice of the Jewish victims. Public officials as well as Jewish leaders were finally discussing the antisemitic nature of the Nazi occupation of Rome.

As for Priebke himself, there followed, after an appeal, a second proceeding, before the military tribunal, in which Priebke was again found guilty, but this time his crime was found punishable. Upon learning of that verdict, the president of the Jewish Community of Rome made the following statement, which echoed the very concerns Giacomo Debenedetti had voiced about half a century earlier. Jews had died as part of the Roman family, and should be remembered as such: "The drama of the Fosse Ardeatine concerns us Jews only in a small part; on the day (in 1944) above all, many, many Romans died. And I believe that we Jews will have won our battle for historical memory the day in which all of civil society realizes that Nazism was a tragedy for all, and not just for the Jews."[14]

The drama did not end there. Priebke's sentence of life imprisonment was reduced to twenty months, given his age and time served. That sentence was appealed, and ultimately Priebke was sentenced to life imprisonment under house arrest. He lived another fifteen years, dying in Rome in 2013 at age one hundred. During his trial and incarceration, as with Kappler's, intermittent antisemitic graffiti marred the streets of Rome.[15]

CELEBRATION AT THE ARCH OF TITUS

If the Shoah was a continuing trauma for the Jews of Rome, the creation of the State of Israel was an occasion for profound celebration. On November 29, 1947, the United Nations General Assembly, meeting in Lake Success, New York, had approved the partition of Palestine and the creation of a Jewish state with a vote of thirty-three in favor (including Italy), thirteen against, ten abstentions, and one absent. Days later, on the afternoon of December 2, Jews from all over the city, some Roman natives and some refugees, gathered at the Arch of Titus, which almost two thousand years earlier had celebrated the destruction of Jerusalem and proclaimed an end to the Jewish nation, if not the Jewish people. Nearby, other triumphal arches in the city—the Arch of Septimius Severus, the Arch of Constantine, as well as memorial columns of Trajan and Marcus Aurelius—stood as congratulatory memorials to the Roman Empire's destruction of the Parthians, the "tyrant Maxentius," the Dacians, and the Sarmatians respectively, all individuals or groups the empire had indeed erased long ago. Tourists from around the world visiting those arches and columns often knew little to nothing about the victims—"Who were the Dacians?"—but tourists at the Arch of Titus were not similarly stumped. In fact, they were far more familiar with the Jews than they were with Titus. In 1947, having long survived the empire, a new generation of Jews now stood under the arch dedicated in part to their demise as a people.

Jews celebrated this circumstance, along with the newly minted Jewish state, on December 2, 1947. A blue and white banner hung from the arch bore the words "Ninth of Ab, 70 CE and December 2, 1947," the two dates marking the destruction of the last Jewish state and the establishment

FIG. 10. Celebration at the Arch of Titus, December 2, 1947. Archivo Storico della Comunità Ebraica di Roma, Archivio fotografico, Rav.

of the present one. The revelers listened to speeches, and placed a laurel wreath next to the reliefs depicting Roman soldiers carrying the Temple menorah in their own celebration almost two thousand years before. The chief rabbi of Rome, David Prato, led the crowd in singing "Hatikvah" (The hope) that was to become the Israeli national anthem. Then, something remarkable happened. Men, women, and children, waving Star of David flags, strutted beneath the arch from west to east. They were deliberately dancing in reverse, in the opposite direction from that of the Jews who were led from Jerusalem to Rome in slavery. They were symbolically undoing the events depicted in the arch, as if to say, "We will unravel the spool of time and erase our misfortunes of two thousand years."

Decades later, Valeria Spizzichino would recall that momentous day:

We had been forbidden by our rabbis to walk under the Arch of Titus, because it represented the great shame, the great sorrow of the destruction of the Temple and then the great diaspora under Titus. When the State of Israel was proclaimed we went. The chief rabbi led the way, dressed in all the vestments just as in the temple, and after him came all the rabbis, and then practically all of Jewish Rome. And we stayed up until three, four A.M. dancing around the bonfires, in the Jewish quarter. I remember it perfectly, it was wonderful.[16]

The spontaneous celebration nonetheless had to be tempered for public consumption in postwar Rome, lest it be construed as a rejection of the Italian nation. Consequently, on November 29, 1947, Raffaele Cantoni, president of the Union of Italian Jewish Communities, wrote a letter to Enrico de Nicola, Italy's provisional head of state, attempting to assure him that Italian Jewish loyalties were to Italy as much as to Israel:

At this solemn moment in the long and tragic history of Israel, the Jews of Italy believe it is their duty to reaffirm their love for the land in which they have lived for centuries and of which they are and remain free and loyal citizens. Because of their participation in Italy's fate, even during the most difficult moments, and because of the proof they have always given of their ability to fulfill their duty towards this country, they feel that they have no need to make promises or give assurances.

Their ties with the new Jewish State, which is emerging at this moment in the land of their faith, will be of the same nature as the ties that unite the millions of Italians spread throughout the world to their land of origin.[17]

Thus, in Rome, the creation of Israel highlighted for Jews their dual status as both Jews and Romans, intimates and strangers. It allowed them to remain enthusiastic Italians but with a certain distance created by their loyalty to the new Jewish state.

THE ROSE GARDEN

Within walking distance from the Arch of Titus is the Aventine Hill, which had served as Roman Jewry's cemetery for about two hundred years, beginning around 1645, when Pope Innocent X had granted the Jewish Confraternity of Death and Charity permission to buy land for a cemetery on the hill. That said, the church permitted grave markers on the site only starting in 1846, during Pope Pius IX's early inclination toward reform. Jews continued to be buried there until 1934, when the Fascist regime expropriated the land to build a wide street, Via del Circo Massimo, for a parade commemorating Mussolini's March on Rome. Thereafter, Rome's Jews were to be buried in the large municipal cemetery at Campo Verano, with the Jews previously buried on the Aventine exhumed and transported to Campo Verano. However, the exhumation was carried out in a hurried and haphazard fashion—sometimes on the Sabbath without Jewish supervision—leaving numerous graves still in place, but paved over. During World War II, due to a shortage of food, the Aventine and what was left of the Jewish cemetery there became a vegetable garden.

After the war, around 1950, an American expatriate, Mary Senni, along with the Rome city council, proposed that a municipal rose garden be established on the site of the former cemetery. Although the Jewish community was consulted, there was little they could do. They could not turn back the clock and reestablish a half-paved cemetery that was no longer home to many of its former "inhabitants."

Nonetheless, the Jewish history of the Aventine was to be remembered. The garden was designed with paths in the shape of a seven-branched menorah referencing the menorah carved in the Arch of Titus a few blocks away. Today, visitors wending their way through the garden in spring arrive at a hill on its west end, and from there take in the full scene: two *menorot* and more than eleven hundred species of roses in bloom. A commemorative plaque in the shape of the Ten Commandments tablets also informs visitors of the garden's Jewish history.[18]

Nevertheless, as a matter of Jewish law, the area is still a cemetery with numerous Jewish graves, and the laws of Jewish cemeteries still obtain. No Jews from a priestly family (*Kohen*) may enter the garden, just as they are prohibited from entering any Jewish cemetery. Many Jews avoid the garden in order not to tread on the Jewish graves. So echoing the perennial give-and-take of Roman Jewish history, while the garden is marked out with the shape of the most Roman of Jewish symbols, few Roman Jews walk these paths.

NOSTRA AETATE

One more post–World War II event appeared to put a cap on the history of Jews and Catholics in Rome. On October 28, 1965, Pope Paul VI issued a Declaration of the Relation of the Church to Non-Christian Religions entitled *Nostra aetate* (In our time), which upended the church's long-standing doctrine of blaming Jews as a whole for Jesus' crucifixion. *Nostra aetate* was a product of the Second Vatican Council (1962–65), itself the brainchild of Pope John XXIII (Angelo Roncalli), who had succeeded Pius XII nineteen days after Pius's death on October 9, 1958.

Roncalli had been born into a peasant family in northern Italy. Ordained in Rome in 1904, he served as a chaplain in the Italian army during World War I. Starting in 1935 he was appointed apostolic delegate to Turkey and Greece, his offices in Istanbul. Taking advantage of his role as a racial certification agent—the church gave Nazis throughout the Reich ascertainments concerning persons of Aryan or Jewish "race"—Roncalli provided Jews with false identity documents so they could pass as Catholics and avoid deportation and death.[19]

Roncalli's creation of false baptismal certificates should be seen in the context of the church's attempts in the previous centuries to forcibly baptize Jews. In the 1940s, thousands of Jews were given official church documents that proved they were Catholics when Roncalli well knew that they were not. After the war, these beneficiaries were never pressured to convert. Furthermore, his work was not a secret to either Catholics or Jews when, in November 1958, he was elevated to the papacy. Three months into his pontificate, he announced his intent to convene the council.

The Catholic Church had held councils for almost two thousand years. These assemblies of bishops were to make decisions binding on the entire church in accordance with papal teachings. It was believed that the Holy Spirit guided the councils. The Code of Canon Law of 1917 asserted at canon 222 that an ecumenical council like Vatican II had to be convened by a pope. Once convened, however, it had exceptional power. Canon 228 stated: "An ecumenical council enjoys supreme power over the universal church."

Vatican II was called to cover a wide range of topics, including the use of the vernacular in the liturgy, the role of the laity, the unity of the church, and the sources of revelation. However, John XXIII had expressed a desire to also grapple with the church's fraught relationship with the Jews.[20] In 1959 he had changed the wording of the Good Friday prayer for the conversion of the Jews to omit the adjectives "faithless" and "perfidious" when referring to Jews.[21] Nonetheless, the prayer still asked God to remove the blindness from the Jews in hopes they would become Catholic.

Pope John was influenced by his friendship with the French Jewish scholar Jules Isaac (1877–1963), who had written two books dealing with Catholic doctrinal attitudes toward Jews and had attempted to dissuade the pope from the doctrines that the Jews had committed deicide by crucifying Christ, that God had punished them for that transgression by dispersing them throughout the world, and that the Jewish religion by Jesus' time had become a dead collection of meaningless laws. Isaac may have had some success. Pope John had strong feelings about Jewish-Catholic relations, and he did try to steer the church and council in a more tolerant direction.[22]

However, Pope John XXIII died on June 3, 1963. In that year the church posthumously published John XXIII's encyclical *Pacem in terris* (Peace on earth), addressed "to all men and women of goodwill." (Prior encyclicals had been directed solely to the church.) Contradicting the position of previous popes, especially Pius IX, *Pacem in terris* endorsed freedom of speech, freedom of the press, and freedom of religion, the latter being "the right of being able to worship God in accordance with the right dictates of one's conscience and to profess one's religion both in private and public."[23]

At the conclave that immediately followed John XXIII's death, Giovanni Battista Montini, archbishop of Milan, was elected pope on the sixth ballot. He took the papal name of Paul VI.[24] Paul VI had an intellectual connection with Judaism. An enthusiast of the Jewish philosopher Martin Buber, Paul had chosen Buber's idea of dialogue to frame the controversy about the church's hierarchical nature in his first encyclical, *Ecclesiam suam* (His church). When during the continuation of Vatican II select church leaders proposed issuing a positive declaration concerning the Jews, he would play a considerable part in the contentious debate.

Opponents attacked the very idea of the Vatican's issuing a positive statement concerning the Jews from two directions. On the theological front, they argued that those who were in error—that is, Jews and other non-Christians—were not worthy of honor. (Thus the idea that Jews lacked honor, prevalent in the Middle Ages, had survived into the 1960s.) Jews might be worthy of tolerance and charity, but not honor. Any declaration beyond tolerance was going too far. On the political front, opponents protested that Arab nations might take any statement concerning the Jews as support for Israel. Should the council make a favorable declaration concerning Jews, some Arab governments might close their embassies to the Vatican. Instead, a general statement about non-Christian religions ought to be issued, without reference to any specific religion, such as Judaism.[25]

Standing against those arguments and supporting a strong statement exonerating Jews of deicide was the German Jesuit Augustin Bea (1881–1968). Bea had been in personal contact with Rabbi Abraham Heschel, an almost prophetic teacher of Judaism at both the Hebrew Union College in Cincinnati and the Jewish Theological Seminary in New York. Bea had warmly received Heschel's conviction that Vatican II had to reject the long-held Christian accusation that Jews had killed Jesus. Bea pointed out to the council that even if a small minority of Jews in the first century CE were responsible for Jesus' death—a position he himself rejected—those Jews could not have knowingly killed God, because Jesus himself had said, "Forgive them father for they know not what they do" (Luke 23:34). According to Bea, in that one sentence, Jesus had refuted both the notion that the Jews intended deicide and the contention that Jews should be blamed for the purported deicide in perpetuity. Meanwhile, other council members urged acceptance of the declaration concerning the Jews for political reasons, because it would help "defend the memory" of Pope Pius XII, whose response to the Shoah was under attack.[26] After debate had ended, procedural matters delayed a vote on the final wording, which would need to take place in 1965.

In early 1965, two Sundays before Easter and approximately five months before the council was to reconvene, Paul VI entered the fray in a ham-handed way. He gave a sermon in a Roman church asserting that the Jews had rejected Jesus as the Messiah and had killed Christ: "The Gospel tells us, in fact, of the confrontation between Jesus and the Jewish people. This people, destined to receive the Messiah, whom they were expecting for thousands of years, and who were completely preoccupied with that hope and assurance, at the perfect moment when, that is, Christ came, in their words and deeds, not only failed to recognize him, but fought him, slandered him, insulted him and in the end killed him."[27]

With these strong words, which drew protests from the chief rabbi of Rome and the president of the Italian Jewish Communities, Paul was not necessarily opposing the issuance of any positive statement about the Jews per se. Paul was making the point that that any positive declaration concerning the Jews had to include an acknowledgment that some Jews had killed Jesus. Otherwise, the church's two-thousand-year teaching would have been in total error. He would not admit that.

The revised text was brought up on October 14. By now the statement also included a long section on Muslims, to placate the Arab nations. Two weeks later, on October 28, 1965, the council approved *Nostra aetate* by a vote of 2,234 to 88. For Jews, these were the crucial lines:

> Since the spiritual patrimony common to Christians and Jews is thus so great, this sacred synod wants to foster and recommend that mutual understanding and respect which is the fruit, above all, of biblical and theological studies as well as of fraternal dialogues.
>
> True, the Jewish authorities and those who followed their lead pressed for the death of Christ; still, what happened in his passion cannot be charged against all the Jews, without distinction, then alive, nor against the Jews of today. Although the Church is the new people of God, the Jews should not be presented as rejected or accursed by God, as if this followed from the Holy Scriptures. . . .
>
> Furthermore, in her rejection of every persecution against any man, the Church, mindful of the patrimony she shares with the Jews and moved not by political reasons but by the Gospel's spiritual love, decries hatred, persecutions, displays of anti-Semitism, directed against Jews at any time and by anyone.[28]

With that, old prejudices fell. All Jews from the time of Jesus to the present could no longer be tarred with accusations of deicide. Equally important was the statement in article 4 of the declaration that Jews are not a community superseded by Catholicism or rejected by God. However, the limited nature of *Nostra aetate*, specifically its failure to address antisemitism in the Catholic tradition, has drawn considerable attention.[29]

In the years following 1965, when Rome became the home of 42 percent of all Italian Jews, the city became the site of numerous events meant to solidify a new and mutually beneficial relationship between the Catholic Church and the Jewish community.[30] Popes John Paul II and Benedict XVI visited the Great Synagogue in Rome, and in 1986, during the first visit by a pope to the synagogue, Pope John Paul reiterated John XXIII's declaration of Jewish-Catholic brotherhood, proclaiming to the assembled Jews: "You are our dearly beloved brothers, and in a certain way it could be said you are our older brothers."[31]

John Paul also visited the Fosse Ardeatine, and in 1982 he went again to meet with Elio Toaff, the chief rabbi of Rome, on the anniversary of the massacre.[32] Before him, Pope Paul VI had paid a commemorative visit to the site, and every pope since then has come to the Fosse Ardeatine to remember the Jewish and non-Jewish Italians who died there.

In 2020, Pope Francis and Riccardo Di Segni, the chief rabbi of Rome, exchanged greetings commemorating both Passover and Easter; and in 2016, Francis visited the Great Synagogue, telling the assembled Jews, "You are our elder brothers and sisters in the faith. We all belong to a single family, the family of God."[33]

Yet even when intentions are good, the possibility for a misstep remains.[34] On August 11, 2021, during his usual Wednesday public audience, Pope Francis delivered an address on Paul's "Letter to the Galatians" that said that the Jewish Law, the Torah, was no longer life-giving. In response, Rabbi Rason Arussi, speaking for the chief rabbinate of Israel, and Rabbi David Sandmel, representing the International Jewish Committee for Interreligious Connections, sent letters of protest to Cardinal Kurt Koch, president of the Holy See's Commission for Religious Relations with the Jews, criticizing the pope for apparently abrogating article 4 of *Nostra aetate* by having claimed that Jesus had superseded the Torah as the only source of human redemption. The chief rabbi of Rome, Riccardo Di Segni, made a similar point in a letter published in the Italian newspaper *La repubblica*.

On September 15, 2021, Cardinal Koch responded, first by saying that Francis had deep respect for Jews, Judaism, and their continuing spiritual relevance. Second, the pope's words needed to be put in context. Pope Francis was not addressing modern Jews. For them, the pope understood, the Torah is undeniably a spiritual source of life. Nor was Francis expressing his own view of the Torah. He was, rather, describing the views of St. Paul as stated in the first-century author's New Testament letter to the Galatians. St. Paul had been addressing a budding first-century Christian community consisting of people who were not, and never were, Jewish. For Catholics and especially a nascent church in the first century CE, the focus, according to St. Paul, had to be on Jesus.

Then, on September 29, 2021, Francis gave an address to a general audience proclaiming that it would be wrong to think that the Mosaic law had lost its value. In a reaffirmation of article 4, he stated the Torah remains an irrevocable gift from God: "We must not, however, conclude that, for Paul, the Mosaic Law had lost its value; rather, it remains an irrevocable gift from God. It is as the Apostle writes, 'holy.' Rom. 7:12."[35]

The popes' attitude toward Rome's Jews has of course changed considerably since the Middle Ages. Given his visits to the Great Synagogue in Rome, his willingness to engage in dialogue with the chief rabbi Riccardo Di Segni, and even his knowledge of Jewish eateries in the Ghetto area (see the conclusion), today's Jewish leaders largely trust that Francis's goodwill guides his relationship with the Jewish community. In the past, a modest number of Roman Jews could feel proud to be papal physicians, or to be granted a place at the table of the vicar's police captain. But only since *Nostra aetate* has a respectful, mutual admiration grown between Rome's Jewish community and the popes in the Vatican.

All of this is not to deny the continuing ambiguous nature of the Catholic-Jewish relationship in Rome. Without diminishing the goodwill of all concerned, the church's failure to confront its role in spreading antisemitism has continued. *Nostra aetate* is still viewed as limited, specifically because it did not address longstanding antisemitism in the Catholic tradition.[36]

Most notable is the church's 1998 report, "We Remember: A Reflection on the Shoah." In 1987, one year after John Paul II's visit to the Great Synagogue, a papal commission had been tasked with determining what responsibility, if any, the Catholic Church bore for the Shoah. Eleven years later, the commission presented Pope John Paul II with a document no longer than three pages. "We Remember" exonerated the church by drawing a distinction between anti-Judaism, which admittedly had been a church tradition, and racial antisemitism, which had fueled the Shoah but which the church had rejected. When evaluating the horrific events of the mid-twentieth century, the insufficiency and sheer inaccuracy of such a formal distinction was apparent. Compelled to respond, the preeminent scholar of the modern papacy, David Kertzer, wrote *The Popes against the Jews: The Vatican's Role in the Rise of Modern Anti-Semitism*, a study of how nineteenth- and twentieth-century church antisemitism—explicitly on display in the Catholic newspapers *Civiltà cattolica* and *L'osservatore Romano*, among other places—played an influential role in the circumstances leading up to the Shoah.

All in all, the paradoxical nature of the Jewish-Catholic encounter in Rome remains. The continuity of the same themes in Jewish-Catholic Rome from the earliest times to the present cannot be denied.

Conclusion

A Walk through the Ghetto

One can stroll through the area of Rome that was once the Ghetto in about half an hour. Depending on your interests, you can be taken back to the time of Titus, or the Cinque Scole, or the *ghettarello*. But you can also take a more contemporary tour through the twentieth and twenty-first centuries. To end this book, that is the tour we need to take.

THE VIA DELLA REGINELLA *STOLPERSTEINE*

The small street called Via della Reginella was added to the Ghetto in the nineteenth century. In the space of two blocks it connects the Piazza Mattei on the north (just outside the Ghetto boundaries) with the Via del Portico d'Ottavia to the south (in the heart of the Ghetto).

Embedded in the cobblestones outside number 10 Via della Reginella are several *Stolpersteine*, or "stumbling blocks," sitting at street level at the feet of passers-by. Each 10-centimeter brass tube (driven into the ground) bears a plate inscribed with the name and crucial dates of a person killed during the Shoah. Placed in the street next to the house of the victim, every *Stolperstein* marks the home from which that individual was deported for extermination. Gunther Demnig, German and not Jewish, initiated the *Stolperstein* project in 1992 as a way of memorializing each victim of the Shoah, Jewish or gentile, and today more than forty thousand *Stolpersteine* can be found across the nations of Europe from the Netherlands and

Germany to Hungary and Austria. *Stolpersteine* appear throughout the city of Rome, though many cluster in the Ghetto area. The inscriptions are small, and you have to bend down, even kneel, to read the names of the dead, but doing so is in itself an act of remembrance.

At the entrance to number 10 Via della Reginella, one *Stolperstein* reads:

Qui abitava
Zaccaria Di Capua
Nato 1899
Arrestato 16.3.1944
Assassinato 24.3.1944
Fosse Ardeatine

Who lived here
Zaccaria Di Capua
Born 1899
Arrested 16.3.1944
Killed 24.3.1944
Fosse Ardeatine

Down the street at number 2 Via della Reginella, another *Stolperstein* says:

Qui abitava
Ada Spizzichino
Nata 1915
Arrestata 16.10.1943
Deportata Auschwitz
Assassinata 23.10.1943

In the space of a few housefronts we are confronted, almost face-to-face, with two victims of the Nazis, one taken during the October 16 roundup and the other murdered at the Fosse Ardeatine; a man and a woman, one forty-five and the other twenty-eight years old.

FIG. 11. *Stolperstein* commemorating the murder of Antonio Roazzi in the Fosse Ardeatine by the Nazi occupiers of Rome. Insidefoto/Alamy.

Once you have read one *Stolperstein*, it is difficult not to keep your gaze to the ground to discover more, and on the Via della Reginella there are many more. *Stolpersteine* are also evident on other streets in the former Ghetto. They are like gold-colored leaves scattered over the sidewalks. Most people walk past them, or over them, without noticing.

THE LIBYAN EATERIES ON VIA DEL PORTICO D'OTTAVIA

The end of Via della Reginella intersects with Via del Portico d'Ottavia, the main drag through the Ghetto area. At that corner is the restaurant Ba Ghetto Milky. A block east is Pasticceria Boccione, an Orthodox Jewish bakery famous for its fruit cakes, but Ba Ghetto is more pertinent to our tour.

Since kosher cooking requires the separation of milk and meat, two Ba Ghetto restaurants make their home on Via del Portico d'Ottavia: Ba

Ghetto (serving meat dishes) and Ba Ghetto Milky (strictly dairy). Both are run by the Dabush family, emigrants, by way of Israel, from Libya.

There is evidence of Jews residing in Libya at least two thousand years ago. Josephus notes that in approximately 85 BCE Cyrene, a city in ancient Cyrenaica, now Libya, comprised citizens, farmers, resident aliens, and Jews.[1] One such Jew, Jason, supposedly authored a lost five-volume work on the Maccabaean revolt: "In five books, Jason of Cyrene has set out the history of Judas Maccabaeus and his brothers. . . . These five books of Jason I shall try to summarize in a single work."[2]

Thus Libya, like Rome, had a Jewish presence as far back as the first century BCE, and it continued uninterrupted for two thousand years. However, approximately thirteen thousand Jews reside today in Rome, but not a single Jew lives in Libya. The last Jew to leave was eighty-one-year-old Rina Debach. In 1982, during the regime of Muammar Gaddafi, she flew from Libya to Rome, where she joined a community of Libyan Jews, many having emigrated to Italy in 1967, during Israel's Six-Day War.[3]

Prior to emigration, the Jewish community in Libya had enjoyed an almost one hundred–year-old connection with Italy and Rome. After Italy's unification in 1870, the new nation had harbored hopes of recreating an empire in the Mediterranean. Italians began colonizing Libya in 1880, and military occupation followed thirty years later. While certain Italians would allege that "international Jewry" opposed the Libyan war, much of the actual Jewish community in Libya welcomed the modern European economic and educational opportunities offered by the occupation, such as the opening of Italian-Jewish schools, and careers in banking and engineering. In 1912, the Jewish community in Libya joined the Union of Italian Jewish Communities.[4]

While attempting to assimilate an imported Italian worldview, Libyan Jews became stuck between two worlds. In one instance, a somewhat Italianized Jewish man courted a fifteen-year-old girl from a similarly European-leaning family. Out of frustration, given her resistance, he abducted her and performed a *kiddushin* ceremony wherein he placed a ring on her finger as two of his male friends witnessed the events, and thus insured that she had to marry him (see chapter 6 for such ceremonies in early modern Rome). Her parents sought help from Rabbi Gustavo Castelbolognese from Padua, whom the Italian Union of Jewish Communities had previously sent to Italy to bring the Libyan community into the contemporary world. Castelbolognese, himself a thoroughly modern official, nevertheless refused to go against a tradition long recognized in Libya.[5]

With the rise of Fascism in 1922, Italy moved to fully integrate Libya as the nineteenth region of the kingdom, a project never to be fully realized. Visiting Libya in 1937, Mussolini reassured the Jewish community that Fascism would respect their traditions, but the following year, all foreign Jews living in Libya were ordered to leave the colony. The Racial Laws of 1938 did not become effective in Libya until 1940, and British victories in North Africa soon thereafter protected the approximately thirty-six thousand Libyan Jews.

In 1948, anti-Israel riots in Tripoli protesting the State of Israel's establishment forced thirty thousand Libyan Jews to emigrate to the new nation. In 1967, after riots again erupted, the Jewish community asked King Idris's government to allow the entire Jewish community to leave the country "temporarily," but en masse. The king agreed, with the stipulation that each family could leave with only the equivalent of twenty pounds sterling. With the help of an airlift and the Italian navy, six thousand Jews left Libya in one month. Two-thirds of those émigrés eventually went to Israel, but two thousand stayed in Rome and Milan. Some of the Jews who remained identified as Italians as well as Jews, and found living in Rome familiar, especially because they were familiar with the Italian language. They chose Italy in part because their children could continue their education in a language they already knew.[6] As one of those children, Yosef Netanya, would later recall: "Every morning in the school before entering the classroom, we used to sing a song in Italian which I forgot now. But it was a song entitled 'Viva il re' (long live the King) in honor of Vittorio Emanuele. Afterwards, with Mussolini and Fascism, we stopped with Vittorio Emanuele—of whom in any case there was a picture in every Jewish household, rich and poor alike. And there were also the pictures of Vittorio Emanuele III, of Umberto of Savoia and the Queen of Italy: three pictures."[7]

By 2014, 777 Jews residing in Rome had been born in Libya. With their children and grandchildren, Roman Jews of Libyan descent numbered close to four thousand, or almost 30 percent of the Roman Jewish population.[8] Today, Libyan Jews are found throughout Rome, both integrated and not integrated into the Jewish community. Libyan Jews have their own neighborhoods and synagogues, but there have also been marriages between Libyan Jews and Jews of non-Libyan descent. Many Libyan Jews identify more as Jews than as Romans. The Dabush family's kosher restaurant business, serving Jews from both communities, extends beyond Rome to Milan and Florence. Their efforts are well-known enough that when Pope Francis's Jewish friends arrived from Argentina, the Vatican contacted Ilan Dabush to provide them with traditional Jewish meals.

The Libyan Jewish presence in Rome is historically significant. A two thousand–year-old culture continues today only in Israel and Italy. There is something both tragic and hopeful in the fact that because the Roman Jewish community persisted over millennia, it was able to give refuge to the Libyan community that, after two thousand years, had to give up its own home.[9]

Similarly, Roman Jews took in refugees from the Spanish expulsion in 1492 and, later, Jews expelled from other cities in the Papal States eventually settled in Rome, as we saw in previous chapters. Viewed in its historical context, Roman Jewry's future is both continuous with the past and a new beginning.

LARGO STEFANO GAJ TACHÈ

If we turn south off Via del Portico d'Ottavia onto Via del Tempio, we are heading toward the Tiber and the Great Synagogue. A block before the river is the Largo Stefano Gaj Tachè, a piazza in front of the synagogue. Unlike the namesakes of other landmarks in Rome, Stefano was not an artist, a revolutionary, or an emperor. He was a two-year-old boy.

On October 9, 1982, a Sabbath coinciding with the holiday of Shemini Atzeret, Libyan terrorists attacked the Great Synagogue with submachine guns and hand grenades, wounding forty people and killing one, Stefano. The purported reason for the atrocity was the Israeli war in Lebanon. All the killers escaped to Libya, Italian requests for extradition were denied, and none of the perpetrators were ever punished.

In 2007 the mayor of Rome, Walter Veltroni, authorized the naming of Largo Stefano Gaj Tachè. A stone monument in the piazza at the synagogue entrance reads in Italian: "After prayer and in front of this Synagogue Stefano Gaj Tachè, 2 years old, was murdered and 40 Jews wounded at the hands of assassins due to antisemitic hatred." This memorial is several yards from a similar one inscribed in memory of the Jews captured on October 16, 1943, for deportation to Auschwitz.

On February 3, 2015, as Italy's President Sergio Mattarella addressed the parliament, he had this to say about Stefano. "[Italy] has paid several times, in a not too distant past, the price of hate and intolerance. I want to remember only one name: Stefano Tachè who was killed in the cowardly terrorist attack on the Synagogue in Rome on October 1982. He was only two years old. He was our baby, an Italian baby."[10]

It is unlikely that when Mattarella told parliament "he was our baby," he intended to echo John XXIII's declaration, "I am your brother," but the connection between the two statements is unavoidable. In both instances, a president and a pope attempted to create an unrealized family of Catholics and Jews, an Italian family that included both. The family is unrealized because the intermittent good feelings between the two peoples alternate with times of harrowing alienation.

The following January, Pope Francis began his visit to the Great Synagogue by laying wreaths at the foot of both the Holocaust memorial and Stefano's memorial, and speaking privately with Stefano's mother, father, and brother. Inside the synagogue, Rome's Chief Rabbi Riccardo Di Segni welcomed Francis by noting that according to rabbinic tradition, an act that is repeated three times—in this case, the papal visits to the Great Synagogue

FIG. 12. Pope Francis shakes hands with Chief Rabbi of Rome Riccardo Di Segni during his visit to the Great Synagogue, January 17, 2016. Pacific Press Media Production Corp. / Alamy.

of Popes John Paul II, Benedict XVI, and now Francis—becomes a *chazaqà*, a set habit. Consequently, he looked forward to further visits and continuing goodwill between the Vatican and the Jewish community in Rome.

In his address, the pope began by looking backward. He acknowledged the Shoah, particularly the events in Rome on October 16, 1943. He recalled John Paul II's earlier visit and his embrace of Jews as elder brothers. He added: "In fact you are our brothers and sisters in the faith. We all belong to one family, the family of God."

Yet Pope Francis was making an even larger point. On the one hand, there was the theology of *Nostra aetate*, a conceptual necessity. On the other, there was the reality of family, a human necessity. By remembering a two-year-old child's shocking death, by speaking to the child's parents, and by invoking the language of family regarding Catholics and Jews, the pope was endeavoring to concretize half a century of Jewish and Catholic efforts at reconciliation.

After exhorting the congregation to act in furtherance of interreligious understanding, peace, and love of God's creation, the pope ended with a version of the Priestly Blessing (Num. 6:24–26): "May the Lord bless you and keep you. May the Lord let his face shine upon you, and be gracious to you. May the Lord look upon you kindly and give you peace." He had begun his remarks with a few words in Hebrew: "Toda Rabbah" (Many thanks); he concluded with "Shalom Aleichem" (Peace upon you all).

CHIEF RABBI DR. RICCARDO DI SEGNI

Since its founding in 1904, the Great Synagogue has housed the congregation of Rome's chief rabbi. The present chief rabbi, Rav Dr. Riccardo Di Segni (b. 1949), is also a radiologist and former chair of the radiology department at Rome's San Giovanni Hospital. He became chief rabbi in 2001.

Rabbi Di Segni's family has been in Rome for centuries, but, he told me, that longtime residency almost came to an end in 1943 during the Shoah. His father, Dr. Mosè Mario Di Segni, also a physician, had served as a military doctor in Spain during the Spanish Civil War when Fascist Italy supported Francisco Franco. After two years of service, the Italian army expelled Mosè pursuant to the 1938 Racial Laws that prohibited Jews from being in the military. As the Nazis approached Rome, a non-Jewish journalist warned him to flee the city. Mosè hid his wife, two children, and a sister and brother in San Severino south of Rome and then joined the Italian partisans to resist the Nazi occupiers. His son Riccardo, born after the war, completed his rabbinical studies in 1973 and became chief rabbi some three decades later.[11]

During his tenure as chief rabbi, there have been three successive popes: John Paul II, Benedict XVI, and Francis. Shortly after his appointment, on February 13, 2003, John Paul II wrote him a letter congratulating him, recalling his own 1986 visit to the Great Synagogue, and speaking of the good faith created between the Catholic and Jewish communities by *Nostra aetate*.[12] Rabbi Di Segni responded publicly in a 2003 interview on the twenty-fifth anniversary of John Paul II's pontificate, saying, "There has been no Pope in history who has fostered such good relations between Judaism and the Catholic Church as John Paul II."[13] The pope then wrote a second letter to the chief rabbi on May 22, 2004, the one hundredth anniversary of the Great Synagogue.[14] Pope Benedict XVI also greeted the chief rabbi with a letter on January 16, 2006; Benedict visited the synagogue and met with the chief rabbi on January 17, 2010; and (as noted above) Pope Francis visited the synagogue on January 16, 2017.

Through all of these ceremonial acts and more, Rabbi Di Segni has been in a unique position. He is a participant in a historic moment wherein the official Catholic Church, headquartered in Rome, feels compelled to live up to its words in *Nostra aetate*. He is also well aware of the church's struggles to keep its word. In a 2021 article for the American Jewish magazine *Tablet*, Rabbi Di Segni praised John Paul II, especially for his 1986 visit to the Great Synagogue, which he recognized as a break with two thousand years of Catholic policy toward Jews, but he also highlighted that pope's ambivalent relationship to Judaism. The pope's much-vaunted statement in the Great Synagogue, "You are our elder brothers," could be read in two ways. First, the statement affirms a common family of Jews and Catholics. But second, it reminds us that "elder brothers in the Bible, starting from Cain to Esau and forward, are the bad guys and those who lose their birthright." Perhaps the church's millennia-long belief that it had superseded Judaism could not be avoided.[15]

THE JOINT EXHIBIT

If we walk behind the Great Synagogue, taking the Via Catalana until it intersects with the winding Via del Portico d'Ottavia, we end up facing the entrance to the Museo Ebraico di Roma. Founded in 1960, the Jewish Museum of Rome is relatively small (about twenty-three hundred square feet) and situated in the Great Synagogue basement (with its own entrance). Still, it houses an extensive collection of ritual objects such as *menorot*, Torah covers, and *parochot* (fabric curtains for the Torah cabinet) dating from the seventeenth to the twentieth century. What is more, the fabrics, ritual objects, and trappings of the Spanish Synagogue preserved from the time of the Cinque Scole (the five synagogues housed in one building in the former Ghetto) are now part of an exhibit that recreates the Spanish Synagogue within the museum.

Also in the collection is a bizarre artifact purporting to be a gravestone. Its inscription, in both Latin and Hebrew, reads: "Here lie the three brothers of Jewish Faith, Natanel, Ammon and Eliau, who found the relics of Jerusalem, the candelabrum and the ark, in the Tiber, where they still are, three hundred and seventy five steps under the island in correspondence with the promontory of the Palatine, they were beheaded by public axe under the Emperor Honorius."[16]

The "gravestone," found beneath a heap of marble fragments in the synagogue garden, is a blatant forgery telling a concocted story. Although claiming to be from the time of Emperor Honorius (395–423 BCE), it resembles no other funerary inscription from that era in Jewish Rome. According to a chemical analysis of its patina, it was created at the end of the nineteenth or the beginning of the twentieth century. The aim of the forgery remains a mystery, but a seven-branched menorah carved on the back of the stone, complementing the inscription on the stone's face, evidences a two-thousand-year-long fascination with the Temple menorah that was carved on the inside of the Arch of Titus and has since become an enduring symbol for Jews worldwide.

From the forgery came the idea to mount a museum exhibit dedicated to the menorah. The Museo Ebraico put together such an exhibit in 2008. Then in 2013 Pope Francis wrote a letter to the Jewish Community of Rome: "I strongly hope to be able to contribute to the progress that the relations between Jews and Catholics have known since the Second Vatican Council, in a spirit of renewed collaboration and in the service of a world that can always be in more harmony with the will of the Creator."[17]

From that letter arose the idea for a joint exhibit, curated by Catholics and Jews from the Vatican Museum and the Jewish Museum, celebrating the menorah in art, history, and legend, and putting on display Jewish and Catholic depictions and visions of the menorah from around the world.

A year after Pope Francis's visit to the Great Synagogue, the Jewish Museum and the Vatican Museum cocreated just such an exhibit, entitled

La menorà: Culto, storia e mito (The menorah: Religion, history and myth). Both museums gathered paintings, artifacts, and inscriptions of the Temple menorah, showcasing its different depictions worldwide over two millennia. And in an intentional display of interreligious cooperation, each museum displayed artifacts from both traditions. As visitors entered the Carlo Magno wing, the Vatican exhibit site, they were greeted by the Magdala Stone (100 BCE–100 CE), a stone found in an ancient synagogue excavated in Migdal, on the shores of Lake Tiberias (the Kinneret) in Israel. A relief carved into the stone depicts a seven-branched menorah, possibly the oldest depiction of the Temple menorah known today. At the entrance to the Jewish Museum visitors encountered a replica, a cast, of the *Tabula Magna Lateranensis*, a mosaic inscription from the time of Pope Nicholas IV (1288–92) listing boastfully and falsely the treasures then allegedly housed in the Lateran Church, which supposedly included the Temple menorah (*Candelabrum aurelium*).

Unlike the first-century menorah carved in stone, the menorah mentioned in the Lateran inscription was only an idea. But it was a powerful idea shared by both Judaism and Catholicism for centuries. The joint exhibit used that shared idea to serve a greater purpose: "The legendary menorah . . . would be able to contribute . . . to giving the road to mutual understanding a more solid foundation."[18] Situated, appropriately, in the city of Rome—home of the worldwide Catholic Church, home of the oldest Jewish diaspora community, and the longtime resting place of the Temple menorah itself—the joint exhibit aimed to make public and tangible a new spirit that recognized the conjoint heritage of Judaism and Christianity. While the exhibit itself had a brief life—after a few months the artifacts were returned to the institutions that had loaned them—the cooperation between Jews and Catholics that had made this possible was based on an aspiration that the Jewish-Catholic encounter in Rome would continue henceforth in steadfast goodwill.

In 2016, the menorah appeared again on the banks of the Tiber in the work of the South African artist William Kentridge. Entitled *Triumphs and Laments: A Project for Rome*, Kentridge's grand work of public art was a mural along the river embankment running five hundred meters from the Ponte Sisto to Ponte Mazzini, in which eighty fantastic figures—some ten meters tall—enacted well-known episodes from the last two thousand years of Roman history. The mural was not painted on the Tiber's concrete banks. It was created by scratching and selectively removing portions of the patina of salt and dirt that had accreted on that concrete embankment. By removing only some of the accretions and leaving the rest, images were created. The "triumph" in the title was Titus's march through Rome after sacking Jerusalem as seen in the Arch of Titus. The mural's centerpiece depicted Roman soldiers holding the Temple menorah high. This was Kentridge's point: Titus's triumph, like many subsequent Roman vanities, including his own mural, was ephemeral. Over the years since 2016, the patina has returned, obscuring his work, as he probably intended.

FUTURE OF ROMAN JEWRY

Our tour through the heart of present-day Jewish Rome ends at the banks of the Tiber, a good place to contemplate the future of Judaism in Rome.

Today, approximately 13,500 Jews live in Rome. Probably several thousand more live here as well but do not affiliate or register with the Jewish community. If so, then today's community, bolstered by the 1967 influx of Libyan Jews, is numerically in line with Rome's Jewish population at the time of the Racial Laws (1938): 12,000 registered and another 4,000 unaffiliated. After World War II the Jewish population of Rome approximated 11,300.

Even so, the Jewish population of Rome remains precarious. While there has been steady immigration into Rome from much smaller Italian Jewish communities, Roman Jewry has a low birthrate: 1.8 children on average. Italy's birthrate is falling (from 576,659 babies born in 2008 to 404,892 in 2020), and the Jewish community is no exception to that trend.

Nonetheless, the present religious, social, and cultural condition of the Jewish community is encouraging. Presently, eighteen synagogues, including two Libyan synagogues, serve the community. The synagogues are spread throughout Rome, given that Jews live in all areas of the city.

A variety of institutions promote Jewish participation in community life, among them the Jewish Museum, the Jewish Archive, the Roman branch of WIZO (Women's International Zionist Organization), the Ospedale Israelitico (Jewish Hospital), and the Casa di Risposo Ebraica di Rome (Jewish Rest Home of Rome)—the last two originating in the 1600s.

All in all, the Roman Jewish community has a unique circumstance. After two thousand years, it remains situated in the center of one of the great cities of the world, across the river from a sovereign nation similarly embedded in the long history of Rome. The events of the last two thousand years have led to a convergence of interests and mutual respect and admiration between a tiny representative of a minority community and a worldwide institution. Even when the church ghettoized the Jews, it was of mutual interest for a Jewish musician and the captain of the vicar's police to exchange information over the course of a Friday night meal. Presently, it is of greater but still mutual benefit that the head of the Universal Catholic Church visits the Great Synagogue in his neighborhood. Neither group is willing to sever ties that have existed for generations. The question for both groups is how to incorporate that troubled history into a forward-looking relationship of trust and understanding. The future always confronts the past and often reconceptualizes it to suit present concerns. A responsible and evolving understanding of the past is necessary for Catholics and Jews in Rome, still intimate strangers, to live and change together in the Eternal City.

NOTES

INTRODUCTION

1. For figures on Jewish deportation throughout Italy during the Shoah see Picciotto, "Shoah in Italy," 210–21; also see Klein, *Italy's Jews from Emancipation to Fascism*; Sullam, *Italian Executioners.*

2. Bassani, *Garden of the Finzi-Continis,* 4–5.

3. Judaeo-Roman may not be its own dialect. It may be less than that, a manner of speaking like "Brooklynese." See Kenneth Stow, "Writing in Hebrew."

4. For the Jewish high school at Villa Celimontana see Della Seta, *Tiber Afire.*

5. Della Seta, *Tiber Afire,* 5.

6. K. Stow, *Jews in Rome,* vol. 2, 115, 188, 604, 605, 618, and 622—documents 310, 474, 1415, 1416, 1443, and 1451 respectively.

7. R. Cohen, "State Origins."

8. Levi-Strauss, *Raw and the Cooked,* 82–83.

9. Cooperman, "Early Modern Ghetto," 67.

10. Nirenberg, *Communities of Violence,* xii, xiii. Also see Funkenstein, "Dialectics of Assimilation."

1. AN INCONVENIENT LIAISON

1. Suetonius, *Lives of the Caesars,* Augustus 29; Zanker, *Power of Images,* 138 fig. 113, 146 fig. 118.

2. The circus is the Circus Flaminius, which underlies much of what is today's Ghetto.

3. Josephus, *Jewish War* 7.123–31. Our witness to Titus's triumph is Flavius Josephus, a Judaean who found favor in the emperor's court and wrote several historical works, one concerning the Jewish revolt.

4. Beard, *Roman Triumph.*

5. For Elephantine see Porten et al., *Elephantine Papyri in English.*

6. Josephus, *Jewish War* 6.241.

7. Sulpicius Severus, *Chronica* 2, no. 30, 6–7.

8. For a capsule biography of Josephus see Goodman, *Rome and Jerusalem*, 3–5; Goodman, *Josephus's "The Jewish War."*

9. Josephus, *Jewish War* 6.252.

10. Josephus, *Jewish War* 7.139–44, 146.

11. Josephus, *Jewish War* 7.148–50.

12. Watkin, *Roman Forum*, 59–60.

13. Shelley, "Notes on Sculptures in Rome and Florence."

14. Dessau, *Inscriptiones latinae selectae*, 264; Goodman, *Rome and Jerusalem*, 432–33.

15. Cappelletti, *Jewish Community*, 101–9, 117.

16. Acts 25:13–26:32.

17. Josephus, *Jewish War* 2.271–308.

18. Josephus, *Jewish War* 2.310–14.

19. Josephus, *Jewish War* 2.333–42.

20. Josephus, *Jewish War* 2.344–401.

21. Josephus, *Jewish War* 2.426.

22. Marcus Julius Alexander had his own minor celebrity. He was the nephew of Philo Judaeus, the Alexandrian philosopher who argued forcefully for an allegorical and Platonic understanding of the Bible. See Goodman, *History of Judaism*, 171.

23. Josephus, *Jewish Antiquities* 20.145–46. Juvenal in *Satires* 6, 160, speaks of "a diamond of great renown, made precious by the finger of Berenice. It was given as a present long ago by the barbarian Agrippa to his incestuous sister, in that country where kings celebrate festal Sabbaths with bare feet and where a long-established clemency suffers pigs to attain old age."

24. Tacitus, *Histories* 2.81.

25. Suetonius, *Lives of the Caesars*, Galba, Otho, and Vitellius.

26. Cassius Dio, *Roman History* 65.15.

27. Quintilian, *Institutio Oratoria* 4.1.19. As historical fact, this seems unlikely; according to Crook ("Titus and Berenice"), judging her own case would have been too scandalous to be true. Instead, she may have been a spectator to her own case.

28. But see Kraemer, "On the Meaning of the Term 'Jew,'" 40, stating that the matrilineal principle was a late addition to Rabbinic Judaism. However, Goodman, *History of Judaism*, xxv, places the matrilineal tradition in Judaism in the first century CE.

29. Goodman, "Nerva," states that the idea of pagans becoming Jews is not found before 96 CE.

30. Horace, *Satires* 1.4.139–43.

31. Augustine, *The City of God* 6.11, quoting Seneca the Younger, *Concerning Superstition*.

32. Cassius Dio, *Roman History* 65.15.
33. Suetonius, *Lives of the Caesars*, Titus 7.
34. Babylonian Talmud, *Gittin* 56b; *Avodah Zarah* 11a.
35. Crook, "Titus and Berenice," 162–75.
36. See, for example, Racine, *Berenice*; Corneille, *Tite et Berenice*; Mozart, *La clemenza di Tito*; Masefield, *Berenice*; and Fast, *Agrippa's Daughter*.
37. Babylonian Talmud, *Gittin* 56 a and b. For analysis of this legend see Saldarini, "Johanan Ben Zakkai's Escape from Jerusalem."
38. Tacitus, *Annals* 15.28; Tacitus, *Histories* 1.2; Goodman, *Rome and Jerusalem*, 151–52.
39. Juvenal, *Satires* 1, 130–31.
40. *Canticles Rabbah* 1, 42.
41. For a review of the debate on Solomon's Egyptian bride see Van Seters, "Israel and Egypt in the Age of Solomon," 199 et seq.
42. G. Cohen, "Esau as Symbol in Early Medieval Thought," 42; Glatzer, "Attitude towards Rome in Third-Century Judaism," 247; Rieger, "Foundation of Rome in the Talmud." Alternative talmudic traditions have Rome founded when Jeroboam established the Golden Calves at Bethel and Dan or when Manasseh put an idol in the Temple. Babylonian Talmud, *Megillah* 6b.
43. Joshua Ben Levi, Jerusalem Talmud, *Taanit* 64a.
44. Babylonian Talmud, *Sanhedrin* 98a.
45. Not all the rabbinic stories about the founding of Rome are self-deprecating. In *Canticles Rabbah*, an alternate story is told of how the rude huts that constituted the earliest Roman settlement kept collapsing. A Jewish sage, Abba Kolon, surely legendary, advised the earliest Romans that their city would never endure without bricks made with water drawn from the Euphrates River. Traveling to Mesopotamia, Abba Kolon brought back casks of river water that guaranteed the strength of Roman construction. Vogelstein, *Rome*, 2.
46. *Leviticus Rabbah* 22:3. This tale is not without its later Jewish skeptics. The Ferrarese scholar Azariah de Rossi, in his *Me'or Enayim* (*The Light of the Eyes*) (1573), called it a "puerile fable." Schama, *Story of the Jews*, 70; Yerushalmi, "Clio and the Jews," 211 et seq.
47. Probably, this story was not intended as an explicit commentary on the story of Berenice and Titus. Rather, it is part of a universe of tales all inspired by the underlying story of the destruction of Jerusalem. In such a universe of narratives, each story mutually informs all the others. Accordingly, the story of Berenice and the Rabbinic story of Titus are connected thematically and symbolically and, in a manner, comment on each other. See K. Stow, *Jewish Dogs*, 102, for the understanding that some Jewish stories are inversions of gentile tales and that both stories need to be read together. See also Levi-Strauss, *Structural Anthropology*,

232–41, wherein Pawnee myths are understood to be structural inversions of the myths and rituals of neighboring Mandan and Hidatsa tribes.

48. Goodenough, *Jewish Symbols in the Graeco-Roman Period*, 8:27ff. See also Levinson, "'Tragedies Naturally Performed.'"

49. The present author's knowledge of the legends recounted here comes from Levinson, "'Tragedies Naturally Performed,'" and Glatzer, "Attitude towards Rome in Third-Century Judaism." Stringing together the legends into a somewhat coherent narrative is his own creation, for which the same license exercised, say, by Levi-Strauss in *The Raw and the Cooked*, and *From Honey to Ashes*, has herein been employed to extrapolate a new world of meaning from individual narratives. Finally, the date when the cited traditions circulated cannot be definitively ascertained from the date they were compiled and preserved as Rabbinic literature, which Glatzer gives as the third century CE. In all likelihood, given the long lifespan of oral traditions in the Mishnah and Talmud, these traditions circulated at an earlier date.

2. "WHO IS A JEW?"

1. Leon, *Jews of Ancient Rome*, 60–61, 205; Laurenzi, *La catacomba*, 55–65.
2. Leon, *Jews of Ancient Rome*, 205; Gutmann, *Dura Europos Synagogue*.
3. Garrucci, *Il cimitero*, 156; Vismara, "I cimiteri ebraici di Roma," 351–89.
4. Cappelletti, *Jewish Community*, 61–62.
5. Goodenough, *Jewish Symbols in the Graeco-Roman Period*, 2:30–32; Leon, *Jews of Ancient Rome*, 60.
6. Goodman, *History of Judaism*, 295–96.
7. Babylonian Talmud, *Sanhedrin* 47a.
8. Vogelstein, *Rome*, 17, first thought that the Jewish population of ancient Rome was forty thousand, but he later reduced that number to twenty thousand. This is also the estimate of Penna, "Les Juifs," 328. Various scholars have offered estimates of forty to sixty thousand. Leon, *Jews of Ancient Rome*, 135n1.
9. Fuks, "Where Have All the Freedmen Gone?"
10. Leon, *Jews of Ancient Rome*, 166.
11. Leon, *Jews of Ancient Rome*, 135–66; Cappelletti, *Jewish Community*, 3ff; Bickerman, "Altars of the Gentiles."
12. A synagogue from the same period was found at Ostia Antica 25 kilometers (15.5 miles) southwest of Rome. Hermansen, *Ostia*, 55–89; and White, "Synagogue and Society."
13. Cappelletti, *Jewish Community*, 8.
14. Goodenough, *Jewish Symbols II*, 16; Cappelletti, *The Jewish Community*, 153n67; but see, Goodman, *History of Judaism*, 296, where he argues that it was only

at the end of the first millennium that Jews felt constrained to be buried with other Jews.

15. Goodenough, *Jewish Symbols in the Graeco-Roman Period*, 2:15–17; Leon, *Jews of Ancient Rome*, 55–57; Cappelletti, *Jewish Community*, 153; Laurenzi, *La catacomba*, 43–48.

16. Leon, *Jews of Ancient Rome*, 75–92.

17. Goodenough, *Jewish Symbols in the Graeco-Roman Period*, 2:5–7. A *lulav* is a palm branch and an *etrog* is a small fruit. Both are used symbolically in the celebration of Sukkot, the Jewish holiday commemorating both the wandering of the Hebrews in the desert and the fall harvest.

18. Goodenough, *Jewish Symbols in the Graeco-Roman Period*, 2:5, 9–10, 14.

19. Leon, *Jews of Ancient Rome*, 233, inscription nos. 109 and 210.

20. Goodenough, *Jewish Symbols in the Graeco-Roman Period*, 2:26–27, 37, 42–43; Laurenzi, *La catacomba*, 70–84.

21. Goodenough, *Jewish Symbols in the Graeco-Roman Period*, 2:26–27; see also Leon, *Jews of Ancient Rome*, 212, 215.

22. Rutgers, *Jews of Late Ancient Rome*, 92–99; Goodman, *History of Judaism*, 294.

23. This statement must be tempered by the fact that during or just before the reign of Magnus Maximus, emperor of the Western Roman Empire (383–88 CE), Christians had destroyed a synagogue in Rome. When the emperor ordered it rebuilt, Christians mocked him, saying he had become a Jew. Langmuir, *Toward a Definition*, 68; Vogelstein, *Rome*, 109.

24. For a comparison of the catacombs with contemporary Jewish burials in Palestine see Williams, "Organisation of Jewish Burials."

25. The Hebrew inscriptions in Leon's catalogue are nos. 289, 292, 293, 296, 319, 349, 497. One unpublished Hebrew inscription from the Nomentana catacomb reads "shalom al Yisra'el." Leon, *Jews of Ancient Rome*, 76.

26. Goodenough, *Jewish Symbols in the Graeco-Roman Period*, 2:40.

27. Feldman and Reinhold, *Jewish Life and Thought*, 314. The text by Valerius Maximus comes to us only in summary form from the Roman historians Julius Paris (fourth century CE) and Januarius Nepotianus (fourth or fifth centuries CE).

28. But see Bickerman, "Altars of the Gentiles," which makes the case that even as Jews in the Roman world worshiped their universal and singular God, they were not shy about referring to God in terms understandable to their gentile neighbors.

29. For a Sabazian tomb in Rome see Goodenough, *Jewish Symbols in the Graeco-Roman Period*, 2:45–50.

30. Leon, *Jews of Ancient Rome*, 3.

31. 1 Macc. 8:17–32 and 12:1–2; Josephus, *Jewish Antiquities* 12.10.414–19, 5.13.163–65.

32. Roth, *History of the Jews of Italy*, 4.

33. Goodman, *Rome and Jerusalem*, 371–73.

34. Cicero, *Defense of Flaccus* 28.66.

35. Leon, *Jews of Ancient Rome*, 8.

36. Philo, *Legatio* 23.155.

37. *Psalms of Solomon* 2:4–6. The *Psalms of Solomon* ostensibly describe the destruction of the First Temple in 587 BCE, but it is believed that at least the second psalm reflects Pompey's desecration of the Second Temple, which, according to Josephus (*Jewish Antiquities* 14.66), occurred on the Day of Atonement. Brilliant, "Jewish Art and Culture in Ancient Italy," 67–68.

38. Josephus, *Jewish Antiquities* 14.127–36; Josephus, *Jewish War* 1.9.187–94.

39. Josephus, *Jewish Antiquities* 14.215–16.

40. Josephus *Jewish Antiquities* 14.10.185–216.

41. Philo, *Legatio*, 155–57.

42. For Livia's Jewish handmaid see Josephus, *Jewish Antiquities* 17.6.141; Josephus, *Jewish War* 1.32.641. For Augustus's erroneous belief about the Sabbath see Suetonius, *Augustus* 76.2.

43. See Persius, *Satires* 5.179–84, where the Sabbath is also called "the sabbath of the circumcised."

44. Ovid, *Ars Amatoria* 1.415–16; Ovid, *Remedia Amoris*, 219–20.

45. Tacitus, *Histories* 5.2–5.

46. Tacitus, *Annals* 2.85.

47. Suetonius, *Lives of the Caesars*, Tiberius 36.

48. Cassius Dio, *Roman History* 57.18.5a.

49. Josephus, *Jewish Antiquities* 18.3.81–84.

50. Goodman, "Nerva," 43.

51. Seneca the Younger, *Moral Epistles* 108.22.

52. Suetonius, *Lives of the Caesars*, Claudius 25.4.

53. Cassius Dio, *Roman History* 60.6.6.

54. This understanding of the contradictory evidence is outlined by Leon, *Jews of Ancient Rome*, 23–27.

55. Vogelstein, *Rome*, 53–54; Goodman, *History of Judaism*, 104.

56. Josephus, *Jewish Antiquities* 20.8.195.

57. Hopkins and Beard, *Colosseum*, 32–34. See also Alföldy, "Eine Bauinschrift," 195–226. In fact, the original inscription had been entirely replaced with another. However, in a brilliant bit of archaeological detective work, the dowel holes that held the original letters to the marble block were traced to show what letters had been affixed there. It is possible then, that the inscription may now be readable despite the absence of the original letters. Hopkins and Beard express a mild

skepticism concerning the reading of the inscription, but they agree that "the Roman Colosseum was the fruit of Roman victory over the Jews."

58. Cassius Dio, *Roman History* 66.7.2.

59. While the tax was commonly known as the *fiscus judaicus*, technically the *fiscus judaicus* was the fund created by the tax payments paid by the Jews, rather than the tax itself. Goodman, "Nerva," 40. Nevertheless, when this author refers to the *fiscus judaicus*, he is referring to the tax.

60. Leon, *Jews of Ancient Rome*, 31.

61. Suetonius, *Domitian* 12.2.

62. Cappelletti, *Jewish Community*, 124n5.

63. Smallwood, "Domitian's Attitudes towards the Jews and Judaism," 3; Goodman, "Nerva," 42. But see Kraabel, "Disappearance of the 'God-Fearers,'" 113–26. The fact that women could not be circumcised would have allowed them a certain fluidity when it came to choosing whether to convert or to just remain a sympathizer or God-Fearer.

64. Rajak, "Jewish Community and Its Boundaries."

65. Cassius Dio, *Roman History* 66.7.2. For Cassius Dio's possible backdating of who had to pay the tax, see Goodman, "Nerva," 41.

66. Smallwood, "Domitian's Attitudes towards the Jews and Judaism," 2–4.

67. Cassius Dio, *Roman History* 67.14.1–2.

68. Smallwood, "Domitian's Attitudes towards the Jews and Judaism," 5–6.

69. Babylonian Talmud, *Avodah Zarah* 10b and 11a, Gittim 56b, and Midrash *Deuteronomy Rabbah* 2, 24.

70. Rajak, "Jews and Christians as Groups in a Pagan World."

71. Goodman, "Nerva," 41.

72. Leon, "Jews of Ancient Rome," 36; Goodman, *Rome and Jerusalem*, 447.

73. Goodman, *Rome and Jerusalem*, 447; Goodman, "Nerva," 44.

74. Goodman, *Rome and Jerusalem*, 448. Sybils were ancient Greek prophetesses.

75. Goodman, *Rome and Jerusalem*, 453–57.

76. Roth, *History of the Jews of Italy*, 17–19.

77. Leon, "Jews of Ancient Rome," 43n5, citing Momigliano, "Severo Alessandro Archisynagogus."

78. Brilliant, "Jewish Art and Culture in Ancient Italy," 69.

79. An early mention of Roman proselytes to Judaism comes from Acts 2:10, where a description of the Jews visiting Jerusalem during the festival of Shavuot (Pentecost) includes, "visitors from Rome, both Jews and proselytes." At least for the author of Acts, a proselyte is not quite a Jew and has an ambiguous position.

80. Leon, *Jews of Ancient Rome*, 341.

81. Leon, *Jews of Ancient Rome*, 361.

82. Leon, *Jews of Ancient Rome*, 332. Alternative and plausible readings are analyzed in Kraemer, "On the Meaning."

83. Leon, *Jews of Ancient Rome*, 273–74.

84. Juvenal, *Satires*, 14, 96–106.

85. Leon, *Jews of Ancient Rome*, 135–66. As Leon admits, the meanings of some of the synagogue names are obscure.

86. Petronius, *Satyricon* 68.8.

87. *Palestinian Talmud*, Sevi'it 4.2.

88. Suetonius, *Augustus* 76.2; Tacitus, *Histories* 5.4.3–4; Ovid, *Remedies of Love*, 217–20.

89. Macrobius, *Saturnalia* 2.4.11.

90. Tacitus, *Annals* 2.85.

91. Tacitus, *Histories* 5.3.

92. Seneca the Younger, *Concerning Superstition*, cited by Augustine, *City of God* 6.11.

93. Juvenal, *Satires*, 14, 96–106.

94. Juvenal, *Satires*, 3, 10–16; Livy, *Early History of Rome* 1.21.

95. Juvenal, *Satires*, 6, 542–47.

96. *Scriptores Historiae Augustae, Alexander Severus* 45.7, 51.7–8.

97. Leon, *Jews of Ancient Rome*, 286, 303.

3. A TORAH FOR THE POPE

1. Milano, *Il ghetto*, 215–19; K. Stow, *Jews in Rome*, vol. 1, xlii n73; D. Di Castro, *Et ecce gaudium*, 16. For the possibility of a sixth synagogue outside the Ghetto walls in a second smaller ghetto or "ghettarello" see Spizzichino, *La scomparsa*.

2. A "Potemkin village" is a construction intended to deceive by providing an external façade and nothing more. It is named after Grigory Potemkin's purported efforts to impress the Russian Empress Catherine II by creating a portable village for her in 1787.

3. Twyman, *Papal Ceremonial*, 197; Wasner, "Pope's Veneration of the Torah," 278; Linder, "'Jews Too Were Not Absent,'" 338.

4. Boniface VIII was elected to the papacy on December 24, 1294, but his coronation took place on January 23, 1295.

5. Wasner, "Pope's Veneration of the Torah," 284. This is a recollection and not a verbatim transcription.

6. Coulet, "De l'intégration à l'exclusion," 677; O'Malley, *What Happened at Vatican II*, 143.

7. Davis, *Gift in Sixteenth Century France*, 44.

8. Wasner, "Pope's Veneration of the Torah," 285.

9. Parione is a Roman neighborhood where the Jewish encounter with the popes usually happened.
10. Wasner, "Pope's Veneration of the Torah," 281. A similar translation is found at Linder, "'Jews Too Were Not Absent,'" 349–50.
11. D. Di Castro, "Jews of Rome," 24; Linder, "'Jews Too Were Not Absent,'" 341.
12. Coulet, "De l'integration à l'exclusion," 672–73. For a different translation see Linder, "'Jews Too Were Not Absent," 350, quoting Cancellieri, *Storia de' solenni possessi*, 25–26.
13. Vogelstein, *Rome*, 129.
14. D. Di Castro, "Jews of Rome," 24. But see Wasner, "Pope's Veneration of the Torah," 282, who believes the tossing of the Torah behind the pope took place only once. Linder, "'Jews Too Were Not Absent,'" 362, reaches the same conclusion based upon Cancellieri, *Storia de' solenni possessi*, 71.
15. Linder, "'Jews Too Were Not Absent,'" 362; Partner, *Renaissance Rome*, 193.
16. Linder, "'Jews Too Were Not Absent,'" 362.
17. Cancellieri, *Storia de' solenni possessi*, 71.
18. Linder, "'Jews Too Were Not Absent,'" 362–71.
19. Davis, *Gift in Sixteenth Century France*, 55–56, figs. 4, 5.
20. In the *Codex balduini trevirensis*, reproduced in Vogelstein, *Rome*, 202.
21. At this early date there is no mention of gifts to the pope.
22. Linder "'Jews Too Were Not Absent,'" 334–35.
23. Linder "'Jews Too Were Not Absent,'" 359; Rist, *Popes and Jews*, 237–38.
24. Bergeron, *English Civic Pageantry*, 21. For a description of the parade see Geertz, *Local Knowledge*, 125–29.
25. Mauss, *Gift*, 2–3. Mauss came to his conclusion concerning gifts by studying Vedic, Icelandic, and Scandinavian traditions as well as tribal societies in Australia, Polynesia, and the Americas. Douglas affirmed Mauss's insight in her foreword to the 1990 republication of *Gift*, i–xv. More recently, Davis in *Gift in Sixteenth Century France* has made use of Mauss's ideas to analyze early modern gifts in France. With regard to Italy, see Bestor, "Marriage Transactions in Renaissance Italy." Most recently, T. Cohen in *Roman Tales*, 34–35, applies Mauss's concept to the world of Jewish-Christian relations in early modern Rome.
26. Thomas of Chobham, *Summa confessiorum*, 504, cited in Le Goff, *Your Money or Your Life*, 18.
27. Davis, *Gift in Sixteenth Century France*, 64, 94, 128.
28. The pattern of lauding the pope, giving the Torah, receiving payment, and again giving pepper and cinnamon is taken from several medieval documents, including the *Basel ordo, London ordo*, the *Gesta pauperis scolaris* by Cardinal Albinus,

and the *Liber censuum* by Cencius Camerarius. Linder, "'Jews Too Were Not Absent,'" 356–58. It is very unlikely that the ceremonies remained unchanged for centuries, but the granular changes that probably occurred are not fully known. For the theoretical possibility of an unending cycle of gifting and reciprocation see Davis, *Gift in Sixteenth Century France*, 66.

29. Mauss, *Gift*, 84n3; Davis, *Gift in Sixteenth Century France*, 24.

30. Poliakov, *Jewish Bankers*, 36.

31. Bonfil, *Jewish Life in Renaissance Italy*, 85.

32. Roth, *History of the Jews of Italy*, 111.

33. K. Stow, "Good of the Church," 248.

34. Vogelstein, *Rome*, 238.

35. K. Stow, *Alienated Minority*; Twyman, *Papal Ceremonial*, 204. *Sicut* was based on papal decisions undertaken by Pope Gregory the Great (590–604) that in turn went back to laws concerning Jews in the Theodosian Code (ca. 438). Stow, *Catholic Thought and Papal Jewry Policy*, xix; Rist, *Popes and Jews*, 78–81.

36. Marcus, *Jew in the Medieval World*, 170–72. From the version of the bull decreed by Gregory X in 1272.

37. Solomon Grayzel has pointed out that a subsequent encyclical, *Turbato corde*, issued in 1267, itself reaffirmed many times, undercut *Sicut judaeis* by making Jews liable for any activity that induced a Christian to convert to Judaism. Grayzel, "Popes, Jews, and Inquisition," 151–88. For a possible but unproven hypothesis that the Pierleoni family called upon Calixtus to issue *Sicut judaeis* see K. Stow, *Jews in Rome*, vol. 1, xxii; Rist, *Popes and Jews*, 230.

38. Rist, *Popes and Jews*, 110–15.

39. Rist, *Popes and Jews*, 79–80.

40. Rist, *Popes and Jews*, 16–17, 79–80.

41. K. Stow, *Catholic Thought and Papal Jewry Policy*, 278n1, 285–88.

42. Grayzel, "Popes, Jews, and Inquisition," 156; Rist, *Popes and Jews*, 232.

43. Rist, *Popes and Jews*, 240–41.

44. Grayzel, "Popes, Jews, and Inquisition," 173–74.

45. Grayzel, "Popes, Jews, and Inquisition," 174–75.

46. Grayzel, "Popes, Jews, and Inquisition," 176–78.

47. Grayzel, "Popes, Jews, and Inquisition," 186.

48. Vogelstein, *Rome*, 183; Grayzel, "Popes, Jews, and Inquisition," 187.

49. Grayzel, "Popes, Jews, and Inquisition," 188.

50. Babylonian Talmud, *Bava Metzi'a* 71b.

51. Poliakov, *Jewish Bankers*, 16.

52. Poliakov, *Jewish Bankers*, 17.

53. K. Stow, "Papal and Royal Attitudes," 166–69.

54. K. Stow, *Catholic Thought and Papal Jewry Policy*, 87.

55. Poliakov, *Jewish Bankers*, 15; Le Goff, *Your Money*, 9.

56. Poliakov, *Jewish Bankers*, 26.

57. Poliakov, *Jewish Bankers*, 27.

58. Bonfil, *Jewish Life in Renaissance Italy*, 46.

59. K. Stow, "Papal and Royal Attitudes," 162.

60. K. Stow, "Papal and Royal Attitudes," 162.

61. Roth, "History of the Jews of Italy," 109.

62. K. Stow, *Catholic Thought and Papal Jewry Policy*, 87–88.

63. Rist, *Popes and Jews*, 144.

64. Rist, *Popes and Jews*, 136–37.

65. Poliakov, *Jewish Bankers*, 151.

66. Bonfil, *Jewish Life in Renaissance Italy*, 34.

67. K. Stow, *Jews in Rome*, vol. 1, 192, document 486.

68. Poliakov, *Jewish Bankers*, 150.

69. Bonfil, *Jewish Life in Renaissance Italy*, 34–35.

70. Poliakov, *Jewish Bankers*, 82.

71. K. Stow, "Good of the Church," 245.

72. Le Goff, *Your Money or Your Life*, 8.

73. Hunt, *Vacant See in Early Modern Rome*, 174–75.

74. K. Stow, *Catholic Thought and Papal Jewry Policy*, 81, 117.

75. K. Stow, *Jewish Life in Early Modern Rome*, ix.

4. HOUSEGUESTS AND HUMANISTS

1. Most likely, whoever compiled the *Yosippon* was from southern Italy. Tradition has it that Joseph ben Gorion was that compiler. The first compilation comes from the tenth century. Later versions from the twelfth and thirteenth centuries evidence additional editors or compilers. Rist, *Popes and Jews*, 36.

2. The *Yosippon* may be a translation of the Greek original or a translation of a Latin version of Josephus's works. The Italian Jewish scholar Azariah de' Rossi (ca. 1511–78) claimed that the *Yosippon* was a paraphrase of a Greek text of Josephus preserved by the Catholic Church. Goodman, *History of Judaism*, 367; K. Stow, *Alienated Minority*, 78.

3. Yerushalmi, "Clio and the Jews," 199.

4. In Genesis 10:4, the Kittim are identified as descendants of Japhet, son of Noah. Later, Jeremiah (2:10) mentions them as possible inhabitants of the Aegean islands. Their mention in the book of Daniel (11:30) may be figurative, referring to Rome. Josephus identifies the Kittim with Cyprus and islands further west (*Jewish Antiquities* 1.6.1).

5. Flusser, *Sefer Yosippon*; K. Stow, *Alienated Minority*, 77–80; G. Cohen, "*Esau as Symbol in Early Medieval Thought*," 40–44.

6. The *Yosippon* contradicts the Rabbinic tradition (discussed in chapter 1) that Rome was founded as a punishment for Solomon's marriage to the Pharaoh's daughter. Cohen, "Esau as Symbol in Early Medieval Thought," 42.

7. Christians also needed to connect Roman history with the Bible. By the thirteenth century, legends circulating in Italy credited the founding of Rome to one of Noah's descendants through his son Japhet. Brentano, *Rome before Avignon*, 81–82.

8. Boccaccio, *Decameron*, 38–42.

9. Scholem, *Major Trends in Jewish Mysticism*, 128.

10. Rist, *Popes and Jews*, 60–61. For the phenomenon of the vacant see in general see Nussdorfer, "Vacant See," 173–79.

11. Gaster, *Ma'aseh Book*, vol. 2, 410–18, no. 188. Gaster's volume is a translation of the Yiddish *Mayse Bukh* from 1602. In the Yiddish volume the referenced story is no. 187. See also Raspe, "Payyetanim," 354–69; Rist, *Popes and Jews*, 33–36.

12. Zimmels, "Rabbi Peter," 51–52; Raspe, "Payyetanim as Heroes of Medieval Folk Narrative," 359.

13. Ruderman, "At the Intersection of Cultures," 1.

14. Ruderman, "At the Intersection of Cultures," 4.

15. Mann, "Art of Jewish Italy," 46.

16. For Benjamin of Tudela's own penchant for exaggeration see Stow, *Jews in Rome*, vol. 1, xxvi.

17. The prologue to *The Itinerary of Benjamin of Tudela* indicates that the information contained therein came from members of the Jewish communities he visited, but a late twelfth- or early thirteenth-century editor added that prologue to the text. Champagne and Boustan, "Walking in the Shadows of the Past," 469.

18. Stroll, *Jewish Pope*, 156–68.

19. Simonsohn, *Apostolic See and the Jews*, 409; Rist, *Popes and Jews*, 170.

20. Grayzel, *Church and the Jews*, 309.

21. K. Stow, *Alienated Minority*, 248; Nirenberg, *Anti-Judaism*, 222.

22. K. Stow, *Jewish Dogs*, has documented the history of the Christian understanding of Jewish impurity. For the most influential anthropological understanding of impurity see Douglas, *Purity and Danger*.

23. K. Stow, *Jewish Dogs*, 62ff.

24. K. Stow, *Jews in Rome*, vol. 1, 136, doc. 360.

25. Roth, *History of the Jews of Italy*, 139.

26. Roth, *History of the Jews of Italy*, 139.

27. E. Cohen, "Seen and Known."

28. Benedict, *Marvels of Rome*, 29.

29. Adler, *Itinerary of Benjamin of Tudela*, quoted in Champagne and Boustan, "Walking in the Shadows of the Past," 477. To set the biblical record straight, Solomon purportedly built the columns Jachin and Boaz in the First Temple. They did not survive the Babylonian destruction in 587 BCE (2 Kings 25:13, Jer. 52:17). The Second Temple had no such columns, and therefore Titus could not have brought them to Rome in 70 CE. The Lateran columns probably date to Constantinian construction and were moved to their present location during the time of Pope Gregory XIII (1572–85). Carroll, *Constantine's Sword*, 481n54.

30. Champagne and Boustan, "Walking in the Shadows of the Past," 479; Brentano, *Rome before Avignon*, 60.

31. K. Stow, *Alienated Minority*, 249.

32. K. Stow, *Jewish Dogs*, 66–70. Regarding Jewish profanation of the Host, see Rubin, *Gentile Tales*.

33. In the thirteenth century, the anonymous apologetic work *Nizzahon yashan* (*The Old Book of Victory*) declared that the Torah commands Jews to give the unkosher cuts to gentiles. K. Stow, *Jewish Dogs*, 143.

34. K. Stow, *Jewish Dogs*, 157.

35. K. Stow, *Jewish Dogs*, 153.

36. Burke, *Historical Anthropology of Early Modern Europe*, 95–109; Blok, "Rams and Billy Goats"; Peristiany, *Honour and Shame*; Gilmore, "Anthropology of the Mediterranean Area"; Mitzman, "The Civilizing Offensive"; T. Cohen and E. Cohen, *Words and Deeds in Renaissance Rome*; Baroja, "Honour and Shame"; E. Cohen, "Honor and Gender," 597–625.

37. Gilmore, "Anthropology of the Mediterranean Area," 191; T. Cohen and E. Cohen, *Words and Deeds*, 23–25.

38. T. Cohen and E. Cohen, *Words and Deeds*, 25.

39. T. Cohen and E. Cohen, *Words and Deeds*, 23; Baroja, "Honor and Shame," 87.

40. E. Cohen, "Honor and Gender," 617.

41. K. Stow, *Catholic Thought and Papal Jewry Policy*, 104, 112.

42. See Bonfil, *Jewish Life in Renaissance Italy*, 45–47, for conceptual connections between Jews and prostitutes.

43. E. Cohen, "Seen and Known," 402–4; K. Stow, "Consciousness of Closure," 392–93; E. Cohen, "Honor and Gender," 611.

44. Petrarch, *Revolution of Cola Di Rienzo*, 172. See also Wright, *Life of Cola di Rienzo*, 151–53.

45. Roth, *History of the Jews of Italy*, 140.

46. Boiteux, "Les juifs," 747.

47. Article 72 of book 3 of the Statutes of Rome (1469) established the races.
48. Boiteux, "Les juifs," 750; Roth, *History of the Jews of Italy*, 386–87. In 1513 the Florentine poet Jacopo Penni described the same scene in rhyme. J.-J. Penni, *Magnifica et sumptuosa festa fatti dalla signori Romani per il carnevale*.
49. Montaigne, *Journal of Montaigne's Travels*.
50. During the pontificate of Paul II (1464–71) the race course was changed to the street today known as the Corso. Earlier the races were at the Piazza Navona. Over the years the precise location changed. Vogelstein, *Rome*, 233; Boiteux "Les juifs," 750–51; Munday, *English Roman Life*, 61–64.
51. Vogelstein, *Rome*, 232.
52. Boiteux, "Les juifs," 751–53.
53. Vogelstein, *Rome*, 233.
54. Vogelstein, *Rome*, 233; K. Stow, *Jews in Rome*, vol. 1, 17, doc. 47; Boiteux, "Les juifs," 747.
55. Boiteux, "Les juifs," 753; Vogelstein, *Rome*, 282–83.
56. Gunzberg, *Strangers at Home*, 91–92; Schama, *Story of the Jews*, 69–70. For the term "virtual Jews" in this context see Linder, "'Jews Too Were Not Absent,'" 347. For the prohibitions against Jews leaving their homes during Holy Week see K. Stow, *Jewish Dogs*, 70.
57. Lent is a Christian period of repentance prior to the Good Friday and Easter holidays. Carnival directly precedes Lent as a week of revelry before the time of repentance begins.
58. Boiteux, "Les juifs," 57–64. For a carnival outside Rome in medieval France see Ladurie, *Carnival in Romans*. For the Roman Carnival see Clementi, *Il carnevale romano*.
59. Boiteux, "Les juifs," 753, 784.
60. Brentano, *Rome before Avignon*, 47.
61. Roth, *History of the Jews of Italy*, 149.
62. The Spanish historian and physician Shelomo ibn Verga is said to have composed *Shevet Yehuda* (The sceptre of Judah) from which this account may have been taken. The title refers to "The scepter shall not depart from Judah" (Gen. 49:10). Yet *Shevet Yehuda* appears to have been the work not only of Shelomo but also his son Joseph ibn Verga, and with a significant part copied from the notes of his relative, Judah ibn Verga. As history, *Shevet Yehuda* may be less that accurate. Indeed, the story about the Jewish petition to Pope Alexander VI has a legendary quality. For a second, Christian source on this story see Infessiera, *Diario della citta di Roma*.
63. K. Stow, "Ethnic Rivalry or Melting Pot," 286–87; Roth, *History of the Jews of Italy*, 180, 192.
64. O'Malley, *Giles of Viterbo on Church and Reform*, 14, 70.

65. Lesley, "Jewish Adaptation," 50.

66. Adler, *Jewish Travellers in the Middle Ages*, 268–84.

67. S. Stow, "Harara," 80–81; see also K. Stow, *Alienated Minority*, 70. The reference is to the round baked bread. Pizza as we know it had to await the tomato's introduction into Italy from Peru in 1548.

68. Sermoneta, "Prophecy," 352–53, 373.

69. Sermoneta, "Prophecy," 152.

70. Ben Solomon, *Tophet and Eden*. *Tophet* is a biblical term describing the Hinnom Valley south of Jerusalem where children were allegedly sacrificed to the Canaanite Gods of Baal and Molech. Jer. 7:31–32, 19:5–6.

71. Brener, "*Scroll of Love* by Immanuel of Rome," 156. Gilgal and Shittin are two locations identified in the Bible. The former is the first place the Israelites settled after they crossed into the Land of Israel (Josh. 4:19). The latter, spelled *Shittim* in Josh. 2:1, was the last place the Israelites camped before they crossed the Jordan River. In other words, Immanuel is making erotic use of biblical geography, while predating Rudyard Kipling's poem "The Ballad of East and West"—"East is East and West is West and never the twain shall meet"—by some 554 years.

72. Roth, *Jews in the Renaissance*, 196, 205; Bemporad, "Jewish Ceremonial Art in the Era of the Ghettos," 123.

73. Vasari, *Lives of the Artists*, 434.

74. Kneale, *Rome*, 154–217; Bell, *Street Life in Renaissance Rome*, 97–105.

5. DIVORCE, ROMAN STYLE

1. The story is recorded in the *Avvisi*, anonymous records found in the Biblioteca Apostolica Vaticana Codex Urb. Lat., as well as Merkle, ed., *Diary of A. Massarelli* and the *Diary of Firmani* in the same volume. The diary entries are summarized in K. Stow, *Catholic Thought and Papal Jewry Policy*, 4–15 and 15n36, and K. Stow, *Theater of Acculturation*, 41. See also Setton, *Papacy and the Levant*, 719. What purports to be an eyewitness account by a Jew is found in Mampieri, *Living under the Evil Pope*.

2. Pasquinade 155, line 15–20, in Marucci, *Pasquinate*, 245. A pasquinade was an anonymous satirical poem concerning current events that was posted near the "statue of Pasquino." It was purported, humorously, that the statue authored the poems. "Pasquino" (which is actually a broken, third-century BCE statue of a scene from book 17 of Homer's *Iliad*, Menelaus holding the dead Patroclus) was the first of several "talking statues" in Renaissance Rome. Pasquino's statue in Rome is located in a piazza next door to the more famous Piazza Navona.

3. Setton, *Papacy and the Levant*, 719. For the practice of casting bodies into the Tiber see Sprenger, "Tiara in the Tiber."

4. Stow, *Catholic Thought and Papal Jewry Policy*, 14–15.

5. T. Cohen and E. Cohen, *Words and Deeds*.

6. Record of the ensuing trial may be found in the *Archivio di stato di Roma tribunale criminale del governatore processi*, sec. 17, b.174, c.374r. The trial has been analyzed in Feci, "Death of a Miller."

7. Roth, *Ritual Murder Libel and the Jew*.

8. K. Stow, "Consciousness of Closure," 392.

9. *New Catholic Encyclopedia*, 2nd ed. (2002), s.v. "Pope Formosus."

10. Duchesne, *Le liber pontificalis*, 252, 259.

11. Sprenger, "Tiara in the Tiber," 163–67.

12. Gucciardini, *Sack of Rome*, 92–93.

13. Kneale, *Rome*, 201. For a depiction of a papal impersonator being paraded through Rome see Gottfried, *Historical Chronicle*, or its reproduction in Kneale, *Rome*, 202.

14. But see Vogelstein, *Rome*, 277. Vogelstein was not convinced of the details concerning the Jew Hat.

15. Setton, *The Papacy and the Levant*, 719.

16. T. Cohen and E. Cohen, *Words and Deeds*, 94: For the vacant see in general see Hunt, *The Vacant See in Early Modern Rome*; Nussdorfer, "The Vacant See," 176; C. Ginzburg with the Bologna Seminar, "Ritual Pillages."

17. K. Stow, *Theater of Acculturation*, 49.

18. T. Cohen, "Case of the Mysterious Coil of Rope," 209.

19. Boksenboim, *Iggerot R. Yehudah Aryeh Modena*, 134–38.

20. Delicado, *La lozana andaluza*, 138, wherein Jewish women teach young Roman brides how to insure pregnancy in the first year of marriage.

21. Milano, *Il ghetto*, 71.

22. Bonfil, *History and Folklore*, 15.

23. K. Stow, *Alienated Minority*, 18–19.

24. Kneale, *Rome*, 217. The earlier and more well known Spanish Inquisition, created by papal bull under Pope Sixtus IV, was less an exercise in papal authority and more a way for the Spanish monarchy, Ferdinand and Isabella, to assert power separate from Rome. Milano, *Il ghetto*, 53.

25. Aquinas, *Summa theologica*, 2a, 2ae, questions 10–12.

26. Wendehorst, "Roman Inquisition," 203.

27. K. Stow, "Burning of the Talmud," 435.

28. Kertzer, *Popes against the Jews*, 139.

29. The account of the Talmud burning in Rome appears in poetry by Moses ben Abraham Anav. See also Vogelstein, *Rome*, 167.

30. Today, the Campo de'Fiore is the site of an open market where fresh food is available daily in the shadow of a statue of the immolated Bruno. A plaque in memory of the Talmud burning was unveiled in the piazza in 2011. Engraved on the plaque is a passage from the elegy "Sha'ali serufah ba esh" (Inquire you who are burned by fire) composed by Rabbi Meir ben Baruch (ca. 1215–93) that recounts the earlier burning of the Talmud in Paris. Ashkenazic Jewish communities recite this elegy on Tisha b'Av.

31. Stow, *Jews in Rome*, vol. 2, 695, doc. 1607.

32. Stow, "Burning of the Talmud," 441.

33. We know of Paul IV's out-of-character interest only from a court case concerning the alleged theft of the messianic books. Archivio di Stato, Roma Tribunale del Governatore, Criminale, Costitui 38 fol. 11–13, March 2, 1552, cited in Stow, "Neofiti and Their Families," 106.

34. K. Stow, "Burning of the Talmud," 443.

35. There are numerous translations of *Cum nimis absurdum*. The selected translation is by K. Stow, *Catholic Thought and Papal Jewry Policy*, 294–95. When it was issued, *Cum nimis* only applied to the Jews of the papal states. In 1566, Pope Pius V extended its scope to make it universal. K. Stow, *Catholic Thought and Papal Jewry Policy*, 168.

36. The story is told in a manuscript in the Archivio di Stato, Roma Tribunale del Governatore, Criminale, Processi, bust 16 (1551). T. Cohen retells it with analysis in "Case of the Mysterious Coil of Rope."

37. Cardinal Lorenzo Ganganelli told this story in his report to Pope Benedict XIV concerning accusations that Jews murdered Christian children to obtain blood for their Passover rituals. His report would clear the Jewish community of the blood libel. Ganganelli, who did not find it problematic that Roman Jews and Catholics could be mistaken for one another, would be elected Pope Clement XIV ten years later.

38. Pope Benedict XIII's bull of 1415, *Etsi doctoris gentium* (Although the teacher of the gentiles), a precursor to *Cum nimis*, set forth most if not all the elements of Jewry policy stated in Paul IV's bull. However, Benedict XIII was declared a schismatic and excommunicated from the church in 1417, and the new Pope Martin V repealed any legislation based upon *Etsi doctoris*. K. Stow, *Catholic Thought and Papal Jewry Policy*, 284–87, 278n1.

39. Quoted in K. Stow, *Catholic Thought and Papal Jewry Policy*, 295. *Cum nimis* recognizes the possibility of there being more than one ghetto in Rome. Indeed, there was a second, smaller ghetto termed the "Ghettarello" (small ghetto) near the main one. See Spizzichino, *La scomparsa*. Limited archaeological excavations

that may reveal a portion of the Ghettarello can be seen on the Lungotevere Dei Cenci where it intersects Portico d'Ottavia street.

40. Stow, *Catholic Thought and Papal Jewry Policy*, 94. Previous attempts to separate Jews by identifying garb were known elsewhere in Europe. The Fourth Lateran Council ordered identifying dress in 1215. Crouzet-Pavan, "Venice between Jerusalem," 178n81. Earlier, in 887, a Muslim ruler had ordered a Jew-badge in Sicily; at that time Christians had to wear identifiable clothing as well. Roth, *History of the Jews of Italy*, 56. There had also been a ghetto in Venice since 1516.

41. Stow, *Catholic Thought and Papal Jewry Policy*, 185.

42. Vogelstein, *Rome*, 269.

43. Milano, *Il ghetto*, 97.

44. Calabi, *Venice and Its Jews*, 27. The Venice ghetto was less harsh and more open than its successor in Rome. See, generally, Crouzet-Pavan, "Venice between Jerusalem."

45. For the ghetto of prostitutes see E. Cohen, "Honor and Gender," 396.

46. Stow, "Sanctity and the Construction of Space," 58. The first use of the word "ghetto" in Christian sources appears in 1562 in Pius IV's bull *Dudum a felicis*. Ravid, "From Geographical Realia to Historiographical Symbol," 337.

47. Kneale, *Rome*, 217; Setton, *Papacy and the Levant*, 710–19.

48. Partner, *Renaissance Rome*, 45–46; T. Cohen, *Roman Tales*, 64.

49. See Belli's sonnet of a later date, "L'ingegno dell'omo" ("The Ingenuity of Man"), which describes an assignation in a confessional inside the Church of St. Ignatius of Loyola.

50. For a description of his hatred of the Franciscan friars see Partner, *Renaissance Rome*, 214–15.

51. G. Cohen, "Esau as Symbol in Early Medieval Thought."

52. K. Stow, "End of Confessionalism," 41; G. Cohen, "Esau as Symbol in Early Medieval Thought," 33.

53. Rist, *Popes and Jews*, 74.

54. K. Stow, *Alienated Minority*, 18–19.

55. K. Stow, "Fruit of Ambivalence," 8. Saint Ambrose of Milan, Augustine's contemporary, expressed the same ambivalence. For Ambrose, while persecution of Jews was not the church's proper role, civil authorities or laypersons could legitimately engage in such activities, including the burning of synagogues. Langmuir, "Toward a Definition of Antisemitism," 75.

56. K. Stow, *Catholic Thought and Papal Jewry Policy*, 5, 186; Roth, *History of the Jews of Italy*, 306–19.

57. For visual evidence of that ambivalence, see Danny Smith, "Painted into a Corner," which demonstrates Jews' constricted social position in medieval and early modern Rome through their depiction in church paintings.

58. K. Stow, *Alienated Minority*, 304; Stow, "Sanctity and the Construction of Space"; Ravid, "How 'Other' Really Was the Jewish Other?" 43.

59. K. Stow, *Alienated Minority*, 100–101, 115, 232.

60. For the paradoxical nature of the Ghetto see Stow, "The Consciousness of Closure"; Cooperman, "Early Modern Ghetto." Also see, generally, K. Stow, *Theater of Acculturation*.

61. K. Stow, *Alienated Minority*, 54–76.

62. K. Stow, "Sanctity and the Construction of Space," 74n32; Stow, *Theater of Acculturation*, 21.

63. Feci, "Death of a Miller," 22.

6. LOVE, DEATH, AND MONEY

1. Kenneth Stow has collected, translated, and annotated a portion of those records covering the years 1536–57 in *Jews in Rome*. The present case appears as document 1902 in vol. 2.

2. K. Stow, *Jews in Rome*, vol. 2, 836; see also doc. 1905. Stow notes that in some ways the Ghetto was a "litigious family." Given the Catholic participation in the litigation, it seems that often that family included Christians.

3. K. Stow, *Catholic Thought and Papal Jewry Policy*, 23.

4. K. Stow, *Jews in Rome*, vol. 2, doc. 1307.

5. K. Stow, *Jews in Rome*, vol. 1, doc. 887.

6. K. Stow, *Jews in Rome*, vol. 2, doc. 1866.

7. K. Stow, *Jews in Rome*, vol. 1, doc. 665.

8. K. Stow, *Jews in Rome*, vol. 1, doc. 988; vol. 2 docs. 1322, 1340.

9. K. Stow, *Jews in Rome*, vol. 2, docs. 1267, 1283.

10. K. Stow, *Jews in Rome*, vol. 2, doc. 1714.

11. K. Stow, *Jews in Rome*, vol. 1, doc. 895; vol. 2, docs. 1799, 895, 1453.

12. K. Stow, *Jews in Rome*, vol. 2, doc. 1743.

13. K. Stow, *Jews in Rome*, vol. 2, doc. 1755.

14. K. Stow, *Jews in Rome*, vol. 2, doc. 1853.

15. K. Stow, "Writing in Hebrew." Milano, *Il ghetto*, 435–71, includes a glossary of Judaeo-Roman words and phrases.

16. K. Stow, "Jewish Pre-Emancipation," 8.

17. T. Cohen, *Roman Tales*, 16–39.

18. K. Stow, *Jews in Rome*, vol. 2, doc. 1996.

19. K. Stow, *Jews in Rome* vol. 2, 820; K. Stow, *Popes, Church, and Jews*, 44.

20. K. Stow, *Jews in Rome*, vol. 1, doc. 844.

21. K. Stow, *Jews in Rome*, vol. 1, doc. 899.

22. K. Stow, *Jews in Rome*, vol. 1, xxxii.

23. K. Stow, *Jews in Rome*, vol. 2, doc. 1099. See also Franzone, "Considerazione." 33.

24. K. Stow, *Jews in Rome*, vol. 2, doc. 1615.

25. K. Stow, *Jews in Rome* vol. 1, xix.

26. K. Stow, *Jews in Rome*, vol. 1, docs. 332, 871.

27. K. Stow, *Jews in Rome*, vol. 1, 543; vol. 2, doc. 1286.

28. K. Stow, *Jews in Rome*, vol. 1, doc. 734.

29. K. Stow, *Jews in Rome*, vol. l, docs. 5, 768, 773.

30. K. Stow, *Jews in Rome*, vol. 1, doc. 866.

31. In 1946, Cecil Roth estimated that a *scudo* was worth about $2.50, with the understanding that $2.50 bought much more in sixteenth-century Rome than it does today. Roth, *History of the Jews of Italy*, x.

32. K. Stow, *Catholic Thought and Papal Jewry Policy*, 17.

33. K. Stow, *Jews in Rome*, vol. 2, doc. 1011.

34. K. Stow, *Catholic Thought and Papal Jewry Policy*, 83.

35. Stow, *Jews in Rome*, vol. 2, doc. 1936; Milano, *Il ghetto*, 89–90.

36. Milano, *Il ghetto*, 89–90.

37. Roth, *History of the Jews of Italy*, 375.

38. K. Stow, *Jews in Rome*, vol. l, docs. 657, 765, 995.

39. K. Stow, *Jews in Rome*, vol. 1, doc. 770; vol. 2, doc. 1161.

40. K. Stow, *Jews in Rome*, vol. 1, doc. 64.

41. K. Stow, *Jews in Rome*, vol. 2, doc. 1375.

42. K. Stow, "Papacy and the Jews," 269–70; K. Stow, "Good of the Church," 248.

43. K. Stow, "Consciousness of Closure," 388–89.

44. K. Stow, *Anna and Tranquillo*, 192n22.

45. Spizzichino, *La scomparsa*, 28.

46. K. Stow, "Good of the Church," 245–47; K. Stow, *Jews in Rome*, vol. 1, docs. 486, 735; K. Stow, *Catholic Thought and Papal Jewry Policy*, 226–27.

47. K. Stow, *Catholic Thought and Papal Jewry Policy*, 226–27.

48. K. Stow, "Good of the Church," 245–52.

49. K. Stow, "Good of the Church," 248.

50. K. Stow, *Anna and Tranquillo*, 115.

51. Colzi, "Angelo Mortera," 97–109.

52. Partner, *Renaissance Rome*, 102–4; Roth, *History of the Jews of Italy*, 103, 127, 229, 198–99.

53. K. Stow, *Jews in Rome*, vol. 1, docs. 551, 559, 565.

54. Brentano, *Rome before Avignon*, 52–53; K. Stow, *Jews in Rome*, vol. 1, doc. 559.

55. K. Stow, *Jews in Rome*, vol. 1, docs. 559, 223.

56. K. Stow, *Jews in Rome*, vol. 1, docs. 581, 234.

57. K. Stow, *Theater of Acculturation*, 61.

58. K. Stow, *Jews in Rome*, vol. 2, docs. 1626, 1408, 1413.

59. K. Stow, *Jews in Rome*, vol. 1, doc. 355.

60. K. Stow, *Jews in Rome*, vol. 1, doc. 486. In the same document the lenders tacked on a requirement that all lenders lend two hundred scudi to the poor interest-free, probably in response to competition from the Catholic Monti di Pietà that had similar practices.

61. See, for example, K. Stow, *Jews in Rome*, vol. 1, doc. 747.

62. K. Stow, *Jews in Rome*, vol. 1, doc. 735.

63. K. Stow, *Jews in Rome*, vol. 2, doc. 1155.

64. K. Stow, *Jews in Rome*, vol. 2, docs. 1629, 1791.

65. K. Stow, *Catholic Thought and Papal Jewry Policy*, 90, 106.

66. K. Stow, "Knotty Problem of Shem Tov Sopporto," 148–49; K. Stow, "Marriages Are Made in Heaven."

67. K. Stow, *Jews in Rome*, vol. 2, docs. 1470, 1714.

68. K. Stow, *Jews in Rome*, vol. 1, doc. 26. The date of Shabbat "Nahamu" refers to the Sabbath just after the Jewish holiday of Tisha b'Av that commemorates the destruction of both the First and Second Temples. Nahamu refers to Isaiah 40:1–26, which reads "Nachamu nachamu ami," "Comfort, o comfort my people."

69. K. Stow, "Marriages Are Made in Heaven," 453–54.

70. K. Stow, "Marriages Are Made in Heaven," 452.

71. K. Stow, "Marriages Are Made in Heaven," 452–53.

72. K. Stow, "Marriages Are Made in Heaven," 486–88. The enhanced rights of women in sixteenth-century Jewish Rome is highlighted throughout Stow, *Jews in Rome*, vols. 1 and 2. Francisco Delicado's *La Lozana Andaluza* (Lozana from Andalusia), a fictional account of Rome written in 1528, provides some evidence of a separate women's synagogue. At sketch no. 16, the title character is guided through the Jewish neighborhood—"This synagogue is for the Catalan men, and the one further along is for their women"—(excerpted in Bell, *Street Life in Renaissance Rome*, 113), but even if this were the case, it may or may not demonstrate any enhanced rights for Jewish women. See also K. Stow, *Anna and Tranquillo*, 52n169. Additionally, the sixteenth-century Roman Jewish poet Deborah Ascarelli translated traditional Jewish liturgy into Italian and included some of her poems in her book *L'abitacolo degli oranti* (The abode of the supplicants).

73. K. Stow, "Marriages Are Made in Heaven," 481.

74. Caffiero, *Forced Baptism*, 228–30.

75. K. Stow, *Jews in Rome*, vol. 1, doc. 791.

76. The Catholic view of a dowry is similar. K. Stow, *Catholic Thought and Papal Jewry Policy*, 103.

77. K. Stow, *Jews in Rome*, vol. 1, doc. 539.

78. K. Stow, *Jews in Rome*, vol. 1, docs. 93, 137, 394.

79. K. Stow, *Jews in Rome*, vol. 1, doc. 292.

80. K. Stow, *Jews in Rome*, vol. 1, docs. 428, 414, 696, 860, 943, 954; vol. 2, docs. 1252, 1349.

81. K. Stow, *Jews in Rome*, vol. 2, doc. 1419.

82. K. Stow, *Jews in Rome*, vol. 2, docs. 1086, 1089, 1090, 1092.

83. On European beliefs about "tying" see Ladurie, "Aiguillette."

84. K. Stow, *Jews in Rome*, vol. 2, docs. 1107, 1236, 1567, 1113, 1163.

85. K. Stow, *Jews in Rome* vol. 2, 583, and also vol. 2, docs. 1634, 1370; K. Stow, *Theater of Acculturation*, 45–46.

86. Hunt, *Vacant See in Early Modern Rome*, 232.

87. Hunt, *Vacant See in Early Modern Rome*, 227.

88. Hunt, *Vacant See in Early Modern Rome*, 237–38; T. Cohen, *Roman Tales*, 93, 110.

89. Hunt, *Vacant See in Early Modern Rome*, 232–34.

90. Hunt, "Conclave from the 'Outside In,'" 372n58.

91. K. Stow, *Catholic Thought and Papal Jewry Policy*, 22; K. Stow, "Consciousness of Closure," 392.

92. Mampieri, *Living under the Evil Pope*, 277, 280–82.

93. K. Stow, *Jews in Rome*, vol. 1, doc. 764.

94. K. Stow, *Jews in Rome*, vol. 2, doc. 1728.

95. K. Stow, *Jews in Rome*, vol. 2, doc. 1981.

96. K. Stow, *Jews in Rome*, vol. 1, doc. 909.

97. K. Stow, *Jews in Rome*, vol. 1, doc. 621.

98. K. Stow, *Jews in Rome*, vol. 1, doc. 768.

99. K. Stow, *Jews in Rome*, vol 2, doc. 1617.

100. Vogelstein, *Rome*, 274.

101. K. Stow, *Jews in Rome*, vol. 2, docs. 1266, 1693, 1043.

102. K. Stow, *Jews in Rome*, vol. 2, doc. 1905. Burying one person on top of another is not a customary Jewish practice. However, when the Jewish graveyard on the Aventine Hill (in use from 1645 through 1934) had to be moved, two layers of graves were found. One set of graves, at a "reasonable depth" (six feet?) beneath the surface, sat atop a second set of graves below the fifteen-foot mark. It is not known whether the lower stratum of graves evidenced earlier Jewish burials or non-Jewish graves that predated 1645. See Spizzichino, "La gestione," 214.

103. Elizabetta Povoledo, "'Here Lies': A Clue in Hebrew Points to Rome's Medieval Jewish Cemetery," *New York Times*, March 28, 2017.

104. K. Stow, *Catholic Thought and Papal Jewry Policy*, 82.

105. Spizzichino, "La gestione," 207–9.

106. K. Stow, *Jews in Rome*, vol. 2, doc. 1274.

107. K. Stow, *Jews in Rome*, vol. 2, doc. 1632.

108. K. Stow, *Jews in Rome*, vol. 1, doc. 526, 527, 53; vol. 2, docs. 1176, 1632. Traditionally the days of the Omer (the seven weeks between the end of Passover and Shavuot) are counted every year.

7. "TILL THE CONVERSION OF THE JEWS"

1. MacDonald, *Poems of Andrew Marvell*, 21.

2. K. Stow, *Catholic Thought and Papal Jewry Policy*, xx–xxi.

3. Anna's name appears in the census of 1733, the *Descriptio Hebreorum* (Description of the Hebrews) at family no. 397, no. 1814: "Anna, o sia Graziosa altra figlia d'anno uno, e mezzo" ("Anna or Graziosa other daughter [of Benedetto] one and a half years"). Gruppi, *Gli abitanti*, 228. See also K. Stow, preface to *Gli abitanti*, 17.

4. In 1793, after Anna's death, her brother Tranquillo circulated her "diary," entitled the *Ratto* (Abduction), in handwritten form, but first he appears to have edited her text for polemical purposes. By 1793, Tranquillo was aware of the French Revolution (1789) through Jewish contacts in Amsterdam, and he was agitating for reforms in Roman Jewish life such as had occurred in northern Europe. There is no doubt that the *Ratto* we have is laced with his ideas, though most likely "the bulk of what the diary has to tell us is real" (K. Stow, *Anna and Tranquillo*, 13).

5. K. Stow, *Anna and Tranquillo*, 20. Stow translated Anna's diary and has provided notes and commentary as well as a historical context for her kidnapping.

6. Caffiero, *Forced Baptism*, 212. Although here the subject is only the Catecumeni in Rome, *Case dei catecumeni* were also located in Bologna, Pesaro, Ferrara, and Avignon, within the Papal States, and outside the Papal States in Florence, Modena, Venice, Mantua, Milan, and Genoa. Stow, *Anna and Tranquillo*, 204 n.1.

7. K. Stow, *Catholic Thought and Papal Jewry Policy*, 187.

8. Caffiero, *Forced Baptism*, 9–10, 212; K. Stow, *Anna and Tranquillo*, 2, 68.

9. Caffiero, *Forced Baptism*, 203.

10. K. Stow, *Anna and Tranquillo*, 22.

11. K. Stow, *Anna and Tranquillo*, 26.

12. For a summary of the *Libellus* see K. Stow, *Catholic Thought and Papal Jewry Policy*, 217–20.

13. Hostiensis, *Summa aurea*, book 5, col. 1519, quoted in Rist, *Popes and Jews*, 186–88.

14. Quoted and translated in K. Stow, *Catholic Thought and Papal Jewry Policy*, 219.

15. Quoted and translated in K. Stow, *Catholic Thought and Papal Jewry Policy*, 219. For a summary of the *Lectione* as it refers to conversion see K. Stow, *Catholic Thought and Papal Jewry Policy*, 211–17.

16. K. Stow, *Catholic Thought and Papal Jewry Policy*, 214. Perhaps Torres was recalling the stance of Innocent III (1198–1216) and Boniface VIII (1294–1303) on the issue

of forced baptism. They agreed that a person should not come to the faith by force. However, if through threat of violence or lost possessions a person agreed, even reluctantly, to be baptized, that conversion would be legitimate. Only if a person was baptized despite unabated objections could a baptism be considered ineffective. Rist, *Popes and Jews*, 78.

17. K. Stow, *Catholic Thought and Papal Jewry Policy*, is a commentary on *De judaeis*. Stow, *Catholic Thought and Papal Jewry Policy*, xiii. Stow, "Church, Conversion and Tradition," 30.

18. Stow, *Catholic Thought and Papal Jewry Policy*, 45.

19. The bull *Vineam Sorec* (Vineyard of Sorek) refers to the valley between Judah and Philistia mentioned at Judges 16:4.

20. K. Stow, *Catholic Thought and Papal Jewry Policy*, 278n1.

21. K. Stow, *Catholic Thought and Papal Jewry Policy*, 208–9.

22. K. Stow, *Catholic Thought and Papal Jewry Policy*, 19.

23. Milano, *Il ghetto*, 272.

24. Montaigne, *Journal of Montaigne's Travels*.

25. Milano, *Il ghetto*, 271.

26. K. Stow, *Catholic Thought and Papal Jewry Policy*, 21, 36.

27. Milano, *Il ghetto*, 275–77.

28. Milano, *Il ghetto*, 277.

29. Milano, *Il ghetto*, 279.

30. Milano, *Il ghetto*, 273–74.

31. K. Stow, *Catholic Thought and Papal Jewry Policy*, 187.

32. Quoted in K. Stow, *Catholic Thought and Papal Jewry Policy*, 27.

33. K. Stow, *Catholic Thought and Papal Jewry Policy*, 11, 28.

34. Caffiero, *Forced Baptism*, 48.

35. The story of Ferdinando and Leocadia, found in the Manuscript Collection of the Vatican Library, was translated into English with notes in Leiphart, "Case of Ferdinando Alvarez."

36. Caffiero, *Forced Baptism*, 49–51.

37. Caffiero, *Forced Baptism*, 53.

38. K. Stow, *Catholic Thought and Papal Jewry Policy*, 181.

39. Caffiero, *Forced Baptism*, 53–54.

40. Caffiero, *Forced Baptism*, 58–60. The case may be found in the Archivio della Congregazione per la Dottrina della Fede (ACDF) *Sant'Officio*, Stanza storica CC4-b 1755.

41. Caffiero, *Forced Baptism*, 62–65.

42. Caffiero, *Forced Baptism*, 70. The case may be found in the ACDF *Sant'Officio*, Stanza storica CC4-b 1758.

43. Caffiero, *Forced Baptism*, 67–72.

44. Caffiero, *Forced Baptism*, 105. The case may be found in the ACDF *Sant'Officio,* Stanza storica BBI-f 1758.

45. Caffiero, *Forced Baptism*, 103–8.

46. Caffiero, *Forced Baptism*, 116–24.

47. Caffiero, *Forced Baptism*, 117.

48. Caffiero, *Forced Baptism*, 88–89.

49. Caffiero, *Forced Baptism*, 165–72.

50. Caffiero, *Forced Baptism*, 124–31.

51. Caffiero, *Forced Baptism*, 88, 116–31, 196–202.

52. Caffiero, *Forced Baptism*, 164–65.

53. Caffiero, *Forced Baptism*, 174. For the full story of Mazaldò see Caffiero, *Forced Baptism*, 173–79. The case may be found at ACDF, *Sant'Officio*, Stanza storica, BBI-c.

54. Caffiero, *Forced Baptism*, 203.

55. K. Stow, *Theater of Acculturation*, 136–38n11; Sonino and Spizzichino, "La demografia," 80, graph 1.

56. On the rites of conversion see Caffiero, *Forced Baptism*, 196–214.

57. Caffiero, *Forced Baptism*, 204–7.

58. Caffiero, *Forced Baptism*, 204.

59. A description of Pope Urban VIII's baptism of Salomone Tullio and his baby sister Emma is inscribed in the Catecumeni's baptismal records. Caffiero, *Forced Baptism*, 210.

60. Caffiero, *Forced Baptism*, 214–19.

61. Caffiero, *Forced Baptism*, 204.

62. The father's wishes were immaterial. In fact, a father of a convert was legally bound to support his children despite baptism, and also bound to provide a dowry for his converted daughter. K. Stow, *Catholic Thought and Papal Jewry Policy*, 176–81.

63. However they often had to work with their former coreligionists because that was the commercial world they knew. Caffiero, *Forced Baptism*, 241.

64. K. Stow, *Catholic Thought and Papal Jewry Policy*, 172–78.

65. Caffiero, *Forced Baptism*, 238–44.

66. Mauss, *Gift*, 38, 84n3.

67. Douglas, *No Free Gifts*, viii–ix.

8. TRADING PLACES

1. The August 4, 1881, edition of the Vatican newspaper, *L'osservatore Romano*, stated that the new Italian government had imprisoned the pope: "The Pope is a prisoner, the Italian government his jailer." Similarly, in October 1870, the archbishop of

Cologne sent a letter to the Prussian king protesting that the pope "had become a prisoner in his own home." Kertzer, *Prisoner of the Vatican*, 194, 69.

2. Between 529 and 534 CE the Byzantine Emperor Justinian I ordered a collection of jurisprudential works that have come to be known as Justinian's Code.

3. K. Stow, *Catholic Thought and Papal Jewry Policy*, 17; K. Stow, "Jewish Pre-Emancipation." *Ius commune* was a Roman and Christianized version of common law that should not be confused with British common law. K. Stow, *Anna and Tranquillo*, 218n79.

4. K. Stow, "Jewish Pre-Emancipation," 6–8.

5. K. Stow, *Catholic Thought and Papal Jewry Policy*, 102–24. Stow is commenting on De Susannis's 1558 writing. But the notion that Jews were citizens and subject to *ius commune* goes back to the jurist Bartolo of Saxoferato in the fourteenth century.

6. K. Stow, *Anna and Tranquillo*, 156.

7. Virtual Roma, Language and Poetry 4, "G. Berneri Meo Patacca" at Canto 12:8, http://roma.andreapollett.com/S8/romabe14.htm.

8. Virtual Roma, Language and Poetry 4, "G. Berneri Meo Patacca" at Canto 12:28, http://roma.andreapollett.com/S8/romabe14.htm.

9. Virtual Roma, Language and Poetry 4, "G. Berneri Meo Patacca" at Canto 12:54, http://roma.andreapollett.com/S8/romabe14.htm.

10. Wasner, "Pope's Veneration of the Torah," 281.

11. Spizzichino, "Ghetto and the Authorities," 17–21; Roth, *History of the Jews of Italy*, 426; Vogelstein, *Rome*, 328.

12. The Directory was the five-person governing committee for the First French Republic from 1795 to 1799.

13. K. Stow, *Anna and Tranquillo*, 156.

14. Beales and Biagini, *Risorgimento and the Unification of Italy*, 24.

15. Vogelstein, *Rome*, 329.

16. Vogelstein, *Rome*, 330.

17. Vogelstein, *Rome*, 331.

18. Gunzberg, *Strangers at Home*, 37.

19. K. Stow, *Anna and Tranquillo*, 4, 90; Beales and Biagini, *Risorgimento and the Unification of Italy*, 25; Vogelstein, *Rome*, 332.

20. Schama, *Story of the Jews*, 415ff.

21. Schama, *Story of the Jews*, 419–20. For a discussion of the Sanhedrin see J. Katz, *Exclusiveness and Tolerance*, 182–96.

22. Lang, "Politics of Conversion," 215–16.

23. Roth, *History of the Jews of Italy*, 440.

24. Beales and Biagini, *Risorgimento and the Unification of Italy*, 26; Vogelstein, *Rome*, 332.
25. Roth, *History of the Jews of Italy*, 444.
26. For descriptions of the burials of Roman rabbis at Verano see Di Segni, "I rabbini."
27. Riall, *Risorgimento*, 53–56.
28. D. Di Castro, "Jews of Rome," 34–35, which includes a photograph of the ring.
29. Procaccia, "Storia economica," 37.
30. Procaccia, "Storia economica," 8–39.
31. Caffiero, "Tra repressione," 375.
32. Roth *History of the Jews of Italy*, 450; Vogelstein *Rome*, 334, 352.
33. Caffiero, "Tra repressione," 384–85.
34. Caffiero, "Tra repressione," 378–84. Later in the century the population of the Rione de Borgo appears to have been significantly anticlerical. Kertzer, *Prisoner*, 62–63.
35. Caffiero, "Tra repressione," 378–80.
36. Vogelstein, *Rome*, 334; Roth, *History of the Jews of Italy*, 451; Procaccia, "Storia economica," 40–41; Caffiero, "Tra repressione," 384.
37. Procaccia, "Storia economica," 38–39.
38. Roth, *History of the Jews of Italy*, 456; Vogelstein, *Rome*, 335.
39. Beales and Biagini, *Risorgimento and the Unification of Italy*, 43–46.
40. No one should look to *Nabucco* for even a scintilla of historical accuracy. Its importance lies in its understanding of Italian, not Israelite, history.
41. Verdi and Solera, *Nabucco* 3.4.
42. Toscano, "Italian Jewish Identity."
43. Leone, "L'ottocento," 260–67, and n. 263, fig. 2.
44. For summaries of the vitriol in Filippo Aminta's *L'ebraismo senza replica e sconfito colle sue stesse armi*, Ferdinand Jabalot's *Degli ebrei nel loro rapport colle nazioni cristiani*, and the anonymous *Dissertazione sopra il commercio, usure, e condotta degli ebrei nello Stato Ponntificio*, see Caffiero, "Tra repressione," 385–94.
45. All translations of Belli's sonnets unless otherwise noted are from Gunzberg, *Strangers at Home*.
46. Gunzberg, *Strangers at Home*, 134–35. As Gunzberg explains, Belli did not use the term "rabbi"; rather, he used the Judaeo-Roman word for wise man, *cacàmme*, from the Hebrew *hakham*, in order to invest his poetry with a scatological pun, because in Italian *cacàmme* sounds like and is related to *caccare*, to defecate. Consequently, Belli was insulting both the pope and rabbis with the same word.
47. Quoted in Di Segni, "I rabbini," 134, and translated into English by this author.
48. Gunzberg, *Strangers at Home*, 136.

49. Gunzberg, *Strangers at Home*, 138.

50. Gunzberg, *Strangers at Home*, 141.

51. Gunzberg *Strangers at Home*, 122–23.

52. See *Hebrew-English Tanakh: The Traditional Hebrew Text and the New JPS Translation*, 2nd edition (Philadelphia: The Jewish Publication Society, 2003).

53. Gunzberg, *Strangers at Home*, 122–23.

54. Gunzberg, *Strangers at Home*, 123.

55. Kertzer, *Pope Who Would Be King*, 21, 27, 29–30.

56. Roth, *History of the Jews of Italy*, 459; Spizzichino, "Pio IX," 281. Rome's Guardia Civica was a force organized to keep order and maintain obedience to law.

57. Spizzichino, "Pio IX," 283–84.

58. Monsagrati, "La Roma papale," 19n29.

59. Kertzer, *Kidnapping of Edgardo Mortara*, 75; Kertzer, *Popes against the Jews*, 114.

60. Kertzer, *Popes against the Jews*, 110.

61. The handbill's contents are quoted and summarized in Kertzer, *Popes against the Jews*, 109–10, and Spizzichino "Pio IX," 284n12. Roth writes of a similar occurrence taking place a few months earlier during Passover, with embellishments, but does not provide documentation for this version of events other than a poem by a David Levi, for which no citation is given: *History of the Jews of Italy*, 459.

62. In *History of the Jews of Italy*, Roth appears to have conflated the story of these events with the stories about Brunetti. A more accurate story is told by Kertzer, *Pope Who Would Be King*, 75 and 369.

63. Vogelstein, *Rome*, 340.

64. Spizzichino, "Pio IX," 293–95.

65. Vogelstein, *Rome*, 340.

66. Vogelstein, *Rome*, 340; Kneale, *Rome*, 259.

67. Kertzer, *Pope Who Would Be King*, 97–98.

68. Kertzer, *Popes against the Jews*, 113; Spizzichino, "Pio IX," 291–92; Kertzer, *Pope Who Would Be King*, 102–21.

69. For the events leading up to the Roman Republic's 1849 establishment see Beales and Biagini, *Risorgimento and the Unification of Italy*, 87–95, 238–45; Kertzer, *Popes against the Jews*, 13; Kneale, *Rome*, 219–31; and Riall, *Risorgimento*, 60.

70. For excerpts from the constitution of the Roman Republic see Beales and Biagini, *Risorgimento and the Unification of Italy*, 245–46. The constitution the pope had agreed to sign was much less generous to the Jews, requiring at article 25 that persons enjoying political rights had to "profess the Catholic religion." Spizzichino, "Pio IX," 288–89.

71. Kertzer, *Pope Who Would Be King*, 306.

72. Kertzer, *Pope Who Would Be King*, 158–89.

73. For descriptions of the French siege of Rome see Kneale, *Rome*, 219–76, and Kertzer, *Pope Who Would Be King*, 190–206.

74. Riall, *Garibaldi*, 98; Kneale, *Rome*, 269.

75. Kertzer, *Pope Who Would Be King*, 143–44, 384–85n7.

76. Kertzer, *Popes against the Jews*, 114–15; Kertzer, *Pope Who Would Be King*, 318–19.

77. Spizzichino, "Pio IX," 329–32; Kertzer, *Pope Who Would Be King*, 305–6.

78. Gregorovius, *Ghetto and the Jews of Rome*, 14.

79. Nineteenth-century Italy, like the rest of the liberal world, was never a true democracy. First, it had a king. Second, while the general populace was consulted through plebiscites concerning unification, voting thereafter was restricted to 2 percent of the population. Riall, *Risorgimento*, 27. See also the Piedmontese constitution (1848), excerpted in Beales and Biagini, *Risorgimento and the Unification of Italy*, 254. The considerable historical work on the Risorgimento is analyzed and reviewed by Riall, *Risorgimento*, 7–52.

80. Kertzer, *Kidnapping of Edgardo Mortara*, 39–41.

81. Caffiero, *Forced Baptism*, 49, 55.

82. It is not clear if the articles ostensibly in favor of Edgardo were in fact motivated by anti-Catholicism.

83. Kertzer, *Kidnapping of Edgardo Mortara*, 127.

84. Kertzer, *Kidnapping of Edgardo Mortara*, 297–98.

85. Kertzer, *Prisoner of the Vatican*, 33.

86. Kertzer, *Prisoner of the Vatican*, 33.

87. Kertzer, *Prisoner of the Vatican*, 53.

88. Dainotto, "Emancipation," 131.

89. Kertzer, *Prisoner of the Vatican*, 55–56.

90. Roth, *History of the Jews of Italy*, 473.

91. Kertzer, *Pope and Mussolini*, 137.

9. BACKYARD EXILES

1. Tuck, *Woman of Rome*, 175.

2. Castronuovo, *Natalia Ginzburg*, 1.

3. Pekelis, *My Version of the Facts*, 6; Klein, *Italy's Jews from Emancipation to Fascism*, 31. From 1840 to 1931, the Jewish population in Rome rose from 3,811 to 12,316.

4. Kertzer, *Popes against the Jews*, 106–30; Kertzer, *Pope and Mussolini*, 3–18.

5. Stille, "Double Bind of Italian Jews," 25.

6. Walter Littlefield, "Man Who Would Not 'Embalm,'" *New York Times*, May 17, 1914.

7. Franzone, "Considerazioni," 35; Melasecchi, "Artisti," 125; Capuzzo, "L'élite," 94–95; Hughes, *Prisoners of Hope*, 13. Freemasonry refers to fraternal organizations that trace their origins to stonemason guilds of the Middle Ages.

8. *Civiltà cattolica* (1880) 4:108–9, quoted in Kertzer, *Popes against the Jews*, 136.

9. *Civiltà cattolica* (1881) 1:727, cited in Kertzer, *Popes against the Jews*, 138.

10. *Civiltà cattolica* (1893) 1:145 et seq, cited in Kertzer, *Popes against the Jews*, 145.

11. *Civiltà cattolica* (1893) 1:145 et seq, cited in Kertzer, *Popes against the Jews*, 145.

12. De Felice, *Jews in Fascist Italy*, 36.

13. *L'osservatore Romano*, July 1, 1892, 1, cited in Kertzer, *Popes against the Jews*, 147–48. As late as 1914, the church was circumspect in denying the veracity of the libel that Jews killed Christian children to make ritual use of their blood. The Vatican affirmed that it had conducted investigations and had found no evidence of Jewish ritual murder, but Catholic publications like *Civiltà cattolica* insisted in vicious terms that the "blood libel" was true. Kertzer, *Popes against the Jews*, 227–36; Perry and Schweitzer, *Antisemitism*, 68.

14. Gunzberg, *Strangers at Home*, 184–218.

15. Klein, *Italy's Jews from Emancipation to Fascism*, 77.

16. De Felice, *Jews in Fascist Italy*, 13.

17. Gunzberg, "Assimilation," 141; Klein, *Italy's Jews from Emancipation to Fascism*, 32.

18. De Felice, *Jews in Fascist Italy*, 14; Zimmerman, introduction to *Jews in Italy*, 4.

19. Di Segni, "I rabbini," 143.

20. Di Segni, "I rabbini," 145–46.

21. Di Segni, "I rabbini," 152; Franzone, "Considerazione," 33.

22. Cava and Terracina, "Transformazione," 246–56.

23. This information comes from lists of gifts to the Jewish community for building the Great Synagogue as well as from dowry lists from 1822 through 1890.

24. Osti Guerrazzi, "Professioni," 73–77.

25. Procaccia, "Il 'Tempio di via Balbo.'"

26. S. Stow, "I sonetti," 37–39; Garvin, "Crescenzo Del Monte," 24–27; Capuzzo, "L'élite," 93–94.

27. Sarfatti, *Jews in Mussolini's Italy*, 7.

28. Toscano, "Italian Jewish Identity," 39; Sarfatti, *Jews in Mussolini's Italy*, 7.

29. Jews had volunteered to fight for the pope's army of 1848 when Rome was nominally a republic. Spizzichino, "Pio IX," 291–92.

30. Toscano, "Italian Jewish Identity," 46.

31. De Felice, *Jews in Fascist Italy*, 18, 24–25.

32. Fabre, "Mussolini and the Jews," 56–57.

33. Mussolini, *Opera Omnia*, 13:69, quoted in Sarfatti, *Jews in Mussolini's Italy*, 40.

34. De Felice, *Jews in Fascist Italy*, 70; Sarfatti, *Jews in Mussolini's Italy*, 10, 17; Kertzer, *Pope and Mussolini*, 31–33.

35. Kertzer, *Pope and Mussolini*, 34.

36. De Felice, *Jews in Fascist Italy*, 71n37.

37. Michaelis, *Mussolini and the Jews*, 30n3.

38. Michaelis, *Mussolini and the Jews*, 30–31.

39. Michaelis, *Mussolini and the Jews*, 30.

40. Michaelis, *Mussolini and the Jews*, 3.

41. Segre, *Memories of Jewish Life*, 87–88.

42. Sarfatti, *Jews in Mussolini's Italy*, 11.

43. Michaelis, *Mussolini and the Jews*, 13–14; De Felice, *Jews in Fascist Italy*, 54–55, 109–10.

44. Michaelis, *Mussolini and the Jews*, 14; De Felice, *Jews in Fascist Italy*, 57, 109–10.

45. Castelnuovo, *Moncalvos*, 51.

46. De Felice, *Jews in Fascist Italy*, 90–91n7; Michaelis, *Mussolini and the Jews*, 5–26.

47. Michaelis, *Mussolini and the Jews*, 26; Sarfatti, *Jews in Mussolini's Italy*, 50–51; De Felice, *Jews in Fascist Italy*, 90.

48. De Felice, *Jews in Fascist Italy*, 90–91.

49. De Felice, *Jews in Fascist Italy*, 171–72, 174–77; Sarfatti, *Jews in Mussolini's Italy*, 63–67.

50. De Felice, *Jews in Fascist Italy*, 94.

51. Segre, *Memories of Jewish Life*, 167.

52. "Una soluzione" (A solution), published in *Il popolo d'Italia*, February 17, 1934, cited in Sarfatti, *Jews in Mussolini's Italy*, 67–68. Mussolini's article came a month after the Rome Zionist Group met on January 8, 1934.

53. Sarfatti, *Jews in Mussolini's Italy*, 60.

54. Michaelis, *Mussolini and the Jews*, 14–15.

55. Kertzer, *Pope and Mussolini*, 99.

56. Kertzer, *Pope and Mussolini*, 99.

57. Sarfatti, *Jews in Mussolini's Italy*, 44–45, 48.

58. Kertzer, *Pope and Mussolini*, 107.

59. De Felice, *Jews in Fascist Italy*, 96.

60. De Felice, *Jews in Fascist Italy*, 97.

61. The legislation, authored in part by a committee comprising Jews, is published in English in De Felice, *Jews in Fascist Italy*, 485–94.

62. Klein, *Italy's Jews from Emancipation to Fascism*, 83–84, fig. 2.1.

63. Sarfatti, *Jews in Mussolini's Italy*, 57–58.

64. It was falsely reported that as he crossed the border, Mario called back to the guards, "Italian dogs, cowards." Sarfatti, *Jews in Mussolini's Italy*, 69–70; Nemeth, "First Anti-Semitic Campaign," 252–53.
65. Stille, *Benevolence and Betrayal*, 104–17; Pugliese, *Carlo Rosselli*, 121–42, 194.
66. Sodi, foreword, viii.
67. C. Levi, *Christ Stopped at Eboli*. The title refers to a saying in the town of his exile. The people there felt outside the civilized world. They used to say "Christ stopped at Eboli," a nearby town, meaning that civilization had reached Eboli but had never come as far as their remote village. Hughes, *Prisoners of Hope*, 65–73.
68. Sarfatti, *Jews in Mussolini's Italy*, 25–26.
69. Voigt, "Children of Villa Emma," 185.
70. De Felice, *Jews in Fascist Italy*, 86–87.
71. Natalia Ginzburg describes Turati hiding in her home in Turin and being spirited out of the country by Carlo Rosselli in her novelized memoir, *Family Lexicon*, 71–74.
72. De Felice, *Jews in Fascist Italy*, 429; Sarfatti, "Characteristics and Objectives," 47; Kertzer, *Pope and Mussolini*, 262, 469n28.
73. Ben-Ghiat, *Strongmen*, 170.
74. De Felice, *Jews in Fascist Italy*, 181; Sarfatti, *Jews in Mussolini's Italy*, 97.
75. De Felice, *Jews in Fascist Italy*, 197–98.
76. Stille, *Benevolence and Betrayal*, 58.
77. Stille, *Benevolence and Betrayal*, 57–58; Kertzer, *Pope and Mussolini*, 228–29.
78. De Felice, *Jews in Fascist Italy*, 98–199.
79. Michaelis, *Mussolini and the Jews*, 88, 181, 195–97.
80. De Felice, *Jews in Fascist Italy*, 503.
81. De Felice, *Jews in Fascist Italy*, 504.
82. A plebiscite is a direct vote by members of an electorate on an important public question.
83. De Felice, *Jews in Fascist Italy*, 139–40, 509, 511.
84. De Felice, *Jews in Fascist Italy*, 511.
85. The alliance was initiated in 1936 through a protocol signed by Germany and Italy, after which Mussolini declared that all of Europe would rotate around the Berlin-Rome Axis.
86. Kertzer, *Pope and Mussolini*, 283–86; Michaelis, *Mussolini and the Jews*, 147–48.
87. Klein, *Italy's Jews from Emancipation to Fascism*, 99. Italian Fascists were also not above derogatorily casting Pius XI as a Jew. On August 3, 1938, the Fascist politician Roberto Farinacci wrote to Mussolini asking, "Is it true that the Pope's mother is a Jew?" Kertzer, *Pope and Mussolini*, 480n8.

88. Kertzer, *Pope and Mussolini*, 258–60.

89. Lewy, *Catholic Church and Nazi Germany*, 156–58; Kertzer, *Pope and Mussolini*, 259–60.

90. Kertzer, *Pope and Mussolini*, 282.

91. De Felice, *Jews in Fascist Italy*, 277; Michaelis, *Mussolini and the Jews*, 141–42.

92. De Felice, *Jews in Fascist Italy*, 540–42.

93. De Felice, *Jews in Fascist Italy*, 541.

94. Sarfatti, *Jews in Mussolini's Italy*, 98–99.

95. De Felice, *Jews in Fascist Italy*, 281–82.

96. Servi, "Building a Racial State."

97. Loy, *First Words*, 43. Mussolini counted the years of his "reign" from 1922, the year of his March on Rome—hence the use of "XVI" as a secondary designation of the year 1938.

98. Venzo, "Fascism and the Racial Laws"; Sarfatti, *Jews in Mussolini's Italy*, 131–35; Michaelis, *Mussolini and the Jews*, 171–72. English translations of the underlying documents and the November 17, 1938, decrees are in De Felice, *Jews in Fascist Italy*, 550–62.

99. Sarfatti, *Jews in Mussolini's Italy*, 152.

100. Klein, *Italy's Jews from Emancipation to Fascism*, 94–95.

101. Sarfatti, *Il cielo*, 41.

102. Venzo, "Fascism and the Racial Laws," 13–15; Sarfatti, *Jews in Mussolini's Italy*, 135–37.

103. Sarfatti, *Jews in Mussolini's Italy*, 134; Michaelis, *Mussolini and the Jews*, 255.

104. Stille, *Benevolence and Betrayal*, 72.

105. Osti Guerrazzi, "La persecuzione," 54.

106. Stille, *Benevolence and Betrayal*, 73.

107. Stille, *Benevolence and Betrayal*, 84–89.

108. Cannistraro and Sullivan, *Il Duce's Other Woman*, 566.

109. Published in Italian as *Dux*, Latin for Duce, her book was published in English as *The Life of Benito Mussolini* in 1925.

110. Kertzer, *Pope and Mussolini*, 24, 174–75, 196; Michaelis, *Mussolini and the Jews*, 52.

111. De Felice, *Jews in Fascist Italy*, 334–35.

112. Nidam-Orvieto, "Impact of Anti-Jewish Legislation," 165; Sarfatti, *Jews in Mussolini's Italy*, 64; Ben-Ghiat, *Strongmen*, 24.

113. Nidam-Orvieto, "Impact of Anti-Jewish Legislation," 171.

114. Kertzer, *Pope and Mussolini*, 320.

115. Kertzer, *Pope and Mussolini*, 320.

116. Kertzer, *Pope and Mussolini*, 332–51.

117. Arendt, *Eichmann in Jerusalem*, 160. Klein reviews the pertinent historiographical issues: *Italy's Jews from Emancipation to Fascism*, 1–18.

118. Klein, *Italy's Jews from Emancipation to Fascism*, 97, 101.

119. Segre, *Memories*, 116.

120. Sarfatti, *Jews in Mussolini's Italy*, 173. Even today there are many Jewish street vendors in Rome, many of whom have monopolized the sale of Catholic souvenirs in Vatican City. For photographs of these vendors see Brenner, *Diaspora*, 1:170 and 2:76–77.

121. Osti Guerrazzi, "La persecuzione," 61.

122. Klein, *Italy's Jews from Emancipation to Fascism*, 98, 105.

123. Nidam-Orvieto, "Impact of Anti-Jewish Legislation," 161.

124. Michaelis, *Mussolini and the Jews*, 292; Osti Guerrazzi, "La persecuzione," 61.

125. Servi, "Building a Racial State," 147–48; Sarfatti, *Jews in Mussolini's Italy*, 164.

126. Osti Guerrazzi, "La persecuzione," 54–55; Della Seta, *Tiber Afire*, 1–11.

127. Della Seta, *Tiber Afire*, 98–99; Zuccotti, *Italians and the Holocaust*, 105–6.

128. De Felice, *Jews in Fascist Italy*, 371.

129. N. Ginzburg, *Place to Live*, "Winter in the Abruzzi," loc. 473 of 3166, Kindle.

130. Pugliese, *Carlo Rosselli*, 91–92.

131. Osti Guerrazzi, "La persecuzione," 119–20.

132. Sarfatti, *Jews in Mussolini's Italy*, 149; De Felice, *Jews in Fascist Italy*, 373.

133. Kertzer, *Pope and Mussolini*, 391–92; Michaelis, *Mussolini and the Jews*, 341.

134. R. Katz, *Fatal Silence*, 21.

135. Klein, *Italy's Jews from Emancipation to Fascism*, 111; Calamandrei, *Diario 1939–1945*, 161 (regarding August 2, 1943); Franzone, "La complicata abrogazione," 110. There is some evidence that Badoglio met with the Jewish community during his administration (Michaelis, *Mussolini and the Jews*, 342), but the Unione comunità israelitiche archives include no record of such a meeting taking place (Calimani, *Storia degli ebrei*, 453).

136. Klein, *Italy's Jews from Emancipation to Fascism*, 112.

10. THE OTHER KNOCK ON THE DOOR

1. Osti Guerrazzi, "La persecuzione," 199; Portelli, *Order Has Been Carried Out*, 103.

2. Osti Guerrazzi, "La persecuzione," 68.

3. R. Katz, "Möllhausen Telegram," 230.

4. R. Katz, "Möllhausen Telegram," 227.

5. Michaelis, *Mussolini and the Jews*, 353–54; R. Katz, "Möllhausen Telegram," 227.

6. R. Katz, *Fatal Silence*, 79.

7. Historians' knowledge of the Nazi reaction to the *Judenaktion* order comes from Kappler's testimony at the trial of Adolf Eichmann, his testimony at his own trial before the Military Tribunal of Rome in 1948, and Möllhausen's 1948 memoir, *La carte perdente* (The lost map). More recently, new CIA-OSS documents have also come to light. See R. Katz, "MöllhausenTelegram."

8. According to both Foà and Almansi in reports to the Union of Italian Jewish Communities in 1943 and 1944 respectively. Kappler also testified at his 1948 trial that he threatened the entire Jewish community. R. Katz, *Fatal Silence*, 69.

9. R. Katz, *Fatal Silence*, 71.

10. Michaelis, *Mussolini and the Jews*, 356–57.

11. Stille, *Benevolence and Betrayal*, 196.

12. R. Katz, *Fatal Silence*, 74; Michaelis, *Mussolini and the Jews*, 356–57; Debenedetti, *October 16*, 30.

13. R. Katz, *Fatal Silence*, 230.

14. R. Katz, *Fatal Silence*, 74; R. Katz, "The Möllhausen Telegram," 230.

15. Debenedetti, *October 16*, 33–34; R. Katz, *Fatal Silence*, 84.

16. Debenedetti, *October 16*, 34–35; Michaelis, *Mussolini and the Jews*, 59; De Felice, *Jews in Fascist Italy*, 464.

17. Gilson, "Fate of the Roman Jewish Libraries," 91–93.

18. *Il Nazareno-Studi de esegesi neotestamentaria alla luce dell'aramaico e del pensiero rabbinico* (Udin: Instituto delle Edizionei Academiche, 1938/XVI).

19. Antonucci and Procaccia, introduction to *Dopo il 16 ottobre*, 26.

20. Sillanpoa and Weisbord, "Baptized Rabbi of Rome," 77–78.

21. Osti Guerrazzi, "La persecuzione," 201.

22. Debenedetti, *October 16*, 39.

23. Today the site is an antiquities garden with markers explaining the ancient remains. There is no mention of the October 16 round-up.

24. The description of the October 16 roundup relies on Debenedetti, *October 16*, 38–50; R. Katz, *Fatal Silence*, 100–116; Zuccotti, *Italians and the Holocaust*, 101–38.

25. Antonucci and Procaccia, introduction to *Dopo il 16 ottobre*, 29.

26. Interview with Claudio Fano as reported in Portelli, *Order Has Been Carried Out*, 88.

27. "Interview of Father Libero Raganella and Mr. Dell'Ariccia," in Caracciolo, *Uncertain Refuge*, 46. The interviews in this volume are tendentious given the interviewer's interest in painting a rosy picture. Nonetheless, the testimony is compelling.

28. Debenedetti, *October 16*, 42–53; R. Katz, *Fatal Silence*, 102; Zuccotti, *Italians and the Holocaust*, 102, 104; Loy, *First Words*, 157–58.

29. Zuccotti, *Italians and the Holocaust*, 116.

30. Debenedetti, *October 16*, 60, says that two women gave birth that night. Sarfatti, *Il cielo*, 52, says that one child was born after the mother's arrest. Antonucci and Procaccia, "Un profilo," 300, say that one child, the son of Cesare Di Veroli and Marcella Perugia, was born in the military college.

31. Morante, *History: A Novel*, 269–70. Morante's description is not an eyewitness account but is based upon such accounts as noted by Sodi, *Narrative and Imperative*, 190.

32. Antonucci and Procaccia, introduction to *Dopo il 16 ottobre*, 27; Sarfatti, *Il cielo*, 52.

33. Picciotto, "Shoah in Italy," 213.

34. Zuccotti, *Italians and the Holocaust*, 123.

35. Zuccotti, *Italians and the Holocaust*, 126.

36. Michaelis, *Mussolini and the Jews*, 368.

37. Osti Guerrazzi, "La persecuzione," 79–80. The Fascist woman was probably protecting Jews. The Nazis had her address listed as a Jewish dwelling, but she kept them at bay with papers showing it was owned by an Aryan.

38. Zuccotti, *Italians and the Holocaust*, 125; Kertzer, *Pope at War*, 365–67.

39. De Felice, *Jews in Fascist Italy*, 475.

40. Zuccotti, *Under His Very Windows*, 177–78.

41. Osti Guerrazzi, "La persecuzione," 201; Klein, *Italy's Jews from Emancipation to Fascism*, 122.

42. Loy, *First Words*, 157–58.

43. Father Benedetto taught Hebrew at a Capuchin seminary. With the establishment of the Vichy government in France, his monastery became a refuge for Jews and anti-Nazi activists. Zuccotti, *Italians and the Holocaust*, 209.

44. Segre, *Memories*, 240.

45. Klein, *Italy's Jews from Emancipation to Fascism*, 122.

46. Zuccotti, "Pius XII," 290, 296; Sarfatti, *Jews in Mussolini's Italy*, 208n166. In appendix 4, 261–69, Sarfatti presents a "Report to the Women's Sections of DELASEM," 1941, which states, among other things, that DELASEM was founded on December 1, 1939. Zuccotti, *Italians and the Holocaust*, 201–10; Kertzer, *Pope at War*, 185–86.

47. Zuccotti, *Under His Very Windows*, 183–86.

48. Zuccotti, *Under His Very Windows*, 202–5.

49. Zuccotti, *Under His Very Windows*, 212–23.

50. Kertzer, *Pope at War*, 403–4.

51. Zuccotti, *Italians and the Holocaust*, 217. A list of the 155 Catholic institutions that sheltered Jews can be found as an appendix in De Felice, *Jews in Fascist Italy*, 601–5.

52. Antonucci and Procaccia, introduction to *Dopo il 16 ottobre*, 22; Wildvang, "The Enemy Next Door," 189–204.

53. Kertzer, *Pope at War*, 380–81.

54. Osti Guerrazzi, "La persecuzione," 112.

55. Klein, *Italy's Jews from Emancipation to Fascism*, 125, reports on the grateful women in Milan. Similar thanks were probably given in Rome.

56. Wildvang, "Enemy Next Door," 196; Michaelis, *Mussolini and the Jews*, 389; Osti Guerrazzi, "La persecuzione," 202–9.

57. Wildvang, "Enemy Next Door," 199; Sullam, *Italian Executioners*, 72, 123.

58. Wildvang, "Enemy Next Door," 199; Osti Guerrazzi, "La persecuzione," 81.

59. Wildvang, "Enemy Next Door," 191–93.

60. Sullam, *Italian Executioners*, 29–30; Wildvang, "Enemy Next Door," 193.

61. Osti Guerrazzi, "La persecuzione," 160, 163–64.

62. Today that apartment building houses the Museum of the Liberation of Rome.

63. Zuccotti, *Italians and the Holocaust*, 217–18.

64. Wildvang, "Enemy Next Door," 193–94; Osti Guerrazzi, "La persecuzione," 113–18, 135.

65. Zuccotti, *Under His Very Windows*, 223–24; Osti Guerazzi, "La persecuzione," 153.

66. Antonucci and Procaccia, introduction to *Dopo il 16 ottobre*, 23.

67. Osti Guerrazzi, "La persecuzione," 88.

68. The description of the Partisan ambush is taken from R. Katz, *Fatal Silence*; Debenedetti, *October 16*; and Portelli, *Order Has Been Carried Out*.

69. Portelli, *Order Has Been Carried Out*, 33, 59.

70. Debenedetti, *October 16*, 63.

71. R. Katz, *Fatal Silence*, 382n12.

72. Portelli, *Order Has Been Carried Out*, 72–79.

73. Portelli, *Order Has Been Carried Out*, 100.

74. Klein, *Italy's Jews from Emancipation to Fascism*, 196.

75. Portelli, *Order Has Been Carried Out*, 28.

76. For the Di Consiglio family see Osti Guerrazzi, "La persecuzione," 182–83; Portelli, *Order Has Been Carried Out*, 89–90.

77. Osti Guerrazzi, "La persecuzione," 179.

78. Debenedetti, *October 16*, 84.

79. In a historical conundrum outside the scope of this book, forty-one years later, Hochuth publicly supported the notorious Holocaust denier David Irving during his trial in London against historian Deborah Lipstadt.

80. R. Katz, *Fatal Silence*, 353–54.

81. Zucotti, *Under His Very Windows*, 93–112.

82. Zucotti, *Under His Very Windows*, 102.

83. Kertzer, *Pope at War*, 214–16, 237–43.

84. Zuccotti, *Under His Very Windows*, 157.

85. Zuccotti, *Under His Very Windows*, 159; R. Katz, *Fatal Silence*, 105.

86. Zuccotti, *Italians and the Holocaust*, 129.

87. R. Katz, *Fatal Silence*, 241.

88. Zuccotti, *Under His Very Windows*, 163–64. See the pope's words in *Summi pontificatus*, issued October 20, 1939, and *Mystici Corpus Christi*, issued June 29, 1943, in Ihm, *Papal Encyclicals*, 5–22, 37–63.

89. Zuccotti, *Under His Very Windows*, 163–64.

90. While the Catholic Church remembers those children as the first martyrs, it is widely believed that the New Testament story is a legend.

91. Zuccotti, *Under His Very Windows*, 161–65.

92. Zuccotti, "Pius XII," 287–307. Additional documents from Pius XII's papacy are still being revealed; see for example Kertzer, "The Pope, the Jews, and the Secrets in the Archives," https://www.theatlantic.com/ideas/archive/2020/08/the -popes-jews/615736/. However, no written directive from Pius XII ordering efforts to save Jews has yet been found.

93. Kertzer, *Pope at War*, 165.

94. Zuccotti, *Under His Very Windows*, 97.

95. Lewy, *The Catholic Church*, 227.

96. Kertzer, *Pope at War*, 83-85, 95, 180, 265–66.

97. Zuccotti, "Pius XII and the Rescue of Jews from Italy," 300.

98. Michaelis, *Mussolini and the Jews*, 395–96.

99. Kertzer, *Pope at War*, 278; De Felice, *Jews*, 401.

100. Kertzer, *Pope at War*, 275–76.

101. Kertzer, *Pope at War*, 213, 331, 340, 356.

102. Michaelis, *Mussolini and the Jews*, 372.

103. R. Katz, *Fatal Silence*, 110–15; Zuccotti, *Under His Very Windows*, 156–69.

104. Picciotto, *Shoah in Italy*, 209–10.

105. Antonucci and Procaccia, introduction to *Dopo il 16 ottobre*, 30–31.

106. De Felice, *Jews in Fascist Italy*, 601–5.

107. Osti Guerrazzi, "La persecuzione," 185. Osti Guerrazzi echoes the statement made by Piero Terracina, who was deported to Auschwitz but survived, unlike his parents, grandfather, two uncles, and four brothers and sisters. Portelli, *Order Has Been Carried Out*, 86, quotes Terracina as saying, "There is no doubt that behind each Jew who survived there is a non-Jew who helped him, even at the risk of his life; but behind each Jew who was deported, there is a Fascist who turned him in. There is no doubt about that."

108. De Felice, *Jews in Fascist Italy*, 467–68. A similar ceremony took place in Rome in January 1945 when a person identified in the press as Mrs. Mandel, speaking on behalf of "all the Jews," thanked Catholic priests in Rome for giving Jews shelter in monasteries and convents. Klein, *Italy's Jews from Emancipation to Fascism*, 223.

109. De Felice, a Jewish historian, is also the author of a multivolume biography of Mussolini and has been accused of an attempted rehabilitation of Fascism. Pugliese, *Bitter Spring*, 300, 306; Ledeen, "Renzo De Felice."

110. Ben-Ghiat, "Secret Histories," 341–42; Portelli, *Order Has Been Carried Out*, 241; and Klein, *Italy's Jews from Emancipation to Fascism*, 2–8, for a thorough investigation of this issue.

111. Klein, *Italy's Jews from Emancipation to Fascism*, 215–27; Arendt, *Eichmann in Jerusalem*, 160–61; Ben-Ghiat, "The Secret Histories," 330–49.

11. THE ARCH OF TITUS REDUX

1. R. Katz, *Fatal Silence*, 340–41.

2. Sands, *Ratline*, 228–29; Sereny, *Into That Darkness*, 315. Presently it would be imprudent to reach any conclusion concerning Pius XII's knowledge and support of the Ratline, given that the Vatican has only recently opened access to many of the pope's documents.

3. See Loftus and Aarons, *Secret War against the Jews*, and Sands, *Ratline*, for details of the extensive postwar operations to save Nazis.

4. Zuccotti, "Pius XII and the Rescue of Jews from Italy," 297.

5. Klein, *Italy's Jews from Emancipation to Fascism*, 184–86.

6. Sillanpoa and Weisbord, "Baptized Rabbi of Rome," 89.

7. Sillanpoa and Weisbord, "Zolli Conversion," 205; Zolli, *Before the Dawn*. See also Newman, *"Chief Rabbi" of Rome Becomes a Catholic*, for an evaluation of Zolli's conversion from the perspective of a New York City rabbi who was Zolli's contemporary.

8. Sillanpoa and Weisbord, "Zolli Conversion," 212–13.

9. Pezzino and Schwarz, "From Kappler to Priebke," 307–11.

10. Pezzino and Schwarz, "From Kappler to Priebke," 299–328; Portelli, *Order Has Been Carried Out*, 257.

11. Sands, *Ratline*, 229–30. Pezzino and Schwarz, "From Kappler to Priebke," 319, indicate that Father Pancrazio Pfeiffer, Pius XII's personal liaison with the German military command in Rome, also played a part in Priebke's escape.

12. Pezzino and Schwarz, "From Kappler to Priebke," 324.

13. Pezzino and Schwarz, "From Kappler to Priebke," 324–25.

14. *La repubblica*, 30 June 1997.

15. The story of Priebke's trial is told in Travis, "The Priebke Trial(s)," and in Pezzino and Schwarz, "From Kappler to Priebke," 319–26; Portelli, *Order Has Been Carried Out*, 254.

16. Interview of Valeria Spizzichino quoted in Portelli, *Order Has Been Carried Out*, 253.

17. Segre, *Memories*, 386. For another description of the events at the Arch of Titus see Fine, *Menorah from the Bible to Modern Israel*, 132.

18. Rossella Tercatin, "The Not-So-Rosy History of Rome's Public Rose Garden," *Times of Israel*, May 20, 2016, https://www.timesofisrael.com/the-not-so-rosy -history-of-romes-public-rose-garden/. Further information can be gathered about Mary Senni in Origo, *Chill in the Air*, 83, 138. For a history of the Aventine Cemetery see Spizzichino, "La gestione dei cimiteri."

19. O'Malley, *What Happened at Vatican II*, 103; Carroll, *Constantine's Sword*, 532.

20. O'Malley, *What Happened at Vatican II*, 195.

21. Carroll, *Constantine's Sword*, 550. Rabbi and eventual convert Eugenio Zolli claims to have unsuccessfully requested the specific liturgical change from Pope Pius XII (Sillanpoa and Weisbord, "Zolli Conversion," 214), but the liturgical change would occur only later, by John XXIII's order.

22. O'Malley, *What Happened at Vatican II*, 219; Isaac, *Jesus and Israel*, and also *Teaching of Contempt*.

23. O'Malley, *What Happened at Vatican II*, 165.

24. O'Malley, *What Happened at Vatican II*, 105–6.

25. O'Malley, *What Happened at Vatican II*, 216, 223, 225.

26. Rynne, *Vatican Council II*, 303–5.

27. O'Malley, *What Happened at Vatican II*, 251, and 368n12, translation by the author.

28. The full text of *Nostra aetate* is found in Barrens, *In Our Time*, 78–88, among other places.

29. Carroll, *Constantine's Sword* (a profound meditation on the ongoing history of church antisemitism), 41–43, 552–53.

30. For the 42 percent figure see Klein, *Italy's Jews from Emancipation to Fascism*, 199.

31. "Text of Pope's Speech at Rome Synagogue: 'You Are Our Elder Brothers,'" *New York Times/UPI*, April 4, 1986.

32. Portelli, *Order Has Been Carried Out*, 253.

33. "Address of His Holiness Pope Francis Sunday 17 January 2016," Holy See, http:// www.vatican.va.

34. See John Pawlikowski and Malka Simkovich, "Pope Francis and the Jewish Law," *Sightings*, October 14, 2021; and Carol Glatz, "Vatican Publishes Letters to Rabbis," *Catholic National Reporter*, September 15, 2021.

35. "General Audience of 29 September 2021: Catechesis on the Letter to the Galatians: 9. Life of Faith," Holy See, http://www.vatican.va. Addressing Catholics in this audience, Pope Francis reminded them that for them "justification" came through Jesus Christ.

36. Carroll, *Constantine's Sword*, 41–43, 552–53.

CONCLUSION

1. Josephus, *Jewish Antiquities* 14.7.2.

2. 2 Macc. 2:19,23–24.

3. Ruth Gruber, "Libyan Immigrants a Force in Italian Jewry," *Jewish Telegraphic Agency*, October 11, 2004; Rosetto, "'We Were All Italian!'"

4. Michaelis, *Mussolini and the Jews*, 135, 292–93.

5. Goldberg, "Tradition with Modernity," 74–79.

6. Rosetto, "'We Were All Italian!'"

7. Rosetto, "'We Were All Italian!'" Yosef Netanya's recollection is taken from Piera Rosetto's interview with Netanya, July 1, 2012.

8. Natale and Toscano, "Libyan Jews in Rome."

9. For a concise description of the Libyan Jewish community, see Reguer, *Most Tenacious of Minorities*, 146–50.

10. "New Italian President Remembers a Young Jewish Victim of Rome Terrorism," Jewish Telegraphic Agency, February 4, 2015, https://www.jta.org/2015/02/04 /global/new-italian-president-remembers-young-jewish-victim-of-rome-terror -attack-2.

11. The author interviewed Chief Rabbi Riccardo Di Segni on December 6, 2021.

12. "Address of John Paul II to the Chief Rabbi of Rome, Dr. Riccardo Di Segni," Holy See, https://www.vatican.va/content/john-paul-ii/en/speeches/2003/february /documents/hf_jp-ii_spe_20030213_rabbino-roma.html.

13. Lapin and Di Segni, "Jewish Leaders Assess John Paul II's Pontificate."

14. "Message of John Paul II to the Chief Rabbi of Rome Dr. Riccardo Di Segni for the Centenary of the Great Synagogue of Rome," Holy See, https://www.vatican .va/content/john-paul-ii/en/speeches/2004/may/documents/hf_jp-ii_spe _20040523_rabbino-segni.html.

15. Riccardo Di Segni, "When Pope John Paul II Came to the Great Synagogue of Rome," *Tablet*, May 18, 2021, https://www.tabletmag.com/sections/history /articles/when-pope-john-paul-came-to-the-great-synagogue-of-rome.

16. D. Di Castro, *From Jerusalem to Rome and Back*, 62–63.

17. Koch, "Introductory Remarks."

18. A. Di Castro, Leone, and Nesselrath, "Reason for the Exhibition," 26.

BIBLIOGRAPHY

Adler, E. N., ed. *Jewish Travellers in the Middle Ages: Nineteen Firsthand Accounts*. New York: Dover, 1987.

Alföldy, Geza. "Eine Bauenschrift aus dem Colosseum." *Zeitschrift für Papyrologie und Epigraphik* 109 (1995): 195–226.

Alighieri, Dante. *The Divine Comedy*. Vol. 3, *Paradise*. Translated by Mark Musa. London: Penguin Classics, 1986.

Antonucci, Silvia Haia, and Claudio Procaccia, eds. *Dopo il 16 ottobre gli ebrei a Roma tra occupazione, resistenza, accoglienza e delazioni (1943–1944)*. Rome: Viella, 2017.

————. "Un profilo dei deportat." In *Dopo il 16 ottobre gli ebrei a Roma tra occupazione, resistenza, accoglienza e delazioni (1943–1944)*, edited by Silvia Haia Antonucci and Claudio Procaccia, 289–306. Rome: Viella, 2017.

Arendt, Hannah. *Eichmann in Jerusalem*. New York: Viking Press, 1963.

Bankier, David, and Dan Michman, eds. *Holocaust and Justice: Representation and Historiography of the Holocaust in Post-War Trials*. New York and Jerusalem: Bergahn Books / Yad Vashem, 2010.

Banti, Alberto Mario. *La nazione del Risorgimento: Parentela, santità e honore alle origine dell'Italia unita*. Turin: Einaudi, 2000.

Banti, Alberto Mario, and Paul Ginsborg, eds. *Storia d'Italia*. Annals 22: *Il Risorgimento*. Turin: Einaudi, 2000.

Baroja, Julio C. "Honour and Shame: A Historical Account of Several Conflicts." In *Honour and Shame: The Values of Mediterranean Society*, edited by John G. Peristiany, 81–137. London: Weidenfeld and Nicholson, 1965.

Barrens, James M. *In Our Time (Nostra Aetate): How Catholics and Jews Built a New Relationship*. St. Petersburg FL: Mr. Media Books, 2015.

Bassani, Giorgio. *The Garden of the Finzi-Continis*. Translated by William Weaver. New York: Harcourt, 1977.

Beales, Derek, and Eugenio Biagini. *The Risorgimento and the Unification of Italy*. 2nd ed. Edinburgh: Pearson Education, 2002.

Beard, Mary. *The Roman Triumph*. Cambridge MA: Belknap Press, 2009.

Beer, Giuliana Piperno. "Le scuole per I giovani ebrei di Roma negli anni delle legge per la difesa della razza (1938–1954)." In *La legge razziale e la persecuzione degli ebrei a Roma 1938–1945*, edited by S. H. Antonucci, P. Ferarra, M. Folin, and M. I. Venzo, 45–53. Rome: Museo della Memoria Locale di Cerreto Guidi and Archivio Storico della Communità Ebraica di Roma, 2012.

Bell, Rudolph M. *Street Life in Renaissance Rome: A Brief History with Documents*. Boston: St. Martins, 2013.

Belli, Giuseppe Gioacchino. *Sonnets*. Translated and edited by Mike Stocks. Richmond, U.K.: Alma Classics, 2015.

Bemporad, Dora Liscia. "Jewish Ceremonial Art in the Era of the Ghettos." In *Gardens and Ghettos: The Art of Jewish Life in Italy*, edited by Vivian Mann, 111–35. Berkeley: University of California Press, 1989.

Benedict, Master. *The Marvels of Rome (Mirabilia Urbis Roma)*. Translated by Francis Morgan Nichols. New York: Italica Press, 1986.

Ben-Ghiat, Ruth. "The Secret Histories of Roberto Benigni's *Life is Beautiful*." In *Jews in Italy under Fascist and Nazi Rule*, edited by Joshua Zimmerman, 330–49. Cambridge: Cambridge University Press, 2005.

———. *Strongmen: Mussolini to the Present*. New York: W. W. Norton, 2020.

Ben Solomon, Immanuel Romi. *Tophet and Eden (Hell and Paradise) in Imitation of Dante's "Inferno" and "Paradiso."* Translated by Hermann Gollancz. London: University of London Press, 1921.

Bergeron, David M. *English Civic Pageantry, 1558–1642*. Columbia: University of South Carolina Press, 1971.

Bestor, Jane. "Marriage Transactions in Renaissance Italy and Mauss' *Essay on the Gift*." *Past and Present* 164 (1999): 6–46.

Bickerman, Elias. "The Altars of the Gentiles: A Note on the Jewish 'Ius Sacrum.'" *Studies in Jewish and Christian History* 3: 596–617. Leiden, Neth.: Brill, 1986.

Blok, Anton. "Rams and Billy Goats: A Key to the Mediterranean Code of Honour." *Man*, 16 (1981): 427–40.

Boccaccio, Giovanni. *The Decameron*. Translated by Mark Musa and Peter Bondanella. New York: New American Library, 2010.

Boiteux, Martine. "Coromania e carnevale a Roma nel medioevo." *Ricerca folkorica* 6 (1982): 57–64.

———. "Les juifs dans le carneval de la Rome moderne (XVe–XVIIIe siècles)." *Mélanges de l'école française de Rome: Moyen âge–temps modernes* 8 (1976): 745–87.

Boksenboim, Yacov, ed. *Iggerot R. Yehudah Aryeh Modena*. Tel Aviv: Tel Aviv University, 1984.

Bonella, Anna L., Augusto Pompeo, and Manola Venza, eds. *Roma fra la restaurazione e l'elezione di Pio IX: Administrazione, economia, società e cultura*. Rome: Herder, 1997.

Bonfil, Robert. *History and Folklore in a Medieval Jewish Chronicle: The Family Chronicle of Ahima'az ben Paltiel*. Leiden, Neth.: Brill, 2009.

———. *Jewish Life in Renaissance Italy*. Berkeley: University of California Press, 1994.

Brener, Ann. "The *Scroll of Love* by Immanuel of Rome: A Hebrew Parody of Dante's *Vita Nuova*." *Prooftexts* 32 (2012): 149–75.

Brenner, Frédéric. *Diaspora: Homelands in Exile*. New York: HarperCollins, 2003.

Brentano, Robert. *Rome before Avignon: A Social History of Thirteenth Century Rome*. Berkeley: University of California Press, 1990.

Brilliant, Richard. "Jewish Art and Culture in Ancient Italy." In *Gardens and Ghettos: The Art of Jewish Life in Italy*, edited by Vivian Mann, 67–90. Berkeley: University of California Press, 1989.

Burke, Peter. *The Historical Anthropology of Early Modern Europe*. Cambridge: Cambridge University Press, 1987.

Caffiero, Marina. *Forced Baptism: Histories of Jews, Christians, and Converts in Papal Rome*. Berkeley: University of California Press, 2005.

———. "The Magic of the Menorah in the Modern Era: From an Object of Devotion to the Kabbalah." In *La menorà: Culto, storia e mito*, edited by Franceso Leone, 92–103. Milan: Skira, 2017.

———. "Tra repressione e conversioni: La 'restaurazione' degli ebrei." In *Roma fra la restaurazione e l'elezione di Pio IX: Administrazione, economia, società e cultura*, edited by Anna L. Bonella, Augusto Pompeo, and Manola Venza, 375–95. Rome: Herder, 1997.

Calabi, Donatello. *Venice and Its Jews: 500 Years since the Founding of the Ghetto*. Bologna: SEPS, 2017.

Calamandrei, Piero. *Diario 1939–1945*. Edited by G. Agosti. Florence: La Nuova Italia, 1997.

Calimani, Riccardo. *Storia degli ebrei di Roma*. Milan: Mondadori, 2017.

Cancellieri, Francesco. *Storia de' solenni possessi de' Sommi Pontefici*. Rome: Presso Luigi Lazzarini, 1802.

Cannistraro, Philip V., and Brian R. Sullivan. *Il Duce's Other Woman: The Untold Story of Margherita Sarfatti, Benito Mussolini's Jewish Mistress, and How She Helped Him Come to Power*. New York: William Morrow, 1993.

Cappelletti, Silvia. *The Jewish Community of Rome from the Second Century B.C. to the Third Century C.E.* Leiden, Neth.: Brill, 2006.

Capuzzo, Ester. "L'élite ebraica Romana: Samuele Alatri, Crescenzo Del Monte, Ernesto Nathan." In *Ebrei a Roma tra risorgimento ed emancipazione (1814–1914)*, edited by Claudio Procaccia, 91–95. Rome: Gangemi, 2013.

Caracciolo, Nicola, ed. *Uncertain Refuge: Italy and the Jews during the Holocaust*. Urbana and Chicago: University of Illinois Press, 1995.

Carroll, James. *Constantine's Sword: The Church and the Jews*. Boston: Houghton Mifflin, 2001.

Castelnuovo, Enrico. *The Moncalvos*. Translated by Brenda Webster and Gabriella Romani. San Antonio: Wings Press, 2017.

Castronuovo, Nadia. *Natalia Ginzburg: Jewishness as Moral Identity*. Leicester, U.K.: Troubador, 2010.

Cava, Sara, and Sergio Amedeo Terracina. "Transformazione urbanistica ed edilizia tra ottocento e novecento dell'area dell'ex ghetto." In *Ebrei a Roma tra risorgimento ed emancipazione (1814–1914)*, edited by Claudio Procaccia, 239–58. Rome: Gangemi, 2013.

Champagne, Marie-Thérèse, and Ra'anan S. Boustan. "Walking in the Shadows of the Past: The Jewish Experience of Rome in the Twelfth Century." *Medieval Encounters* 17 (2011): 464–94.

Chobham, Thomas. *Summa confessiorum*. Edited by F. Broomfield. Paris: Editions Béatrice Nauwelaerts, 1968.

Clementi, F. *Il carnevale romano*. Città di Castello: Edizioni R.O.R.E—Niruf, 1938–39.

Cohen, Elizabeth. "Honor and Gender in the Streets of Early Modern Rome." *Journal of Interdisciplinary Studies* 22 (1992): 597–625.

———. "Seen and Known: Prostitutes in the Cityscape of Late Sixteenth Century Rome." *Renaissance Studies* 12 (1998): 392–409.

Cohen, Gerson. "Esau as Symbol in Early Medieval Thought." In *Jewish Medieval and Renaissance Studies*, edited by Alexander Altmann, 19–48. Cambridge MA: Harvard University Press, 1967.

Cohen, Ronald. "State Origins: A Reappraisal." In *The Early State*, edited by H. Claessen and P. Skalnik, 31–75. The Hague: De Gruyter Mouton, 1978.

Cohen, Thomas V. "The Case of the Mysterious Coil of Rope: Street Life and Jewish Persona in Rome in the Middle of the Sixteenth Century." *Sixteenth Century Journal* 19 (1988): 209–21.

———. *Love and Death in Renaissance Italy*. Chicago: University of Chicago Press, 2004.

———. *Roman Tales: A Reader's Guide to the Art of Microhistory*. London and New York: Routledge, 2019.

Cohen, Thomas V., and Elizabeth S. Cohen. *Words and Deeds in Renaissance Rome: Trials before the Papal Magistrates*. Toronto: University of Toronto Press, 1993.

Colzi, Francesco. "Angelo Mortera e la Banca Romana: Un operatore ebreo nella tempest finanziaria italiana della fine del XIX secolo." In *Ebrei a Roma tra risorgimento ed emancipazione (1814–1914)*, edited by Claudio Procaccia, 97–109. Rome: Gangemi, 2013.

Cooperman, Bernard Dov. "The Early Modern Ghetto: A Study in Urban Real Estate." In *The Ghetto in Global History, 1500 to the Present*, edited by Wendy Z. Goldman and Joe William Trotter, 57–73. London: Routledge, 2018.

Corneille, Pierre. *Tite et Berenice*. Scotts Valley CA: CreateSpace Independent Publishing Platform, 2015.

Coulet, Noël. "De l'intégration à l'exclusion: La place des juifs dans les cérémonies d'entrée solennelle au Moyen Age." *Annales: Histoire, Sciences Sociales* 34 (1979): 672–83.

Crook, John A. "Titus and Berenice." *American Journal of Philology* 72 (1952): 169–70.

Crouzet-Pavan, Elizabeth. "Venice between Jerusalem, Byzantium, and Divine Retribution: The Origins of the Ghetto." *Mediterranean Historical Review* 6 (1991): 163–79.

Dainotto, Robert Maria. "Emancipation and Jewish Literature in the Italian Canon." In *The Most Ancient of Minorities: The Jews of Italy*, edited by Stanislao Pugliese, 131–37. Westport CT: Greenwood Press, 2002.

David, Abraham. "The Expulsion from the Papal States (1569) in Light of Hebrew Sources." In *The Most Ancient of Minorities: The Jews of Italy*, edited by Stanislao G. Pugliese, 91–99. Westport CT: Greenwood Press, 2002.

Davis, Natalie Zemon. *The Gift in Sixteenth Century France*. Madison: University of Wisconsin Press, 2000.

Debenedetti, Giacomo. *October 16, 1943: Eight Jews*. Notre Dame IN: University of Notre Dame Press, 2001.

De Felice, Renzo. *The Jews in Fascist Italy: A History*. New York: Enigma Books, 2001.

Delicado, Francisco. *La Lozana Andaluza*. Translated by Bruno Damiani. Potomac: Scripta Humanistica, 1987.

Della Seta, Fabio. *The Tiber Afire*. Marlboro VT: The Marlboro Press, 1991.

Dessau, H., ed. *Inscriptiones latinae selectae*. Chicago: Ares Publishers, 1892.

Di Castro, Alessandara, Francesco Leone, and Arnold Neselrath. "The Reason for the Exhibition." In *La menorà: Culto, storia e mito*, edited by Francesco Leone, 26–29. Milan: Skira Editore, 2017.

Di Castro, Daniela, ed. *Et ecce gaudium: The Roman Jews and the Investiture of the Popes*. Rome: Araldo De Luca, 2010.

———. *From Jerusalem to Rome and Back: The Journey of the Menorah from Fact to Myth, An Exhibition of the Jewish Museum of Rome*. Rome: Araldo De Luca, 2008.

———. "The Jews of Rome, the Solemn Possession Ceremonies of the Popes and Fourteen Ephemeral Displays of the Eighteenth Century." In *Et ecce gaudium: The*

Roman Jews and the Investiture of the Popes, edited by Daniela Di Castro, 22–36. Rome: Araldo De Luca Editore, 2010.

Di Segni, David Gioanfranco. "I rabbini di Roma nell'ottocento e agli inizi del novecento." In *Ebrei a Roma tra risorgimento ed emancipazione (1814–1914),* edited by Claudio Procaccia, 131–62. Rome: Gangemi Editore, 2013.

Douglas, Mary. "No Free Gifts." In *The Gift: The Form and Reason for Exchange in Archaic Societies,* by Marcel Mauss, vii–xv. London: Routledge, 1990.

———. *Purity and Danger.* London: Hammondsworth, 1970.

Duchesne, L., ed. *Le liber pontificalis.* Vol. 2. Lyon: E. Thorin, 1886.

Dumont, Louis. *Homo Hierarchicus: The Caste System and Its Implications.* 2nd ed. Chicago: University of Chicago Press, 1980.

Fabre, Giorgio. "Mussolini and the Jews on the Eve of the March on Rome." In *Jews in Italy under Fascist and Nazi Rule,* edited by J. Zimmerman, 55–68. Cambridge: Cambridge University Press, 2005.

Fast, Howard. *Agrippa's Daughter: The Story of an Extraordinary Woman.* New York: Doubleday, 1964.

Feci, Simona. "The Death of a Miller: A Trial *Contra Hebreos* in Baroque Rome." *Jewish History* 7 (1993): 9–27.

Feinstein, Wiley. *The Civilization of the Holocaust in Italy: Artists, Saints, Anti-Semites.* Madison NJ: Fairleigh Dickinson Press, 2003.

Feldman, Louis H., and Meyer Reinhold, eds. *Jewish Life and Thought among the Greeks and Romans: Primary Readings.* Minneapolis MN: Fortress Press, 1996.

Fine, Steven. *The Menorah from the Bible to Modern Israel.* Cambridge MA: Harvard University Press, 2016.

Flusser, D., ed. *Sefer Yosippon.* Jerusalem: n.p., 1979.

Franzone, Gabriella Yael. "Considerazione per una storia politica e institutzionale della Communità Ebraica di Roma." In *Ebrei a Roma tra risorgimento ed emancipazione (1814–1914),* edited by Claudio Procaccia, 27–36. Rome: Gangemi Editore, 2013.

———. "La complicata abrogazione delle leggi razziali." In *Le leggi razziali e la persecuzione degli ebrei a Roma, 1938–1945,* edited by Silvia Haia Antonucci, Pierina Ferrara, Marco Folin, and Manola Ida Venzo, 107–59. Rome: Mumeloc, 2012.

Fuks, G. "Where Have All the Freedmen Gone? On an Anomaly in the Jewish Grave Inscriptions from Rome." *Journal of Jewish Studies* 36 (1985): 25–32.

Funkenstein, Amos. "The Dialectics of Assimilation." *Jewish Social Studies* 1 (1995): 1–14.

Garrucci, R. *Il cimitero degla antichi ebrei scoperto recentemente in Vigna Randanini.* Rome: n.p., 1862.

Garvin, Barbara. "Crescenzo Del Monte: Poet of the Roman Ghetto." *Jewish Quarterly Review* 27 (1979): 24–27.

Gaster, Moses, trans. *Ma'aseh Book: Book of Jewish Tales and Legends*. 2 vols. Philadel-phia: The Jewish Publication Society of America, 1934.

Geertz, Clifford. *Local Knowledge: Further Essays in Interpretive Archaeology*. New York: Basic Books, 1983.

Giardina, A., ed. *Società romana ed impero tardo-antica*. Bari, Italy: Laterza, 1986.

Gilmore, David. "Anthropology of the Mediterranean Area." *Annual Review of Anthropology* 11 (1982): 175–205.

Gilson, Estelle. "The Fate of the Roman Jewish Libraries." In *October 16, 1943: Eight Jews*, edited by Giacomo Debenedetti, 91–100. Notre Dame IN: University of Notre Dame Press, 2001.

Ginzburg, Carlo, in coordination with the Bologna Seminar. "Ritual Pillages: A Preface to Research in Progress." In *Microhistory and the Lost Peoples of Europe*, edited by Edward Muir and Guido Ruggiero, 20–41. Baltimore MD: Johns Hopkins University Press, 1991.

Ginzburg, Natalia. *Family Lexicon*. New York: New York Review Books, 1963.

———. *A Place to Live*. Translated by Lynne Sharon Schwartz. New York: Seven Stories Press, 2002. Kindle.

Glatzer, Nahum. "The Attitude towards Rome in Third-Century Judaism." In *Politische Ordnung und menschliche Existenz: Festgabe für Eric Vögelin*, edited by Alois Dempf, 243–57. Munich: Beck, 1962.

Goldberg, Harvey. "Tradition with Modernity from Ottoman Times (1835–1911) to Italian Encounters (1900–)." In *Jewish Libya: Memory and Identity in Text and Image*, edited by Jacques Roumani, David Meghnagi, and Judith Roumani, 68–84. Syracuse NY: Syracuse University Press, 2018.

Goldman, Wendy Z., and Joe William Trotter, eds. *The Ghetto in Global History, 1500 to the Present*. London: Routledge, 2018.

Goodenough, Erwin. *Jewish Symbols in the Graeco-Roman Period*. 12 vols. New York: Pantheon Books, 1953–69.

Goodman, Martin. *A History of Judaism*. Princeton NJ: Princeton University Press, 2018.

———. *Josephus's "The Jewish War": A Biography*. Princeton NJ: Princeton University Press, 2019.

———. "Nerva: The *Fiscus Judaicus* and Jewish Identity." *Journal of Roman Studies* 79 (1989): 40–44.

———. *Rome and Jerusalem: The Clash of Ancient Civilizations*. New York: Vintage Books, 2008.

Grayzel, Solomon. *The Church and the Jews in the Thirteenth Century*. Edited by Ken-neth Stow. New York: Jewish Theological Seminary Press, 2012.

————. "Popes, Jews, and Inquisition, from 'Sicut' to 'Turbato corde.'" In *Essays on the Occasion of the Seventieth Anniversary of Dropsie University*, edited by A. Katsch and L. Nemoy, 151–88. Philadelphia PA: Dropsie University, 1977.

Gregorovius, Ferdinand. *The Ghetto and the Jews of Rome*. Translated by Moses Hadas. New York: Schocken Books, 1948.

Gruppi, Angela, ed. *Gli abitanti del ghetto di Roma: La Descriptio Hebreorum del 1733*. Rome: Viella, 2014.

Gucciardini, Luigi. *The Sack of Rome*. Translated and edited by James H. McGregor. New York: Italica Press, 1933.

Gunzberg, Lynn. "Assimilation and Identity in an Italian-Jewish Novel." In *The Most Ancient of Minorities: The Jews of Italy*, edited by Stanislao Pugliese, 139–46. Westport CT: Greenwood Press, 2002.

————. *Strangers at Home: Jews in the Italian Literary Imagination*. Berkeley: University of California Press, 1992.

Gutmann, J., ed. *The Dura Europos Synagogue: A Reevaluation (1932–1992)*. Tampa: University of South Florida, 1992.

Hermann, Klaus, et al., eds. *Jewish Studies between the Disciplines (Judaistik zwischen den Disziplinen): Papers in Honor of Peter Schäfer on the Occasion of His Sixtieth Birthday*. Leiden, Neth.: Brill, 2003.

Hermansen, G. *Ostia: Aspects of Roman City Life*. Edmonton, Can.: University of Alberta Press, 1982.

Herzer, Ivo, ed. *The Italian Refuge*. Washington DC: Catholic University of America Press, 1989.

Hochuth, Rolf. *The Deputy*. New York: Grove Press, 1964.

Hopkins, Keith, and Mary Beard. *The Colosseum*. London: Profile Books, 2011.

Hughes, H. Stuart. *Prisoners of Hope: The Silver Age of Italian Jews, 1924–1974*. Cambridge MA: Harvard University Press, 1983.

Hunt, John M. "The Conclave from the 'Outside In': Rumor, Speculation, and Disorder in Rome." *Journal of Early Modern History* 16 (2012): 355–82.

————. *The Vacant See in Early Modern Rome: A Social History of the Papal Interregnum*. Leiden, Neth.: Brill, 2016.

Ihm, Claudia Carlen, ed. *The Papal Encyclicals*. Vol. 4, *1939–1958*. Raleigh NC: McGrath, 1981.

Infessiera, Stephan. *Diario della citta di Roma*. Edited by O. Tommasini. Rome: 1890.

Isaac, Jules. *Jesus and Israel*. New York: Holt, Rinehart and Winston, 1971.

————. *The Teaching of Contempt: Christian Roots of Anti-Semitism*. New York: Holt, Rinehart and Winston, 1964.

Katsch, A., and L. Nemoy, eds. *Essays on the Occasion of the Seventieth Anniversary of Dropsie University*. Philadelphia PA: Dropsie University, 1979.

Katz, Jacob. *Exclusiveness and Tolerance: Studies in Jewish-Gentile Relations in Medieval and Modern Times*. New York: Schocken Books, 1962.

Katz, Robert. *Death in Rome*. New York: Macmillan, 1967.

———. *Fatal Silence: The Pope, the Resistance and the German Occupation of Rome*. London: Cassel, 2004.

———. "The Möllhausen Telegram, the Kappler Decodes, and the Deportation of the Jews of Rome: The New CIA-OSS Documents, 2000–2002." In *Jews in Italy under Fascist and Nazi Rule*, edited by J. Zimmerman, 224–42. Cambridge: Cambridge University Press, 2005.

Kertzer, David. *The Kidnapping of Edgardo Mortara*. New York: Random House, 1997.

———. *The Pope and Mussolini: The Secret History of Pius XI and the Rise of Fascism in Europe*. New York: Random House, 2014.

———. *The Pope at War: The Secret History of Pius XII, Mussolini, and Hitler*. New York: Random House, 2022.

———. *The Popes against the Jews: The Vatican's Role in the Rise of Modern Anti-Semitism*. New York: Random House, 2001.

———. *The Pope Who Would Be King: The Exile of Pius IX and the Emergence of Modern Europe*. New York: Random House, 2018.

———. *Prisoner of the Vatican: The Popes, the Kings and Garibaldi's Rebels in the Struggle to Rule Modern Italy*. New York: Houghton Mifflin, 2004.

Klein, Shira. *Italy's Jews from Emancipation to Fascism*. Cambridge: Cambridge University Press, 2018.

Kneale, Matthew. *Rome: A History in Seven Sackings*. New York: Simon and Schuster, 2017.

Koch, Cardinal Kurt, "Introductory Remarks." In *La menorà: Culto, storia e mito*, edited by Francesco Leone. Milan: Skira editore, 2017.

Kraabel, A. T. "The Disappearance of the 'God-Fearers.'" *Numen* 28 (1981): 113–26.

Kraemer, Ross. "On the Meaning of the Term 'Jew' in Greco-Roman Inscriptions." *Harvard Theological Review* 82 (1989): 35–53.

Ladurie, Emmanuel Le Roy. "The Aiguillette: Castration by Magic." In *The Mind and Method of the Historian*, translated by Sian and Ben Reynolds, 84–96. Chicago: University of Chicago Press, 1981.

———. *Carnival in Romans: Mayhem and Massacre in a French City*. New York: George Braziller, 1980.

Lamet, Eric. *A Child al Confino: The True Story of a Boy and His Mother in Mussolini's Italy*. Avon MA: Adams Media, 2011.

Lang, Ariella. "The Politics of Conversion: Jews and Inquisition Law in Nineteenth-Century Italy." In *The Roman Inquisition, the Index, and the Jews: Contexts, Sources, and Perspectives*, edited by Stephen Wendehorst, 215–34. Leiden, Neth.: Brill, 2000.

Langmuir, Gavin. *History, Religion, and Antisemitism*. Berkeley: University of California Press, 1990.

———. *Toward a Definition of Antisemitism*. Berkeley: University of California: Press, 1990.

Lapin, Daniel, and Riccardo Di Segni. "Jewish Leaders Assess John Paul II's Pontificate." *Religion and Liberty* 15 no. 1 (July 20, 2010), Acton Institute, https://www.acton.org/pub/religion-liberty/volume-15-number-1/jewish-leaders-assess-john-paul-iis-pontificate.

Laurenzi, Elsa. *Jewish Catacombs: The Jews of Rome, Funeral Rites and Customs*. Rome: Gangemi, 2013.

———. *La catacomba ebraica di Vigna Randanini*. Rome: Gangemi, 1999.

Ledeen, Michael. "Renzo De Felice and the Historiography of Italian Fascism." *Journal of Contemporary History* 11 (1976): 269–83.

Le Goff, Jacques. *Your Money or Your Life: Economy and Religion in the Middle Ages*. New York: Zone Books, 1988.

Leiphart, Nancy Goldsmith. "The Case of Ferdinando Alvarez and His Wife Leocadia of Rome (1637–1643)." In *The Most Ancient of Minorities: The Jews of Italy*, edited by Stanislao Pugliese, 101–4. Westport CT: Greenwood Press, 2002.

Leon, Harry J. *The Jews of Ancient Rome*. Updated edition. Peabody MA: Hendrickson, 1995.

Leone, Francesco, ed. *La menorà: Culto, storia e mito*. Milan: Skira, 2017.

———. "L'ottocento: L'ethos neoclassico, il pathos romantico, le istanze risorgimentali italiane, il vero e il suo supramento verso il simbolismo di fine secolo." In *La menorà: Culto, storia e mito*, edited by Franceso Leone, 260–67. Milan: Skira, 2017.

Lesley, Arthur. "Jewish Adaptation of Humanist Concepts in Fifteenth and Sixteenth Century Italy." In *Essential Papers on Jewish Culture in Renaissance and Baroque Italy*, edited by David Ruderman, 45–62. New York: New York University Press, 1992.

Levi, Carlo. *Christ Stopped at Eboli*. New York: Farrar, Straus and Giroux, 1947.

Levi, Lia. *The Jewish Husband*. New York: Europa Editions, 2009.

Levinson, Joshua. "'Tragedies Naturally Performed': Fatal Charades, Parodia Sacra, and the Death of Titus." In *Interdisciplinary Studies in Ancient Culture 3: Jewish Culture and Society under the Christian Roman Empire*, edited by Richard Kalman and Seth Schwartz, 349–82. Leuven, Belg.: Peeters, 2003.

Levi-Strauss, Claude. *From Honey to Ashes: Introduction to a Science of Mythology*. Vol. 2. Translated by John and Doreen Weightman. New York: Harper and Row, 1973.

———. *The Raw and the Cooked: Introduction to a Science of Mythology*. Vol. 1. Translated by John and Doreen Weightman. New York: Harper and Row, 1969.

———. *Structural Anthropology*. New York: Basic Books, 1963.

Levita, Elijah. *Massoreth ha-Massoreth*. Edited and translated by C. D. Ginsburg, 1867. Books on Demand, 2013.

Lewy, Guenter. *The Catholic Church and Nazi Germany*. New York: Da Capo Press, 2000.

Lieu, Judith, John North, and Tessa Rajak, eds. *The Jews among Pagans and Christians in the Roman Empire*. London: Routledge, 1992.

Linder, Amnon. "'The Jews Too Were Not Absent . . . Carrying Moses's Law on Their Shoulders': The Ritual Encounter of Pope and Jews from the Middle Ages to Modern Times." *Jewish Quarterly Review* 99 (2009): 323–95.

Livi, Livio. *Gli ebrei alle luce della statistica*. Vol. 2. Bologna: Arnaldo Forni, 1918–29.

Loftus, John, and Mark Aarons. *The Secret War against the Jews: How Western Espionage Betrayed the Jewish People*. New York: St. Martin's, 1994.

Loy, Rosetta. *First Words: A Childhood in Fascist Italy*. New York: Henry Holt, 2000.

MacDonald, Hugh, ed. *Poems of Andrew Marvell*. 2nd ed. Cambridge MA: Harvard University Press, 1956.

Mampieri, Martina, ed. *Living under the Evil Pope: The Hebrew Chronicle of Pope Paul IV by Benjamin Nehemiah ben Elnatan from Civitanova Marche*. Leiden, Neth.: Brill, 2019.

Mann, Vivian. "The Art of Jewish Italy." In *Gardens and Ghettos: The Art of Jewish Life in Italy*, edited by Vivian Mann, 45–65. Berkeley: University of California Press, 1989.

———, ed. *Gardens and Ghettos: The Art of Jewish Life in Italy*. Berkeley: University of California Press, 1989.

Marcus, Jacob Rader, ed. *Jew in the Medieval World: A Sourcebook: 315–1791*. Cincinnati OH: Hebrew Union College Press, 1999.

Marucci, Valerio, ed. *Pasquinate el cinque e seicento*. Rome: Salerno Editrice, 1988.

Mauss, Marcel. *The Gift: The Form and Reason for Exchange in Archaic Societies*. London: Routledge 1990.

Melasecchi, Olga. "Artisti e committenti ebrei a Roma nella *belle epoque*." In *Ebrei a Roma tra risorgimento ed emancipazione (1814–1914)*, edited by Claudio Procaccia, 119–27. Rome: Gangemi Editore, 2013.

Michaelis, Meir. *Mussolini and the Jews: German-Italian Relations and the Jewish Question in Italy, 1922–1945*. Oxford: Clarendon Press, 1978.

Milano, Attilio. *Il ghetto di Roma*. Rome: Carruci, 1988.

Mitzman, Arthur. "The Civilizing Offensive, Mentalities, High Culture and Individual Psyches." *Journal of Social History* 20 (1986): 663–87.

Modigliani, Piero. *I nazisti a Roma: Dal diario di un ebreo*. Rome: Citta Nuova Editrice, 1984.

Momigliano, Arnoldo. "Severo Alessandro Archisynagogus." *Athenaeum*, n.s., 12 (1934): 151–53.

Monsagrati, Giuseppe. "La Roma papale e gli ebrei alle fine del potere temporale" In *Ebrei a Roma tra risorgimento ed emancipazione (1814–1914)*, edited by Claudio Procaccia, 13–22. Rome: Gangemi, 2013.

Montaigne, Michel Eyquem de. *The Journal of Montaigne's Travels in Italy by Way of Switzerland and Germany in 1580 and 1581*. Translated by W. G. Waters. London: John Murray, 1903.

Morante, Elsa. *History: A Novel*. Translated by William Weaver. Hanover NH: Steerforth Press, 2000.

Muir, Edward, and Guido Ruggiero, eds. *Microhistory and the Lost Peoples of Europe*. Baltimore MD: Johns Hopkins University Press, 1991.

Munday, Anthony. *The English Roman Life*. London: John Charlwoode, 1590.

Myers, David, et al., eds. *Acculturation and Its Discontents: The Italian Jewish Experience between Exclusion and Inclusion*. Toronto: University of Toronto Press, 2008.

Natale, Luisa, and Pia Toscano. "Libyan Jews in Rome: Integration and Impact on the Roman Jewish Community." *Studi emigrazione / Migration Studies* 194 (2014): 275–95.

Nemeth, Luc. "The First Anti-Semitic Campaign of the Fascist Regime." In *The Most Ancient of Minorities: The Jews of Italy*, edited by Stanislao Pugliese, 247–58. Westport CT: Greenwood Press, 2002.

Neusner, Jacob, and Ernest Frerichs, eds. *To See Ourselves as Others See Us: Christians, Jews and Others in Late Antiquity*. Chico CA: Scholars Press, 1985.

Newman, Louis I. *The "Chief Rabbi" of Rome Becomes a Catholic: A Study in Fright and Spite*. New York: Renascence Press, 1945.

Nidam-Orvieto, Iael. "The Impact of the Anti-Jewish Legislation." In *Jews in Italy under Fascist and Nazi Rule*, edited by J. Zimmerman, 158–81. Cambridge: Cambridge University Press, 2005.

Nirenberg, David. *Anti-Judaism: The Western Tradition*. New York: W. W. Norton, 2013.

———. *Communities of Violence: Persecution of Minorities in the Middle Ages*. Princeton NJ: Princeton University Press, 1998.

Nussdorfer, Laurie. "The Vacant See: Ritual and Protest in Early Modern Rome." *Sixteenth Century Journal* (1987): 73–179.

O'Malley, John W. *Giles of Viterbo on Church and Reform: A Study in Renaissance Thought*. Leiden, Neth.: Brill, 1968.

———. *What Happened at Vatican II*. Cambridge MA: Belknap Press, 2008.

Origo, Iris. *A Chill in the Air: An Italian War Diary, 1939–1940*. New York: New York Review Books, 2017.

Osti Guerrazzi, Amedeo. *Caino a Roma: I complici Romani della Shoah*. Rome: Cooper, 2006.

————. "La persecuzione degli ebrei a Roma, carefici e vittime." In *Dopo il 16 ottobre gli ebrei a Roma tra occupazione, resistenza, accoglienza e delazioni (1943–1944)*, edited by Silvia Haia Antonucci and Claudio Procaccia, 35–271. Rome: Viella, 2017.

————. "Professioni e radicamento su territorio degli ebrei di Roma dall' emancipazione all prima guerra mondiale." In *Ebrei a Roma tra risorgimento ed emancipazione (1814–1914)*, edited by Claudio Procaccia, 73–77. Rome: Gangemi Editore, 2013.

Partner, Peter. *Renaissance Rome, 1500–1559: Portrait of a Society*. Berkeley: University of California Press, 1976.

Pekelis, Carla. *My Version of the Facts*. Evanston IL: Northwestern University Press, 2004.

Penna, Roman. "Les juifs à Rome au temps de l'apotre Paul." *New Testament Studies* 28 (1982): 321–47.

Peristiany, John G., ed. *Honour and Shame: The Values of Mediterranean Society*. London: Weidenfeld and Nicholson, 1965.

Perry, Marvin, and Frederick M. Schweitzer. *Antisemitism: Myth and Hate from Antiquity to the Present*. New York: Palgrave Macmillan, 2002.

Petrarch. *The Revolution of Cola Di Rienzo*. 3rd ed. Edited by Mario Emilio Cosenza. New York: Italica Press, 1996.

Pezzino, Paolo, and Guri Schwarz. "From Kappler to Priebke: Holocaust Trials and Seasons of Memory in Italy." In *Holocaust and Justice: Representation and Historiography of the Holocaust in Post-War Trials*, edited by David Bankier and Dan Michman, 299–328. New York and Jerusalem: Berghahn Books / Yad Vashem, 2010.

Picciotto, Liliana. "The Jews during the German Occupation and the Italian Social Republic." In *The Italian Refuge*, edited by Ivo Herzer, 109–38. Washington DC: Catholic University of America Press, 1989.

————. "The Shoah in Italy: Its History and Characteristics." In *The Jews in Italy under Fascist and Nazi Rule*, edited by J. Zimmerman, 209–23. Cambridge: Cambridge University Press, 2005.

Poliakov, Leon. *The History of Anti-Semitism*. 4 vols. Philadelphia: University of Pennsylvania Press, 2003.

————. *Jewish Bankers and the Holy See from the Thirteenth to the Seventeenth Century*. London: Routledge and Kegan Paul, 1977.

Portelli, Alessandro. *The Order Has Been Carried Out: History, Memory, and Meaning of a Nazi Massacre in Rome*. New York: Palgrave Macmillan, 2003.

Porten, Bezalel, et al. *The Elephantine Papyri in English: Three Millennia of Cross-Cultural Continuity and Change*. 2nd ed. Atlanta GA: Society of Biblical Literature, 2011.

Procaccia, Claudio, ed. *Ebrei a Roma tra risorgimento ed emancipazione (1814–1914)*. Rome: Gangemi Editore, 2013.

————. "Il 'Tempio di via Balbo' e la comunita ebraica di Roma (1914–2014): Linee di sintesi e spunti di riflessione." In *L'Oratorio Di Castro: Cento anno di ebraismo a Roma (1914–2014)*, edited by Claudio Procaccia, 13–28. Rome: Gangemi Editore, 2014.

———. "Storia economica e sociale degli ebrei a Roma: Tra retaggio e metamorfosi (1814–1914)." In *Ebrei a Roma tra risorgimento ed emancipazione (1814–1914)*, edited by Claudio Procaccia, 37–71. Rome: Gangemi, 2013.

Pugliese, Stanslao. *Bitter Spring: A Life of Ignazio Silone*. New York: Farrar, Strauss and Giroux, 2009.

———. *Carlo Rosselli: Socialist Heretic and Antifascist Exile*. Cambridge MA: Harvard University Press, 1999.

———, ed. *The Most Ancient of Minorities: The Jews of Italy*. Westport CT: Greenwood Press, 2002.

Racine, Jean. *Berenice*. Kindle, 2019.

Rajak, Tessa. "Jew and Christians as Groups in a Pagan World." In *To See Ourselves as Others See Us: Christians, Jews and Others in Late Antiquity*, edited by Jacob Neusner and Ernest Frerichs, 247–62. Chico CA: Scholars Press, 1985.

———. "The Jewish Community and Its Boundaries." In *The Jews among Pagans and Christians in the Roman Empire*, edited by Judith Lieu, John North, and Tessa Rajak, 9–28. London: Routledge, 1992.

Raspe, Lucia. "Payyetanim as Heroes of Medieval Folk Narrative: The Case of Rabbi Shimon B. Yishaq of Mainz." In *Jewish Studies between the Disciplines (Judaistik zwischen den Disziplinen): Papers in Honor of Peter Schäfer on the Occasion of His Sixtieth Birthday*, edited by Klaus Hermann et al., 354–69. Leiden, Neth.: Brill, 2003.

Ravid, Benjamin. "From Geographical Realia to Historiographical Symbol: The Odyssey of the Word *Ghetto*." In *Essential Papers on Jewish Culture in Renaissance and Baroque Italy*, edited by David Ruderman, 373–85. New York: New York University Press, 1992.

———. "Ghetto Etymology, Original Definition, Reality and Diffusion." In *The Ghetto in Global History, 1500 to the Present*, edited by Wendy Z. Goldman and Joe William Trotter Jr., 23–39. London: Routledge, 2018.

———. "How 'Other' Really Was the Jewish Other? The Evidence from Venice." In *Acculturation and Its Discontents: The Italian Jewish Experience between Exclusion and Inclusion*, edited by David Myers, Massimo Ciavolella, Peter H. Reill, and Geoffrey Symcox, 19–54. Toronto: University of Toronto Press, 2008.

Reguer, Sara. *The Most Tenacious of Minorities: The Jews of Italy*. Brighton MA: Academic Studies Press, 2013.

Riall, Lucy. *Garibaldi: Invention of a Hero*. New Haven CT: Yale University Press, 2007.

———. *Risorgimento: The History of Italy from Napoleon to Nation State*. New York: Palgrave Macmillan, 2009.

Rieger, Paul. "The Foundation of Rome in the Talmud: A Contribution to the Folklore of Antiquity." *Jewish Quarterly Review* 16 (1926): 227–35.

Rist, Rebecca. *Popes and Jews, 1095–1291.* Oxford: Oxford University Press, 2016.

Rosetto, Piera. "'We Were All Italian!': The Construction of a 'Sense of Italianness' among Jews from Libya (1920s–1960s)." Taylor and Francis Online, January 14, 2021, https://www.Tanfonline.com.

Rossi, Azariah de. *Me'or Enayim: The Light of the Eyes.* Translated by Joanna Weinberg. New Haven CT: Yale University Press, 2001.

Roth, Cecil. *The History of the Jews of Italy.* Philadelphia: The Jewish Publication Society of America, 1946.

———. *The Jews in the Renaissance.* Philadelphia: The Jewish Publication Society of America, 1959.

———, ed. *The Ritual Murder Libel and the Jew: The Report by Cardinal Ganganelli (Pope Clement XIV).* London: Woburn Press, 1935.

Rubin, Miri. *Gentile Tales: The Narrative Assault on Late Medieval Jews.* Philadelphia: University of Pennsylvania Press, 1999.

Ruderman, David. "At the Intersection of Cultures: The Historical Legacy of Italian Jewry." In *Gardens and Ghettos: The Art of Jewish Life in Italy,* edited by Vivian Mann, 1–23. Berkeley: University of California Press, 1989.

———, ed. *Essential Papers on Jewish Culture in Renaissance and Baroque Italy.* New York: New York University Press, 1992.

———, ed. *Preachers of the Italian Ghetto.* Berkeley: University of California Press, 1992.

Rutgers, L. V. *The Hidden Heritage of Diaspora Judaism.* Leiden, Neth.: Peeters, 1998.

———. *Jews of Late Ancient Rome: Evidence of Cultural Interaction in the Roman Diaspora.* Leiden, Neth.: Brill, 1995.

Rynne, Xavier. *Vatican Council II.* New York: Farrar, Straus and Giroux, 1968.

Saldarini, Anthony J. "Johanan Ben Zakkai's Escape from Jerusalem: Origin and Development of a Rabbinic Story." *Journal for the Study of Judaism in the Persian, Hellenistic and Roman Period* 6 (1975): 189–204.

Sanchez, Jose M. *Pius XII and the Holocaust: Understanding the Controversy.* Washington DC: Catholic University of America Press, 2002.

Sands, Philippe. *The Ratline: The Exalted Life and Death of a Nazi Fugitive.* New York: Alfred A. Knopf, 2021.

Sarfatti, Michele. "Characteristics and Objectives of the Anti-Jewish Racial Laws in Fascist Italy, 1938–1943." In *Jews in Italy under Fascist and Nazi Rule, 1922–1945,* edited by Joshua D. Zimmerman, 71–80. Cambridge: Cambridge University Press 2005.

——— *Il cielo sereno e l'ombra della Shoah: Otto stereotipi sulla persecuzione antiebraica nell'Italia fascista.* Rome: Viella, 2020.

———. *The Jews in Mussolini's Italy from Equality to Persecution.* Madison: University of Wisconsin Press, 2006.

Schama, Simon. *The Story of the Jews.* Vol. 2: *Belonging: 1492–1900.* New York: Harper Collins, 2017.

Scholem, Gershom. *Major Trends in Jewish Mysticism.* New York: Schocken Press, 1961.

Schweitzer, Frederick M. "Why Was Italy So Impervious to Anti-Semitism (to 1938)?" In *The Most Ancient of Minorities: The Jews of Italy,* edited by Stanislao Pugliese, 259–73. Westport CT: Greenwood Press, 2002.

Segre, Augusto. *Memories of Jewish Life from Italy to Jerusalem, 1918–1960.* Lincoln: University of Nebraska Press, 2008.

Sereny, Gitta. *Into That Darkness: An Examination of Conscience.* New York: Vintage, 1983.

Sermoneta, Giuseppe. "Prophecy in the Writings of R. Yehudah Romano." In *Studies in Medieval Jewish History and Literature,* vol. 2, edited by Isadore Twersky, 337–74. Cambridge MA: Harvard University Press, 1984.

Servi, Sandro. "Building a Racial State: Images of the Jew in the Illustrated Fascist Magazine, *La difesa della razza,* 1938–1943." In *Jews in Italy under Fascist and Nazi Rule,* edited by Joshua Zimmerman, 114–57. Cambridge: Cambridge University Press, 2005.

Setton, Kenneth M. *The Papacy and the Levant, 1204–1571.* Vol. 4: *The Sixteenth Century.* Philadelphia: American Philosophical Society, 1984.

Shelley, Percy Bysshe. "Notes on Sculptures in Rome and Florence: Rome, the Arch of Titus." *Athenaeum* 5 (September 29, 1832): 633.

Sillanpoa, Wallace P., and Robert G. Weisbord. "The Baptized Rabbi of Rome: The Zolli Case." *Judaism* 38 (1989): 74–91.

———. "The Zolli Conversion: Background and Motives." *Judaism* 38 (1989): 203–15.

Simonsohn, Shlomo. *The Apostolic See and the Jews.* Toronto: UTP Pontifical Institute of Medieval Studies, 1991.

Smallwood, E. Mary. "Domitian's Attitudes towards the Jews and Judaism." *Classical Philology* 51 (1956): 1–13.

Smith, Danny. "Painted into a Corner: Seeing Jews in Medieval Rome." *AJS Perspectives* (Fall 2021): 54–55.

Smith, D. Mack. *Cavour and Garibaldi 1860: A Study in Political Conflict.* Cambridge: Cambridge University Press, 1954.

Smith, Jonathan Z. *To Take Place: Toward Theory in Ritual.* Chicago: University of Chicago Press, 1987.

Sodi, Risa. Foreword to *A Child al Confino: The True Story of a Boy and His Mother in Mussolini's Italy,* by Eric Lamet, vii–x. Avon MA: Adams Media, 2011.

———. *Narrative and Imperative: The First Fifty Years of Italian Holocaust Writing, 1944–1994.* New York: Peter Lang, 2007.

Sonino, Eugenio, and Daniele Spizzichino. "La demografia degli ebrei di Roma: Un focus al 1868." In *Ebrei a Roma tra risorgimento ed emancipazione (1814–1914)*, edited by Claudio Procaccia, 79–87. Rome: Gangemi Editore, 2013.

Spizzichino, Giancarlo. "The Ghetto and the Authorities: Difficult Coexistence." In *Et ecce gaudium: The Roman Jews and the Investiture of the Popes*, edited by Daniela Di Castro, 17–21. Rome: Araldo De Luca Editore, 2010.

———. "La gestione dei cimiteri: La confraternita *ghemilut chasadim*." In *L'Aventino dal rinascimento ad oggi: Arte e architectura*, edited by Mario Bevilacqua and Daniela Gallavotti Cavallero, 204–19. Rome: Artemide, 2011.

———. *La scomparsa della sesta Scola: La sinagoga Portaleone*. Rome: Gangemi, 2011.

———. "Pio IX e l'università degli ebrei di Roma: Speranze e delusione (1846–1850)." In *Ebrei a Roma tra risorgimento ed emancipazione (1814–1914)*, edited by Claudio Procaccia, 265–338. Rome: Gangemi Editore, 265–338.

Sprenger, Kai-Michael. "The Tiara in the Tiber: An Essay on the *damnatio in memoria* of Clement III (1084–1100) and Rome's River as a Place of Oblivion and Memory." *Reti Medievali Rivista* 13 (2012): 153–74.

Stille, Alexander. *Benevolence and Betrayal: Five Italian Jewish Families under Fascism*. New York: Simon and Schuster, 1991.

———. "The Double Bind of Italian Jews: Acceptance and Assimilation." In *Jews in Italy under Fascist and Nazi Rule, 1922–1945*, edited by Joshua D. Zimmerman, 19–34. Cambridge: Cambridge University Press, 2005.

Stow, Kenneth. *Alienated Minority: The Jews of Medieval Latin Europe*. Cambridge MA: Harvard University Press, 1992.

———. *Anna and Tranquillo: Catholic Anxiety and Jewish Protest in the Age of Revolutions*. New Haven CT: Yale University Press, 2016.

———. "The Burning of the Talmud in 1553 in the Light of Sixteenth-Century Catholic Attitudes towards the Talmud." *Bibliotheque D'Humanisme et Renaissance* 34 (1972): 435–59.

———. *Catholic Thought and Papal Jewry Policy, 1555–1593*. New York: Jewish Theological Seminary, 1977.

———. "Church, Conversion and Tradition: The Problem of Jewish Conversion in Sixteenth-Century Italy." *Dimensione e problemi della ricerca storica* 2 (1996): 25–34.

———. "The Consciousness of Closure: Roman Jewry and its *Ghet*." In *Essential Papers on Jewish Culture in Renaissance and Baroque Italy*, edited by David Ruderman, 386–400. New York: New York University Press, 1992.

———. "Emotion and Acculturation: Masquerading Emotion in the Roman Ghetto." In *Acculturation and Its Discontents: The Italian Jewish Experience between Exclusion and Inclusion*, edited by David Myers et al., 56–71. Toronto: University of Toronto Press, 2008.

———. "The End of Confessionalism: Jews, Law and the Roman Ghetto." In *The Ghetto in Global History, 1500 to the Present*, edited by Wendy Z. Goldman and Joe W. Trotter, 40–56. London: Routledge, 2018.

———. "Ethnic Amalgamation, Like It or Not: Inheritance in Early Modern Jewish Rome." *Jewish History* 16 (2002): 107–21.

———. "Ethnic Rivalry or Melting Pot: The 'Edot' in the Roman Ghetto." *Judaism* 41 (1992): 286–96.

———. "The Fruit of Ambivalence: Papal Jewry Policies over the Centuries." In *The Roman Inquisition, the Index, and the Jews: Contexts, Sources, and Perspectives*, edited by Stephen Wendehorst, 3–17. Leiden, Neth.: Brill, 2000.

———. "The Good of the Church, The Good of the State: The Popes and Jewish Money." In *Christianity and Judaism: Studies in Church History*, vol. 29, edited by Diana Wood, 237–52. Oxford: Blackwell, 1992.

———. *Jewish Dogs: An Image and Its Interpreters in the Catholic Jewish Encounter*. Stanford CA: Stanford University Press, 2006.

———. *Jewish Life in Early Modern Rome: Challenge, Conversion and Private Life*. Burlington VT: Ashgate, 2007.

———. "Jewish Pre-Emancipation: *Ius Commune*, The Roman Communitá, and Marriage in the Early Papal State." In *Tov Elem: Memory, Community, and Gender in Medieval and Early Modern Jewish Culture: Festschrift for Robert Bonfil*, edited by Elisheva Baumgarten, Amnon Raz-Krakotzin, and Roni Weinstein, 1–24. Jerusalem: Mossad Bialik, 2007.

———. *The Jews in Rome*. Vol. 1, 1536–51. Vol. 2, 1551–57. Leiden, Neth.: Brill, 1995, 1997.

———. "The Knotty Problem of Shem Tov Sopporto: Male Honor, Marital Initiation, and Disciplinary Structures in Mid-Sixteenth Century Jewish Rome." *Italia* 13–15 (2001): 137–49.

———. "Marriages Are Made in Heaven: Marriage and the Individual in the Roman Jewish Ghetto." *Renaissance Quarterly* 42 (1995): 445–91.

———. "Neofiti and Their Families: Or Perhaps the Good of the State." *Leo Baeck Yearbook* 47 (2002): 105–13.

———. "The Papacy and the Jews: Catholic Reformation and Beyond." *Jewish History* 6 (1992): 257–78.

———. "Papal and Royal Attitudes toward Jewish Lending in the Thirteenth Century." *AJS Review* 6 (1981): 166–69.

———. *Popes, Church, and Jews in the Middle Ages: Confrontation and Response*. Burlington VT: Ashgate, 2007.

———. Preface to *Gli abitanti del ghetto di Roma: La Descriptio Hebreorum del 1733*, edited by Angela Gruppi, 15–24. Rome: Viella, 2014.

———. "Sanctity and the Construction of Space: The Roman Ghetto as Sacred Space."
In *Jewish Assimilation, Acculturation, and Accommodation*, edited by Menachem
Mor, 54–76. New York: University Press of America, 1991.

———. *Theater of Acculturation: The Roman Ghetto in the Sixteenth Century*. Seattle:
University of Washington Press, 2001.

———. "Writing in Hebrew, Thinking in Italian." In *Jewish Life in Early Modern
Rome: Challenge, Conversion and Private Life*, 1–14. Burlington VT: Ashgate, 2007.

Stow, Sandra Debenedetti. "Harara, pizza, nel XIV secolo." *Archivio glottologia italiano*
68 (1983): 80–81.

———. "I sonetti di Crescenzo del Monte." In *Appartenenza e differenza: Ebrei d'italia
e letteratura*, edited by Jacques Montefiore and Sandra Debenedetti Stow, 34–42.
Florence: Giuntina, 1998.

Stroll, Mary. *The Jewish Pope: Ideology and Politics in the Papal Schism of 1130*. Leiden,
Neth.: Brill, 1987.

Sullam, Simon Lewis. *The Italian Executioners: The Genocide of the Jews in Italy*. Princeton NJ: Princeton University Press, 2018.

Thomas, Gordon. *The Pope's Jews: The Vatican's Secret Plans to Save Jews from the Nazis*.
New York: St. Martin's Press, 2012.

Thomas, William. "The History of Italy." In *Street Life in Renaissance Rome*, edited by
Rudolph Bell, 75–79. New York: Bedford/St. Martin's, 2013.

Toscano, Mario. "Italian Jewish Identity from the Risorgimento to Fascism, 1848–
1938." In *Jews in Italy under Fascist and Nazi Rule, 1922–1945*, edited by Joshua D.
Zimmerman, 35–54. Cambridge: Cambridge University Press, 2005.

Travis, David. "The Priebke Trial(s)." In *The Most Ancient of Minorities: The Jews of
Italy*, edited by Stanislao Pugliese, 289–300. London: Greenwood Press 2002.

Tuck, Lily. *Woman of Rome: A Life of Elsa Morante*. New York: Harper Collins, 2008.

Twyman, Susan. *Papal Ceremonial at Rome in the Twelfth Century*. London: Henry
Bradshaw Society, 2002.

Van Seters, John. "Israel and Egypt in the Age of Solomon." In *Walls of the Prince:
Egyptian Interaction with Southwest Asia in Antiquity: Essays in Honor of John S.
Holladay, Jr.*, edited by Timothy P. Harrison, Edward B. Banning, and Stanley
Klassen, 199–211. Leiden, Neth.: Brill, 2015.

Vasari, Giorgio. *Lives of the Artists*, translated by Julia Conaway Bondanella and Peter
Bondanella. Oxford: Oxford University Pres, 1991.

Venzo, Manola Ida. "Fascism and the Racial Laws." In *The Racial Laws and the Jewish
Community of Rome, 1938–1945*, edited by Manola Ida Venzo and Bice Migliau,
10–23. Rome: Gangemi Editore, 2003.

Venzo, Manola Ida, and Bice Migliau, eds. *The Racial Laws and the Jewish Community
of Rome, 1938–1945*. Rome: Gangemi Editore, 2003.

Verdi, Giuseppe, and Temistocle Solera. *Nabucco: Libretto*. Italian and English edition. Scotts Valley CA: CreateSpace Independent Publishing Platform, 2016.

Vismara, C. "I cimiteri ebraici di Roma." In *Società romana ed impero tardo-antica*, vol. 2, edited by A. Giardina, 51–392, 490–503. Rome: Bari, 1986.

Vogelstein, Hermann. *Rome*. Jewish Communities Series. Philadelphia: The Jewish Publication Society of America, 1940.

Voigt, Klaus. "The Children of Villa Emma at Nonantola." In *Jews in Italy under Fascist and Nazi Rule, 1922–1945*, edited by Joshua Zimmerman, 182–98. Cambridge: Cambridge University Press, 2005.

Wasner, Franz. "The Pope's Veneration of the Torah." In *The Bridge: A Yearbook of Judaeo-Christian Studies*, vol. 4, edited by John M. Oesterreicher, 274–93. New York: Pantheon, 1962.

Watkin, David. *The Roman Forum*. Cambridge MA: Harvard University Press, 2009.

Weinberg, Joanna. "Preaching in the Venetian Ghetto." In *Preachers of the Italian Ghetto*, edited by David Ruderman, 105–28. Berkeley: University of California Press, 1992.

Wendehorst, Stephen, ed. *The Roman Inquisition, the Index, and the Jews: Contexts, Sources, and Perspectives*. Leiden, Neth.: Brill, 2000.

———. "The Roman Inquisition, the Index, and the Jews: New Perspectives for Research." *Jewish History* 17 (2003): 201–14.

White, L. Michael. "Synagogue and Society in Imperial Ostia: Archaeological and Epigraphic Evidence." *Harvard Theological Review* 90 (1997): 23–58.

Wickham, Chris. *Medieval Rome: Stability and Crisis of a City, 900–1150*. Oxford: Oxford University Press, 2015.

Wieseltier, Leon, *Kaddish*. New York: Alfred A. Knopf, 1998.

Wildvang, Frauke. "The Enemy Next Door: Italian Collaboration in Deporting Jews during the German Occupation of Rome." *Modern Italy* 12 (2007): 189–204.

Williams, Mary. "The Organisation of Jewish Burials in Ancient Rome in the Light of Evidence from Palestine and the Diaspora." *Classical Philology* 51 (1956): 165–82.

Wood, Diana, ed. *Christianity and Judaism: Studies in Church History*. Vol. 29. Oxford: Blackwell Publishers, 1992.

Wright, John, trans. *The Life of Cola di Rienzo*. Toronto: Pontifical Institute of Medieval Studies, 1975.

Yerushalmi, Yosef Hayim. "Clio and the Jews: Reflections on Jewish Historiography in the Sixteenth Century." In *Essential Papers on Jewish Culture in Renaissance and Baroque Italy*, edited by David Ruderman, 191–218. New York: New York University Press, 1992.

Zanker, Paul. *The Power of Images in the Age of Augustus*. Ann Arbor: University of Michigan Press, 1990.

Zimmels, H. J. "Rabbi Peter the Tosaphist." *Jewish Quarterly Review* 48 (1957): 51–52.

Zimmerman, Joshua D., ed. *Jews in Italy under Fascist and Nazi Rule, 1922–1945*. Cambridge: Cambridge University Press, 2005.

Zolli, Eugenio. *Before the Dawn: Autobiographical Reflections*. San Francisco: Ignatius Press, 1954.

Zuccotti, Susan. *The Italians and the Holocaust: Persecution and Survival*. Lincoln: University of Nebraska Press, 1987.

———. "Pius XII and the Rescue of Jews from Italy." In *Jews in Italy under Fascist and Nazi Rule, 1922–1945*, edited by Joshua Zimmerman, 287–307. Cambridge: Cambridge University Press, 2005.

———. *Under His Very Windows: The Vatican and the Holocaust in Italy*. New Haven CT: Yale University Press, 2000.

INDEX

Page numbers in italics indicate illustrations.

Bassani, Giorgio, 3–5
bat mitzvah ceremony, 188
Battista, Juan, 113
Bava Metzi'a, 112
Bayer, Karl, 249
Bea, Augustin, 261
Beèr, Rabbi Moisè Sabbato, 168–69
Belli, Giuseppe Gioachino, 168–73, 187, 307n46
ben Azariah, Eleazar, 42
Benedetto, Maria, 226–28, 316n43
Benedict XIII (pope), 65, 143, 297n38
Benedict XIV (pope), 121, 146–48
Benedict XVI (pope), 263, 274, 275–76
ben Elnatan, Benjamin Nehemiah, 133–34
Ben-Ghiat, Ruth, 246
ben Gorion, Joseph, 74, 291n1
Benjamin of Tudela, 77–78
ben Jose, Rabbi Eliezer, 43
Benoît, Marie, 226
Bentivegna, Rosario, 233
ben Yehiel, Rabbi Nathan, 77
ben Yishaq, Rabbi Shim'on, 76
ben Yohai, Rabbi Simeon, 43
ben Zakkai, Rabbi Yohanan, 19–20
Berenice, 16–20, 22–24, 282n23, 283n47
Berlin-Rome Axis, 200, 312n85
Bernard of Clairvaux, St., 53
Berneri, Giuseppe, 157–59
Berthier, Louis-Alexandre, 160–61
Beta Israel (House of Israel), 199
betrothal (*qiddushin*), 124–25
Bible, 21, 55, 60, 69, 89, 109, 114, 124, 292n7
Biblioteca del Collegio Rabbinico, 218–19
Biblioteca della Comunità Ebraica, 218–19

Bina, Joshua, 135
Bina, Simha, 135
Boaz, 80, 293n29
Boccaccio, Giovanni, 75
body of Christ, 78–79
bombings, 232–34
Bondi, Romeo, 5
Bonfil, Robert, 98–99
Boniface VII (pope), 97
Boniface VIII (pope), 54, 55–56, 61, 67, 288n4, 303–4n16
The Book of Testimony (Abulafia), 76
Borromeo, Charles, 143
Brunetti, Angelo, 174–75, 177, 308n62
Brunetti, Luigi, 176–77
Bruno, Giordano, 99–100
Buber, Martin, 260
Buchanan, James, 180
burials in Rome, 27–31, 135–36, 163, 257–58, 302n102
businesses, 62–63, 86, 119–21, 163–65
Buzi, Leopoldo, 50, 52–53

Caligula, 38–39
Calixtus II (pope), 63–64
Calò, Mirella, 225–26
cambio (exchange), 144
Campidoglio piazza, 95, 102–3
Campo de'Fiore, 96, 100, 297n30
Campo Verano, 163, 257
Campus Martius, 83
canon law, 156–57, 259
Canticles Rabbah, 21, 283n45
Cantoni, Raffaele, 256–57
"Canzonetta nuova sopra gli ebrei," 161
capitalism, 71–72
Capitoline Chamber, 83
Capitoline Hill, 16, 39
Capon, Augusto, 222

Capponi, Carla, 233

Caracalla, 10

Carafa, Gian Pietro. *See* Paul IV (pope)

Cardinal della Valle, 94

carnevale giudeo (Jewish carnival),
  102–3

Carnival, 83–86, 163, 173, 294n57

Caruso, Pietro, 230–31

Casa dei Catecumeni. *See* Catecumeni

Cassius Dio, 19, 36, 38, 41

Castelbolognese, Gustavo, 271

Castel Gandolfo, 194, 201

Castelnuovo, Enrico, 192

Castelnuovo, Silvana Ascarelli, 225

Castel Sant'Angelo, 54–55, 94

Castilian Synagogue, 122–23

Castle of S. Angelo, 83–84

catacombs, 26–31, 40, 44–46, 49, 77

Catecumeni, 122, 138–39, 145–47, 149–51,
  152–53, 163, 180, 251, 303n6, 306n59

Catholic Bible, 55

Catholic Ring Day, 125

Catholics: as artists, 91–92; and banks,
  121–22; and baptism, 179–80; and
  betrayal and protection of Jews, 3,
  225–31, 242–48; and burials, 135;
  and business partnerships, 119–20;
  and the chief rabbi of Rome, 250–51,
  275–76; and divorce, 126–27; and
  Fascism, 207–8; and the Ghetto,
  101–5, 110–11; and the Ghetto
  economy, 120–21, 163–66; and
  Giuseppe Belli's sonnets, 171; and
  greeting the pope, 59; and guilds,
  122–23; and hatred of Paul IV, 105–7;
  and holidays, 144; as informers,
  228–30; and the Inquisition, 99–101;
  and jails, 133; and Jew-Badges,
  79–82; and Jewish assimilation,

75–77, 98–99; and Jewish family
  life, 128; and Jewish honor, 82–86;
  and the joint exhibit, 276–79; and
  language of family, 2–7, 66, 274; and
  the Lateran Accords, 194–95; and
  liberalism, 173–75; and marriage,
  124–26, 187; and money lending,
  68–70; and Nazi occupation of
  Rome, 214–36; and *Nostra aetate*,
  258–65, 275; and policy toward Jews,
  140–42; and power differential
  between vicar and Jewish community, 115–17; as property owners,
  118–19; and Racial Laws, 203–7, 217;
  and Renaissance Jews, 88–90; and
  response to the Jews' gift, 61; and
  Roman hierarchy, 73; and the sack
  of Rome, 92–94; and sexual abuse,
  130–31; and Vatican antisemitism,
  184–86; and Zionism, 192–93. *See
  also* conversion(s); papacy

Cavalieri, Alina, 222

cazagas, 118–19

celebratory conversions, 151–53

Cellini, Benvenuto, 91

Cencius Camerarius, 59, 290n28

Charles V (emperor), 87, 92–94

Charles X, 166

chief rabbi of Rome, 250–51, 275–76

children, baptism of, 146–49. *See also*
  maternal conversion

children, sexual abuse of, 129–31

children of mixed marriages, 204

Christian heretics, 99. *See also*
  Inquisition

Christian sarcophagi, 29–30

Christmas, 136

Christ Stopped at Eboli (Levi), 196,
  312n67

Fascism (*continued*)

Lateran Accords, 194–95; and Libya, 271; and militarism, 198–200; and papal reception of Hitler, 200–201; and Racial Laws, 201–7, 208–12; and Roman Jews, 3, 187–90; and Roman resistance, 232–37; and Vatican antisemitism, 184–87; and Zionism, 191–94. *See also* antisemitism

fattori (Jewish community leaders), 84, 100, 134–35

favor fidei (favor of the faith), 146–49

Ferdinand II, 176

Ferrara, 109, 303n6

fetal baptisms, 147–50

fifty kilos of gold, 216–18, 252

Finzi, Aldo, 234

Fiorina, 130–31

First Crusade, 63–64

First Vatican Council, 181

fiscus Alexandrinus (tax on Alexandrians), 39

fiscus asiaticus (tax on Asiatics), 39

fiscus judaicus (tax on Jews), 39–43, 287n59

Flaccus, Lucius Valerius, 32–34

Foà, Ugo, 216–20, 315n8

forced baptism, 145–51, 173, 304n16

forced labor programs, 211

foreign Jews, 197, 202, 226, 271

Forma Urbis (ancient map of Rome), 9

Formosus (pope), 97

Fort Bravetta, 234

Fosse Ardeatine, 235, 236–37, 238, 247, 247–48, 251–53, 263, 268–69

Fourth Lateran Council, 69–70, 78, 298n40

France, 88, 107–9, 160–63, 166, 175–79, 181, 199, 243–44, 316n43

Francis (emperor), 92

Francis (pope), 238, 263–64, 272–77, 274, 321n35

Franco, Francisco, 207, 275

François I, 57

French Republic, 52, 159–60, 162, 306n12

funerals in Rome, 27–31, 135–36, 163, 302n102

funerary inscriptions. *See* inscriptions

Fuscus, Aristius, 35

Gabrini, Nicola. *See* di Rienzo, Cola

Galilee, 17–18

Gallio, Tolomeo, 133

Gallov, Joseph, 249

Gallus, Cestius, 17

Gamaliel II, 42

gambling, 132–33

Ganganelli, Lorenzo, 297n37

The Garden of the Finzi-Continis (Bassani), 3–5

Garibaldi, Giuseppe, 176

Gelasius II, 59

General Proclamation of 1555, 107

Genesis, 108, 291n4

Gerarchia, 206

German Jews, 196–98, 200

Germany, Nazi. *See* Nazis

Gershom, Rabbi, 118

Gessius Florus, 17

Gestapo, 201, 215, 229, 231

get (bill of divorce), 105, 126–27

get zeman, 126

ghettarello (small ghetto), 121, 288n1, 297–98n39

Ghetto, 9, 51–53, 95–96, *106*; economy of, 120–21, 163–66; establishment of, 101–5, 141–42; and Jewish conversion, 137, 145–51; and Jewish honor, 83–86; and Jewish professions and partnerships, 119–20; liberation from, 155–56, 182, 187–89; *Meo Patacca* describing, 157–60; money lending in, 123–24; and the Napoleonic Code, 163; and papal restoration, 161; and Pius IX, 173–75, 178–79; and property, 119; and the vicar, 116; a walk through, 267–69

The Ghetto and the Jews of Rome (Gergorovius), 179

ghettoization, 57, 107–11, 120–21, 138, 163, 172–73

"The Gift" (Mauss), 60, 289n25

gifts: anthropological interpretations of, 60–67, 289n25; and conversions, 152, 154–55; and Fascism, 198–99; in *Meo Patacca*, 159; and ritual presentation of the Torah, 53–59; and role of the pope, 72–73

Giles of Viterbo, 87–88, 94, 131, 140

Ginzburg, Leone, 196, 210, 224, 231

Ginzburg, Natalia, 183, 206, 210–11, 312n71

Giornata della fede, 198

"Giovanezza" (Youth), 198

giudate (anti-Jewish street theatre), 85

Giustizia e Libertà, 196, 197

Glossario giudeo-italiano dei termini difficili che si trovano ne Mishna Tora (Maimonides), 89

God-Fearers, 40–45, 287n63

goi, 112, 114, 118, 132

gold. *See* fifty kilos of gold

Golden Rule, 48

Goldman, Nahum, 199–200

good and bad antisemitism, 186

Gramar, Christoforo, 130–31

Grand Council of Fascism, 211

Grandi, Dino, 211

Grayzel, Solomon, 290n37

Great Britain, 192–93, 198, 242

Great Synagogue, 51–52, 188, 217, 218–19, 263–65, 272–77, 280, 310n23

Gregorovius, Ferdinand, 179

Gregory I (pope), 141

Gregory IX (pope), 100

Gregory X (pope), 66–67, 290n36

Gregory XII (pope), 56

Gregory XIII (pope), 117, 143, 151, 293n29

Gregory XIV (pope), 133

Gregory XV (pope), 151

Gregory XVI (pope), 166, 168–70, 173

Gruppi di Azione Patriottica (GAP), 233

Guerrazzi, Osti, 318n107

Guicciardini, Luigi, 94

guilds, 91, 122–23, 310n7

Hadrian, 43, 54

Hadriel, Rabbi, 118

halizah, 127

Hanukkah, 144

Hayez, Francesco, 167–68

Hebrew Bible, 55, 109, 114

Hebrew language, 87

Henry VII, 57–58

Henry of Segusio, 141

Heras, 19

Hérissé, Monsignor, 227

Herod of Chalcis, 18

Herod the Great, 11

Herzl, Theodor, 191

Heschel, Rabbi Abraham, 261

Hillel, 48

Himmler, Heinrich, 214–16

Hispalus, 32

Histories (Tacitus), 12

Jabotinsky, Ze'ev, 193

Jachin, 80, 293n29

Jacob, 74–75, 108

jails, 97, 133–34

Janiculum Hill, 234

Jason of Cyrene, 270

Jerome, Saint, 55, 91

Jerusalem/Jerusalem Temple: and
Berenice, 16–20; and destruction of
Jerusalem, 10, 12, 16, 19–20, 22–24,
283n47; and destruction of Jewish
Temple, 10, 14, 19–20, 22–24, 39; and
history of Jerusalem Temple, 11–13;
and Jews during the early empire,
33–39; and Josephus, 13–15; and
Rome, 20–24

Jesus' death, 261–62

Jew-Badge (sciamanno), 78–82, 141

Jew Hat, 95, 98, 104, 141

Jewish Antiquities (Josephus), 13, 74

Jewish banks in Rome, 157, 209

Jewish Confraternity of Death and
Charity, 257

Jewish Ghetto. See Ghetto

Jewish Museum, 276–78

Jewish revolt (115–16 CE), 43

Jewish revolt (1830), 166

Jewish revolt against Rome (66–70 CE),
11–12, 39, 167

Jewish usury, 68–72, 82, 109, 141, 153

The Jewish War (Josephus), 10, 12–13,
74, 281n3

Jews: and absolution, 145; and Anna
del Monte, 138–40; as anti-Fascists,
195–96; and arbiters of troubled
marriages, 128–29; assimilation and
acculturation of, 46, 78, 98–99, 184,
188–90, 192–93, 196, 270–71; and

banks, 121–22; becoming Italians,
187–90; betrayal and protection
of, 3, 225–31, 242–48; and burials
in Rome, 27–31, 135–36, 163,
257–58, 302n102; and catacomb
inscriptions, 26–31, 40, 44–46, 49,
77; and Catholic artists, 91–92; and
celebratory conversions, 151–53; and
the chief rabbi of Rome, 250–51,
275–76; church's policy toward,
140–42; and conversionary sermons,
143–44; conversion of, 137–55; and
the creation of the State of Israel,
254–57; and Cum nimis absurdum,
101–5; and customs, 46–49; and
Debenedetti's statements, 236–37;
and divorce, 126–27; and dowries,
127–28; during the early empire,
31–39; emancipation of, 156–82;
expulsion of, 31–39, 47, 107–11; in
Fascist Rome, 183–213; and fifty kilos
of gold, 216–18; and forced baptism,
145–47; future of, 279–80; and
gambling, 132–33; in Giuseppe Belli's
sonnets, 168–73; and guilds, 122–23;
and honor, 82–86; and identity,
40–44; immigration of, 196–98;
and impugned wife trial, 131–32;
and the Inquisition, 99–101; and
Israel Zolli's warning, 219–20; under
ius commune jurisdiction, 156–57;
and jails, 133–34; and Jew-Badges,
78–82; and the Joint, 250; and
the joint exhibit, 276–79; and the
Lateran Accords, 195; and legends
of Jewish popes, 75–77; libraries of,
218–19; in Libya, 269–73, 279; and
luoghi di monti (bonds), 120–21;

202–6; and militarism, 198–200; and Racial Laws, 201–7; and Zionism, 192–94

pagan tombs, 26–27, 29–31

pageants, 14–15

Palazzini, Pietro, 227–28, 241, 250

Palazzo Leonori, 135–36

Palazzo Tittoni, 233

Palermo, Sicily, 176

Palestine, 30, 191–94, 199, 202, 243, 254

Pallantieri, Alessandro, 130–31

Pantera Nera, 229, 234

papacy: and the French Republic, 162; and gifts of conversion, 154–55; and Jewish notaries, 113; and law in papal Rome, 156–57; and money lending, 67–72, 123–24; and papal bulls, 62–67, 96, 100, 101–2, 113, 117, 119, 133, 137, 138, 142, 143, 170, 200–201, 297n38; and papal processions, 53–73; and policy toward conversion, 137–38; and posthumous papal trials, 97–98; and protection of Jews, 61–65; as restored, 163–66; and role of the pope, 72–73; and the Roman Republic, 161; and Rome's Jews, 98–99, 105; and temporal powers, 177, 181. See also individual popes

Papal Curia, 86

Papal States, 72, 84, 109–10, 122, 143, 156, 164, 170, 174, 176–77, 195, 272

Pappagallo, Pietro, 234

pardon, 145

Parione, 289n9

Paris, France, 53, 100, 162, 181, 197, 216, 297n30

Parthians, 254

partition of Palestine, 254

Paschal II (pope), 59, 97

pasquinade, 295n2

Passover, 144, 175, 187, 263, 297n37, 308n61

Pasticceria Boccione, 269

Pastoris eternis vices (Julius III), 138

patria potestas (ancestral power), 146–47

Patrizi, Agostini, 55

Paul (apostle), 38, 107–8, 263–64

Paul II (pope), 83, 294n50

Paul III (pope), 123, 138, 145

Paul IV (pope), 9, 51, 95–107, 110–11, 119, 123, 141–42, 155, 297n33. See also *Cum nimis absurdum* (Paul IV)

Paul VI (pope), 239, 241, 258, 260–63

peddlers' licenses, 209–10

Pekelis, Carla, 183

People's Crusade, 63

Persius, 35

Perugia, 71

Peter, St., 76–77, 80

Petit, Solomon, 86

Petronius, 45

Pfeiffer, Pancrazio, 241, 319n11

Pharaoh of Egypt, 21–22

Philip II of Spain, 105–7

Philo of Alexandria, 33, 38

philosemitic statements, 191

Phoenicia, 44

Piazza Giudea, 96, 102

Piazza Mattei, 160, 267

Piazza Mercatello, 51

Piazza Pasquino, 95

Piazza Pescaria, 96

Piazza San Pietro, 83–84

Picart, Bernard, 57, 58

Picciotto, Liliana, 245

Pierantoni, Amadeo, 220

Pierleoni, Peter, 78

Pierleoni family, 63, 78, 290n37

"Pio ottavo" ("Pius VIII") (Belli), 168

Piperno, Sergio, 246

and second roundup of Rome's
Jews, 230–32; and *Sicut Judaeis*,
62–67; and Titus's triumph, 10; and
Vatican antisemitism, 184–87; and
the Via della Reginella, 267–69; and
war crimes trials, 251–54; and the
Yosippon, 74–75. *See also* Ghetto
Rome Zionist Group, 194
Romulus, 75
Roncalli, Angelo. *See* John XXIII
  (pope)
Rondina, Saverio, 186
Roselli, Ermindo, 228
Roselli, Marion, 211
Rosh Hashanah, 100, 144
Rosselli, Carlo, 312n71
Rosselli, Carlo and Nello, 197–98
Rossi, Pellegrino, 176
Rothschild, James, 178
Rothschild, Karl, 170
Rothschild, Salomon, 173
Rothschild family, 165, 174, 178
Royal Savoy March, 198
Rutelli, Francesco, 252–53
Rychlak, Ronald, 241

Saar Valley, 199
Sabbath, 34–35, 46–47, 143–44
sack of Rome, 88, 92–94
The Sack of Rome (Guicciardini), 94
Salomone (maestro), 115
Salò Republic, 212, 228
Sanchez, José M., 238
Sancta mater ecclesia (Gregory XIII),
  143
Sandmel, Rabbi David, 263
San Girolamo degli Illirici Seminary,
  249
Sanhedrin, 162

Santa Maria Ausiliatrice, 225
Santissima Trinità dei Pellegrini, 144
Sapienza (University of Rome), 164
sarcophagi, 29–30, 44–45
Sardinia, 36, 176
Sarfatti, Margherita, 206–7
Sarmatians, 254
Scavizzi, Pirro, 238–39
Scechina (Giles), 87
Schanzer, Carlo, 194
scholae of Rome, 59
sciamanno (Jew-Badge), 78–82
Scola Nova, 117
Scola Tempio, 123, 132
Season Sarcophagus, 30
secondary burial, 135
second roundup of Rome's Jews, 230–32
Second Temple, 11, 80, 167, 286n37,
  293n29
Second Vatican Council, 258
Sede vacante. *See* Vacant See
Segre, Augusto, 188
Segre, Sion, 195–96
Seminario Lombardo, 228
Seneca the Younger, 19, 37–38, 44, 47
Senni, Mary, 257
serraglio, 105
"Sesto, nun formicà" ("Sixth
  [Commandment]") (Belli), 172
Severa, Alexandria, 49
Severus, Alexander (emperor), 43,
  48–49
Severus, Septimius (emperor), 10, 43
Severus, Sulpicius, 12
sexual abuse of children, 129–31
sexual mores, 107
sexual relations, 172, 187
shadchan (matchmaker), 124
Shekhina, 87

Victor Emmanuel III, King, 188, 191–92, 211–12

Vigna Randanini, 26–28, 234

Villa Celimontana, 5, 210

Villa Torlonia, 5, 28, 45

Vineam Sorec (Nicholas III), 143, 304n19

Virgil, 57, 75

virginity, 129–32

Vogelstein, H., 175

von Kessel, Albrecht, 215

von Weizsäcker, Ernst, 215, 239–40

Vows (*Nedarim*), 17

Walters Art Museum, 10

war crimes trials, 251–54

Warsaw Ghetto, 104, 239

Waterloo, 163

weekly attendance mandate, 143–44

Weizmann, Chaim, 193, 199

"We Remember," 265

wills, 134–35

Wolff, Karl, 224, 232

women, 79, 83, 118, 120, 146–50, 165, 188, 221, 224, 229, 301n72

World War I, 188–90

World War II, 25–26, 210, 257

written contract. See *condotte* (contract)

Yad Vashem, 228, 241

Yehiel, 77–78

yitush (mosquito), 23–24

Yosippon, Book of, 74–75, 291nn1–2, 292n6

Zarfati, Samuele Levi, 134

Zavattari, Edoardo, 202

Zepho, 74–75

Zevi, Tullia, 253

Zionism, 191–94, 197

Zohar, 87

Zolli, Emma Maionica, 250

Zolli, Rabbi Israel, 219–20, 250–51, 320n21

Zucotti, Susan, 242